FIFTH EDITION

AMERICA'S Musical LANDSCAPE

JEAN FERRIS

Professor Emerita, Arizona
State University

McGraw Hill **Higher Education**

Boston   Burr Ridge, IL   Dubuque, IA   Madison, WI   New York   San Francisco   St. Louis
Bangkok   Bogotá   Caracas   Kuala Lumpur   Lisbon   London   Madrid   Mexico City
Milan   Montreal   New Delhi   Santiago   Seoul   Singapore   Sydney   Taipei   Toronto

Higher Education

AMERICA'S MUSICAL LANDSCAPE

Published by McGraw-Hill, a business unit of The McGraw-Hill Companies, Inc., 1221 Avenue of the Americas, New York, NY, 10020. Copyright © 2006, 2002, 1998, 1993, 1990 by The McGraw-Hill Companies, Inc. All rights reserved. No part of this publication may be reproduced or distributed in any form or by any means, or stored in a database or retrieval system, without the prior written consent of The McGraw-Hill Companies, Inc., including, but not limited to, in any network or other electronic storage or transmission, or broadcast for distance learning. Some ancillaries, including electronic and print components, may not be available to customers outside the United States.

This book is printed on acid-free paper.

2 3 4 5 6 7 8 9 0 DOC/DOC 0 9 8 7 6

ISBN-13: 978-0-07-298919-9
ISBN-10: 0-07-298919-X

Editor in Chief: *Emily Barrosse*
Publisher: *Lyn Uhl*
Senior Sponsoring Editor: *Melody Marcus*
Executive Marketing Manager: *Suzanna Ellison*
Editorial Coordinator: *Beth S. Ebenstein*
Managing Editor: *Jean Dal Porto*
Lead Project Manager: *Susan Trentacosti*
Manuscript Editor: *Susan Gamer*
Senior Designer (Cover Designer): *Preston Thomas*
Text Designer: *Kay Fulton*
Art Editor: *Emma C. Ghiselli*
Senior Photo Research Coordinator: *Alexandra Ambrose*
Photo Researcher: *Mary Reeg*
Senior Production Supervisor: *Carol A. Bielski*
Lead Media Producer: *Shannon Gattens*
Composition: *10/12 Times by Interactive Composition Corporation*
Printing: *PMS 160, 45# New Era Matte, R. R. Donnelley, Inc./Crawfordsville, IN*

Cover: *Grant Wood,* Landscape, *1930. Oil on paperboard, 12 5/8 × 14 5/8 in. (32.1 × 37.2 cm). Smithsonian American Art Museum, Washington DC / Art Resource, NY*
© Estate of Grant Wood/Licensed by VAGA, New York, NY

Credits: The credits section for this book begins on page C–1 and is considered an extension of the copyright page.

Library of Congress Control Number: 2005932400

The Internet addresses listed in the text were accurate at the time of publication. The inclusion of a Web site does not indicate an endorsement by the authors of McGraw-Hill, and McGraw-Hill does not guarantee the accuracy of the information presented at these sites.
www.mhhe.com

With a song of joy for our new little boy.
Welcome, Jamie.

About the Author

Twenty years after completing a bachelor of music degree in music history and literature at the University of Michigan, I received an MA, also in music history, at Arizona State University, where I then taught music history and appreciation for the next twenty years. *Music: The Art of Listening* and *America's Musical Landscape* evolved for use in my classes, and I am delighted that other instructors have found them useful, too.

My interest in travel and in world cultures began early, encouraged by attending a year-and-a-half of high school in Manila, Philippines, and later by living for nearly a year in Japan with my husband and our four children. I still travel extensively, and when home stay busy playing the piano, cooking, practicing yoga, reading, doing needlework, and of course writing. And there's always time to enjoy our fourteen grandchildren!

Contents

3

Religious Music in the Colonial, Revolutionary, and Federal Periods   49

4

Secular Music in the Colonial, Revolutionary, and Federal Periods   66

The Tumultuous Nineteenth Century   78

5

Religious Music in the Early Nineteenth Century   86

6
Popular Music of the Civil War Era   97

7
Early Concert Music   117

8
American Concert Music Comes of Age: The Late Nineteenth Century   129

12
The Jazz Age   195

13
Jazz 1930–1960   213

14
Jazz since 1960   233

15
Latin Popular Musics   254

16
Rock and Roll   270

17
Popular Music since 1970   290

23
The Avant-Garde, Continued   397

24
The Recent Mainstream   409

Optional Listening Examples

(Listening Guides for the Optional Listening Examples are printed in the Instructor's Manual and may be copied for distribution to students.)

Barber, Samuel: "Knoxville: Summer of 1915"

Beach, Amy Marcy Cheney: "The Year's at the Spring"

Braxton, Anthony: 92 + [30, 32, 139] + [108c, 108d] for Creative Orchestra

Bristow, George: Fourth Symphony (*Arcadian*), Op. 49, third movement ("Indian War Dance")

Cage, John: *Aria* and *Fontana Mix*

Copland, Aaron: Variations on "Simple Gifts" from *Appalachian Spring*

Cowell, Henry: "The Tides of Mananaun"

Gershwin, George: Concerto in F

Gershwin, George: *Rhapsody in Blue*

Gillespie, Dizzy: "Shaw 'Nuff"

Gottschalk, Louis Moreau: "Bamboula"

Hopkinson, Francis: "My Days Have Been So Wondrous Free"

Ives, Charles: *The Unanswered Question*

Joplin, Scott: "A Real Slow Drag" from *Treemonisha*

MacDowell, Edward: "To a Wild Rose" from *Woodland Sketches*

Menotti, Gian-Carlo: "To This We've Come" from *The Consul*

Monroe, Bill: "It's Mighty Dark to Travel"

Parker, Horatio: Fugue in C minor

Reich, Steve: *Drumming*

Rodgers, Jimmie: "Daddy and Home"

Still, William Grant: *Afro-American Symphony,* first movement

"Windsor" (Psalm 15)

Preface

The survey course for which this text is designed affords the same broad coverage of musics—classical and popular, secular and religious, vocal and instrumental—as does the traditional music appreciation course predominantly featuring European examples. Here we tackle the happy task of introducing basic musical terms and concepts using selected examples of outstanding American music.

As suggested in the title of the text, I have often related music to other arts, finding such comparisons to have pedagogical as well as aesthetic value for nonmusicians perhaps more familiar with visual and literary than with aural experience. Asher B. Durand's stunning landscape painting *Kindred Spirits* (p. 83), an eloquent portrayal of the nature poet William Cullen Bryant and the Hudson River School painter Thomas Cole sharing reverent admiration for their country's natural splendors, in fact inspired this text, which seeks to capture some of that painting's expression of the interdependence uniting American art and artists.

The musical landscape we explore stretches from the Pacific to the Atlantic coast between Canada and Mexico, and Hawaii—the areas comprising today's United States. Though influences abound from above and below the northern and southern borders, and though each of the many cultures of North, Central, and South America and Mexico has a rich American musical landscape of its own, time constrains most American music courses to cover only some of the music, of only certain regions, within the United States. Regret for what we cannot cover must encourage us to extend our exploration as soon and as far as possible throughout all of the Americas.

The fifth edition includes up-to-date information on each of the areas of popular and classical music covered in the text. The proportion of vernacular to classical coverage has been expanded in response to requests of users, while the text remains of a practical (short) length. Further, I have divided certain long chapters into shorter ones, easier for students to absorb and for instructors to organize into semester plans.

The Prelude introduces basic technical information concerning texture, form, and notation. Students may browse through the Prelude at the beginning of a term and return to it to refresh their understanding as the concepts recur throughout the course. While instructors will differ in the emphasis they place on the Prelude, I find it as essential a part of the text, and the course, as the prelude of a music composition is to that work.

As in the previous edition, relevant social and cultural information appears before each section in Part Openers, available to those who find them valuable, but unobtrusive for those who choose to leave them out. The Part Openers are not intended as material to be absorbed for test purposes, but rather as enriching and thought-provoking information related to the music covered in the sections that they introduce. They set the context in which music was conceived and first experienced, and they broaden students' perspective of music's place in the cultural environment.

Important terms introduced during a chapter are highlighted and listed in each end-of-chapter section and, of course, in the Glossary. The Critical Thinking topics newly added at the end of each chapter offer students an opportunity to form and articulate opinions, perhaps using vocabulary and information gleaned from the chapter. The Part Summaries use terms and names which students have studied in that section much as those terms and names might appear in a concert program or a newspaper review.

The three CDs accompanying the text offer students generous opportunity to apply their developing listening skills to representative selections of music. Restrictions imposed by recording companies often determine what we may and may not include: It is especially difficult to acquire permission to use current or even recent popular music. Of course students and instructors may wish to supplement class listening experiences with relevant examples from their personal collections, and the Internet offers innumerable opportunities to hear complete pieces or excerpts via computer. Listening guides for pieces listed as Optional Listening Examples are included on the Instructor's CD-ROM, should instructors choose to assign or to play in class some of this music.

The Instructor's CD-ROM is an enhanced Instructor's Manual, including chapter summaries, additional topics for essay or discussion, and a test bank, as well as the Optional Listening guides. The Online Learning Center offers further supplemental material, including Web sites relevant to topics covered in the text. While the listed Web sites may change from time to time, students will be well advised to form the habit of creatively checking the Internet as they study each chapter. Simply entering as keywords the name of a composer, a piece, or an instrument, for example, reveals information to further students' experience and understanding of every topic.

As always, I am indebted to colleagues and friends for invaluable suggestions, and I hope this edition will elicit their further comments and, yes, criticism. I particularly want to thank Professor Warren Gaughan of Warren Wilson College for his expert advice on jazz. I remain extremely grateful to Professor J. Richard Haefer of Arizona State University for the use of his Native American slides. My gratitude to Tom Laskey of Sony Music Special Projects is boundless: He provided examples, answered questions, and tolerated confusions (mine) with patience and generosity. Special thanks, too, to Bill Kane, president of the Spirit of Phoenix barbershop chorus, for his efforts in securing permission for us to use the Phoenicians' splendid recording of George M.

Cohan's "Rose." I'm grateful as well to Professor Glenn Hackbarth of Arizona State University, who made it possible for us to photograph the university's electronic music lab.

And to my editors at McGraw-Hill, I express the most profound respect and gratitude. Expert and diligent as well as patient and kind, they made the process of developing this new edition a completely delightful experience.

Jean Ferris

Chronology of Figures and Events

Date	Cultural Figures and Events	Historical Figures and Events
40,000 B.C.E.		People later known as Native Americans migrate to North America from Asia (ca. 40,000–18,000 B.C.E.)
300 C.E.		Hawaii settled (300 C.E.)
1500		Spanish explorers arrive in American southeast and southwest (1513–1543)
1575		First English settlement established at Roanoke Island (1585)
1600	Anne Bradstreet (1612–1672)	Dutch build New Amsterdam on Manhattan Island (1614)
1625		
1700		Benjamin Franklin (1706–1790)
1725	John Singleton Copley (1738–1815) The Great Awakening (1730s, 1740s) Benjamin Franklin's *Poor Richard's Almanack* first published (1732) Charles Willson Peale (1741–1827)	The Great Awakening (1735) Thomas Jefferson (1743–1826)
1750		French and Indian War (1754–1763) Boston Tea Party (1773)
1775		American Revolution (War of Independence) (1775–1782) Declaration of Independence (1776) Eli Whitney invents the cotton gin (1793)
1800	Edgar Allen Poe (1809–1849) Julia Ward Howe (1819–1910) Second Great Awakening (1820s, 1830s) Hudson River School of artists (1820–1870)	Louisiana Purchase (1803) Frederick Douglass (1818–1895) Harriet Tubman (ca. 1820–1913)
1825	Transcendentalism; the American Renaissance (1840s)	Erie Canal completed (1825) President Andrew Jackson signs the Indian Removal Act (1830) The Cherokee people begin the Trail of Tears (1838) Continental expansion described as Manifest Destiny (1840s)
1850	Publication of *Uncle Tom's Cabin* by Harriet Beecher Stowe (1852) Gertrude Stein (1874–1946)	Underground Railroad rescues fleeing slaves (1850s) Booker T. Washington (1856–1915) John Brown's raid (1859) Civil War (War between the States) (1860–1865)

Musical Events	Musicians	Date
		40,000 B.C.E.
		300 C.E.
		1500
		°
		1575
		1600
Publication of *Bay Psalm Book* (1640)		**1625**
		1700
	John Antes (1740–1811) William Billings (1746–1800)	**1725**
First music shop in America opens in Philadelphia (1759)	Alexander Reinagle (1756–1809) Daniel Read (1757–1836)	**1750**
Philadelphia bans theater and opera (1785)	Lowell Mason (1792–1872)	**1775**
Francis Scott Key writes "The Star Spangled Banner" (words) (1814)	Thomas Dartmouth "Daddy" Rice (1808–1860) Daniel Decatur Emmett (1815–1904)	**1800**
Singing Hutchinson Family become famous (1840s) New York Philharmonic Orchestra, America's oldest symphony orchestra, founded (1842)	Stephen Foster (1826–1864) Louis Moreau Gottschalk (1829–1869) Theodore Thomas (1835–1905) John Knowles Paine (1839–1906)	**1825**
Minstrel shows popular (1850–1870) Julia Ward Howe writes "The Battle Hymn of the Republic" (1862) Fisk University Jubilee Singers tour (1871)	James A. Bland (1854–1911) John Philip Sousa (1854–1932) Edward MacDowell (1861–1908) Harry Thacker Burleigh (1866–1949) Amy Marcy Cheney Beach (1867–1944)	**1850**

Date	Cultural Figures and Events	Historical Figures and Events
1850		First telegraph message sent across the United States (1861) The Emancipation Proclamation (1863) Abraham Lincoln assassinated (1865) Abolition of slavery (1865) First transcontinental railroad linked up (1869)
1875	Eugene O'Neill (1888–1953) Alexander Calder (1898–1976) Ernest Hemingway (1899–1961)	Thomas Edison invents the phonograph (1877) Spanish American War (1898–1899)
1900	Agnes DeMille (1905–1993) Richard Wright (1908–1960) Jackson Pollock (1912–1956) Romare Bearden (1912–1988) Arthur Miller (1915–2005) Saul Bellow (1915–) Jacob Lawrence (1917–2000) Alan Freed (1921–1965) James Baldwin (1924–1987) George Segal (1924–2000) American literature's "Lost Generation" (Stein, Hemingway, Fitzgerald, Pound) (1920s) Peak years of the Harlem Renaissance (1920s–1930s)	Wright brothers' first successful flight (1903) Albert Einstein develops relativity theory (1905) San Francisco earthquake (1906) Model T Ford produced (1908) NAACP formed (1909) Panama Canal opened (1914) World War I (1914–1918) Prohibition (1919–1933) 19th Constitutional Amendment gives women the right to vote (1920)

Musical Events	Musicians	Date
	Scott Joplin (1868–1917) Florenz Ziegfeld (1869–1932) Charles Ives (1874–1954)	**1850**
New York Metropolitan Opera founded (1883) Ragtime popular (1890s) Tin Pan Alley ruled the popular song industry (1890s–ca. 1950)	George M. Cohan (1878–1942) James Reese Europe (1881–1919) Robert Nathaniel Dett (1882–1943) Eubie Blake (1883–1983) James Scott (1886–1938) Gertrude "Ma" Rainey (1886–1939) Huddie "Leadbelly" Ledbetter (1888–1949) Al Jolson (1888–1950) Irving Berlin (1888–1989) Noble Sissle (1889–1975) Ferdinand "Jelly Roll" Morton (1890–1941) Paul Whiteman (1890–1967) Cole Porter (1891–1964) Bessie Smith (1894–1937) James P. Johnson (1894–1955) Jerome Kern (1895–1945) Oscar Hammerstein II (1895–1960) William Grant Still (1895–1978) Virgil Thomson (1896–1989) Jimmie Rodgers (1897–1933) Fletcher Henderson (1897–1952) Henry Cowell (1897–1965) Edward Kennedy "Duke" Ellington (1899–1974)	**1875**

Arthur Farwell's Wa-Wan Press (1901–ca. 1912)
First Broadway musical, George M. Cohan's *Little Johnny Jones* (1904)
Ziegfeld Follies (1907–1932)
Irene and Vernon Castle introduce tango to
   Broadway (1911)
The Jazz Age; Dixieland jazz popular (1920s)
First performance of Gershwin's *Rhapsody in Blue*
   (1924)
	New Orleans jazz (1900–1920s)
	Aaron Copland (1900–1999)
	Louis Armstrong (1900–1971)
	Coleman Hawkins (1901–1969)
	Harry Partch (1901–1974)
	Frederick Loewe (1901–1988)
	Richard Rodgers (1902–1979)
	Bing Crosby (1903–1977)
	Fats Waller (1904–1943)
	Count Basie (1904–1984)
	Bob Wills (1905–1973)
	Joe Turner (1907–1990)
	Lester Young (1909–1959)
	Johnny Mercer (1909–1976)
	Benny Goodman (1909–1996)
	Art Tatum (1910–1956)
	Frank Loesser (1910–1969)
	Samuel Barber (1910–1981)
	Mary Lou Williams (1910–1981)
		1900

Date	Cultural Figures and Events	Historical Figures and Events
1900		
1925	Robert Rauschenberg (1925–) Jasper Johns (1930–) Realism in literature (Faulkner, Steinbeck) (1930s) Toni Morrison (1931–) Andy Warhol (1931–1987) John Updike (1932–) Abstract Expressionism (1946–1960s)	Charles Lindbergh flies solo across Atlantic (1927) New York Stock Market crashes (1929) Lindbergh baby kidnapping (1932) Jesse Owens wins 4 gold medals at Berlin Olympics (1936) America involved in World War II (1941–1945) United Nations founded (1945) Cold War (1945–1991)

Musical Events	Musicians	Date
	William Schuman (1910–1992)	**1900**
	Bill Monroe (1911–1996)	
	Stan Kenton (1912–1979)	
	John Cage (1912–1992)	
	Woodrow Wilson "Woody" Guthrie (1914–1967)	
	Billie Holiday (1915–1959)	
	Frank Sinatra (1915–1998)	
	Milton Babbitt (1916–)	
	John Birks "Dizzy" Gillespie (1917–1993)	
	Alan Jay Lerner (1918–1986)	
	Leonard Bernstein (1918–1990)	
	Ella Fitzgerald (1918–1996)	
	Ray Charles (1918–2004)	
	Pete Seeger (1919–)	
	Charles "Bird" Parker (1920–1955)	
	Thelonious Monk (1920–1982)	
	Charles Mingus (1922–1979)	
	Hank Williams (1923–1953)	
	Paul Desmond (1924–1977)	
	Henry Mancini (1924–1994)	
	Earl Scruggs (1924–)	
Grand Ole Opry begins broadcasting country music (1925)	Chuck Berry (1926–)	**1925**
Jerome Kern's *Show Boat* opens (1927)	John Coltrane (1926–1967)	
New York Philharmonic Orchestra's first radio broadcast (1928)	Miles Davis (1926–1991)	
	Willie Mae "Big Mama" Thornton (1926–)	
Big band jazz (swing) popular (1930s)	Stan Getz (1927–1991)	
Western swing popular (1930s, 1940s)	Ray Charles (1930–2004)	
Many important European composers emigrate to the United States (1930s, 1940s)	Stephen Sondheim (1930–)	
	Ornette Coleman (1930–)	
Gershwin's *Porgy and Bess* opens on Broadway (1934)	Patsy Cline (1932–1963)	
	Johnny Cash (1932–2004)	
Development of bebop (1940s)	John Williams (1932–)	
Cuban music strongly affects jazz (1940s)	James Brown (1933–)	
Rodgers and Hammerstein's *Oklahoma!* Opens (1943)	Loretta Lynn (1934–)	
	Elvis Presley (1935–1977)	
Copland's *Appalachian Spring* choreographed by Martha Graham (1944)	Terry Riley (1935–)	
	Steve Reich (1936–)	
Development of *musique concrète* in Paris (1948)	Philip Glass (1937–)	
Introduction of long-playing records (1948)	Joan Tower (1938–)	
Billboard substitutes "rhythm and blues" for "race records" (1949)	Ellen Taafe Zwillich (1939–)	
	Bob Dylan (1941–)	
	Joan Baez (1941–)	
	Chick Corea (1941–)	
	Paul Simon (1941–)	
	Jimi Hendrix (1942–1970)	
	Aretha Franklin (1942–)	
	Janis Joplin (1943–1970)	
	Diana Ross (1944–)	

Date	Cultural Figures and Events	Historical Figures and Events
1925		
1950	Pop art, minimal, conceptual, and superrealist movements (1960s)	Korean War (1950–1953) America explodes hydrogen bomb (1952) *Brown v. Kansas Board of Education* ends school segregation (1954) John F. Kennedy assassinated (1963) Martin Luther King "I Have a Dream" speech (1963) Vietnam War (1964–1975) Freedom March in Alabama (1965) Martin Luther King and Robert Kennedy assassinated (1968) American astronauts land on moon (1969) *Apollo 13* disaster (1970) 26th Constitutional Amendment lowers voting age from 21 to 18 (1971) Watergate affair begins (1973) *Roe* v. *Wade* legalizes abortion (1973)
1975	Elvis postage stamp (1993) Toni Morrison wins Nobel Prize for Literature for *Jazz* (1993) J. K. Rowling's *Harry Potter and the Sorcerer's Stone* published (1997)	First Dr. Martin Luther King, Jr. national holiday (1986) Space shuttle *Challenger* disaster (1986) Persian Gulf War (1990–1991) Desert Storm war in Iraq (1991) World Trade Center bombing (1993) O. J. Simpson trial (1994–1995) Oklahoma City Federal Building bombed (1995) Dolly the sheep cloned in Scotland (1996) International Space Station assembly begins (1998) Panama Canal returned to Panama (1999)
2000	Christo and his wife Jeanne-Claude create "The Gates" in New York's Central Park (2005)	Terrorist airliner attacks on the World Trade Center and the Pentagon (2001) Iraq War begins (2003)

Musical Events

Cool jazz (ca. 1950)
Nashville sound (1950s)
John Cage develops chance music (1950s)
American experiments in electronic music
    at Columbia University (1952)
Beginning of rock 'n' roll (1955)
Hard bop, funk, soul (late 1950s)
Berry Gordy, Jr. forms Motown (1959)
Ornette Coleman introduces free jazz (1960)
Relationships between jazz and classical music
    explored (1960s)
Bossa nova becomes popular (1960s)
Lincoln Center for the Performing Arts, New York
    (1960s)
Beach Boys formed (1961)
Grateful Dead (1965–1995)
Woodstock Festival (1969)
Reggae popular in the United States (1970s)

John Lennon murdered (1980)
Digital recordings become widely marketed (1980)
Rap movement emerges (1980s)
MTV runs music videos around the clock (1981)
Michael Jackson's album *Thriller* (1982)
Introduction of compact discs (1983)
Bruce Springsteen's *Born in the USA* (1984)
Prince's *Purple Rain* (1984)
Live Aid concert for Ethiopian famine relief (1985)
Dirty Dancing soundtrack (1987)
Rap and alternative music hit mainstream (1988–)
MC Hammer's *Please Hammer, Don't Hurt 'Em*
    (1990)
Grunge movement begins (1991)
Prince changes his name to a symbol (1993)
Woodstock II (1994)
Kurt Cobain commits suicide (1994)
Selena killed (1995)
Saturday Night Fever soundtrack (1996)
Tupac Shakur shot to death (1996)
Macarena dance craze (1996)

Napster is dead (2002)

Musicians

Barry Manilow (1946–)
Carlos Nakai (1946–)
Dolly Parton (1946–)
John Adams (1947–)
Bruce Springsteen (1949–)

Anthony Davis (1951–)
Stevie Wonder (1951–)
Wynton Marsalis (1961–)

Date

1925

1950

1975

2000

Introduction

Most Americans today would find it difficult, perhaps impossible, to experience a day without music, so pervasive is the sound of music in our everyday lives. Music enhances many of our social, religious, and work-related experiences. Music sets rhythms for us to dance or exercise to, keeps us company at work or play, enhances our concentration and our emotional response when we are viewing a film or a musical, accompanies some religious services, helps us go to sleep at night, and makes it easier to wake up in the morning and to prepare for another day filled with the sounds we individually enjoy.

From the wide field of *popular* musics, we generally develop preferences for certain kinds, or styles, over others. That is, from the incredibly rich menu of sounds available today we might choose most often to hear rap, jazz, rock, country, pop—or something else. Some of us enjoy instrumental music; others prefer song. Our tastes change over long periods of time, and our preferences may differ from one moment to another, depending on our mood or circumstance at a given time.

The great world of *classical* music, as it is often called, also encompasses a tremendous range of sounds. Unfortunately, none of the terms generally used to distinguish between the music we call popular and the music we call classical is truly descriptive of the differences we recognize between them. We can agree that music that serves no functional purpose, but simply expresses an abstract concept a composer thought worth sharing—music that requires intense concentration and sometimes a measure of learning and experience on the part of the listener—differs from music that exists primarily as a means of entertainment. It is difficult, however, to describe differences between these two kinds of music without implying unintended and inappropriate judgments of value. Commonly we speak of music that requires extensive training on the part of composers and performers, and that may assume some guided experience on the part of the listener, as *classical, art, concert,* or *serious* music; but none of those terms properly distinguishes between this music and much of the music played by DJs on popular radio sites. No one is more *serious* about music than outstanding singer-songwriters in the popular fields. Many great American songs have survived beyond their days of initial popularity to become *classics* in their own right. *Concerts* are among the most important venues for experiencing so-called popular music of many kinds. And *art* suggests simply a creative means of expression, with no inherent requirement that it be simple or complex or even good or bad. Further confusing the issue, many so-called classical pieces have become so familiar and well-loved that today they are performed in concerts we refer to as *pops*.

The terms italicized above, however, have become inherent parts of the language of music. You will hear and read them in formal and informal discussions of music, and we will use them in this text, although with sensitivity to the unintended connotations they have acquired. Words, after all, serve only to broaden our ideas about music and our knowledge of its history. No words can substitute for the glorious experience of hearing, and understanding, the great and beautiful music of the United States.

The more we understand about musical forms and the elements that constitute the building materials of music, the better we are prepared to enjoy music of all kinds. Recognition of the historical context in which music was conceived, and an awareness of the relationships between music and the other arts of a given period, will enhance our understanding and pleasure. It is my personal wish that your delight in listening to all kinds of music will increase immeasurably as you discover the many and varied aspects of America's musical landscape.

PRELUDE
Basic Properties of Musical Sound

Music, an art of organized sounds, is virtually limitless in variety and in the power to enchant and challenge our ears. However, because it never holds still, and we can neither see nor touch it, understanding music can be an elusive thing, and the world's greatest music may prove challenging to the unprepared listener.

The more we understand the qualities of music, the elements of which it is constructed, the historical-social setting in which a given piece evolved, the intent of the composer, and the contributions of the performer or performers, the greater will be our intellectual, emotional, and aesthetic rewards for listening to any kind of music. One can readily develop a sense of musical form, making it easier to enjoy a piece of some length. And while it's unnecessary to be able to read music in order to enjoy listening to it, some knowledge of how music is notated may be of interest even to the casual listener. The purpose of our Prelude, then, is to explain some basic concepts which may serve as a helpful introduction to your music experience, and to which you may refer throughout your course of study.

The Elements of Music

Musicians generally recognize four **elements of music**—rhythm, melody, harmony, and timbre—as the fundamental materials of which music is composed. As we listen to music, any one of the elements—a memorable tune, a driving rhythm, the unusual sound of an exotic musical instrument—may attract our attention; but more often we respond to the combination of two or more of the elements of music without methodically analyzing the name and proportions of each.

Understanding these building blocks of music enhances our listening and provides a vocabulary with which to discuss a piece in some detail. Further, listening with *awareness* of what we hear greatly increases our capacity to enjoy all kinds of music.

1

TABLE 1   Rhythmic Notation

This table assumes that the quarter note equals 1 beat. Any other note value may equal 1 beat instead, the number of beats per other note values changing proportionately.

Notated Symbol	Name	Rest	Number of Beats per Note	Number of Notes Equal to 4 Beats
ο	Whole note	–	4	1
♩	Half note	–	2	2
♩	Quarter note	≹	1	4
♪	Eighth note	⁊	½	8
♬	Sixteenth note	⁊	¼	16

Rhythm   Because music consists of arrangements of long and short sounds and silences, **rhythm,** having to do with time relationships in music, is the most basic of the elements. The system of music notation used in the Western world indicates the rhythm of music by giving the *proportional* length of each sound and silence; that is, written music dictates the duration of each sound or silence only in relation to other sounds and silences in the piece.

Rhythmic values are expressed in the familiar terminology of fractions (Table 1): the value of a *half note,* for example, is equal to half the value of a *whole note*. But the specific duration of a half note depends upon the **tempo,** or rate of speed, at which the music is performed. *Tempo,* which means time, is one of many Italian words adopted into a virtually universal music language during the sixteenth and seventeenth centuries, when Italians dominated music in the Western world. Foreign musicians studying in Italy absorbed the techniques and much of the terminology of their Italian masters, which they shared with their own students and patrons upon returning to their homelands. Since then, many Italian music terms have been used all over the world, remaining in common use today.

Music listeners quickly become familiar with the most common Italian words for tempos, shown in Table 2, which regularly appear in printed concert programs and often also in newspaper reviews of concerts and recordings.

Meter   Just as language is formed of irregularly occurring accented and un-accented syllables, musical sounds, too, may occur without specific rhythmic organization. If, however, musical sounds are arranged in rhythmic patterns, similar to those of poetry as opposed to prose, we say the music is metered.

Meter organizes rhythm into units called *measures,* each containing a particular number of pulses, or beats. The common meters are *duple* (two

TABLE 2	Common Tempo Indications
Largo	Slow; "broad"
Adagio	Slow; "at ease"
Andante	Moderately slow; "walking" tempo
Moderato	Moderate
Allegro	Fast; cheerful
Presto	Very fast
Vivace	Lively
Molto	Very (*allegro molto* = very fast)
Non troppo	Not too much (*allegro non troppo* = not too fast)
Con brio	With spirit

Duple meter

Triple meter

Quadruple meter

> = Stress, or accent   ⌣ = Secondary accent

FIGURE 1

Common meters, showing accents.

beats per measure), *triple* (three beats per measure), and *quadruple* (four beats per measure). In Western practice—that is, in music based on European traditions of the seventeenth through the nineteenth centuries—the first beat of each measure is normally accented, or stressed; and if there are four or more beats per measure, there is at least one secondary accent as well. For example, in quadruple meter (Figure 1), the secondary accent falls on the third beat.

FIGURE 2

A piano keyboard.

Second

Third

Octave

Melody

Musical sounds, called **tones,** are caused by something vibrating at a particular frequency, or rate of speed. Tones are said to be relatively high or low in **pitch,** depending upon the rate of vibration of the medium producing the sound: The faster a string on a violin or the column of air in a trumpet vibrates, the higher the level of pitch. Much as a sentence is a meaningful succession of words, a **melody** is a meaningful succession of tones of various levels of pitch.

Tones have *letter* names, A through G. The **interval,** or distance, between tones is named according to the *number* of tones it includes; for example, from A to B is a *second,* from A to C, a *third,* and so on (Figure 2). The most basic interval is the *eighth,* called an **octave,** the two tones of which share the same letter name and sound nearly alike. The higher tone of the octave vibrates at exactly twice the rate of the lower tone, the simple relationship of their frequencies (the ratio 2:1) causing minimal tension between them.

All keys on a keyboard that bear the same letter name *look* the same as well, because they occupy the same position relative to other keys. For example, if we start at the left of the keyboard and move up, we see that the last white key before the third of the three black keys is always an A (Figure 2), D is always the white note between the two black notes, and so on.

Scales.

Melodies are based on **scales:** stepwise rising or descending patterns of pitches within the range of an octave. By the seventeenth century, two particular seven-note patterns—the **major** and **minor scales**—had been accepted as those that best served European composers of concert music, and they continue to prevail in Western music today.

The major and minor scales each include two **half steps** (the closest distance between two keys on a keyboard) and five **whole steps** (the equivalent of two half steps). The white notes of the octave from C to C on the keyboard correspond to the pattern of the *major* scale, while the white notes of the octave from A to A correspond to the pattern of the *minor* scale.

Music based on the major scale sounds very different from music that is minor, because of the different order in which the half and whole steps occur (Figure 3). If you can play a keyboard instrument, you might play the first three notes of "Doe, a Deer" from *The Sound of Music,* beginning on C. These are

(a)

W* W H* W W W H

*Whole steps
*Half steps

(b)

W H W W H W W

FIGURE 3

The major and minor scales.
(a) The white notes of the
octave from C to C on the
keyboard correspond to
the pattern of the major
scale. (b) The white notes of
the octave from A to A on the
keyboard correspond to the
pattern of the minor scale.

the first three notes of the major scale. Now *lower* the third tone by a half step, or begin playing on A and use all white keys, and you will hear how the melody would begin if it were based on a minor scale.

Other scales we will encounter in our survey of American music include the **modes**—seven-note patterns whose arrangements of half and whole steps differ from those of either the major or the minor scale. If you start on any white key of a keyboard *other* than C or A, and play up or down an octave using white keys only, you will have played a mode different from the major or minor scale. Notice that although each mode, or scale, has five whole and two half steps, the different order in which they occur strongly affects the "flavor" of the sound. Another popular scale, the basis of many children's songs and much folk music, is the simple **pentatonic** (five-note) pattern, represented by the five black keys on a keyboard. If you can play "by ear," you will find that many tunes can be played using those five tones only.

Further Characteristics of Melody. Melodies of course have rhythm, the tones of a melody occurring in some order of long sounds, short sounds, or both. If a melody, such as a children's song or folk song, is particularly singable and memorable and seems complete in itself, we call it a **tune.** A different kind of melody is a brief, fragmentary melodic idea or **motive,** recurring throughout a piece, particularly in instrumental music. Probably the most famous motive in Western music is the four-note "knocking" pattern that begins Beethoven's Symphony No. 5, identified at least as readily by its rhythm as by its melodic characteristics.

Because we may draw a line up or down from one note of a melody to the next, we think of a melody as *linear* and identify its contour as angular (with large leaps between the tones), smooth (with the tones closely connected), or some combination of angular and smooth. Figure 4 compares, for example, the

FIGURE 4

Melodic contours.

(a) Smooth melody line   (b) Angular melody line

FIGURE 5

Triads on each note of the C major scale.

I   ii   iii   IV   V   vi   vii°   I

smooth contour of "Merrily We Roll Along" with the angular shape of "Westminster Chimes." Other familiar tunes that might further clarify this distinction are "America" ("My Country, 'Tis of Thee") (smooth) and "The Star Spangled Banner" (sharply angular in contour).

Harmony The melodies of European and American music generally are accompanied by simultaneous combinations of tones called **harmony,** defined as the sounding of two or more different tones at once in a logical or meaningful (not necessarily beautiful) manner. The system of harmony that has governed Western music for nearly 400 years, based upon the major and minor scales (the tonal scales), is called **tonality** or the **tonal system.**

Purposeful combinations of *three or more* different tones constitute **chords,** which enrich the sounds of Western music and please Western ears much as linear perspective adds depth and pleases the eyes of lovers of Western art. Indeed, chordal harmony, like linear perspective, is a peculiarly Western concept; both the aural and the visual concepts evolved during the Western Renaissance, and neither has become characteristic of non-Western arts. As shown in Figure 5, the tones of a chord are notated in *vertical* fashion, above and beneath each other.

Consonant and Dissonant Sounds. Certain combinations of musical sounds, which we call **consonant,** have the effect of being passive, or at rest. Other harmonies, sounding relatively tense or active, we call **dissonant.** It is important to understand that dissonance and consonance have nothing to do with "good" or "bad" sounds (composers are hardly likely to choose "bad" sounds for their music), but refer only to the relative degree of activity or tension the composer intends or the listener perceives.

Of course, these concepts are entirely subjective, differing widely from one time, culture, or individual to another. Generally, though, dissonance and consonance work together to provide variety and stability in musical compositions, dissonant sounds creating tension that may (or may not) resolve to consonant harmony, much as a dancer expressively tenses and then relaxes muscles.

Tonal Harmony. The first tone of a major or minor scale, called the **tonic,** represents a kind of home base, from which a piece of music in the Western tradition is likely to begin and on which it is even more likely to end. The tonic names the **key** of a composition; for example, we say a piece is in the key of A major, meaning that the tonic note is A and most of the tones are those of the major scale. For another example, a piece based on the D minor scale is said to be in the key of D minor.

Each of the tones in a major or minor scale bears a specific relationship, relatively distant or close, to the tonic. The fifth step of the scale, called the **dominant,** is the tone most closely related to tonic. It is heard frequently during a piece, and it seems to bear almost a gravitational pull back to tonic, or home base. The second-closest tone to tonic is the fourth step above (or the fifth below) tonic, called the **subdominant.**

The most basic chord in the tonal system, consisting of three alternate tones (or a third piled on top of a third), is called a **triad** (Figure 5). Triads may be built on any tone of the major or minor scale and bear the same relationship to tonic and to each other as the tones upon which they are built. Thus the strongest relationship is between the tonic triad (often represented by the Roman numeral I) and the triad built upon the fifth note of the scale, or the dominant (V). The next-closest chord to tonic is the triad built upon the fourth, or subdominant, step of the scale, which provides a somewhat weaker drive toward tonic. (Perhaps you will notice the increasing levels of dissonance from the *major* chords [I, IV, and V], to the *minor* chords [ii, iii, and vi], and to the vii° chord, called *diminished* and indicated by the small circle to the upper right of the lowercase Roman numeral.)

The I, IV, and V chords, then, provide the cornerstones of tonal harmony. Many simple melodies are effectively accompanied by just these three closely related chords.

Texture. Much as we describe the texture of a piece of fabric according to the way in which its threads are interwoven, so we describe the **texture** of music in terms of its "threads," or melodic lines. The combination of lines of music may or may not achieve harmony, depending on the intentions of the music's creators.

Music consisting only of one line of melody—a Native American song or flute piece, or an ancient folk tune, for example—we call **monophonic** in texture, the prefix *mono* indicating the sounding of one line of music. No matter the number of voices or instruments performing the same melody in **unison**—that is, all sounding the same pitches (not necessarily in the same octave) at the same time—the texture of the music remains monophonic, and there are no harmonic combinations of sound—though a listener's ear may perceive implied harmonic relationships between consecutive tones.

Another music texture, **heterophony,** involving the simultaneous sounding of two or more different versions of the same melody, is often heard in musics outside the Western tradition. Here, too, there is no intention to produce harmony but simply to enrich or enhance—or perform in the most natural and comfortable way—the melodic line.

A piece such as a **round,** in which different melody lines are heard *simultaneously,* is **polyphonic** in texture, the prefix *poly* indicating more than one of something occurring at the same time. In a round, all the voices perform the same melody but enter at different times, producing meaningful combinations of tones, or harmony. Polyphony may instead involve combinations of *different* melodic lines that, when combined, produce harmony.

A fourth music texture, **homophony,** occurs when a melody is accompanied not by one or more other melodic lines, but by chords. In other words, the voices (instrumental or vocal) accompanying the melody produce harmony but are not primarily of melodic interest themselves. Hymns sung by a church congregation are often accompanied by an organ or piano adding chordal harmony; a band provides harmonic accompaniment while the crowd sings "The Star Spangled Banner" at a football game; folk singers may accompany themselves by strumming chords on a musical instrument. All these are examples of homophonic, or **chordal,** texture. (See Figure 6.)

FIGURE 6

Texture in music.

Monophony
One melody line

Heterophony
Two or more versions of the same melody

Polyphony

or

Melody in more than one line

Homophony
A melody accompanied by chords

TABLE 3   Dynamic Levels

Levels of Volume

Italian Term	Abbreviation	English Meaning
Pianissimo	pp	Very soft
Piano	p	Soft
Mezzopiano	mp	Moderately soft
Mezzoforte	mf	Moderately loud
Forte	f	Loud
Fortissimo	ff	Very loud

Timbre   The quality or **timbre** (tam'-breh) of a musical sound depends on characteristics of the medium producing it. Thus musical instruments have distinctive timbres according to their size, the material of which they are made, and the manner in which they are played. For example, the timbre or "color" of the sound produced by a violin differs from that of a flute, and the sound produced by plucking the string of a violin is unlike the sound made when the same string is bowed.

Pitch also affects the timbre of musical sound: Notice how the high tones of a piano differ in timbre as well as pitch from the very low tones of the instrument, and how men's and women's voices are distinguished in terms of timbre as well as the range of their pitches.

Another factor affecting the timbre of a voice or instrument is the loudness or softness of the sound, called its **dynamic level.** Composers often vary the dynamic level within a piece for many reasons: to achieve emotional effects, to illustrate events described in the text of a song, or to achieve extramusical effects in descriptive instrumental music. The Italian words **piano** and **forte,** respectively meaning soft and loud, are among the commonly used dynamic terms included with their abbreviations in Table 3.

Form

When describing a work of art, we often consider the manner in which it is organized—its **form.** There are many approaches to formal design, based upon principles of *repetition* and *contrast,* with repetition lending a work unity, symmetry, and balance, and contrast providing the variety necessary to sustain interest. A play, for example, may have one or several acts, a novel a number of chapters, a poem one or several strophes or stanzas. Similarly, a musical composition may have one or several sections, or **movements.** As each act, chapter, or stanza of a literary work is logically organized within itself, so each movement of a symphony, for example, has a particular design, or form.

The form of a musical piece, or a movement within a piece, depends on the manner in which the composer organizes the elements of music.

Music Notation

Although one may well enjoy listening to and even performing music without necessarily learning to read music notation, some conception of how music is written may be of interest. For centuries, Western music has been written on a **staff** of five lines and four spaces (see Figure 7). Musical pitches and rhythms are written as **notes,** and notated silences are called **rests.** The staff forms a kind of "ladder," with each line and each space representing a particular pitch. A sign called a **clef,** placed at the beginning of the staff, indicates that a particular line represents a specific pitch, thus fixing the relative position of all the other pitches on the staff. For example, the *bass clef* (𝄢), sometimes called the F clef, on which lower tones are notated, indicates that the fourth line of the staff is (a particular) F. The *treble clef* (𝄞), also called the G clef, on which higher tones are notated, indicates that the second line of the staff represents (a particular) G. In other words, placing a clef on the staff provides a reference point that fixes the pitches of all the lines and spaces.

Understanding just these basic concepts of how music is written allows us, without really "reading" music, to follow the ascending and descending patterns of tones written on a page and have an approximate idea of how the music would sound.

Elements of an American Sound

Because America's early settlers came from many different cultures, it took time for music to acquire a characteristic American sound; but surprisingly soon music, like the English language, changed its accent in the New World. The manner in which the elements of music are selected and combined, the choice of timbres, various means of musical expression such as changes in dynamic level and in tempo, and the purpose for which music is intended are among the nearly indefinable qualities that determine a particular composition's characteristic sound, or **style.**

In music, as in fashion, *style* refers to a manner or mode of expression, and again as in fashion, style in music is affected by the time and the culture that produce it. For example, American rhythms often are more flexible than those characteristic of European music; and although the delay or anticipation of accented beats called **syncopation** occurs in music worldwide, its bold and consistent use gives much American classical as well as popular music a distinctive flavor. The long, irregular melodies of pieces such as Samuel Barber's *Adagio for Strings* (Listening Example 76) are sometimes thought to reflect the informality, personal freedom, and lack of physical and cultural boundaries associated with the ideal American life. Jazz musicians, by using traditional instruments in new and unusual ways, caused Americans to alter the timbres of symphonic as well as popular musics, as we hear for example in George Gershwin's *Rhapsody in Blue* (an Optional Listening Example).

Thus, although much American music is stylistically indistinguishable from music by European composers of the same period, perhaps you will sense in some American pieces a certain audacity, a generous expansiveness, a peculiar irregularity, or some other scarcely definable attribute that simply "sounds American."

How to Improve Your Listening Skills

Attendance at live performances as well as repeated and concentrated study of the text's listening examples are essential to furthering your understanding and enjoyment of music, for no read or spoken words can substitute for the impact music makes on our minds and hearts. It is not difficult to develop skills to enhance your listening comprehension and pleasure—not just for now but for the rest of your life.

First, approach each listening experience with expectations of enjoyment. Next, try to memorize music as you hear it so that it will quickly become familiar, and so that you will develop an awareness of a composition's form even as you listen to it for the first time. Remember to apply the knowledge gleaned from your class discussions and from this text to the music you are hearing. By listening actively, even *creatively,* you will participate in the successful collaboration of composer, performer, and listener that makes possible the magnificent experience of enjoying great music.

Listening Example 1, "Love Me Tender," offers the opportunity to apply your developing listening skills to an American song, first popular with the Union army during the Civil War with the title "Aura Lee," and popularized again, with new lyrics, by Elvis Presley, in 1956. The song is in **strophic form,** the most common song form of all, in which two or more stanzas or strophes of text are all set to the same tune. Repetition of the melody lends unity to

"Love Me Tender"

Composer
George R. Poulton (1828–1867)

Lyrics
Elvis Presley

Performer
Marty Robbins

Accompaniment
Guitar, orchestra, softly singing chorus

Meter
Quadruple (4 beats per measure)

Tempo
Slow, relaxed

Form
Strophic. The song follows the classic verse-chorus structure, with each stanza or verse (there are three) followed by a refrain, or chorus.

The performance begins with a lightly syncopated descending melodic phrase played in low range by a flute and echoed by softly singing female voices, as a guitar lightly outlines the harmony. This melodic phrase recurs in the strings before the second verse, and in the voices and strings before the third verse.

The orchestra gradually becomes more involved, other instruments adding melodic comments in the second verse, as the background chorus also increases in volume. The accompaniment thins for the third verse, becoming light and delicate; but the orchestra surges to new significance in the final chorus.

Notice how changes in dynamic level, accompaniment timbres, and harmony affect your emotional response to the song. Notice, too, the steady, light beat and the slight relaxation in tempo just before the end.

Lyrics
1. Love me tender, love me sweet,
   Never let me go.
   You have made my life complete,
   And I love you so.

   (Chorus)

CD 1
Track 1
3:02

—Continued

Listening Example 1—Concluded

"Love Me Tender"

Love me tender, love me true,
All my dreams fulfill.
For my darlin', I love you,
And I always will.

2. Love me tender, love me long,
Take me to your heart.
For it's there that I belong,
And we'll never part.

(Chorus)

3. Love me tender, love me dear,
Tell me you are mine.
I'll be yours through all the years,
Till the end of time.

(Chorus)

Listening Example selections are on the three ninety-minute CDs that accompany this text.

---

the form, while the evolving text gives variety. Like many popular songs, "Love Me Tender" follows the **verse-chorus** structure, with a chorus, having the same words and music, interspersed between verses relating the story or situation.

Each time you listen to this song, try to hear something that escaped your notice before, "stretching your ears" to capture all that the performance offers.

Terms to Review

elements of music   The basic materials of which music is composed.

rhythm   The arrangement of time in music.

tempo   The rate of speed at which music is performed.

meter   The organization of rhythm into patterns of strong and weak beats.

tone   A sound with a specific pitch.

pitch   The highness or lowness of a sound.

melody   A meaningful succession of pitches.

interval   The distance between two tones.

octave   The interval of an eighth.

scales   A stepwise rising or ascending pattern of pitches within the range of an octave.

major, minor scales   The tonal scales.

half step   The smallest interval on a keyboard, and the closest interval in traditional Western music.

whole step   An interval equal to two half steps.

modes   Pretonal seven-note scales whose arrangements of half and whole steps differ from both the major and minor scales.

pentatonic scale   A five-note scale within the range of an octave.

tune   A melody that is easily recognized, memorized, and sung.

motive   A short melodic phrase subject to development.

harmony   The meaningful combination of two or more different tones. /Sand W a specific pitch.

tonality, tonal system   The system of harmony that has governed Western music for about four hundred years.

chord   A meaningful combination of three or more tones.

consonance (**consonant,** adj.)   Musical sounds that seem to be passive or at rest.

dissonance (**dissonant,** adj.)   Musical sounds that imply tension, drive, or activity.

tonic   The first and most important note of the major or minor scale, often indicated by the Roman numeral I.

key   The name of the tonic upon which a tonal piece is based.

dominant   The fifth tone of the major or minor scale, often indicated by the Roman numeral V.

subdominant   The fourth tone of the major or minor scale, often indicated by the Roman numeral IV.

triad   The most basic chord in the tonal system, consisting of three alternate pitches, or two superimposed thirds.

texture   The manner in which melodic lines are used in music—alone, or combined with other melodic lines or with harmony.

monophony (**monophonic,** adj.)   The musical texture consisting of one melodic line only.

unison   The same pitch, at the same or different octaves.

heterophony   The simultaneous sounding of two or more different versions of the same melody.

round   A circular canon, which may be repeated indefinitely.

polyphony (**polyphonic,** adj.)   The simultaneous combination of two or more melodic lines.

homophony (**homophonic,** adj.)   A melody combined with chords, producing harmony. Also called **chordal** texture.

timbre   The characteristic quality of the sound of a voice or instrument.

dynamic level   The level of volume (loudness or softness) of a musical sound.

piano   Soft.

forte   Loud.

form   The organization or formal design of a musical composition.

movement   A section of a complete work that has its own formal design and a degree of independence but is conceived as a part of the whole; usually separated from other movements by a pause.

staff   Five lines and four spaces on which music is notated.

notes   The symbols with which music is written.

rests   Symbols indicating the cessation of musical sound.

clef   A sign placed on the staff that fixes the pitch of each line and space.

style   A characteristic manner of composition or performance.

syncopation   The occurrence of accents in unexpected places.

strophic form   The most common song form: two or more stanzas are set to the same melody.

verse-chorus form   Common song form in which the *verses* relate the story and a tuneful *chorus,* or **refrain,** is repeated after each verse.

Suggestions for Further Listening

Duple meter
John Philip Sousa, "The Stars and Stripes Forever," Listening Example 25, p. 114

Syncopation
Scott Joplin, "Maple Leaf Rag," Listening Example 29, p. 148

European music intended to sound American
Claude Debussy, "Golliwog's Cakewalk" from *Children's Corner*

Darius Milhaud, "La création du monde" ("The Creation of the World")
Maurice Ravel, Violin Sonata
Igor Stravinsky, "Ragtime"

Critical Thinking

What roles does music currently play in your life?

What do you think music contributes to a visual experience, such as watching a film or television?

Has music ever enhanced your ability to remember something—an advertised product, for example? If so, how?

If you are familiar with Elvis Presley's recording of "Love Me Tender," how would you compare his performance and Marty Robbins's, using terms and concepts introduced in this section of the text?

Go to www.mhhe.com/ferrisaml5 for a list of additional Web-based resources that relate to the content in this chapter.

PART

1

Music in Early North America

The Early Years: Historical and Cultural Perspective

Scholars believe that human experience has always included music, although music's sound and its place in society have differed widely from one time and one culture to another. Even today some people differentiate between "music" and "noise"—often disagreeing, however, on which is which—whereas others deny the distinction. Some consider sounds of nature, such as birdcalls or thunder, a kind of music; others do not. For some people, music is art, and for others it is simply an integral part of their everyday experience. Speakers of some languages have no word for music at all, although music is fully integrated into their daily experience. But always, it seems, patterns of sound—one possible concept of what we mean by music—have found a meaningful place in human society.

The Beginnings of Music in America

Although today's American music is rooted in the artistic styles and experiences of European and African cultures, long before the first white settlers or black slaves touched the North American shores the people living here were making music of their own. Even though we have no firsthand knowledge of the music of the early North American Indians, Native American music traditions have evolved so slowly over vast periods of time that we may imagine their early music concepts bore a close relationship to those of today.

Native Americans
Scholars generally believe that the people destined to be called North American Indians or Native Americans began coming to this continent from Asia between 18,000 and 40,000 years ago, crossing the land bridge then existing where the Bering Strait is today, and spreading south from Canada and Alaska into Mexico and Central and South America, and eastward to the Atlantic Ocean and the Gulf of Mexico. New archaeological evidence suggests, however, that the New World may have been colonized on numerous different occasions, beginning thousands of years earlier than previously thought and by people arriving from several different regions of Europe. It is possible, for example, that the people who established an ancient campsite 45 miles south of Richmond, Virginia, recently dated at around 18,000 years old, came by sea across the Atlantic rather than by land from Asia. Still, although fascinating research continues as new discoveries occur, it appears likely that *most* of the people who first arrived on the North American continent came from Siberia by crossing the Bering Sea land bridge.

Whatever their distant heritage, all early American Indian cultures shared a close dependence upon and affinity with the natural world. However, over vast periods of time they developed a very broad linguistic and cultural diversity. Thus when Christopher Columbus arrived in the region of the Bahamas, late in the fifteenth century, well over 300 American Indian cultures with several hundred languages inhabited what is now the United States. Today we generally recognize eight geographic areas, within each of which many tribes share cultural characteristics similar to each other's but distinct from those of Native Americans inhabiting other cultural regions (see Table on p. 18).

Today's descendants of the early Native Americans retain a strong reverence for and a sense of oneness with nature, expressed in their music as in all their arts—although the term "arts" here gives us pause, because traditional American Indian dry (sand) painting, weaving, pottery, basketry, and music all had spiritual and utilitarian significance without which they would have been meaningless. For example, magnificent buckskin shield covers, designed according to divine instruction, protect the wearer as much by the sacred design etched, incised, or painted on them as by the heavy material of which they are made. The Western separation of sacred and secular concepts

Fight scene painted on a Sioux shield cover. The central mounted warrior shows the manner in which shields were held.

17

TABLE Representative Cultures Sharing Music Style Traits

Plains		East	
Northern	*Southern*	*Northeastern*	*Southeastern*
Arapaho	Comanche	Iroquois nations	Cherokee
Blackfoot	Kiowa		Creek
Cheyenne	Western Cherokee	Wabanaki	Seminole
Crow			Shawnee
Dakota (Sioux)			

Great Lakes	Southwest/ Southern California	Athapaskan
Menomini	Hopi/Zuni/Other "mesa" pueblos	Apache
Ojibwa (Chippewa)	Maricopa	Navajo
Winnebago	O'odham (Papago)	
	Pima	
	Rio Grande Pueblos (from three language families)	
	Yavapai	
	Yuma	

Great Basin/ Northern California	Northwest Coast	Eskimo/Inuit and Athapaskans
Paiute	Bella Coola	Eskimos of Alaska, Canada, and Greenland
Pomo	Kwakiutl	Northern Athapaskans (Slave, Kulchin, Dogrib)
Shoshoni	Nootka	
Ute	Salish	
	Tlingit	

has little meaning among Native Americans, for whom religion, art, music, and poetry are the inseparable threads—the warp and woof—of life and culture.

Our brief survey can only generalize about important concepts generally shared by members of different Native American cultures, especially up until the early years of the twentieth century, before which time their cultural expression remained quite consistent. During the last century, acculturation brought about significant changes in Indian music, the changes varying from one region to another; yet many basic tenets of Native American culture retain their ancient values today.

European Emigrants

During the sixteenth century, Europeans began to arrive and settle on the North American continent in large numbers, bringing with them their various musical customs. Missionaries, adventurers, explorers, and settlers traversed the land stretching from Florida to the northern California coast. Maps and pictures drawn by these intrepid travelers, vividly depicting American Indians as they appeared to the newcomers, and the great natural beauty of the newly discovered land, encouraged other Europeans to join them in the vast New World. Soon French Catholics and French Protestants (Huguenots) in the Southeast, and Spanish Catholics and Sir Francis Drake's Protestant Englishmen in the Southwest, were persuading American Indians to join them in singing Christian songs as part of their effort to convert them to Christianity.

The Pilgrims and Puritans arriving in New England early in the seventeenth century were Protestants, whose protests against the Roman Catholic Church included some concerning the performance of religious music. That century also brought English Quakers (members of the Society of Friends) as well as German-speaking Protestants, such as the Mennonites and Moravians.

All these brave settlers left behind them a rich and varied cultural experience. Roman Catholics had enjoyed generous support for their arts, including music, from royalty and the church. The Protestant New England settlers, sharing simple tastes, generally avoided the extravagant characteristics of the music style (*Baroque*) then prevalent in Europe, but many of them loved art and music and made both a significant part of their life. The lyrical folk songs and rollicking dance tunes of various European cultures also traveled with the settlers to become a part of their new experience in their adopted homeland.

Puritan Society

The more we learn about the Puritans, the more we realize how inappropriate is the stereotype of them as plain and wholly serious, for Puritan society included sophisticated men and women of keen wit and high intellect. Some brought with them their personal libraries, but the small ships carrying them to America had scarce room for such luxuries, and before long the colonists began to produce their own new literature, largely consisting of didactic religious tracts but also including memoirs, essays, and poetry.

The New World's first poet, Anne Bradstreet (1612–1672), busy wife of a colonial governor and the mother of eight, composed a significant body of poetry despite her own serious illness and the rigors of colonial life. Though she declared her peers believed "my hand a needle better fits" (than a poet's pen), she was admired then as now for her learned and well-crafted poems. Here is an example:

> *I am obnoxious to each carping tongue,*
> *Who sayes, my hand a needle better fits,*
> *A Poets Pen, all scorne, I should thus wrong;*
> *For such despighte they cast on female wits:*
> *If what i doe prove well, it wo'nt advance,*
> *They'l say its stolen, or else, it was by chance.*

Although the practical early New Englanders had little use for art for art's sake and specifically excluded art from their churches, still their daily experience was rich in artistic expression. For example, the graveyards adjacent to their plainly furnished houses of worship often contained elaborately carved and decorated headstones. They furnished their homes with many functional articles of beauty,

Anne Bradstreet.

covering tables and beds with fine needlework to provide protection from cold New England drafts, while beautifully carved furniture, hand-painted dishes, and toys elaborately constructed for the delight of children lessened the severity of New England colonial life.

Although landscape painting held little attraction for early New Englanders more inclined to tame than to admire natural wonders, portraits served the practical purpose of preserving a likeness and so were highly valued. Most portrait painters were amateur artists who earned their living as farmers, as shopkeepers, or in some other trade, and who thought of themselves simply as craftspeople producing commodities of practical worth. The rather flat or linear quality of American folk art lends it a pleasing flavor distinct from the professional products of their European contemporaries. Ironically, these early artists often painted their subjects dressed in elaborate finery, suggesting an attraction to worldly goods surprising in the staid Puritan society. But how astonished these modest people would be to know the aesthetic and monetary value their work has acquired today.

The African Experience in Early America

Even before the Pilgrims' arrival at Plymouth Rock in 1620, Africans were being forcibly brought to, and made to work in, the New World. At first African slaves constituted a minuscule portion of society in New York or New England, and even in southern colonies; but after 1700 the importation of slaves increased greatly. By the time of the American Revolution, there were slaves in large numbers in the South, where their forced services made possible the great plantations that produced the coffee, tobacco, sugar, rice, and (much later) cotton on which the southern economy relied.

During the eighteenth century, a surge of humanitarian feeling gave rise to strong movements against the continuing slave trade, which finally was prohibited in the United States twenty years after

Gravestone in a colonial churchyard.

Elizabeth Davis, *Mrs. Hezekia Beardsley*, c. 1785–1790.

the ratification of the Constitution. However, the strong protests of Quakers and other religious groups notwithstanding, antislavery sentiment had little effect in this country until well into the nineteenth century. In New England, slavery proved unprofitable and disappeared, but in the South the invention of the cotton gin in 1793 made slavery an even more integral part of the plantation system than before.

Forbidden to practice their familiar African religious rituals and to sing songs, dance, and play musical instruments in their accustomed ways, the brutally uprooted Africans and their American-born progeny, starved for religion, attempted to adapt traditional African musical expression to worship of the white people's Christian god. Their early efforts mostly met with ridicule, because their white owners regarded them as "beasts" unfit to receive religious instruction of any kind; but here as in their fatherland, the slaves integrated music and faith into their daily lives.

Revolution, in Classical Style

Eighteenth-century Americans of European descent reflected a strong European influence, enhanced by increased opportunities for travel and communication from one continent to the other. European artists of this time had adopted the *classical* ideals of ancient Greek sculptors and architects, who strove for perfection of form, balanced designs, and relatively restrained emotional expression. Artists on both sides of the Atlantic, in fact, from about 1750 until 1825 applied order, balance, and emotional restraint to their work, rendering the Age of Reason in social and political affairs the Age of Classicism in the arts. To distinguish eighteenth-century visual works of art rendered in this cool, reasoned manner from their ancient classical models, we call them *neoclassical* in style; but too little ancient music remains to cause confusion in terms, and the eighteenth century is known as the Classical period of music.

Paradoxically, the Age of Reason spawned several violent revolutionary movements, and Americans joined a number of European nations in firmly rejecting rule by absolute authority and establishing a republican form of government. Enlightened intellectuals—hardly impassioned fanatics—led the American Revolution, the classical influence evident, for example, in the cool, reasoned language of the Declaration of Independence, which begins "When in the course of human events it becomes necessary for one people to dissolve the political bonds which have connected them with another..." America's founders, led by Thomas Jefferson and influenced by outstanding French neoclassical architects, designed Washington, D.C., to be an orderly city of wide and regular streets with many grassy parks and shady trees. The simple lines and classical columns of Washington's state buildings, although not constructed until the early years of the nineteenth century, clearly represent the ideals of the Classical period during which they were planned.

Classical influence is reflected in the orderly layout of streets and the prevalence of Greco-Roman architectural style in Washington, D.C.

21

Painting in Eighteenth-Century America

Although American artists during this century had more training and sophistication than the folk artists of the settlers' period, their finest works retained an innocence, honesty, and decorative sense distinguishing them from the more elegant European works of the same era. John Singleton Copley (1738–1815), America's greatest colonial artist, was largely self-taught. He developed a highly personal style rooted in the American tradition and governed by classical order and reserve. Becoming increasingly, though reluctantly, involved in events relating to the impending American Revolution, Copley sailed for Europe in 1774, intending to return to America when peace was attained, but in fact he spent the rest of his life abroad.

In Europe, Copley studied with the famous American expatriate Benjamin West (1738–1820), who encouraged him to paint historical and heroic subjects. Although the subsequent paintings were more elegant and polished than Copley's early American portraits, they were correspondingly less distinctive and interesting. One of Copley's later paintings, *Watson and the Shark* (1778) is of great interest, however, for in it Copley produced a warm and sympathetic portrayal of an African American man attempting to assist a white man—Watson—desperately floundering in the water. The would-be rescuer has thrown a rope, which Watson has missed, as the shark looms menacingly nearby. (Notice how the African American's outstretched arm, mirroring that of Watson, contributes to the symmetry and the drama of this strong painting.) Such a subtle and sympathetic rendering of relations between African Americans and whites was unusual in that time, and Copley's painting is in every way a masterpiece.

Charles Willson Peale (1741–1827) also studied for a time in Europe with Benjamin West, returning to America to become the leading artist in Philadelphia for many years. Peale revealed the classical thirst for knowledge in his boundless curiosity about a broad range of subjects, implementing his ideas (in the practical, classical way) by establishing the first American museum of natural history, in Philadelphia in 1802.

Peale, who fought in the American Revolution, painted fine, lifelike portraits of the leaders of the young nation. His painting *The Staircase Group,* reflecting the eighteenth-century interest in scientific measurement and optical effects, is so realistic a portrayal of Peale's sons standing on a staircase that George Washington is said to have bowed to the boys as he passed by the painting one day.

Today we recognize the dominant effects of many cultures on the evolution of American music, but the traditions and practices of all the early inhabitants—those native to the land, the early European arrivals, and the people brought by force from their African homeland—have deeply colored the complex landscape of American music. From at least the early seventeenth century, the music heard in the widely separated inhabited regions of the continent reflected highly disparate values and sounds. Nevertheless, Indian, African, and European musics had some things in common: all were more likely to be performed by amateurs than by professionals, in intimate (inside or outside) domestic or worship settings than in a concert hall, and often (although not always) with spiritual connotation. The distinctions we draw now between sacred and secular music and between high and low art—and the difficulties we experience in finding appropriate terminology to distinguish one kind of art from another—had little meaning in the early American experience. ♪

John Singleton Copley, *Mrs. Thomas Boylston*, 1766.

John Singleton Copley, *Watson and the Shark*, 1778. Oil on canvas, 72½ in. × 90¼ in. (184 cm × 229.5 cm). Although largely self-taught, Copley effectively captured the seething action and dramatic interplay of emotions between the desperate characters in his masterful painting.

Charles Willson Peale,
The Staircase Group, 1795.

North American Indian Music

Long before European settlers arrived in the New World, North American Indians were practicing their own vital music traditions, essential and integral to their most basic daily experience. Because their music always occurred in association with other activities—dance, religious ritual, prayer, work, recreation—their languages included no word for music itself; yet for American Indians then as today, life without music was unthinkable. even

Songs

Never an independent concept but always a part of dance, celebration, games, work, or prayer, Native American music essentially consists of songs imbued with strong powers to accomplish a given end, such as success in fishing, healing, gambling, or winning a bride. American Indians think of their songs not as *composed,* but as *received,* often in a dream or vision—gifts of power from the spirit world. The owner of a song may sell it or may grant someone else the right to sing it, usually in exchange for a gift; or a song may be included among the items in one's will.

Songs, which are highly valued in American Indian cultures, have been preserved through the ages not by notation but by a rich and vital oral tradition—handed down, that is, from one generation to the next through performance and memorization, stressing the necessity for completely accurate rendition. Navajos, who think of their songs as enriching experiences, sometimes count their wealth in terms of the number of songs they know. And because a basket weaver, for example, sings not only to ease the drudgery of work but more importantly to make a basket pleasing to supernatural spirits, the song must be performed and listened to with propriety.

Native American music certainly does *not* all sound the same to the discriminating ear: The songs of some tribes, for example, are low-pitched, sounding practiced or controlled, whereas songs of others lie very high in the voice, pulsing vibrantly with emotion and energy. Even within a given tribe,

FIGURE 1.1

The pleasing repetition of geometric patterns in this lovely Navajo blanket unifies the design much as melodic repetition unifies a Native American song.

songs for gambling, war dances, lullabies, and healing ceremonies vary widely in their sounds.

Although there are as many kinds of Native American songs as there are Native American cultures, some characteristics do apply to all or most. Songs are usually sung by a solo voice or by men and women singing together in unison (all singing the same notes at the same time). Although men's voices lie an octave lower than women's, and although **call-and-response**—a solo voice alternating with a group—sometimes leads to an overlap between the leader's and the other singers' tones, there is never harmony in the Western sense. Slightly different versions of the same melody performed simultaneously, however, result in *heterophony* (see p. 7). In most Native American cultures, melodic phrases generally begin on a relatively high pitch and descend without wide leaps, approximating the inflection typical of a spoken phrase.

A song often consists simply of many repetitions of one or more phrases or partial phrases, much as designs on baskets, blankets, and other Native American art often consist of repeated geometrical patterns. (See Figure 1.1.) Such aural and visual repetition has a nearly hypnotic effect, enhancing a work's spirituality and artistic coherence while also suggesting the ideal balance of nature for which the Native American constantly strives.

Texts Song texts may be in a native language or, recently, in English. Some texts are simply a series of consonant-vowel clusters or **vocables**—neutral syllables, such as *hey, yeh,* or *neh,* which may in fact convey meaning in themselves. For example, as part of the Navajo Night Way curing ceremony, teams of young men compete in the singing of *Yeibichai (Yeh-be-chy)* songs while masked dancers, personifying the sacred spirits of their grandfathers (*Yei-bi-chai* means "spirits-their-grandfathers"), bring supernatural healing power to help the sick. Every one of the hundreds of Yeibichai songs, consisting entirely of vocables, contains the call of the *Yei: Hi ye, hi ye, ho-ho ho ho,* immediately identifying the song as belonging to this tradition. You will clearly hear the distinctive call in Listening Example 2, an excerpt from a Yeibichai chant song. Notice here the alternation between singing in the normal range of the voice and singing in the extremely high **falsetto** tones, lying above the normal voice range.

Listening Example 2

Yeibichai Chant Song (excerpt)

Form
Strophic. A long phrase is repeated many times with minimal variation.

CD 1
Track 2
0:57

Melody
Repeated high-pitched tones interspersed with even higher cries of indeterminate pitch, producing a rather florid melodic line featuring dramatic upward leaps.

Rhythm
A steady pulse marked by rattle shakes (two to the beat).

Text
Vocables punctuated with the distinctive call of the Yei.

Manner of Performance
On the ninth (last) night of the Night Way ceremony, Yeibichai appears, accompanied by masked dancers shaking their gourd rattles, and by the unearthly call of the gods. The falsetto tones heard here are particularly characteristic of this and of some other Native American songs as well.

Sioux Grass Dance

Perhaps easiest to identify of all Native American styles is the singing of the Plains Indians, whose regions stretch from the foothills of the Rocky Mountains east to the Mississippi River and beyond, and from the Gulf of Mexico north into Canada. High in pitch, tense in quality, and harsh in tone, this sound is entirely distinct from that of European-based American music (Listening Example 3). No less is it distinct, however, from the music of other Native American Cultures, and from other kinds of music (simple lullabies or intimate songs, for example) of the Plains Indians themselves.

Usually referred to today as a grass dance, because of the grass braids the dancers wear at their waists, this is the stirring war dance music heard, or imitated, in countless western movies. The strong pulsations, the very high pitches sung in falsetto range, and the tense quality of the voices enhance the emotional intensity of this exciting music, as do the elaborate costumes and dramatic steps of the dancers. (See Figure 1.2.)

Sound Instruments

Although little music is performed by instruments alone, sound instruments, as they are called, often support or "hold up" a song. Navajo flutes, the primary melody-playing Native American instrument, are usually made of cedar wood

Sioux Grass Dance   (excerpt)

**CD 1
Track 3
0:55**

Form
Strophic. The phrases, some of which are introduced by a leader's "call," are sung in unison by men and women.

Melody
Each phrase begins high in pitch and descends, much as a spoken phrase often ends lower than it began. The melody descends by narrow intervals, the only large leaps occurring from the end of one phrase to the beginning of the next.

Accompaniment
The insistent beat of drums and delicate shaking of rattles accompany the singers, while the yells of observers as well as participants add to the drama and excitement of the dance.

Manner of Performance
Two teams of costumed dancers enter the area, each dancer carrying a tomahawk or another weapon. Facing each other, the teams dance in place, brandishing their weapons in a threatening manner. Next, forming a circle, they move around clockwise, crouching, leaping, and yelping dramatically. Individually, the dancers simulate the motions of battle, alternately forming and breaking the original formation.

and may be elaborately carved and decorated (Figure 1.3). Traditionally the flute was sometimes used as a courting instrument, played by a young man who trusted the wind to carry his flute-song to the woman he loved, and who hoped the sounds of his flute, by their beauty and perhaps by magic as well, would persuade her to become his bride. The Navajo flute, rarely heard during the first three quarters of the twentieth century except among families and occasionally at large intertribal gatherings called **powwows,** is frequently heard today at tribal fairs, powwows, and concerts of traditional music. It has no standard dimensions because its finger holes and air column are based on finger measurements and are therefore never the same. Each flute has its own sound and pitch. The flute repertoire now includes newly composed courting songs as well as Western-influenced classical pieces composed especially for this unique instrument.

Far more common and widespread are percussion instruments, especially container rattles of several kinds: A rattle element, such as pebbles, sacred corn, or beans, placed into a gourd or pot or into a container made of hide or bark, is shaken in time to the rhythm of a song or swung in a circular motion to produce a continuous sound (Figure 1.4). For certain sacred ceremonies, the

FIGURE 1.2
Stirring music performed in the emotional Plains Indian style enhances the drama of the traditional war dance.

FIGURE 1.3
Decorated flute of the Northern Plains Indians. This Kiowa Indian flute with a carved wind cap is decorated with painting, feathers, and braided hair.

FIGURE 1.4

Two Northwest Coast carved wooden rattles from the Tlingit culture, carved with double birds' heads. These date from the late nineteenth century and come from the area around Sitka, Alaska.

shaking of deer hooves or shells suspended from a stick (a suspension rattle) produces quite a different sort of rattling effect.

Rasps, percussion instruments normally made from a long stick of wood into which notches have been carved, are rubbed with another stick or a piece of bone (such as the shoulder blade of a sheep) to make a rasping sound. To amplify the sound, the rasp may be placed on an inverted basket or on a piece of hide over an open hole in the ground.

Drums, carrying great importance in Indian culture, exist in profuse variety. Most are made of wood, with one or two heads of the skin of deer or some other animal. The Zuni, Navajo, and Apache, however, sometimes use less resonant pottery vessels or drum jars. Hollowed-out logs, or *log drums,* tall and thin or short and wide, common to the Plains area, have become the powwow drum of today.

Contemporary Indian Song

The late nineteenth century and the twentieth century witnessed many changes in North American Indian music, as some cultural traditions nearly succumbed to overwhelming influences from modern American life. Among the earliest changes in traditional Native American music practice, for example, was the development of pan-Indian song styles, which evolved as the introduction of the horse and later the automobile increased intertribal contact. Soon Native American peoples from many tribes, speaking various languages, were meeting at powwows to share their dances, songs, and ceremonies with each other and sometimes with a public audience.

The modern powwow is common not only on reservations but also in many cities across the United States. Some Native Americans follow the powwow circuit throughout the year, often traveling many miles to sing, dance, and rodeo. The use of either English or vocables is particularly convenient for singing powwow songs, which unite the people as Native Americans and also as members of a particular tribe, authenticating their ceremonies and helping keep the people in balance with nature. Powwow songs also allow visitors from other cultures not only to view but sometimes even to participate in the wide variety of music, dance, and visual splendor associated with American Indian culture.

Professional Musicians

A recent surge of interest among Native Americans concerning their own heritage, together with new appreciation among other Americans of the rich Indian cultures, has produced a wealth of research and of live and recorded performances of both traditional and new Native American music. Some Native Americans have adopted elements of contemporary popular or vernacular musics, modifying these to suit their needs and desires; and rock bands, country-western groups, and gospel quartets flourish on many reservations today.

Other Native American musicians have chosen an academic route, studying music at universities and conservatories and applying their native gifts and experience to composing and performing concert music within the Western music tradition. Among the most prominent of these is **Carlos Nakai** (b. 1946, Figure 1.5), a classically trained cornet and trumpet player who became fascinated with the haunting sounds of the Navajo-style flute and made an exhaustive study of the instrument, which he calls "a sound sculpture—a piece of art that also creates sound." Today Nakai collaborates with musicians in many fields, finding new expression for the Navajo flute in jazz ensembles, in piano-guitar combinations, and in the concert hall. He even uses electronic techniques, including the electronic synthesizer and digital delay, together with the cedar flute.

To many American listeners, Native American music sounds more "foreign" than the music of many distant cultures. However, Americans are becoming more aware of and sensitive to the values of a music born and nurtured in this land we all share. The end-of-chapter list here includes only a few of today's

FIGURE 1.5

R. Carlos Nakai—Native American flutist, composer, and educator.

many prolific and successful professional Native American musicians, but a search on the Internet for "Native American music" will yield innumerable examples of contemporary American Indian popular and concert musicians and their music, and you may follow the links that pique your interest or arouse your curiosity.

Louis Ballard, a prestigious composer, music educator, and music journalist of Cherokee, Quapaw, Scottish, French, and English heritage, once said in reference to the uniqueness of each Navajo flute, "Don't ever let 'different' be 'alien.'" His comment applies as well to our approach to the music of Native Americans, who freely share the arts by which all humankind receives the most gracious blessings.

Terms to Review

call-and-response   A leader's solo voice alternating with a chorus of singers.

vocables   Neutral syllables, sometimes called consonant-vowel clusters.

falsetto   The singing voice above the normal (full, or chest voice) range.

powwow   A contemporary pan-Indian gathering for singing, dancing, rodeo, carnival, and other celebrations.

Key Figures

Carlos Nakai (flutist, composer)

Louis Ballard (composer, music educator, music journalist)

Other Figures in Classical Music

Edward Wapp (composer, scholar, professor)

John Kim Bell (conductor, composer)

Brent Michael Davids (Mohegan composer)

Other Figures in Popular Music

John Trudell (poet, songwriter, spoken-word performer)

Black Lodge Singers (Blackfoot drum group)

Burning Sky (guitar, Native American flute, percussion)

December Wind (vocals accompanied by guitars, drums)

Sharon Burch (singer, in Navajo and English)

Joanne Shenandoah (singer, songwriter)

XIT (hard rock)

Keith Secola (songwriter, folk rocker)

Karen Therese (singer, of mixed Cherokee, Chikasaw, Choctaw, and African-American heritage)

Clan/destine (six members, combining progressive rock, reggae, jazz, blues, and Latin sounds with their own Native American perspective)

Suggestions for Further Listening

Records produced by:

Canyon Records, 4143 North Sixteenth Street, Phoenix,
   AZ 85016

Indian House, P.O. Box 472, Taos, NM

Smithsonian Folkways, Smithsonian Institution, L'Enfant
   Plaza, Washington, DC

AKINA Productions, P.O. Box 1595, Tempe, AZ 85280

Sound of America Records, P.O. Box 8606, Albuquerque,
   NM 87198

Suggestions for Viewing

Discovering American Indian Music, Barr Films

*American Indian Dance Theater: Dances for the New
   Generation* (Canyon)

(Also see on the Internet: North American Indian Videos
   at the University of Arizona)

Critical Thinking

What specific characteristics of the Native American
music you have heard distinguish it from the European
or American classical or popular music you are familiar
with?

What influences in modern American life can you suggest
that may have affected Native American music? What
changes would such influences cause?

**Go to www.mhhe.com/ferrisaml5 for a list of additional
Web-based resources that relate to the content in this chapter.**

Folk Music

Folk music refers to simple songs and instrumental pieces whose origin has been lost or forgotten, or to music composed in an informal style traditional in certain cultures. Unpretentious, easy to remember and to perform, folk music appeals to inexperienced listeners and sophisticated musicians alike.

The folk music of the United States springs from many ethnic and cultural sources: English, Irish, Scottish, Welsh, German, and other European influences abound. Africa, too—particularly West Africa—introduced an immeasurable wealth of musical sounds and traditions to folk as well as to other musics in America. Much of the recent urban and country folk music we shall consider in Chapters 10 and 11 is deeply rooted in the traditional music introduced here.

Spanish Traditions

The Spanish founded St. Augustine, Florida, in 1565. It is the oldest European settlement in the United States, and Spanish music traditions remain strong in that area of the country. (A historian recently pointed out that not until 2055 will the flag of the United States have flown over St. Augustine as long as the Spanish flag did.) In regions of the Southwest as well, one still hears Spanish folk songs and dances and folk **hymns** (religious songs) reflecting their origins in seventeenth-century Spain or more recent Mexico. Missionary priests taught Indians to sing hymns, for example, and Spanish troops guarding forts near the Christian missions sang ballads and love songs at their work. Vendors' songs, work songs, lullabies, and all manner of Spanish folk dances, or *bailes,* formed an ordinary part of the Spanish settlers' lives in the New World.

Performed now as in years past to celebrate engagements, weddings, birthdays, and other happy social events, such rollicking dance tunes as *El Cutilio* (Listening Example 4) lighten the hearts of those who hear them—though few remember how to dance the intricate steps popular 150 years ago.

El Cutilio   (The Cotillion)

Composer

Anonymous

**CD 1
Track 4
1:15**

Unlike the stately ballroom cotillion, performed by formally dressed dancers in elegant settings, the lively *cutilio* is the last of a set of square dances popularly danced in New Mexico through the nineteenth century. The dance posed a challenge to dancers to keep up with its fast tempo and complex steps.

Instrument

A fiddle

Melody

The tune—one of many to which people danced *El Cutilio*—has two melodic sections (A and B), heard in the order AABBAABB.

Meter

Duple

Section A (0:00) begins with an upward leap and continues with a rising inflection. Section A is repeated.

Section B (0:21) begins with a downward inflection. Section B is repeated.

Notice that each section includes four phrases, with an irregular number of beats. For example, if you count each "stomp" as a beat and hear where the accents fall in the music, you will hear the four phrases of A alternating between 6 beats and 4 beats (6-4-6-4). The beats of the four phrases of section B occur as 4-4-3-3, with a "free" beat between repetitions of the section, and another "free" beat before returning to section A. There is also one "free" beat after the last playing of section A.

Alabados   One of the first kinds of religious music in California, Texas, and New Mexico was the **alabado,** a Spanish hymn, or religious song (*alabado sea* means "praised be"). Alabados became part of a thriving Spanish folk tradition that survives today in remote villages of the American Southwest. Long and invariably sad, alabados project the profound loneliness of the beautiful but remote regions inhabited by those who sing them.

Some alabados, probably introduced by Franciscan priests, are related musically to the modal chants of the Roman Catholic church; newer alabados use tonal scales (see p. 6). Like chant, the religious texts are sung without measure, the rhythm conforming to that of the words. Alabados performed during religious processions are sung in unison, unaccompanied except perhaps by flute figures evocative, some say, of the tears of Mary, and a twirling rattle. Alternatively, alabados may be sung by a solo voice or by a lead singer, often a priest, alternating verses with group responses. The latter method offers missionary priests, for example, a prime opportunity to teach the stories of the Bible in song.

Many examples of alabados may be heard on the Web.

British Traditions

The early English settlers who arrived in the New World around the turn of the seventeenth century brought few musical instruments with them; but in time, as violins and other, mostly stringed, instruments became available, the settlers and colonists played the fiddle tunes and dances familiar from their British childhood. Many traditional songs acquired new words and altered melodies, reflecting American dialects and New World experience as they were handed down from one generation to the next.

These folk music traditions survive today in rural and mountain areas, where the style of singing and playing instruments is remarkably close to that of seventeenth-century Britain. Simple lullabies, such as "The Mockingbird" ("Hush, little baby, don't say a word, Papa's gonna buy you a mockingbird"), delightfully silly and entertaining nonsense songs, various work songs, and singing games ("Did You Ever See a Lassie," "Go in and out the Window") all belong to the American folk song repertoire.

Folk Ballads
Most common of all folk songs are **ballads,** or stories told in song. Delivered from memory by a solo voice, with or without accompaniment, ballads offer little background information about the stories they relate, presenting the essential elements and allowing the listener's imagination free rein to flesh out the details. Although the events described often are of a dramatic, even tragic, nature, ballads are presented in a simple, direct, nearly emotionless manner, time and place remaining pleasantly abstract.

Ballads, strophic in form, were a major source of entertainment in early America (Figure 2.1). Sung by amateurs for their own or their families' and friends' pleasure, they often included a very large number of stanzas, so that the entertainment might last as long as possible. Having survived through oral tradition, their authors unknown or forgotten, they evolved as the product of many people over long periods of time, remaining subject to alteration today. Thus ballad singers often add, alter, or delete stanzas as they perform, lending a song local or timely relevance, or simply expressing the irrepressible creativity of the balladeer.

Among the most popular subjects for ballads is the ill-fated love affair, such as the one described in the very famous "Barbara Allen" (Listening Example 5). A favorite song of President George Washington, this is one of a great number of folk ballads that have survived apparently intact since their

FIGURE 2.1

Early Americans gather to enjoy informal music and dance.

British (in this case probably Scottish) origin. Some of these very old songs seem to have been better preserved in America, in fact, than in the land that introduced them, and they have long been adopted into the American folk repertoire.

Early American Folk Music

Early emigrants also reflected the influence of another kind of British folk tradition, the **broadside,** written and printed on a very large sheet suitable for public display, or sometimes printed in a newspaper (Figure 2.2). As early as the seventeenth century, Americans began to alter traditional ballads to fit their new experiences, setting original words to old tunes. For subjects, some broadsides took historical or topical events, such as mine disasters, famous murders, or train wrecks; some offered moral instruction or delivered impassioned political commentary. Much like the World Wide Web today, broadsides offered an opportunity to state one's case anonymously, often in brutally satirical terms, free from censorship or retaliation.

The first stanza and chorus of a famous patriotic ballad of the Revolutionary period, "The Liberty Song," exemplify the inflammatory character of political broadsides. (Interestingly, the author of these fervent words, set to an English air called "Heart of Oak," had urged appeasement with England and long staunchly opposed revolution.)

"Barbara Allen"

CD 1
Track 5
2:48

Composer

Anonymous. The ballad, sometimes called "Barbry Ellen" or another similar name, probably originated in Scotland in the early seventeenth century.

Form

Strophic. As in most ballads, there are several four-line stanzas.

Text

The story is of the young "Sweet William," who is dying for love of "hard-hearted Barbara Allen." She loves him, too, of course, and—remorseful for having repulsed his advances—soon joins him in death. A red rose and a green briar miraculously grow and join above the ill-fated lovers' adjacent graves. The words vary from one performance to another, the song having been handed down through centuries by oral tradition.

Melody

The melody, like the words, exists in several versions. It is based upon a pentatonic scale that uses only the tones of the five black notes of a keyboard. Many children's songs and folk melodies are based upon this simple scale.

Texture

This song is often performed with no accompaniment. Sometimes simple chords are strummed on a guitar, a banjo, or another instrument. A piano may provide accompaniment if a chordal texture is desired.

Rhythm

There is a steady underlying pulse, and a general sense of triple meter. The rhythm is refreshingly irregular, and the phrases are sometimes asymmetrical, adapted to suit the informal text.

The Liberty Song

(AMERICAN WORDS BY JOHN DICKINSON)

Come, join hand in hand,
Brave Americans all!
And rouse your bold hearts
At fair Liberty's call;
No tyrannous acts shall
Suppress your just claim,

Or stain with dishonor
America's name.

(Chorus—*repeated between the stanzas of the song*)
In freedom we're born,
And in freedom we'll live!
Our purses are ready,
Steady, friends, steady;
Not as slaves, but as free men,
Our money we'll give.

Less objective, abstract, and timeless than ancient ballads, American broadsides proved less likely to survive beyond the period that introduced them; thus few of the American folk ballads we remember and enjoy today were written before the second half of the nineteenth century. But even before that time, each geographical area of America was producing songs and instrumental pieces expressing the typical local experience. Frontier people sang songs about freedom, equality, danger, and the beauty of nature in the wild. Ballads commemorated the opening of the Erie Canal (1825), the gold rush in California (1849), and other events of intense local concern. Slaves produced their own music, expressive of their particular loneliness and suffering. And songs of miners, farmers, railroad workers, and even outlaws also joined the American folk repertoire. Lullabies served every segment of the population, and play and party songs entertained adults as well as children. Performed in the same plain, direct manner as their British counterparts, American ballads reflect in their titles—such as "John Henry," "Billy the Kid," "The Erie Canal," "The John B. Sails," or "Casey Jones" (Listening Example 35, p. 171)—their uniquely American source and character.

Sailors' work songs or **chanteys** appeared as New Englanders became heavily involved in sea trade and traffic, and as sailors working on the rivers, too, developed songs about their trade. The origin of the hauntingly beautiful "Shenandoah" (Listening Example 6) is sketchy, but the song seems to have originated in the early nineteenth century in the areas of the Missouri and the Mississippi rivers and eventually to have made its way down the Mississippi to the open ocean, where deep-sea sailors adopted its rolling melody as their own. (Shenandoah was the name of an Indian chief living on the Missouri River.) It has remained one of America's favorite folk songs.

African Traditions

Unlike the European settlers, who arrived in the New World of their own free will, Africans were forcibly brought to America in European slave ships, beginning early in the seventeenth century—about the time the Pilgrims arrived at Plymouth Rock. By 1700 slavery had become common throughout the thirteen colonies.

Many slaveholders harshly discouraged references to African gods and religions in any traditional song or dance. Especially British Protestants, who considered African music customs savage and heathen, did everything possible to eradicate their slaves' native religion and culture. Partly to this end, the first babies born to slaves in this country (unlike those in other areas of the New World, such as Haiti, Cuba, or Brazil) often were separated from their families to be raised on other plantations. There they learned African lore and language from older Africans, of course, but they also began to accrue experience with America and with English.

Slaves in New England worked much as slaves worked in the South but were treated with more leniency, often enjoying a measure of free time in which to entertain themselves and their masters by singing, dancing, and playing musical instruments. The admiration they excited by their music was not always to the slaves' advantage, however: Newspaper lists of slaves for sale and of runaways often referred to their outstanding musical abilities, adding to their desirability as commodities to be owned and abused.

As adults, the first generation of slaves born here began to develop their own music, rooted in African customs and sounds, but genuinely African *American,* expressing their new experience in a new sort of African American language. Whereas the first slaves had sung in African dialects, work songs and

"Shenandoah"

CD 1
Track 6
1:48

Composer
Anonymous

Performer
Pete Seeger

Form
Strophic. Note the refrain at the end of each verse.

Meter
Quadruple (four beats per measure). The relaxed tempo and somewhat irregular accents, closely following the natural rhythm of the text, suggest the roll of waves and the easy sway of a ship.

Tempo
Slow

Accompaniment
Very sparse strumming of a few supportive guitar tones and simple chords.

Text
This lovely, plaintive ballad tells of a white (Canadian or American) trader who courted the daughter of Shenandoah, an American Indian chieftain, and carried her off in his canoe, only to abandon her later on the banks of the Missouri River. A favorite song of sailors—some of whom must have experienced similar conquests and subsequent remorse, and who loved to sing it while away on long, lonely voyages—the song is sometimes thought of as a chantey.

Oh Shenandoah, I love your daughter.
Wa–ay, you rollin' river.
Oh Shenandoah, I love your daughter.
Away, we're bound away
'Cross the wide Missoura.

Oh Shenandoah, I long to see you.
Wa–ay, you rollin' river.
Oh, Shenandoah, I'll not deceive you.
Away, we're bound away
'Cross the wide Missoura.

For seven years I've been a rover.
Wa–ay, you rollin' river.
For seven years I've been a rover.
Away, we're bound away
'Cross the wide Missoura.

FIGURE 2.3

In a Cotton Field. Wood
engraving, drawn by Horace
Bradley, 1887.

other songs gradually came to be sung more in English, pronounced, however,
with African rhythms. For a long time, some African words continued to be
used, perhaps for the purpose of obscuring seditious meaning from white people. When even the blacks could no longer understand the African languages,
meaningless but rhythmic syllables were used as well.

Field Hollers

Most of the slaves forced to work on the plantations in
what is now the southeastern United States came from West Africa, where
they had commonly integrated music with their daily work. Particular kinds
of songs became associated with certain tasks, such as fishing, weaving, hunt-
ing, or tilling their farms. In America, the familiar fishing, weaving, and hunt-
ing songs lost relevance, but slaves, such as those pictured in Figure 2.3,
poured all the anguish of their new, tragic experience into **field hollers**—loud,
rhythmically flexible, emotionally expressive chants or cries sung by a solitary voice. Some field hollers had words ("Where *are* you-u-u . . .?") but
most, as in Listening Example 7, used neutral syllables easily heard over
distances. In this way the singer established wordless but heartwarming contact with fellow workers who, hearing the poignant cries, could respond with
expressive hollers of their own.

Listening Example 8, a father's field call or holler, illustrates the high
falsetto range, lying above the normal, full, chest voice, which enhanced the
ability to call over long distances.

The "bent," or slurred, melodically ambiguous **blue notes** later applied by
jazz musicians and other black musicians to their instruments or voices also colored the hollers and complaint songs, as heard in Listening Example 9. It is easy

Listening Example 7

Field Holler

Timbre
Solo male voice

Rhythm
Free, flexible

Melody
A simple, narrow, mournful phrase on three tones, repeated.

Text
Neutral syllables, easy to sing and to hear over distances.

CD 1
Track 7
1:15

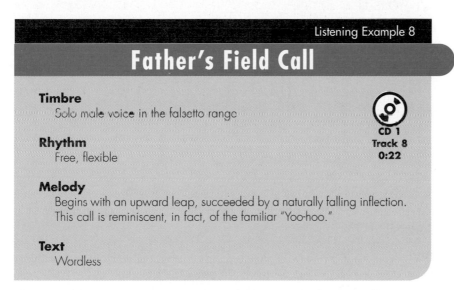

Listening Example 8

Father's Field Call

Timbre
Solo male voice in the falsetto range

Rhythm
Free, flexible

Melody
Begins with an upward leap, succeeded by a naturally falling inflection. This call is reminiscent, in fact, of the familiar "Yoo-hoo."

Text
Wordless

CD 1
Track 8
0:22

to recognize connections from this music to the *blues* (see pp. 196–203), soon to evolve on the work farms and in the cotton fields of the post-Civil War South.

Ring Shouts Another African tradition translated to an African American experience was the religious **shout,** or **ring shout,** performed at religious services or camp meetings. The "shouters" formed a ring and shuffled energetically to the singing of a spiritual (see pp. 88–91) or hymn. Though careful to hardly lift their feet from the floor (lifting the feet would constitute dancing, a forbidden entertainment at services), the shouters, accompanied by singers and

Complaint Call

Timbre
Solo male voice

Rhythm
Free, flexible, accommodating the text

CD 1
Track 9
0:40

Melody
Based on a five-note, or pentatonic, scale, the melody begins high, then falls to lower pitches. Notice the manner in which some of the pitches touch and linger slightly below the normal tones of the western scale, as do the expressive blue notes of African music.

Text

> Oh, da time don't get no better here
> I'm goin down the road
> I'm goin' away to leave ya
> If the time don't get no better here
> Down the road I'm goin'.
>
> If the time don't get no better
> If the time don't get no better
> Down the road I'm goin'.

sometimes singing themselves, gradually quickened their pace, as they became caught up in an ecstasy of religious fervor that often kept them moving until they fell from sheer exhaustion.

Work Songs In Africa, another kind of song, the **work song,** accompanied such rhythmic tasks as rowing, hoeing, or chopping trees. Traditional work songs expressed joy and pride in hard work for one's family and land, and gratitude to the gods for their help.

In America, too, slaves made up, or **improvised,** work songs as they labored in pain and sorrow, adapting the words, however, to their tragic new condition. Work songs often accompanied American plantation slaves, setting the pace and synchronizing the movements of groups of forced laborers. The songs, strophic in form, were performed in the characteristic West African music practice known as call-and-response, in which the leading lines of each verse, sung by a single voice, alternate with a repeated phrase, or refrain, sung by the group.

Listening Example 10, "Hammer Ring," recorded at a state penitentiary in Texas in 1934, indicates how work songs facilitate the movements and lighten the mood of laborers working under the most difficult and depressing conditions.

"Hammer, Ring" (excerpt)

**CD 1
Track 10
2:36**

Performers

Jesse Bradley and group at State Penitentiary, Huntsville, Texas, 1934.

Form

Strophic. Each verse consists of a line of text, repeated, with the refrain "Hammer, ring!" interspersed between lines. The leader sings each line; the hammering men sing the refrain (call-and-response). Occasionally the leader repeats the chorus, which begins the song.

Meter

Duple

Hammer songs accompanied men driving the spikes that fastened long steel rails to wooden railroad ties. From the dramatic Bible story of Noah and the ark, the leader of this hammer song improvises simple lines of text, to which the men—swinging ten-pound hammers freely from the shoulder in a complete circle about the head—rhythmically respond, "Hammer, ring!" The relentless rhythm and driving energy of the piece support and reinforce the regular rhythm of the hammering men.

Notice occasional variations in the inflection of the melody line, which add emphasis or emotional intensity to the delivery. Notice, too, the occasional calls, cries, or shouts of the workers. While their response is generally sung in unison, occasional flights of creativity among individuals vary the texture of their singing.

Chorus

Won't you ring, old hammer?
  Hammer, ring!
Won't you ring, old hammer?
  Hammer, ring!

Verses

1. *Broke the handle on my hammer,*
     Hammer, ring.
   Broke the handle on my hammer,
     Hammer, ring.
2. *Got to hammerin' in the Bible.*
3. *Gon'ta talk about Norah [Noah].*
4. *Well, God told Norah.*
5. *You is a-goin' in the timber.*
6. *You argue some Bible.*
7. *Well, Norah got worried.*
8. *What you want with the timber?*

—Continued

"Hammer, Ring" (excerpt)

9. Won't you build me an ark, sir?
10. Well, Norah asked God, sir.
11. How high do you want it?
12. Build it forty-two cubits.
13. Every cubit have a window.
14. Well, it started in to rainin'.
15. Old Norah got worried.
16. He called in his children.
17. Well, Norah told God, sir.
18. This is a very fine hammer.
19. Got the same old hammer.
20. Got to hammerin' in the timber. . . .

Musical Instruments In Africa, drums often accompanied work songs, sometimes providing two or three different underlying rhythmic patterns in a complexity difficult for Western ears even to hear. Using drums for communication as well as for music, West Africans developed an extremely fine sense of changes in tone and timbre, together with truly remarkable rhythmic techniques.

Many slaves brought small drums and simple string instruments with them on the slave ships, where their captors sometimes compelled them to perform music to keep them occupied and while away the time; but slaveholders on southern plantations generally banned the use of African drums, fearing that the thrilling drumbeats might incite revolt. Slaves compensated for the loss of their drums by improvising percussive instruments from empty oil drums, metal washbasins, and whatever else might be available and by clapping, body-slapping, and stamping the rhythms of their songs and dances. Rattles or bits of shell or bone added to simple instruments further enhanced the driving beat.

West African gourd **banjos** (variously called *banjar, banza,* and other similar names) arrived in the American colonies by way of the slave trade in the late seventeenth century. Developed from ancient Arab prototypes, the African banjo typically had four strings, three long and one short, the short string providing a rhythmic and harmonic **drone** (a repeated tone of constant pitch). By stretching an animal skin across the open side of a hollowed-out gourd or calabash, slaves created their own primitive banjos, destined in more sophisticated form (such as the four-string banjo seen in Figure 2.4) to provide limitless entertainment for Americans and others of assorted ethnicity and culture.

What of African Music Survives Today? Today's African American musics are deeply rooted in African traditions that arrived in the New World with the first slaves. Call-and-response, for example, became a

FIGURE 2.4
A 4-string banjo.

basic characteristic of African American vocal and instrumental music, as we shall see when we study blues, vocal and instrumental jazz, the religious folk songs called *spirituals,* and many other kinds of contemporary black music. Improvisation is inherent in the concept of jazz and colors much other music as well. Much African American music is still based on the "bent" or flexible tones of the *blues* scale (see p. 197), unheard in this country until the first West Africans arrived. Even more apparent is the emphasis in African American music on rhythm over melody, and the complexity of African rhythms compared with those of Western (European) music.

Terms to Review

folk music   Usually music of unknown origin, orally transmitted.

hymn   A religious song, suitable for congregational singing.

alabado   A religious song of praise, belonging to Spanish and Mexican folk traditions.

ballad   A folk story-song, strophic in form.

broadside   A topical ballad, printed on a large sheet or on sets of sheets called *songsters.*

chantey   Sailors' work song.

field hollers   Loud, rhythmically flexible, emotionally expressive chants or cries sung by a solitary voice, forming a kind of communication between slaves.

blue notes   Flexible tones derived from African scales.

shout, ring shout   A lively dance, performed at religious services with shuffling but rigorous steps by dancers in a ring, accompanied by the singing of a religious song.

work songs   Songs sung by groups of slaves to set the pace and synchronize the movements of rhythmic tasks performed in unison.

improvised   Simultaneously invented and performed.

banjo   A string instrument derived in America from West African instruments.

drone   A single tone, sounded continuously or repeated.

Suggestions for Further Listening

Folk Songs

"The Riddle" ("I Gave My Love a Cherry That Has No Stone")

"Arkansas Traveler"

"Down in the Valley"

Useful Collections of Folk Songs

Anthology of American Folk Music. Folkways 2951/3.

Folk Music in America. Library of Congress.

Folk Music U.S.A. Folkways 4530.

Roots of American Music. Arhoolie 2001/2.

Critical Thinking

What opportunities do today's political, religious, or personal satirists have to avoid prosecution by those they attack? Compare the potential for free expression in rap lyrics, cartoons, television entertainment, movies, newspapers, and books, and on the Web, with that of the broadsides in colonial and revolutionary America.

In how many ways might you distinguist between African and African American music?

Go to www.mhhe.com/ferrisaml5 for a list of additional Web-based resources that relate to the content in this chapter.

Religious Music in the Colonial, Revolutionary, and Federal Periods

A S early as the sixteenth century, inhabitants of the New World experienced a variety of native and imported musics. These included Roman Catholic music, with which French and Spanish visitors accompanied their own worship and which they taught to Indians in Florida and in parts of the Southwest as part of their effort to convert Native Americans to Roman Catholicism.

Music at the Spanish Missions

Music was an important part of the religious training of American Indians by zealous Spanish missionaries, who taught their more or less willing converts to sing the songs and prayers of the Christian church, usually set to very simple tunes. Soon American Indians were learning to sing in choirs, play in church orchestras, and even make simple European-style musical instruments. They learned traditional Spanish music, religious praise songs or hymns, and even the more difficult *Gregorian chant*. At Christmastime, they participated in musical nativity plays called *Las posadas* (The Lodgings), commemorating the struggles of Mary to find a place in which to deliver the baby Jesus.

The Spanish missions remained active in California, and Catholic church music was regularly performed there by missionaries and by their Native American students, until the Mexican government ordered the missions closed in 1833. A large number of musical instruments, as well as manuscripts of mass settings and other church music of varying levels of complexity, have been found at some of the mission sites, many of which can still be visited.

While Catholic music remained important in regions of the country inhabited by Spanish, French, or Mexican people, the Protestant custom of singing psalms and hymns dominated the religious music experience in this country. These religious songs inspired and comforted urban and rural people in the North and South, but New England's practices exerted the strongest and longest-lasting influence on American music.

Psalm Tunes

In 1517, a German Catholic cleric, Martin Luther (1483–1546), instigated the Protestant Reformation by advocating reform of certain questionable practices by the Roman Catholic church of his day. The movement thus begun stimulated a number of independent-minded people in northern European countries to form their own Protestant sects, each adhering to particular tenets of religious and secular conduct, including the place of music in worship.

Unlike Catholics, whose formal religious music was sung in Latin, Protestants sang their hymns in their vernacular, or common, language. They also preferred simple, folklike tunes, which everyday people could sing, to the elaborate Gregorian chant or complex choir pieces sung by trained Catholic monks.

The Pilgrims and Puritans arriving in New England early in the seventeenth century were Protestants, whose protests against the Roman Catholic church included some concerning religious music. People who followed the strict teachings of the Swiss reformer John Calvin (1509–1564) believed that the *only* texts suitable for singing in a worship service were those of the **psalms,** 150 inspirational verses found in the Old Testament of the Bible. Thus Calvinists forbade the singing in church of hymns, which had freely written texts not necessarily based on passages from the Bible or from church liturgy.

Although poetic in style and expression, however, the psalms as they appear in the Bible are neither metered nor rhymed and therefore do not lend themselves readily to congregational singing. Thus Calvinists retranslated all the psalms into verses having a regular number of lines, with patterns of weak and accented beats, suitable for setting to music.

The Calvinists did not intend their **psalm tunes** to stir emotions or draw attention to the music itself, because they believed the only purpose for music in a church service was to enhance expression of a religious text. Therefore, because musical instruments cannot express words, harmony increases music's sensuous appeal, and neither instruments nor harmony will serve to clarify a text, the Calvinists consistently sang their psalm tunes in church **a cappella** (unaccompanied) and in unison. It is important for us to understand, however, that the separation between sacred and secular experience typical of the modern American experience did not apply in colonial America. Thus it was quite usual for Calvinists to sing the same psalm tunes they performed so austerely in church, in harmony and with elaborate instrumental accompaniment in family and social gatherings at home.

The New Englanders' psalm singing became, in effect, a kind of folk tradition. Psalm tunes were of a folklike nature and generally were learned from oral experience. Strophic in form, most had four-line stanzas, as is common in much folk song, and the ornamentation and variation in the singing of psalm tunes were typical of the manner of singing songs in the folk tradition.

Psalters   The newly metered and rhymed psalm verses were printed in books called **psalters** for use in congregational singing. Some psalters contained notated melodies, whereas others printed no music but only the words of the psalm verses, which could be sung to widely familiar and well-remembered folk, popular, or hymn tunes.

The first collection of psalm tunes was printed in Switzerland in 1539, nearly a century before the Pilgrims and Puritans came to the New World, and the first edition of the famous *Geneva Psalter* appeared in that Swiss city in 1551. (When the Separatists finally settled in the New World, they became known as Pilgrims, and Calvinists coming directly from England were called Puritans.)

Among the tunes in the *Geneva Psalter* was a setting of Psalm 100 (Listening Example 11), which has become the most famous psalm tune of all, known today as "Old Hundred" and sung in Protestant churches of many denominations as the Doxology ("Praise God, from Whom All Blessings Flow"). (Another famous psalm tune, "Windsor," an Optional Listening Example, is also widely sung today with a text beginning "Jesus the very heart of Thee.")

Listening Example 11

"Old Hundred" (excerpt)

Composer
Louis Bourgeois (c. 1510–c. 1560)

CD 1
Track 11
0:23

Form
Strophic. (Only one stanza is heard on the CD.)

Meter
Quadruple. (We have considered meter as defining the number of beats per measure. In another sense, *meter* may refer to the pattern of syllables in a stanza of text. Thus each stanza of the text to "Old Hundred" has four lines, and each line has eight syllables, a pattern called *long meter*. Any psalm in long meter could be sung to any long-meter tune.)

Rhythm
Although the melody has remained unchanged for centuries, the rhythm has been altered. Modern Protestants generally sing "Old Hundred"— so called because of the tune's association with Psalm 100—in the rhythm heard here, or in another equally regular rhythmic pattern, neither pattern having the rhythmic variety, interest, or vigor of the settings enjoyed by early congregations.

Performance
A cappella. The choir, or chorus, sings in four-part harmony (soprano, alto, tenor, bass), with the melody in the high, or soprano, female voices.

An English-language psalter known as *Sternhold and Hopkins* (after the man who had printed the first metrical psalter in English and the man who contributed the most translations to the new version), printed for the use of Calvinists living in England in 1562, became the West's most important religious text next to the Bible for more than a century. It included some tunes from the *Geneva Psalter* as well as several folklike melodies that might have been derived from popular songs of the day, offering seventeen metrical patterns to which the psalm verses could be sung. (It was not considered necessary to provide a separate tune for each of the 150 psalms, because all verses with the same metrical pattern could be sung to the same melody.)

As the sixteenth century progressed, some English Calvinists fled persecution in England to seek religious freedom in Holland, where they became known as Separatists. The psalter they printed for their use during this self-imposed exile, called the *Ainsworth Psalter* (Figure 3.1), included even greater metric variety than *Sternhold and Hopkins.* Both of these famous English-language psalters—*Ainsworth* and *Sternhold and Hopkins*—contain tunes so merry in mood and lively in tempo that skeptics, reminded of the syncopated rhythms of popular Renaissance dances, referred to them as "Geneva jigs." In a similar vein, in *The Winter's Tale,* Shakespeare described a Puritan who "sings psalms to hornpipes."

Many of the English settlers had enjoyed playing and listening to musical instruments in their homes, but few managed to bring any instruments with

FIGURE 3.1

Pages from the *Ainsworth Psalter* (Amsterdam, 1612), showing a psalm tune and the manner in which each verse of the psalm has been retranslated into rhymed and metered verse.

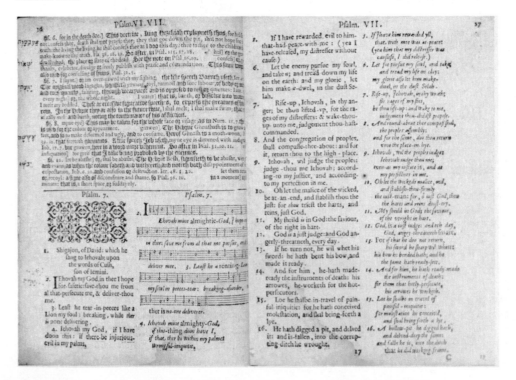

them to the New World. Furthermore, because travel between the continents was costly, time-consuming, and dangerous, the settlers soon lost touch with current music events abroad. They had, of course, brought their psalters with them, and for some time the music experience for both Pilgrims and Puritans consisted of singing psalm tunes a cappella for worship in church and in harmony and accompanied for entertainment at home.

In a surprisingly short time, the settlers developed an American taste and tongue, making the language of their old psalters seem stilted and old-fashioned. Thus only twenty years after landing at Plymouth Rock, in 1640, an American psalter titled *The Whole Booke of Psalms Faithfully Translated into English Metre,* but popularly known as the **Bay Psalm Book,** was printed in Cambridge, Massachusetts, the first book printed in the New World (Figure 3.2).

FIGURE 3.2

Pages from the *Bay Psalm Book,* the first book printed in the American colonies.

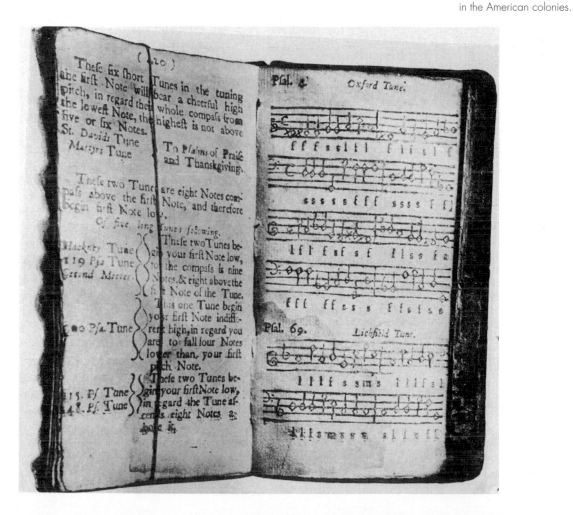

Other Protestant Music

While John Calvin proscribed all music but the singing of psalm tunes in church, Martin Luther encouraged the joyful singing of simple tunes and light-hearted texts in worship, even composing some hymns of his own. Thus while Calvinists confined their worship music to the unaccompanied singing of psalm tunes, American Lutherans sang hymns, many of which (including Luther's best-known hymn, with a sturdy tune and a strong text beginning "A mighty fortress is our God"), appear in hymnals currently used by many Protestant sects.

German-Speaking Protestant Sects
Responding to William Penn's policy of religious toleration, a number of German-speaking Protestants fled persecution in their homelands and came to this country to settle first in Pennsylvania, and later in other regions as well. Here, free from persecution, they kept much of their European culture intact, their language and religious practices largely isolating them from the Protestant Anglo-American mainstream of the thirteen colonies.

Mennonites. The Mennonites (of whom the Amish were a later offshoot) first arrived in 1683, mostly from Germany. From the time of their founding, in the 1520s, their refusal on religious grounds to perform military service and their rejection of a state church led to severe persecution by their Dutch, Swiss, and German hosts.

The Mennonites had their own hymnals and psalters, some containing notated music for hymn and psalm texts. During the last quarter of the eighteenth century, Mennonite schoolmasters also compiled tune books containing traditional texts and tunes for presentation to their pupils as rewards for good work and to provide music instruction. They decorated the title pages of their tune books with a Pennsylvania-German Mennonite folk art called *Fraktur,* a highly ornamental combination of calligraphy and script with flowers, figures, and geometric designs (Figure 3.3). However, the Mennonites seem to have preserved their lovely old hymn tunes largely by oral tradition, singing them today in versions differing widely from written sources such as student notebooks and hymnals.

Moravians. The late seventeenth century and early eighteenth century brought further waves of emigrant Protestants, including members of the English Society of Friends, known as Quakers; and Shakers, a later offshoot from the Quaker sect (so called because of the trembling induced by their religious emotion). Of the new immigrants, however, the German-speaking Moravians had by far the most significant effect upon music in America.

The Moravians arrived in 1735 together with the famous Methodist missionaries and hymn writers John and Charles Wesley. Having been severely persecuted for their religious beliefs and practices in their homelands of Moravia and Bohemia, the Moravians wished to settle in America, where many intended to

FIGURE 3.3

Fraktur. This beautifully illuminated manuscript of the thirty-fourth psalm, made by an anonymous artist in 1802, may have been intended to hang on the wall of a home.

serve as Christian missionaries to African and Native Americans. Settling first in Georgia, the Moravians then moved north to found Bethlehem, Pennsylvania. They also established communities in Salem (Winston-Salem today), North Carolina, and other areas in what is today the eastern United States.

Music had been an important part of the Moravians' experience in Europe, and they continued to compose and perform beautiful music in their new land. Integrating hymn singing and other religious music into their daily lives, some Moravians also wrote secular songs and instrumental music, sophisticated and complex beyond those of other early Americans and revealing their strong German and Czech heritage.

The first important American-born Moravian composer, **John Antes** (1740–1811), composed a number of beautiful religious choral pieces called **anthems**—religious songs, longer and more complex than hymns, intended to be sung by a trained soloist or a choir rather than by the members of a church congregation. The text of an anthem is often biblical, nonmetric, and non-rhyming. The form is usually **through-composed,** meaning that unlike a song in strophic form, in which two or more verses are all set to the same music, through-composed music has little or no repetition of melodic phrases; rather, the text unfolds to new music throughout the piece. A number of anthems by Antes, including "Surely He Has Borne Our Griefs" (Listening Example 12), are still sung today.

"Surely He Has Borne Our Griefs"

CD 1
Track 12
2:42

Composer
John Antes

Form
Through-composed

Meter
Quadruple. Although there is a steady sense of pulse throughout this moving anthem, the tempo is often greatly relaxed at the ends of phrases to heighten the emotional expressiveness of the piece. The term for this expressive "robbing from" and "returning to" the tempo is *rubato*.

Harmony
The anthem is in the key of C minor, meaning that the tonic note is C and most of the melodic and harmonic material is based upon the C minor scale. Notice how Antes varies the effect, however, by occasionally using a major chord, as at the end of the first phrase on the word "griefs."

Also notice how pungent dissonances, as on "wounded" in the third phrase, enhance the meaning of the text by evoking an emotional response. The sopranos' high pitch on "wounded" and in the last phrase on "stripes" also has an emotional impact upon the listener.

Accompaniment
Whereas most early American composers expected accompanying instruments simply to double the voice lines, Antes wrote full instrumental accompanying parts for his anthems. Here there is a four-part accompaniment for string ensemble, although it may be played on an organ or piano instead. There is no instrumental introduction, but the instruments play an interlude between the two large sections (beginning after "iniquities"). Their ending material, with a descending melodic line, slowing of tempo, and lessening of dynamic level, brings the anthem to a moving close.

Text
(from Isaiah 53:4, 5). Nonmetric, nonrhyming.

Surely He has borne our griefs and carried our sorrows. He was wounded for our transgressions. He was bruised for our iniquities. The chastisement of our peace lay upon Him: And with His stripes we are healed.

The Great Awakening
Beginning in 1735, a series of strong religious revival movements known as the Great Awakening swept the eastern seaboard. The movement began in New England cities, where many Puritans perceived a lessening of moral rectitude and an increase in intellectual, as opposed to spiritual, interests. People living on small farms and plantations in remote rural

areas, consumed with scratching a meager living from hard and difficult land, had largely abandoned religious customs fostered by the close communication and churchly discipline of parish life.

But the Great Awakening spread like wildfire from North to South, stirring latent religious fervor and raising concern among urban and rural folk not only for their own redemption, but for that of black slaves and Indians as well. All this religious enthusiasm further stimulated the rise of psalm- and hymn-singing in America.

Early Efforts at Musical Reform

The Moravians' musical influence was strong but limited in scope, and most colonials had no opportunity to hear or to practice good music. Although each edition of the *Bay Psalm Book* printed after 1698 included several notated tunes, few people knew how to read music, and as the old tunes came to be remembered differently in various towns and villages, New Englanders began to disagree as to how they should be sung. In order to learn each tune as they thought it should be rendered, some congregations adopted the practice of **lining out,** in which a more or less musically literate leader sang one line of the psalm, which the congregation then repeated in unison, performing each successive line in this awkward manner.

Lining out satisfied very few. Some of the leaders, with voices untrained and sometimes unattractive as well, began the songs too high or too low, causing people in the congregation to "squeak above" or "grumble below" their comfortable singing ranges. In the effort to improve or enliven the effect, leaders and sometimes congregational members embellished the tunes at will, grossly distorting their original sound. Becoming accustomed to such altered (in a sense Americanized) versions of the old tunes, many people resisted all efforts to impose the "regular" style of singing the tunes as they were written.

The Singing School Movement As the advantages of being able to read music notation became apparent, certain better-educated ministers printed collections of tunes, prefaced by detailed instructions on how to read music notation, and set out to teach New Englanders to read the tunes printed in their psalters. Although the traditional system of music notation is quite easy to learn (you may want to refer to p. 10 of the Prelude), some amateur teachers attempted to devise even simpler methods, including one based on the four syllables then commonly used to sing pitches (*fa, sol, la,* and *mi*) that placed on the staff the first *letter* of each syllable (*f, s, l,* or *m*) instead of the traditional note heads.

The efforts of the teaching ministers soon were supplemented, and eventually assumed, by talented amateur musicians, who became known as **singing school masters.** Some of these self-taught music amateurs, having previously earned their living as shopkeepers, merchants, or farmers, or in other practical trades, became itinerant teachers, traveling from town to town and holding informal singing schools in the local meetinghouse, church, or school for a

Virgil Thomson
"The way to write American music is simple. All you have to do is be an American and then write any kind of music you wish."

limited period of perhaps two or three months. People welcomed the singing school masters to their towns, because singing schools became popular social as well as educational events. Interested men, women, and young people attended the singing lessons several times a week and, at the end of their instruction, gave a performance demonstrating their accomplishments to the town's proud public. Then the singing school master traveled on to another place.

The singing school movement, which began in Boston about 1720 and experienced its greatest activity throughout New England from 1760 to 1800, finally spread north into Canada and south through New York, New Jersey, Pennsylvania, and Maryland, and into the Carolinas. In fact, singing school masters offered widespread instruction and inspiration, especially in rural and remote areas, well into the nineteenth century. Necessarily hardy and independent individuals, the singing school masters devised their own teaching materials, compiled collections of familiar psalm tunes and other religious songs, and composed tunes of their own. Some wrote extensive introductions to their music primers, including information about the syllables to be sung and the elements of music. The first Americans to write music with a distinctively American (at least, non-European) sound, they are collectively referred to as members of the **First New England School** of composers.

A "school" of artists generally includes people living at about the same time, in the same geographic region, and sharing certain artistic goals and similarities of style. The First New England School composers, who lived in late eighteenth-century New England, shared the goals of teaching people to read music and to sing. Most of the simple folklike songs they composed as teaching tools had religious texts and so were also suitable for congregational singing and for private entertainment at home. The best songs of these "Yankee pioneers" were as rugged, naive, and honest as the sturdy tunesmiths who made them because, untouched by the influence of their sophisticated European contemporaries, they relied upon old, familiar techniques and their own honest taste. Colonial Americans, after all, had been out of touch with European music since the early seventeenth century, when tonality first became the harmonic system of the Western world, and the singing school masters had only a rudimentary comprehension of the tonal system. More significantly, they did not feel constrained to conform to *anyone's* rules. Sometimes they turned to pretonal techniques, basing some melodies on modes or on simple pentatonic scales.

William Billings (1746–1800)   **William Billings,** a tanner of hides who became famous as a singing school master and composer, was the first American to produce a book of tunes all of his own composition (see Figure 3.4). Billings's *New England Psalm Singer* was printed (by Paul Revere) in 1770. Although Billings had attended singing school himself and continued to study music throughout his career, he considered "nature" the best teacher and confidently judged the quality of a piece according to how much he liked it. Well aware, for example, of the conventional relationships between consonant and dissonant sounds (see Prelude, p. 6), Billings and other composers

FIGURE 3.4
Circular notation of a canon by William Billings.

of the First New England School often remained independent of such rules, making refreshingly unorthodox musical decisions to please their own ears. (Annoyed at criticism of his music by certain less adventurous listeners, Billings flaunted his unconventional ideas by writing a song titled "Jargon," with flagrantly outrageous harmonies sure to offend the sensibilities of delicate taste.) Considered by his contemporaries to be eccentric but talented above the ordinary, Billings had many admirers; but he failed to realize much profit on his tune books, because there was no effective copyright law in his day. Forced to work as a street cleaner late in life, this remarkable early American composer died a poor man.

A nationalist, in the sense that he wrote to suit his own American tastes and made no attempt to imitate European sounds, Billings produced a number of stirring patriotic songs, some of which describe specific events of the American Revolutionary War. "Chester" (Listening Example 13), a favorite of the Revolutionary period, is sometimes referred to as the first American popular song, because it was widely sung and played by bands and by solo instrumentalists for general pleasure and entertainment. "Chester" appeared with its first verse in the collection printed in 1770, but Billings added defiant topical stanzas after the war broke out.

Unlike most of the music we have studied so far, consisting of one line of melody without harmonic accompaniment, "Chester" was written and is usually performed in chordal, or homophonic, texture (see Prelude, p. 8). In other words, Billings wrote not only the tune, but also its chordal accompaniment. People had long enjoyed singing harmonized versions of their religious songs at home if not in church; and by the time of the First New England School, harmony was no longer excluded from music in the worship service.

"Chester"

CD 1
Track 13
1:28

Composer
William Billings

Form
Strophic. There are three four-line stanzas.

Meter
Quadruple. Suitable in meter and tempo for marching, "Chester" was the principal marching song of the New England troops during the Revolutionary War.

Melody
The strong tune lies within the range of an octave. It begins with the last four notes of the ascending major scale—the third phrase also uses these four notes only. The second phrase uses the lower notes of the octave, and the fourth phrase uses the complete descending major scale.

Texture
Homophonic. The melody lies in the tenor or next-to-the lowest voice, as was the custom in homophonic vocal music of the eighteenth century. We are accustomed to hearing the melody of a song in the soprano (highest) voice, with the alto or contralto (lower female voice), tenor, and bass (lower male voice) providing harmony. Here we must listen carefully to distinguish the melody line from the other voices, which provide harmony and also—with the exception of the alto—have considerable melodic interest of their own.

Timbre
A cappella four-part choral singing.

Text
Three stanzas, written by Billings, indicate the stirring spirit and martial mood of his text.

Let tyrants shake their iron rod,
And Slav'ry clank her galling chains.
We fear them not, we trust in God.
New England's God forever reigns.

The Foe comes on with haughty stride,
Our troops advance with martial noise,
Their vet'runs flee before our youth,
and Generals yield to beardless boys.

What grateful off'ring shall we bring,
What shall we render to the Lord?
Loud Hallelujahs let us Sing
And praise his name on ev'ry Chord.

In our Listening Example, "Chester" is sung a cappella, but it might have been accompanied by one or more instruments doubling the voice parts. The belief that church music must enhance—never detract from—worship had caused strong prejudice against the instrumental accompaniment of church music, since instruments could not express a text but simply added a sensuous dimension to the sound. But, as noted above, this prejudice began to lessen about the time of the First New England School, as some churches accepted accompaniment of congregational singing by organ or by string or wind instruments. The violin, associated with popular dancing and widely condemned as the "devil's fiddle," gained acceptance only slowly, but the bass viol, flute, clarinet, and bassoon increasingly accompanied singing or were even used to play short instrumental passages.

Canons

A **canon** is a melody that forms meaningful harmonies when performed with "staggered entrances"—that is, when successive voices begin the same melody at later times (Figure 3.5). Each voice continues to the end of the melody, simply dropping out at the end of the tune while any remaining voices continue until they drop out in turn. (Here "voice" refers to a line of music, whether sung or played by musical instruments.) Because each of the lines is melodically conceived—in fact, each line is actually the same melody—a canon is polyphonic in texture.

"When Jesus Wept" (Listening Example 14), one of Billings's best-known and best-loved songs, is a circular canon, or round, which continues to make harmonic sense when repeated any number of times.

Fuging Tunes

Late in the eighteenth century, a new kind of song called a **fuging tune** became very popular, and by 1810, about 1,000 of these had been written. A fuging tune consists of two sections, which we will call **A** and **B** (Figure 3.6). The first section (**A**) is chordal, or homophonic, in texture, the melody lying in one voice (usually the tenor) while the other three (soprano, alto, and bass) provide chordal harmony.

The second section of a fuging tune (**B**), which begins with staggered entrances, gives each voice melodic interest; thus the texture is polyphonic. But unlike a canon, in which each voice performs the *same* melody, entering and dropping out in turn, a fuging tune has four similar but *independent* lines of music, which finally end together on a chord. The second section is repeated, rendering the form of a fuging tune **ABB.**

First voice
Second voice
Third voice
Fourth voice

FIGURE 3.5

A canon. Each voice enters in turn, singing the same melody. The resulting combination of tones produces attractive harmonies.

Listening Example 14

"When Jesus Wept"

CD 1
Track 14
1:16

Composer
William Billings

Form
A four-part circular canon or round. There are four phrases, any two or more of which form harmony when performed together.

Texture
Monophonic when the melody is performed in unison: polyphonic when performed in canon.

Meter
Triple

Timbre
The canon may be performed by four women's voices, by four men's voices, or by a mixed chorus of soprano, alto, tenor, and bass.

Text
Billings wrote the words, as well as the music, of this famous canon. The ending is particularly effective, as the last voices sing the moving words in unison, the other voices having dropped out in turn.

When Jesus wept, the falling tear
In mercy flow'd beyond all bound;
When Jesus groan'd, a trembling fear
Seiz'd all the guilty world around.

FIGURE 3.6

A fuging tune. Section A is homophonic in texture, as represented by the dotted vertical lines. Section B begins with staggered entrances (polyphonic texture) but ends with chords. Section B is repeated.

Soprano
Alto
Tenor
Bass

Section A   Section B

Fuging tunes were fun to sing, offering everyone an interesting and varied part and challenging housewives, farmers, shopkeepers, tavern owners, young people—all those who enjoyed music—to put to use their hard-won singing school skills. "Sherburne" (Listening Example 15) by **Daniel Read** (1757–1836), another well-known member of the First New England School of composers,

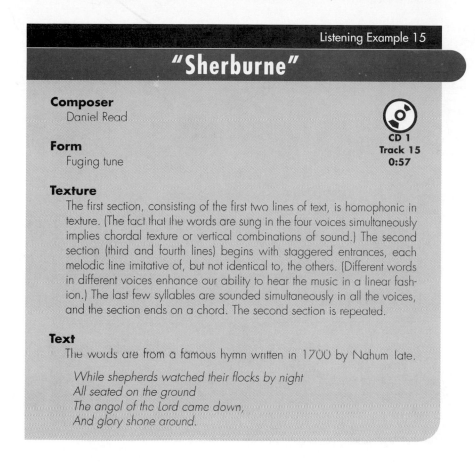

Listening Example 15

"Sherburne"

Composer
Daniel Read

CD 1
Track 15
0:57

Form
Fuging tune

Texture
The first section, consisting of the first two lines of text, is homophonic in texture. (The fact that the words are sung in the four voices simultaneously implies chordal texture or vertical combinations of sound.) The second section (third and fourth lines) begins with staggered entrances, each melodic line imitative of, but not identical to, the others. (Different words in different voices enhance our ability to hear the music in a linear fashion.) The last few syllables are sounded simultaneously in all the voices, and the section ends on a chord. The second section is repeated.

Text
The words are from a famous hymn written in 1700 by Nahum Tate.

*While shepherds watched their flocks by night
All seated on the ground
The angel of the Lord came down,
And glory shone around.*

was an immensely popular fuging tune in late-eighteenth-century America. A comb maker who also owned a general store and taught singing school, Read probably was the most popular composer of fuging tunes. "Sherburne" remained widely known until the Civil War period and still is sung in parts of the country today.

Besides Billings and Read, many singing school masters composed psalm tunes, hymns, canons, and fuging tunes for the edification and enjoyment of their pupils. Although these practical men conceived of their music as teaching material rather than art, we value it today as strong, beautiful, and genuinely American in character, much as we appreciate the work folk artists of the period produced, functional in purpose but beautiful in its own right. (See Figure 3.7.) Recent American composers have used the tunes of the First New England School composers and their contemporaries as inspiration and source material for music of our own period. (Notably, William Schuman, a Pulitzer Prize–winning composer with strong national interests, wrote a symphonic concert piece titled *New England Triptych* based on three of Billings's songs, including "When Jesus Wept" and "Chester." See Listening Example 80.)

FIGURE 3.7

The Sargent Family, American School, 1800, canvas, 0.974 cm × 1.280 cm. Folk artists, like the singing school masters, accomplished highly attractive art in their efforts to provide a practical service— here, to preserve the likenesses of this young American family.

Terms to Review

psalms   One hundred fifty inspirational verses from the Old Testament of the Bible.

psalm tunes   Tuneful settings of the psalms in versions suitable for congregational singing.

a cappella   Unaccompanied (choral singing).

psalter   A printed collection of the psalms translated into metered and rhymed verse, suitable for setting to simple tunes.

Bay Psalm Book   A famous psalter, the first book printed in America (1640).

anthem   A through-composed religious song, usually with a biblical text, for performance by a choir rather than a congregation.

through-composed   A song form containing new music throughout, without the internal repetition characteristic of strophic form.

lining out A method of group singing in which each line of text is sung by a leader and echoed by the group or congregation.

singing school masters Musical amateurs who taught people to read music and to sing.

First New England School America's first composers, also known as Yankee pioneers and singing school masters, who lived in New England in the eighteenth century and the early nineteenth century, and who wrote music to use as teaching tools.

canon A polyphonic composition in which all the voices perform the same melody beginning at different times.

fuging tune A hymn or psalm tune in two sections, the first homophonic and the second polyphonic in texture.

Key Figures

John Antes   William Billings   Daniel Read

Optional Listening Example

"Windsor"—psalm tune

Suggestions for Further Listening

Fuging Tunes and Other Songs by First New England School Composers, Such as the Following
Supply Belcher
Jeremiah Ingalls
Jacob Kimball
Andrew Law
Timothy Swan
Music by the Following Moravian Composers
John Antes
Jeremiah Denckem

Johannes Herbst
Edward W. Leinbach
Johann Friedrich Peter
Modern Compositions Based upon the Music of the First New England School, Including the Following
William Schuman, "New England Triptych" (see Listening Example 80)
Henry Cowell, "Hymns and Fuging Tunes"
Otto Luening, "Fuging Tune for Wind Instruments"
Ross Lee Finney, "Hymn, Fuging, and Holiday"

Critical Thinking

Why do you think twentieth-century American composers such as Henry Cowell, William Schuman, and Otto Luening found fuging tunes a fertile source of inspiration for the composition of concert music?

In what ways might you describe the music of the singing school masters as folk art?

Why do you think many eighteenth-century American Protestants enjoyed singing fuging tunes more than psalm tunes?

Why do you think some of the psalm tunes (including "Old Hundred") remain so well-known and well-loved today?

Go to www.mhhe.com/ferrisaml5 for a list of additional Web-based resources that relate to the content in this chapter.

Secular Music in the Colonial, Revolutionary, and Federal Periods

P
ublic concerts began to be performed in some of the larger American cities beginning in the late 1720s—about the same time they began to be held in Europe. For most of the eighteenth century, however, Americans showed little interest in formal concert music, most remaining largely unaware of the outstanding composers of their time, the Austrians W. A. Mozart (1756–1790) and F. J. Haydn (1732–1809). Because even the best-educated American audience had very limited experience with serious music, early concerts consisted of simple and popular pieces—marches, dance tunes, and stirring **program music** (instrumental pieces purporting to imitate sounds of nature or to "tell" a story) interspersed with folk and popular songs from the contemporary theater. Programmatic battle pieces, imitating on harpsichord, organ, piano, or band and orchestral instruments the sounds of gunfire, marching troops, bugle calls, and other warlike effects, numbered among the most popular concert attractions.

Music in Everyday Experience

Home music, work music, music for entertainment, and music for dancing dominated American music throughout the Revolutionary and federal periods. In rural areas, combined work-social affairs such as barn raisings, maple sugaring, and cornhusking often were accompanied by singing, fiddling, or other musical activities and followed by dancing. Music in New Orleans must have been particularly rich and varied, because African, Native American, Caribbean, French, and Spanish cultures all were part of life in that vibrant city. One prominent New Orleans family was depicted by the artist José Salazar entertaining themselves, and perhaps some friends, with music (Figure 4.1).

Music publishing had become an important business by the latter part of the century, producing quantities of sheet music appropriate for the amateur performer that consisted mostly of simple vocal and piano pieces sometimes referred to as "household music." More and more Americans had musical instruments such as violins, guitars, oboes, and flutes in their homes. Popular

FIGURE 4.1

The Family of Doctor Montegut, José Francisco Xavier de Salazar y Mendoza, 1794–1800, oil on canvas, 59" × 74". Collection of the Louisiana State Museum, loan of Mr. Gustave Pitot.

keyboard instruments included small and often elaborately decorated *virginals* (Figure 4.2) as well as harpsichords and early pianos, called *fortepianos,* some of which were built in America. The fortepiano was smaller and more delicate than the modern instrument, but as its name implies, it was able to produce varied dynamic levels according to the touch of the performer. Children and young women learned to sing and play simple pieces by taking lessons from immigrant professional musicians.

Servants, both African American and white, sometimes were chosen for their musical abilities and expected to contribute to music making in the home. Talented African Americans sometimes supplied music for social dancing and played at dancing schools, in taverns, and for formal balls. The favored instrument to accompany dancing was the *fiddle:* Smaller and lighter than the modern violin and producing a louder and more vibrant sound than was considered appropriate for genteel listening, the eighteenth-century instrument was heard more often in the barnyard or ballroom than in the parlor.

FIGURE 4.2

Double spinet, or virginal, made by Ludovicus Growelus (Lodewijck Grauwels). Early virginals were oblong boxes small enough to be placed on a table, but late in the eighteenth century, the term was applied to various keyboard instruments.

FIGURE 4.3

An eighteenth-century chamber music concert.

Prestigious Musical Amateurs Although Europeans continued to dominate professional music performances, American amateurs became increasingly active in various phases of musical activity. Many joined musical societies founded in a number of larger American cities, which presented instrumental or choral music—mostly written, however, by European composers. Professional foreign musicians often joined the members of amateur societies for their concerts, which lasted for as long as three or more hours. (See Figure 4.3.)

The first performances in America of important European symphonic and choral works were given by Moravian musicians, whose compositions and performances were of the highest quality, for they were amateurs only in the sense that they composed and performed music for the love of it (as the root of the word "amateur" implies) rather than for money. As news spread of the Moravians' outstanding concerts, people traveled long distances from other settlements to hear them. George Washington and Benjamin Franklin numbered among the Moravians' most fervent admirers.

Well-to-do patrons and musical amateurs such as the famous statesman **Thomas Jefferson** (1743–1826) supported the efforts of the musical societies by contributing generously of their time, money, and talent. Jefferson, a fine musician himself, participated enthusiastically in music activities, although he insisted that the arts were meaningful only as they bore relevance to everyday life. An accomplished architect who designed buildings to be beautiful as well as efficient, Jefferson apparently considered the musical arts an essential part of the human experience as well. He played the violin, as did Patrick Henry, who sometimes joined Jefferson in duets to entertain themselves, their friends, and (before the Revolution) illustrious representatives of the king's government in Williamsburg, Virginia. Most early Americans agreed with Jefferson that art—especially American art—must be practical to be worthwhile. John Adams considered even "practical" art a luxury inappropriate for the people of a young democracy, although he admired a well-written sermon, political document, or tract.

Benjamin Franklin (1706–1790), who warned that Americans should not cultivate a taste for the arts before they were able to produce art, clearly considered Europeans superior in this regard. Conceding that poetry, painting, and music might be useful under certain circumstances, he complained that America had no musicians of the caliber of outstanding European performers, and that even concerts performed by Europeans in America were inferior to the performances Franklin heard in England and on the continent.

Franklin wrote verses to set to tunes that he enjoyed, learned to play the guitar and the harp very well, and even invented a musical instrument called the **armonica** or **glass harmonica** (Figure 4.4), which became enormously popular in its day. This instrument consists of a series of hollow, hemispheric glass bowls or bells, each with a short neck. The glasses are mounted on a horizontal spindle, each fitted inside the next largest with a finger width of brim exposed on which to play. The performer keeps the spindle turning through a trough of water by working a pedal, while producing a delicate sound by rubbing the wet rims of the glasses with the fingers.

The mysterious sounds of the glass harmonica were reputed to make women faint, soothe marital disputes, and even wake the dead! (Mozart frequently played the instrument at the Vienna home of the hypnotist Anton Mesmer, who used it to help induce trances in his patients.)

The first secular songs published in America were by Europeans, many from England, and were usually associated with the theater. But about the same time that the singing school masters were writing religious songs to use as teaching tools, other amateur American composers began to write music that had neither a religious nor a practical purpose.

FIGURE 4.4
Benjamin Franklin playing his glass harmonica.

Francis Hopkinson (1737–1791), an extraordinary American who became our first secretary of the navy and was one of the signers of the Declaration of Independence, also was much concerned with the artistic dimension of American life. Hopkinson wrote several **art songs**—songs intended for concert or recital performance (amateur or professional) as opposed to folk or popular pieces. The text of an art song is a poem of literary merit, by a known poet. Because the music is intended to enhance the meaning of the poem, it may be expressive or dramatic rather than necessarily pleasing to the ear. Because the essence of an art song lies in the text, and because translations inevitably lose nuances of meaning and sound, art songs are nearly always performed in the language in which they were written.

A zealous patriot in the political sense, Hopkinson nevertheless conceived his songs in conscientious imitation of the English songs of his day. Unlike the sturdily independent singing school masters, Hopkinson held the "cultivated" eighteenth-century American view that the colonists were inferior in the arts and best advised to emulate European styles, as he did in his song titled "My Days Have Been So Wondrous Free" (Optional Listening Example).

Although Hopkinson appears to have been the first American to attempt songs of this nature, soon other Americans also composed songs European in style, with texts, however, often based upon American subjects—several in honor of George Washington. Most early American art songs, unlike their more demanding European models, were suitable for performance by amateurs.

Professional Composers Many talented and accomplished European musicians who immigrated to the United States greatly enriched the American concert experience before and after the turn of the nineteenth century. An outstanding example, **Benjamin Carr** (1768–1831)—composer, singer, conductor, pianist, organist, and music publisher—arrived in Philadelphia from England soon after the Revolution. One of the first people to be active in the music business in this country, Carr also ran a music store that become the leading center of music activity after the war. Carr and others like him made wide-ranging and long-lasting contributions to music performance, business, and appreciation in North America.

A colleague and near contemporary of Carr's, **Alexander Reinagle** (1756–1809), composed the Philadelphia Sonatas, a set of piano pieces that includes the Sonata II in E, the third movement of which is Listening Example 16. Reinagle, who was raised in Edinburgh by an Austrian father and a Scottish mother, taught music in New York City before settling in Philadelphia as director of a theater company. He also directed a series of concerts in Philadelphia, presenting the music of outstanding European composers as well as his own.

A **sonata** is a large musical form for one or more solo instruments, consisting of several movements. (The number of movements and other characteristics of the form change from one historical period to another.) Reinagle's sonata for pianoforte (an early piano, smaller and lighter than the modern grand) has three movements.

As explained in the Prelude (p. 9), each movement of a multimovement composition is organized according to some formal design, based upon principles of unity and contrast. The third movement of Reinagle's Sonata in E is in the form of a **rondo,** in which the opening melodic material (A) returns to alternate with other material (B, C, etc.). The return of A lends balance and unity to the rondo, while the contrasting sections add interest. We indicate the general concept of the rondo form with the letters **A B A C A,** but a composer may write any number of contrasting sections alternating with the return of A. For example, A B A B A B A and A B A C A D A are among the limitless possibilities for realizing the rondo form. Because the mood of a rondo is typically bright and the tempo fast, this form often provides an effective close to a multimovement work.

Early American Theater

Musical theater became popular in some areas during the 1730s, as growing numbers of European professional musicians became associated with both the theater and the concert hall. Although their songs and instrumental interludes were performed in concert halls as well as in the theater, theatrical performances made their works popular and afforded them a living.

These highly trained professional musicians provided performance and educational opportunities previously denied colonial Americans. Two early centers of music activity—Charleston, North Carolina; and Williamsburg, Virginia—had active theaters well before the middle of the eighteenth century.

Sonata II in E, third movement

Composer
Alexander Reinagle

CD 1
Track 16
6:44

Form
Modified rondo. The letters A B A C A D A outline the form
of this movement, but each contrasting section (B, C, D) is
unusually long and complex.

Tempo
Allegro

Meter
Duple

Key
The key written as a capital letter indicates the major mode. (By contrast,
E minor is written e.)

(A) The bright opening theme includes two 8-measure phrases. Its repetition, with only slight variation, provides classical balance and also
allows the listener to memorize it for recognition upon its return. The
simple left-hand accompaniment includes some measures of the
broken-chord pattern called **Alberti bass.** (By "broken chord,"
we mean that one note of the chord is played at a time.)

(B, 0:26) This extended section, much longer than A, includes graceful
running passages, often accompanied by the Alberti bass. Notice
the strong accents in one passage (0:48–0:56). You will also hear
(1:04–1:17) a simple, mostly descending scale pattern (five steps
down, two up) in the left hand (lower pitches) accompanied by
lightly-running figures in the right hand. A teasing pause anticipates
the return of A.

(A, 1:35) The two 8-measure phrases are heard once.

(C. 1:49) This extended passage includes several sections differing in
melodic material, mood, intensity, accompaniment patterns, and dynamic levels. After its somewhat tentative start, we hear material related to A. Toward the end of the passage (3:32), familiar material
leads to the pause intimating the return of A.

(A, 3:50) The two phrases are heard once.

(D, 4:04) This section includes several statement-and-answer effects, typical of music in the Classical period (about 1750–1825). A slow,
quiet *cadenza*, or solo passage for the right hand alone (5:22), anticipates the return of A.

(A, 6:03) The theme is heard once more, followed by a modest, carefully balanced closing section.

Anglican religious influence prevailed in the South, and the English church authorities—unlike the Calvinists—had largely abandoned Oliver Cromwell's seventeenth-century scruples regarding theatrical performances.

In 1778, however, under wartime stress, the Continental Congress decreed that "frequenting Play Houses and theatrical entertainments has a fatal tendency to divert the minds of people from a due attention to the means necessary for the defence of their country and preservation of their liberties." Accordingly, Congress banned all theater performances.

The lifting of the ban in 1789, and the passing a year later of the first national copyright act, which protected printed materials including music for fourteen years with the possibility of renewal for another fourteen, encouraged a wave of foreign (mostly British) musicians to come to America. They performed onstage and in orchestra pits, taught music to aspiring amateurs, and composed many pieces, including some of America's first popular songs.

Musical theater grew in popularity as interest in music and the theater moved north to New York and then to Philadelphia, which soon dominated the musical scene. There the enthusiasm of such influential patrons as George Washington, who justified his fondness for theater by declaring that it had the practical effect of elevating one's manners, overruled the Quakers' disapproval of theatrical performances. In fact, however, manners were hardly elevated at theatrical performances, where informality to the extent of rowdiness prevailed. Those sitting in the cheaper seats, called the gallery, yelled freely at the actors and musicians, demanding to hear their favorite songs and criticizing the performance in the frankest and rudest terms. They tossed bottles and fruit into the orchestra pit or onto the stage, and despite the presence of soldiers hired to keep order, pandemonium often reigned.

The American stage at this period offered a potpourri of entertainment. Performances, lasting four or five hours, usually included a main drama and also a shorter, lighter, often comic piece. Music was added even to nonmusical plays, with musical entertainment provided between the dramatic pieces and after the comedy. Sometimes a march played at the end led the audience out of the hall to attend a nearby dance.

Most of the plays performed in eighteenth-century America were English pieces adapted to suit American taste. Shorter and lighter than contemporary European works, they also included more comedy. The most popular type of performance, called a **ballad opera,** was a simple, unsophisticated musical play in which spoken dialogue replaced the *recitative* ("sung speech") of serious opera, and popular songs of the day were interspersed throughout the show. John Gay's *Beggar's Opera,* the first musical play of this kind, became as popular in America as it had been in England since it opened in 1728. (The popular song "Mack the Knife" comes from a twentieth-century version of the *Beggar's Opera* called *Threepenny Opera* by Kurt Weill.)

A short musical play credited to Francis Hopkinson in 1781 may have been America's earliest original musical theater work, although Hopkinson probably just set new words to existing music. In any case, foreign professionals such as Alexander Reinagle dominated the American popular music stage for a considerable period, significantly affecting the development of music in America.

FIGURE 4.5
A band of drummers.

Early Bands

In 1777, General George Washington issued an order requiring "every offi-cer, for the credit of his corps," to provide military music to American troops. The first American military bands, established during the Revolutionary War, consisted only of drums and small flutes called *fifes*. The duties of these **fife and drum corps,** many of whose members were African Americans, ex-tended far beyond lifting the spirits and quickening the steps of the amateur soldiers (see Figure 4.5). They also announced the beginning and end of the day, called the troops to meals and other activities, and transmitted com-mands on the battlefield that could not otherwise be heard over the noise of musket fire.

Besides fife and drum corps, some military bands in the colonies began to develop, very gradually, along the lines of those in Europe. In 1792, the first laws were passed standardizing the formation of American military bands to resemble European models, which had long included a variety of woodwinds and brasses as well as percussion instruments in their ensembles. And in 1798, President John Adams signed into law the creation of the United States Marine Corps, which included thirty-two drummers and fifers, a drum major, and a fife major. This early band soon acquired two horns, two clarinets, one bassoon, and a bass drum, in which form it played for the inauguration of Thomas Jefferson in 1801. Early brass instruments, however, lacking valves that allowed players to change pitches manually, were relatively difficult to play, and only after they were fitted with valves, about 1830, did brass instruments assume the significant melodic responsibilities in military and concert bands they hold today.

Throughout the eighteenth century, New Orleans had its own strong musical heritage, in which military-style bands played a prominent role. Black musicians, both slave and free, provided music for balls and parades in that colorful city, and eventually dominated the transition of the traditional military funeral parade to a civic custom. The band attached to the First Battalion of Free Men of Color, which had an active role in defeating the British at the Siege of New Orleans (1815), included people identified as Creole-of-color, meaning that they were partly European and active in the French-dominated culture of the city.

Besides their military functions, early military bands also played to entertain the public at parades and informal concerts. Among the popular tunes included in such programs, a favorite would have been "Yankee Doodle" (Listening Example 17), which has pleased American ears from the time of its origin to the present day. Though perhaps written by an Englishman for the purpose of ridiculing the appearance of New England troops compared with the spit and polish of the British army, it delighted Americans, who added countless verses of text (some say about 190) over the years.

Listening Example 17

"Yankee Doodle" (excerpt)

Tune

The origin of the tune and the meaning of its title are unknown. It was composed some time before the Revolutionary War, either in Britain or in America, and first appeared in print in 1782. (The words, also anonymous, were often changed for partisan purposes. In fact, the British first sang the song to make fun of the Yankees, who later adopted it as their own!)

CD 1
Track 17
0:46

Meter

Duple

Form

Strophic

The high-pitched fifes carry the stirring tune, while the drums mark the rhythm with distinctive beats and rolls. The first section of the tune is played and repeated; then the second section, in a version popular during the Revolutionary War, is played and also repeated. As the example tapers off, the corps begins to sound again the first section of the song.

Terms to Review

program music   Instrumental music describing a story, scene, idea, or event.

armonica or **glass harmonica**   A musical instrument invented by Benjamin Franklin, consisting of tuned, wet glasses that are rubbed to produce a sound.

art song   A secular song, usually with a text of literary merit, intended for concert or recital performance.

sonata   Multimovement form for one or more solo instruments.

rondo   A form of composition, usually fast in tempo and merry in mood, in which various episodes alternate with the opening material (**A B A C A**).

Alberti bass   An accompaniment pattern consisting of rhythmically regular broken chords.

ballad opera   An English form of music theater setting comedy and satire to popular tunes.

fife and drum corps   An early band, consisting of fifes and drums, which performed for military and later for entertainment purposes.

Key Figures

Thomas Jefferson   Francis Hopkinson   Alexander Reinagle
Benjamin Franklin   Benjamin Carr

Optional Listening Example

Francis Hopkinson, "My Days Have Been So Wondrous Free"

Suggestions for Further Listening

Rondo
Mozart, *Adagio and Rondo,* K. 617, for glass harmonica, flute, oboe, viola, and cello
American Instrumental Music in Classical style
Benjamin Carr, *Sonata I,* for piano or harpsichord Carr, *Federal Overture*

Battle Piece
James Hewitt, "Battle of Trenton," for organ

Critical Thinking

What programmatic effects might you expect to hear in a work titled "Spring" Symphony? Violin Sonata for Halloween? Rondo español?

Do you know of any modern statesmen who have been enthusiastic music amateurs?

If you have been to the theater, compare your experience with what the text says about stage entertainment and audience behavior at a typical eighteenth-century American theatrical performance.

Go to www.mhhe.com/ferrisaml5 for a list of additional Web-based resources that relate to the content in this chapter.

PART 1
Summary

The earliest North American music experience was that of American Indians, whose many musics are associated with ritual, dance, ceremony, or work. Most Native American music was and is song, sometimes supported by sound instruments—primarily percussion instruments, such as drums, rattles, and rasps, or their most common melodic instrument, a flute. Contemporary Native American music reflects not only the ancient, traditional songs and dances, but also various new styles, some of which are traditional and some borrowed from North American neighbors. Even the new songs remain a potent source of power in American Indian culture, confirming Indian-ness, validating ceremonies, and helping keep people "right" and in balance with nature and with the deity who controls all.

Beginning in the sixteenth century, as Europeans came to settle in the New World, Native Americans in Florida and in the missions of the Southwest learned to perform Roman Catholic music and some European secular music as well. Soon German- and English-speaking Protestants established permanent settlements in America, bringing with them their hymns and psalm tunes as well as folk and other secular music. The first book printed in the New World was a psalter, the *Bay Psalm Book*. Both African and European Americans enjoyed secular as well as religious music, the settlers singing ballads and playing fiddle tunes, the slaves singing work songs and other songs according to African custom.

Early efforts to improve the quality of singing in New England's churches led to the forming of singing schools, some of whose singing masters wrote their own original tunes, thereby becoming known as members of the First New England School of composers. Their music differed in style and purpose from that of their European contemporaries. William Billings, Daniel Read, and their many Yankee pioneer colleagues produced quantities of psalm tunes, hymns, fuging tunes, and patriotic songs for use at singing school, at church, and in the home.

Americans' musical tastes became more secular and more varied throughout the eighteenth century, as music supplied entertainment in the home, at concerts, and in the theater. Many people learned to play instruments and sing simple songs, and musical societies were formed for the purpose of performing instrumental and choral music. Talented amateurs participated in informal recitals and composed songs and keyboard pieces. Moravians produced music of a complexity and quality unprecedented among other early American compositions.

Public concerts and musical theater had also become popular forms of entertainment by the middle of the century. The important musicians associated with the early American theater were Europeans who adapted popular European plays and ballad operas to suit the less sophisticated American taste. Band music became increasingly popular as fife and drum corps and military bands played public concerts in addition to performing their military functions.

PART 2

The Tumultuous Nineteenth Century

Romanticism in America: Historical and Cultural Perspective

During the nineteenth century, most European writers, painters, and musicians abandoned the coolly reasoned Classical style to reveal in their new art a fierce independence, a fascination with the unknown, and a worshipful love of nature—all characteristics associated with *romanticism* in the arts. From about 1825 to 1900, the emotional, intuitive style called Romanticism (the capital letter distinguishing the nineteenth-century style from romanticism in general) dominated the arts in Europe, and German musicians dominated music in the Western world.

Americans revealed strong romantic tendencies long before the nineteenth century and continue to do so today. Thus the artistic style newly dominant in Europe came quite naturally to this young country, where its spirit seemed always to have been at home. Perhaps the pioneers bred their sense of adventure into later generations of Americans, or perhaps the vast, wild land encouraged the demand for freedom and independence. For whatever reasons, romanticism seemed then, as now, congenial to the American personality.

The Emergence of Characteristically American Art

Although from about the 1830s one could travel from America to Europe by steamship, such travel was neither safe nor reliable, and most Americans remained effectively isolated from European culture. Little diplomatic exchange took place, and few foreigners immigrated to America during the midcentury period. Although many nineteenth-century American musicians shied away from the fresh, original sounds of the Yankee tunesmiths and attempted to emulate European—specifically German—traditions, the young country's literary and visual artists often expressed their romantic ideals in characteristically American ways.

Independence In the early 1800s, Americans defended their new and hard-earned political and military independence by resisting the French and British in assorted skirmishes and vigorously fighting the notorious Barbary pirates. American patriots further manifested their fierce independence by vowing, in the Monroe Doctrine of 1823, to resist foreign interference anywhere in the Western Hemisphere. In 1828, city and frontier folk alike rejected aristocratic leadership by electing a populist hero president of the United States, and under President Andrew Jackson a

new American nationalism evolved as artists and writers, encouraged by their patrons' new interest in American art for art's sake, shed their dependence on Europeans and began to produce works on a wide variety of American subjects.

Claiming a refreshing freedom from European dominance, American literary figures developed their own distinctive ways to express the American experience, and a genuinely American literature evolved. The prolific literary activity of this period reflected a new American nationalism, as poets and novelists wrote on American subjects placed in American settings. James Fenimore Cooper's *The Last of the Mohicans,* for example, was one of many Romantic works featuring the American Indian.

In the mid-nineteenth century, Boston housed an important group of writers and philosophers known as transcendentalists, who in the romantic way trusted intuition, rather than reason, as the guide to truth. Sharing the Protestants' and the frontier people's belief in the integrity and ability of the individual, the transcendentalists also fervently expressed in their literary and philosophical works their love of nature and pride in America's natural beauty.

From the time Abraham Lincoln was elected president in 1860 until he was assassinated in 1865, sermons, speeches, poems, articles, and proclamations addressed all sides of the slavery issue. The famous humorist and author Mark Twain (real name Samuel Clemens, 1835–1910) depicted scenes and described relations between blacks and whites as he remembered them from his boyhood along the Mississippi River. An amateur musician who sang and played the piano, Twain frequently referred in his stories to the singing of simple songs and the playing of keyboard instruments. Twain claimed to particularly dislike the piano, an instrument he may have associated with the upper classes, with whom he did not identify. It is also possible that his sensitive ear was offended by the sound of poorly tuned pianos, since few instruments in his day were afforded the regular attention of a professional tuner. In any case, he often wrote approvingly of a simple and increasingly popular keyboard instrument variously called a *reed organ, parlor organ, cabinet organ, cottage organ,* or *melodeon* (Listening Example 42, "St. Louis Blues"). The reed organ, cheaper and requiring less maintenance than a piano, was very popular in Twain's day.

The Unknown
Romantic curiosity and intrigue with the unknown led pioneer men and women to push America's frontier ever farther west, defying great perils in the high spirit of optimism also characteristic of the romantic personality. During the early years of the nineteenth century, surveyors and engineers explored and carefully mapped the wilderness areas of upstate New York, New England, and the West. The Erie Canal was opened in 1825, and steam railroads soon afforded Americans yet further opportunity to become acquainted with their magnificent land, of which they were justly proud.

Stories and poems concerning abnormal psychology by such writers as Edgar Allan Poe (1809–1849) and Nathaniel Hawthorne (1804–1864) revealed

The Erie Canal.

their fascination with the unknown, whereas some Romantic painters, sharing the interest in science and art expressed during the last century by Charles Willson Peale, explored new fields of study and made discoveries of significant scientific and practical worth. James Audubon (1785–1851) gave unprecedented attention to the study of birds, producing an astonishing number of realistic watercolors of American birds in their natural poses and settings.

Samuel Morse (1791–1872), who like Audubon and C. W. Peale had an interest in and a talent for both science and art, helped make the pre-photographic process known as *daguerreotype* popular with Americans, who often had more interest in something new and mechanical than in objects of purely artistic value. Having studied painting in Europe, Morse produced several fine canvases upon his return to America. Ultimately, however, he became discouraged at Americans' preference for landscapes of local scenery over the large European-style "history paintings" he favored, whereupon he turned his attention to another form of communication and invented the telegraph.

Love of Nature
Nature, formerly viewed as a menacing force to be conquered and tamed, now received reverent admiration in American literature, painting, and music idealizing the natural beauty of the American continent. Writers portraying nature as good and beautiful included the poets William Cullen Bryant and Henry Wadsworth Longfellow

A melodeon. The player of this instrument, the timbre of which could be varied through the use of levers or buttons called *stops,* pumped one or two treadles to produce the wind that made the sound possible.

and the essayists Ralph Waldo Emerson and Henry David Thoreau, each of whom expressed in American ways ideals similar to those of the British Romantic poets.

American painting in the post-Revolutionary, or federal, period also reflected the new American nationalism and the romantic love of nature, as artists captured the clear light, blazing sky, and vast open spaces of the American landscape. Although American viewers lagged behind Europeans in appreciating art for its own, not necessarily functional, sake, American artists produced paintings and sculptural works of unprecedented numbers and variety. In painting, landscapes predominated, but Charles Willson Peale's cousin Margaretta Angelica Peale (1795–1882), one of very few professional women artists, was widely admired as a painter of still lifes, perhaps considered a more seemly subject than landscape for a woman to interpret. The same democratic spirit that elected Andrew Jackson president stimulated appreciation for scenes in art of everyday life, especially as experienced in the idealized countryside: cornhusking, dancing, and all manner of work and play were charmingly depicted by folk and formal artists.

George Catlin, *White Cloud, Head Chief of the Iowas.* Canvas, 58 cm × 71 cm (22⅞ in. × 28 in.)

Painters accompanying explorers and adventurers across the American wilderness depicted the wild beauty of untamed areas, stirring the romantic imagination of city-bound folk. George Catlin (1796–1872), a dedicated artist-explorer, vividly portrayed the vast American wilderness, complete with Indians and wild animals.

Fusion of the Arts

Although comparisons are readily drawn among the various arts of any stylistic period, the relationships between literature, painting, and music of the Romantic period are particularly striking in their strength and significance. Nineteenth-century artists in Europe and America drew inspiration from close association with each other and showed unprecedented interest in each other's work.

In truth, however, in America as well as in Europe, artists were newly dependent on the approval of a public audience, which lacked both the training and

Margaretta Angelica Peale, *Still Life with Watermelon and Peaches,* 1828. Oil on canvas, 13 in. × 19⅛ in. (33 cm × 48.5 cm). (Smith College Museum of Art, Northampton, MA. Purchased with funds given anonymously by a member of the class of 1952.)

Thomas Cole, *Scenes from The Last of the Mohicans.*

the experience of the earlier limited, even private, audiences of church, court, or salon. Thus during the Romantic period, in this country and abroad, artists relied on each other for moral support, and sometimes for more practical support as well.

The first important group of American painters, known as the Hudson River School, was led for a time by Thomas Cole (1801–1848), whose large landscape paintings capture the spaciousness and grandeur of the Catskill and Adirondack mountains of New York state. Reflecting the close association between artists so dear to the great Romantics, Cole based his painting *Scenes from The Last of the Mohicans* on the novel by his friend James Fenimore Cooper, who is sometimes referred to as a Hudson

River painter using prose rather than pigment to depict panoramic American landscapes.

The intertwined relationships among writers and artists is also revealed in *Kindred Spirits* by Asher B. Durand (1796–1886), who succeeded Cole as leader of the Hudson River School. Durand's painting portrays the artist Cole, for whom the painting was a memorial, and the poet William Cullen Bryant sharing admiration for the natural beauty of the Catskill Mountains. Durand intended the painting to depict the rugged moral innocence of the new continent contrasted with what Bryant called the "tamings and softenings of cultivation" that afflicted European culture. Cole, Durand, and Bryant, who knew and admired each other, differed widely in their political

Asher B. Durand, *Kindred Spirits*. In a scene exemplifying the Romantic image, this beautiful painting expresses love of nature, nationalism, and the close mating of the arts.

views, yet shared a patriotic urge to eradicate American feelings of inferiority toward the Old World. *Kindred Spirits* embodies the feeling of Romantic artists of various media that reverence for the natural beauty of their homeland transcended the feelings of more mundane souls.

Music proved a particularly congenial medium for the romantic blending of the arts: An art song, for example, was the setting of a poem to music, and program music often depicted scenes from literature in musical terms. Certain kinds of musical theater, especially operas and operettas, constituted even more complex combinations of visual, literary, and musical arts. While there was no Hudson River School of musicians, leading composers and music performers of the day traveled to the Hudson River Valley, derived inspiration from its physical beauty, and evoked its spirit, if not its name, in their music.

The Civil War Era

The reform movements begun in the early part of the nineteenth century gathered strength in the 1860s, as tension heightened between blacks and whites and

Edmonia Lewis, *Bust of Abraham Lincoln.*

Wooden bucket (c. 1825), whose charming painted designs must have seemed to lighten its load.

between supporters of slavery and of abolition. Workers, increasingly well organized, forced enactment of tough new labor laws; feminists marched and demonstrated, demanding improved educational opportunities for women, liberalized property rights, equitable divorce laws, and the right of women to vote. Whereas urban Northerners found themselves increasingly repelled by slavery, Southerners considered the system essential to the plantation economy upon which they depended, and there seemed no grounds for compromise on this volatile subject.

Finally forced to confront the problems leading inexorably to the Civil War, Americans reflected in their literary, visual, and musical arts every facet of these and other social issues.

From about 1850 to 1875, American painters shared their European colleagues' fascination with the myriad effects of light, which they learned to use as a means of expression in its own right, their best work capturing the clear atmosphere and wide spaciousness characteristic of the American scene. American artists of the period idealized nature in the romantic way, viewing it as morally uplifting and taking pride in the grandeur of their nation's landscape. Andrew Jackson's optimism and the idealism of the American pioneer were reflected in many moving scenes of mountain splendor and rural calm.

But few American patrons shared the artists' appreciation for American art. The best-known American artist of his day, James McNeill Whistler (1834–1903), spent most of his life in Europe, having become discouraged by the lack of a market for serious art in his own country. Highly eccentric in dress and manner but widely admired for his great talent, Whistler became a leading figure in both European and American art.

American still-life painting matured and flourished, largely independent of European influence, and folk art became more individual and expressive than ever. American practicality and craftsmanship produced fine weather vanes, shop signs, furniture, and other wares every bit as beautiful as they were indeed useful.

Americans during this time also produced distinctive sculpture, sometimes laden with messages of social significance. *The Greek Slave* by Hiram Powers (1805–1873) was seen as an American expression of sympathy for the Greek War of Independence as well as for slaves in the American South. Another work revealing its creator's social consciousness was *The Indian* (*The Chief Contemplating the Progress of Civilization*) by Thomas Crawford (1813–1857). Among the few professional women artists of the time, Edmonia Lewis (1845–1909), whose mother was Native American and whose father was black, produced sculpture with social and political relevance, including a stunning bust of Abraham Lincoln in 1867.

Music

Newly liberated from its former semifunctional position in worship or daily life, and newly available to an ever wider public audience, music became an increasingly significant facet of nineteenth-century American life. Religious and secular music, for voices and for instruments, reflected every feature of American experience in that turbulent century. ♪

Religious Music in the Early Nineteenth Century

Consistent with the Romantic emphasis upon individual rights and preferences, the brave men and women of the American frontier developed a fierce (if inconsistent) respect for the integrity of the humblest individual. Puritans, Quakers, and members of other Protestant sects living in the cities of the Northeast, who shared the frontier people's work ethic and concern for the common folk, initiated strong reform movements addressing issues of human and civil rights. Women particularly became active in a number of social causes, including the abolition of slavery, the founding of the American Temperance Society (1826), improvements in the conditions of prisons and asylums, and increased aid to the disabled.

The Great Revival

This zeal for reform spawned the strong religious revival movement known as the Great Revival, or the Second Awakening (see the Great Awakening, p. 56–57), which rapidly attracted rural Presbyterians, Baptists, Methodists, and others by the thousands to huge, emotional camp meetings, each lasting for several days. Itinerant preachers called circuit riders led the praying, shouting, singing, and often a kind of frenzied dancing at these social, recreational, and religious events—refreshingly democratic affairs in which men and women, blacks and whites, adults and children participated with equal enthusiasm (Figure 5.1).

Shape-Note Notation

Music, too, reflected the concern for reform. For example, singing school teachers eager to improve the quality of their students' singing devised and promoted a new method of reading music called **shape-note notation.** While the traditional system of music notation is quite easy to learn (see Prelude, p. 10), shape-note notation proved popular and long-lived.

Shape notes evolved from the system of placing the first letters of the four syllables *fa, sol, la,* and *mi* on the staff instead of traditional note heads. In shape-note notation, each syllable was assigned a different shape (square,

FIGURE 5.1

George Bellows, *Billy Sunday.* This lithograph depicts the famous revivalist preaching to a fervent camp meeting crowd.

FIGURE 5.2

An arrangement of "Old Hundred" in shape-note notation. The words are placed under the melody line.

O come loud   an thems   let   us   sing,

◁ = fa (used for the 1st and 4th degree of scale)
𝓞 = sol (used for the 2nd and 5th degree of scale)
□ = la (used for the 3rd and 6th degree of scale)
◇ = mi (used for the 7th degree of scale)

circle, diamond, or triangle) and placed in appropriate positions on the staff (Figure 5.2). Although never adopted as the usual way of notating music, the shape-note method proved an effective teaching tool and a comfortable means of reading folk hymns and camp-meeting songs.

Vocal quartets hired by shape-note music publishers to popularize their music collections created strong interest in and a demand for shape-note song-books, in which songs were printed in three-part harmony with the melody in the middle voice, according to an old-fashioned custom. (Today we usually place a hymn melody in the top voice, with three lower voices providing harmony.) One of the most popular such songbooks, **The Sacred Harp,** first published in 1844, is still in use today in many rural and some urban and suburban areas. Its first edition included the tunes of popular British ballads, to which Americans had set their favorite religious verses, as well as new American hymns, fuging tunes, and anthems. Southern song compilers printed and circulated the familiar shape-note repertoire after it lost favor in New England, and new shape-note music appeared well into the twentieth century.

Spiritual Songs

Camp meetings occurred not on the strictly regulated and segregated Southern plantations, but in rural and frontier regions, where blacks and whites alike worshiped and socialized freely, sometimes with each other. Virtually isolated from European experience throughout the post-Revolutionary periods, frontier Americans evolved a distinctive music suiting the purposes and pleasing the ears of hardy pioneers. Besides the tuneful ballads with their new religious texts mentioned above, camp meeting songs included hymns with texts by famous English clergymen, and popular American folk hymns and spiritual songs, or **spirituals.** These strophic settings of simple religious texts to folk or popular tunes, available for those who could read music in the popular shape-note notation, became a treasured source of comfort and inspiration for people living a difficult life in the South, in the country, and on the frontier.

Because folk hymns or spiritual songs involved a great deal of repetition, even people who could read neither words nor music learned them quickly and easily. Some songs had many verses, in which only one or a few words changed—"father" becoming "mother," "sisters," "brothers," or "friends" in succeeding stanzas, for example. "There'll Be Joy, Joy, Joy" (Listening Example 18) is typical of the simple but rousing white spirituals sung lustily at nineteenth-century revival camp meetings.

"Amazing Grace"   We do not know who composed "Amazing Grace" (Listening Example 19), surely the favorite of all white spirituals, or folk hymns. The words, written in the 1770s by an English abolitionist preacher and former captain of a slave ship, John Newton, were sung to many different melodies before becoming associated with the lovely American melody called "New Britain." This tune, which appeared in print (in shape-note notation) at least as early as 1831, remains widely known today: It can be found, in fact, on more than 1,100 albums in nearly 1,000 different arrangements. As likely to be performed at times of joy (weddings) as of grief (funerals), the haunting spiritual beautifully expresses our deepest feelings.

Black Spirituals   Especially after the Civil War, many blacks (free or slave) who had been converted to Christianity participated enthusiastically in rousing camp meetings, singing psalm tunes and folk hymns with sincerity and fervor and developing distinctive spirituals of their own. African American spirituals, as simple and folklike as white folk hymns but more rhythmically vibrant, included joyful praise songs accompanied by hand clapping and other

"There'll Be Joy, Joy, Joy"   (excerpt)

**CD 1
Track 18
1:37**

Performers

Carter Family

Sara, with her rich, expressive alto voice, sings the melody, while A. P. and Maybelle add the tight harmony characteristic of mountain music. Their raw southern twang and occasional rhythmic irregularities accentuate the physical and emotional power of the stirring camp meeting spirituals.

Accompaniment

"Mother" Maybelle, as she was called, on guitar and Sara with her autoharp introduce the song and add simple accompaniment to the sung verses. They also play one instrumental verse alone, Sara's autoharp accompanying Maybelle's guitar melody.

Form

Strophic. Only the first phrase of each verse has new text, introduced here by Sara's deep voice. A. P. and Maybelle join her, in call-and-response fashion, for the rest of each verse, which remains the same. Notice how the frequent repetition of words and phrases makes the song seem familiar almost immediately.

Text

There'll be joy, joy, joy
Up in my father's house,
Up in my father's house,
Up in my father's house.
There'll be joy, joy, joy
Up in my father's house,
Where there's peace, sweet peace.

We'll all be happy there . . .

(Instrumental verse)

Don't you want to go up there . . .
There'll be no drunkards there . . .

African effects, such as call-and-response, melodic improvisation, and exciting rhythmic complexities. On the other hand, many black spirituals, such as "Nobody Knows the Trouble I've Seen" (Listening Example 20), expressed the deep sorrow black people experienced in their everyday lives. Referred to by blacks as slave hymns or sorrow songs, black spirituals often contained hidden references to hopes for release or escape—from slavery, from oppression, from the harsh realities of the black experience in America, even from life itself.

"Amazing Grace"

CD 1
Track 19
4:19

Composer
Anonymous

Performer
Judy Collins

Form
Strophic. Judy Collins intersperses the first verse (beginning "Amazing grace") between the other verses, treating it as a chorus or refrain.

Accompaniment
Harp. The performance begins a cappella, the harp entering tentatively when the first verse (or refrain) first recurs and gradually assuming more of a role as the song continues. Notice how the harp slightly varies the accompanying harmonies and finally complements the voice with melodic interest of its own.

Melody
The familiar melody ("New Britain"), using only the notes of the pentatonic scale, is perfection itself; yet it gratefully absorbs interpreters' slides, scoops, and other effects similar to, and sometimes borrowed from, African music.

Meter
Triple

Tempo
Slow

Text
The words, written by John Newton, an English evangelist overwhelmed with remorse for his earlier life as a slave trader, promise God's forgiveness, even for such a "wretch" as he.

Amazing grace, how sweet the sound
That saved a wretch like me.
I once was lost, but now I'm found,
Was blind, but now I see.

Through many dangers, toils, and snares
We have already come.
'Twas grace that brought us safe thus far,
And grace will lead us home.

'Twas grace that taught my heart to fear
And grace my fears relieved.
How precious did that grace appear
The hour I first believed.

"Nobody Knows the Trouble I've Seen" (excerpt)

CD 1
Track 20
1:58

Arranger
Henry Thacker Burleigh. The tune is traditional (anonymous).

Performer
Paul Robeson (bass)

Accompaniment
Piano

Form
Strophic

Melody
The simple tune, based on the pentatonic (five-note) scale, retains its improvisatory flavor in Robeson's polished performance. The words of the verses, too, remain subject to variation by different soloists, to whom a group may respond with the familiar chorus. (The second line of the chorus, in fact, is traditionally sung "Nobody knows but Jesus.")

Text
(Chorus)

Nobody knows the trouble I've seen,
Nobody knows my sorrow.
Nobody knows de trouble I've seen.
Glory, Hallelujah.

(First verse)

Sometimes I'm up, sometimes I'm down,
Oh, yes, Lord.
Sometimes I'm almost to de ground,
Oh, yes, Lord.

(Second verse)

Although you see me goin' along so,
Oh, yes, Lord,
I have my trials here below,
Oh, yes, Lord.

Borrowing familiar imagery from the Old Testament of the Bible, they described their anguish in terms of another oppressed people, the Jews. References to "the promised land" somewhere "over Jordan" could be heard as veiled references to reaching safety in the North, readily understood by fellow slaves but safely obscure to their white owners.

Spirituals as Concert Music   During the Reconstruction era (the period following the Civil War), black spirituals acquired a new dimension in the form of hymn-like choral harmonies. Beginning in 1871, spirituals were introduced to the world in this form by the Jubilee Singers, a small choral group touring to raise funds for their impoverished school, Fisk University in Nashville, Tennessee, one of several schools founded for the education of former slaves.

Soon the black spiritual entered the solo singer's repertoire as a kind of black art song, often performed in moving arrangements written for voice and piano by **Henry (Harry) Thacker Burleigh** (1866–1949). Thus African American spirituals, many originally improvised and performed in the African style of call-and-response, became and remain familiar to and well loved by black people and white people alike.

Singing Conventions

The Great Revival and other strong revival movements gave further impetus to the popularity of the music of the First New England School, which continued to be enjoyed by plain and simple folk in New England, New York, New Jersey, Pennsylvania, Maryland, and the Carolinas—wherever the singing school masters roamed and set up their short-term but highly effective schools. Every summer throughout the nineteenth century, singing conventions attracted shape-note singers in large numbers to come together in churches or campgrounds, where they spent several days singing together, picnicking, and socializing much as in the early days of the singing schools.

But as public schools standardized music instruction, and as improved roads and the automobile brought new travel and entertainment opportunities to young people, musical tastes changed. The eventual purchase of small publishing houses by commercial gospel music companies, more interested in making money than encouraging public singing, contributed to a decline in the number of singing conventions and amateur shape-note singers. Yet singing conventions exist today in rural, urban, and suburban areas across the country, attended in declining numbers but with strong enthusiasm by those who still know and love the traditional songs and the shape-note method of reading them.

Further Movements to Reform Music

Despite the popularity of singing school music and shape-note notation, many educated Americans considered this music inferior to the music of their European contemporaries. Especially, they disparaged the unorthodox music of the First New England School—fuging tunes in particular. The same fervor for reform that gave rise to labor movements and the Temperance Society led many American musicians to scrupulously avoid the irregularities characteristic of the music of the self-taught singing school masters (the very characteristics that render it interesting and attractive to modern ears).

Thus while America's literary figures and visual artists developed indigenous styles of expression, professional American composers turned to Europe for inspiration and instruction, choosing to imitate the German masters who dominated European music at that time. In music collections published in America during the first half of the nineteenth century, European pieces and their American imitations largely replaced indigenous American music; and although faithfully retained by steadfast adherents of the singing school (especially in the South, as noted above), shape notes and other simplified notation systems generally succumbed to the traditional European system of writing music.

Lowell Mason (1792–1872)

A strong proponent of traditional music notation and of music that at least sounded "European," the hymn writer and educator **Lowell Mason** led the movement to reform music in America. The son of a singing school master and schoolteacher, Mason inherited talent both for music and for teaching. Having attended singing school as a child, he continued the study of music as a young man by taking private lessons with a German musician. While making his living by working at a bank, he learned to play several instruments, became a church organist and choirmaster, and began to compose rather conventional but very attractive anthems and hymns.

In 1822, Mason published the first of many editions of the *Boston Handel and Haydn Society Collection of Church Music,* which included some of his own religious songs as well as several that he had arranged from melodies by famous European composers. Amazed at how well the book sold, Mason left his bank job and turned his professional attention to music, a field which previously had not offered Americans significant business opportunities but in which Mason recognized there was money to be made.

Believing that children should not have to depend, as he had depended, on the singing school system for their music education, Mason declared that public schools should provide all American children instruction in reading music and singing. It was, in fact, largely owing to his efforts that the Boston public school curriculum first included music, in 1838, and that other school districts soon followed Boston's example. Mason also pioneered in training for music teachers, made voice lessons readily available to adults and children in the Boston area, conducted performances of choral music, published collections of choral music and hymns, composed religious vocal music, and generally promoted the improvement of musical taste and performance in America.

Toward this worthy end, Mason wrote hymns and other religious music he considered of a better (that is, more European) quality than the works of the Yankee pioneers. However, sensitive to the needs of the relatively unsophisticated public, he revealed a keen business sense, sometimes using (or allowing his publisher to use) shape-note notation, although he clearly preferred that people learn the traditional European system of writing music. Mason also wrote some of his hymns in three-part harmony, more familiar to ordinary people than the modern standard four-part arrangement of soprano, alto, tenor, and bass. He even sometimes placed the melody of a hymn in the middle voice, as the singing school masters had done according to early common practice, instead of in the top voice, as modern listeners were coming to expect (and as we are accustomed to hearing today). Also recognizing the public's fondness for fuging tunes and other early American songs of which he disapproved, Mason wisely included some of them in all the volumes he published, ensuring their commercial success and making himself a wealthy man.

Less daring and less original than the efforts of the Yankee pioneers, Mason's attractive hymns appealed to the sentimental taste of his day, and a number of them remain among the most familiar hymns today. "Nearer, My God, to Thee"(Listening Example 21), "My Faith Looks Up to Thee," "Work, for the Night Is Coming," and "When I Survey the Wondrous Cross" are still widely known and are included in the current hymnals of many denominations.

Listening Example 21

"Nearer, My God, to Thee"

Composer
Lowell Mason

Performers
Mormon Tabernacle Choir

CD 1
Track 21
4:21

Accompaniment
Organ

Form
Strophic

Meter
Quadruple

Melody
Mason's tune, which is called "Bethany," lies comfortably within the range of just over an octave. The high degree of melodic repetition (the four lines of each verse follow the pattern **a a′ b a′**—**a′** indicating a variation of **a,** and **b** a different melodic line), and the recurrence of the same last phrase of text at the end of every verse make the tune easy to sing and to memorize and thus well suited to congregational performance. Notice the contrast with Billings's "Chester" and "When Jesus Wept," in which one syllable of text may run through several notes. Here, Mason almost consistently gives each syllable just one tone.

—Continued

"Nearer, My God, to Thee"

Harmony

Whereas Mason accompanied his melody with simple, academically correct tonal harmonies, based almost entirely on the I, IV, and V chords, this arrangement adds changing harmonies in the choral voices and in the organ accompaniment. Notice, too, the arrangement's varied combinations of voices and alternation between accompanied and a cappella performance.

Text

The words, written by a young American woman, Sarah F. Adams (1805–1848), are based on the Bible story of Jacob, who, while fleeing from his home and his brother Esau, dreamed of seeing angels ascending and descending "steps unto heaven," or to Bethel, "the house of God" (Genesis 28:10–22). Although it makes no reference to Christ, this hymn continues to be found in nearly every published Christian hymnal and is named by many people as their favorite. Set to Mason's tune, it is said to have brought comfort to people aboard the ill-fated *Titanic* as it plunged to its icy grave.

> Nearer, my God, to Thee, nearer to Thee!
> E'en tho it be a cross that raiseth me;
> Still all my song shall be, nearer, my God, to Thee,
> Nearer, my God, to Thee, nearer to Thee!
>
> (Men, a cappella) Tho' like the wanderer, the sun gone down,
> Darkness be over me, my rest a stone,
> Yet in my dreams I'd be nearer, my God, to Thee,
> Nearer, my God, to Thee, nearer to Thee!
>
> (Organ transition, change of key)
>
> There let the way appear, steps into heav'n;
> All that Thou sendest me, in mercy giv'n—
> Angels to beckon me nearer, my God, to Thee,
> Nearer, my God, to Thee, nearer to Thee!
> My God, to Thee!

Terms to Review

shape-note notation   A method of music notation assigning a shape to the pitches *fa, sol, la,* and *mi,* placing them in their normal positions on the staff.

The Sacred Harp   A popular nineteenth-century collection of hymns and spiritual songs.

spiritual   A folklike religious song with a simple tune.

Key Figures

Henry Thacker Burleigh   Lowell Mason

Suggestions for Further Listening

Shape-Note Singing
"American Angels: Songs of Hope, Redemption, and
    Glory" (performed by Anonymous 4)
Spirituals (Slave Hymns or Sorrow Songs)
"Go Down, Moses"
"Deep River"
"Swing Low, Sweet Chariot"

Hymns by Lowell Mason
"My Faith Looks Up to Thee" (tune known as "Olivet")
"Work, for the Night Is Coming" ("Diligence")
"When I Survey the Wondrous Cross" ("Hamburg")
"Watchman, Tell Us of the Night" ("Watchman")

Suggestion for Viewing

Cold Mountain, 2003. Film featuring Sacred Harp singers.

Critical Thinking

If you read music notation, why do you suppose that
many people found shape-note music easier to read than
the traditional method of notating music?

Why do you think the pentatonic pattern playable on the
five black notes of a keyboard has inspired so many
popular melodies, including "Amazing Grace," "Nobody
Knows de Trouble I've Seen," and countless others?

What are some of the reasons American composers might
have turned to Europe for inspiration and instruction at
the same time that American artists, painters, and literary
figures were developing a characteristically American
style of expression?

**Go to www.mhhe.com/ferrisaml5 for a list of additional
Web-based resources that relate to the content in this chapter.**

Popular Music of the Civil War Era

Throughout the nineteenth century, great waves of immigration from various European countries enriched America's popular culture, as Germans, Italians, French, Swedish, and other newcomers poured their secular as well as their religious songs into the American stream. Instrumental music, too, found popularity as dance tunes of various ethnic heritages entertained informal gatherings in every settled region of the country. However, then as now, songs dominated music in the vernacular.

Each geographic area of America also produced and enjoyed new songs and instrumental pieces expressing the typical local experience. On the frontier, for example, people sang songs about freedom, equality, danger, and the beauty of nature in the wild. Songs commemorated the opening of the Erie Canal, the California gold rush, and other events of intense local and national concern. Slaves in the South produced their own characteristic music, expressive of their particular loneliness and suffering. Seamen sang chanteys; and songs of miners, farmers, railroad workers, and even outlaws joined the American repertoire as well. Lullabies served every segment of the population, and play and party songs entertained rural adults as well as children. More and more, music became a part of the day-to-day American experience. (See Figure 6.1.)

Minstrelsy

Most popular of all the songs representative of this fertile period were those sung in **minstrel shows,** a form of entertainment popular in England in the late eighteenth century in which white men, their skin darkened by burnt cork or coal, caricatured African American figures. Minstrel performances soon became a part of American circus and showboat performances and even appeared between the acts of serious plays. Two basic characters emerged: one representing the plantation slave, with ragged clothes, uncouth manner, and thick dialect, named Jim Crow; the other, a fashionable dandy of elegant dress and manners caricaturing a citified Northern black, named Zip Coon. Jim Crow and

FIGURE 6.1

Henry Ossawa Tanner, *Banjo Lesson*

Zip Coon, ridiculous and grotesque, became stock characters in the countless minstrel shows that defied conscience and good taste to remain wildly popular for decades.

A minstrel show began with a rousing grand march, during which the players entered the stage and formed a semicircle, exchanging comic comments (Figure 6.2). The fiddle and the banjo made vital contributions to the entertainment, minstrels radically transforming the four-string plantation banjo to "invent" the five-string banjo that is often called America's only truly indigenous musical instrument (though Native American instruments, including the tom-tom, bone flute, and medicine rattle, among others, are also indigenous). A retired blackface performer (Joel Walker Sweeney, 1810–1860) helped develop the drumlike hoop body and adjustable tensioning brackets familiar today; and about 1880 the placement of strips of material, called **frets,** on the fingerboard allowed players to stop the strings at a specific, rather than an estimated, pitch, making it easier to perform complex and sophisticated music.

FIGURE 6.2

Scene from a minstrel show, with "Mr. Bones" on the left and "Mr. Tambo" on the right.

Minstrel shows also invariably included a **tambourine** (derived from an African percussion instrument) and a pair of **bones** (commonly replaced in more recent times by a pair of linked castanets). Often there was also a small accordion-like instrument called a **concertina,** with a number of buttons on each side that control the pitch. The concertina is played by alternately pushing the sides inward and pulling them out, producing the wind that makes the sound.

Often credited as the first popular hit in America, the minstrel song "Jim Crow" was written by a white man known as the father of American minstrelsy, **Thomas Dartmouth "Daddy" Rice.** ("Jim Crow" later became a hostile term synonymous with discrimination against African Americans.) In 1843, another white man, **Daniel Decatur Emmett** (1815–1904), who had served in the Union army as a fifer at the age of seventeen and later performed in circus minstrel acts, formed the **Virginia Minstrels,** the first completely independent minstrel show. At their debut the Virginia Minstrels, wearing white trousers, striped calico shirts, and blue calico coats with tails, appeared before a wildly enthusiastic audience in New York City. They sang, danced, joked, and told stories in a manner imitative of plantation and Northern blacks as they understood, or misunderstood, them. The **Christy Minstrels,** a four-man troupe formed by E. P. Christy, a famous white minstrel composer and skit writer, toured the American South and West bringing theater (of a sort) to people who had never experienced it in any form before.

Daniel Decatur Emmett wrote one of America's favorite songs, "I Wish I Was in Dixie's Land" (Listening Example 22), conceiving it as a lively plantation song and dance routine called a **walkaround,** performed as the finale of a minstrel show. The troupe stood in a semicircle in front of a plantation background, and when the music started, two or more of the members strutted out and alternately sang a stanza while another "walked around" in the inside of the semicircle. Reaching the center, the singers began to dance, accompanied by a musical interlude, after which the entire troupe joined in the frolic.

Ironically, the song's catchy tune, simple lyrics, and inspiring patriotic chorus ("In Dixie's Land, I'll take my stand, To live and die in Dixie") made it a virtual anthem of the South, though it had been written by a Northerner, was originally sung in "black" dialect by whites, and first became popular in New York City. "Dixie," in fact, was fervently received wherever it was performed in the country, cheered as enthusiastically by Abraham Lincoln in Chicago as by the most zealous Southern patriot. The performance on our CD is more polished than what a minstrel audience would have heard, but we can sense the rousing spirit of the stirring song.

After emancipation, blacks themselves participated in minstrel shows, forming their own companies and writing songs that remain favorites today. The best-known minstrel songs include "Carry Me Back to Ole Virginny," "In the Evening by the Moonlight," "De Golden Wedding," and "Oh, Dem Golden Slippers," all composed by the first well-known black songwriter, **James A. Bland.**

James A. Bland (1854–1911)

The son of a remarkable father, one of the first black men to receive a college education, James Bland attended public school in Washington, D.C. As a teenager, he became a page in the U.S. House of Representatives and enjoyed entertaining himself and Washington notables by singing his own songs to a banjo accompaniment.

After Bland graduated from Howard University with a degree in liberal arts at the age of nineteen, his main ambition was to become a stage performer. Having repeatedly been turned down by minstrel groups that preferred white men playing in blackface, he finally secured a job and for several years toured the country with various minstrel companies. In England with one troupe, he became very popular and even performed for Queen Victoria and the Prince of Wales. Unfortunately, his talent for music was unmatched by good business sense, and though he made a lot of money he died penniless, from tuberculosis, in Philadelphia, Pennsylvania. His grave in a nearby city's cemetery for blacks remained unmarked until 1939, when the American Society of Composers, Authors, and Publishers (ASCAP) found the site, landscaped it, and erected a monument.

In 1940, the Virginia state legislature made "Carry Me Back to Ole Virginny" the official state song.

"I Wish I Was in Dixie's Land"

Composer
Daniel Decatur Emmett

CD 1
Track 22
2:58

The origin of the word "Dixie" is obscure—it probably does not refer to the Mason-Dixon line. Some associate it with a French money note called the *dix* (for "ten").

Accompaniment
Piano. The piano introduces and concludes the song, and plays a brief interlude between the chorus and the second verse.

Meter
Duple

Form
Strophic

Each verse has two sections, each sung by a soloist and followed by a small group responding in unison, "Look away! Look away! Look away! Dixie Land." The chorus ("I wish I was in Dixie . . .") succeeds each verse.

Emmett wrote "Dixie" as a lively plantation song and dance routine called a walkaround, performed as the finale of a minstrel show with the concluding instrumental music accompanying the spritely dance steps.

Text
I wish I was in de land ob cotton,
Old times dar am not forgotten;
Look away! Look away! Look away! Dixie Land.
In Dixie Land whar I was born in.
Early on one frosty mornin';
Look away! Look away! Look away! Dixie Land.

(Chorus)

Den I wish I was in Dixie,
*   Hooray! Hooray!*
In Dixie Land, I'll take my stand,
To live an' die in Dixie,
Away, away.
Away down south in Dixie.

Old Missus marry "Will-de-weaber,"
Willium was a gay deceaber;

But when he put his arm around 'er.
He smiled as fierce as a forty pounder.

(Chorus)

His face was sharp as a butcher's cleaver,
But dat did not seem to grieve 'er;

—Continued

"I Wish I Was in Dixie's Land"

Old Misses acted de foolish part,
And died for a man dat broke her heart.

(Chorus)

Now here's a health to the next old Missus,
An' all de gals dat want to kiss us;

But if you want to drive 'way sorrow,
Come and hear dis song tomorrow.

(Chorus)

The Heritage of Minstrelsy   Although it is offensive by today's standards, minstrelsy constituted a highly popular form of entertainment in the pre– and even post–Civil War periods, offering a refreshing contrast to the sentimental parlor ballads of the age; and much of the music produced by this unlikely medium remains as enchanting as ever. Although derived from African and European customs, minstrel songs and dances were as indigenous to the American experience as were the folk hymns of New England and the South. The best of the minstrel music, often referred to as America's first popular music, had an unselfconscious and highly infectious charm, exemplified by the minstrel fiddle tune "Turkey in the Straw"—possibly derived from an old Irish ballad but known in 1834 as "Old Zip Coon."

Stephen Foster (1826–1864)

By far the outstanding American composer of popular songs of the pre–Civil War period was the gifted, self-taught musician **Stephen Foster.** Born into the genteel society of Pittsburgh, Pennsylvania, the young Foster heard his sisters sing and play the piano and other instruments and soon was picking out tunes himself. (The philosopher George Santayana (1863–1952) coined the term "genteel tradition" to describe that pretentiously noble, decidedly prudish, segment of polite society determined to ignore the unattractive aspects of life—such as the flophouse and the slum—and preserve "culture" as they understood it.) Because music was not considered a respectable profession for a man in his social position, Foster dutifully went to work as a bookkeeper while still in his teens; but he could not resist jotting down some of the tuneful melodies that filled his mind and—to his own amazement—had his first song ("Open Thy Lattice, Love") published when he was just eighteen. Soon he was writing and publishing professionally.

Foster's early sentimental love songs suited the self-conscious gentility of his family and their friends, reflecting and reinforcing the mid-nineteenth-century concept of the female identity: domestic, refined, and well-cared-for by father or spouse. The women in Foster's songs, normally described from a male point of view, are passive creatures, entirely idealized, and often asleep ("Beautiful Dreamer"), or perhaps dead, as suggested in "I Dream of Jeanie with the Light Brown Hair" (Listening Example 23).

Foster's own personal favorite songs were of two types: the lovely "plantation melodies," reminiscent of the songs he heard African Americans singing as they worked on the Pittsburgh riverfronts, and—especially—the rollicking, comic songs he wrote for minstrel shows. Foster, in fact, experienced a devastating conflict between the music he felt he *ought* to write and the music he wrote and loved best. His sentimental songs about home ("Old Folks at Home," for example, and "My Old Kentucky Home"—a nostalgic "remembrance" of the plantation life he never lived inspired by Harriet Beecher Stowe's novel *Uncle Tom's Cabin*)—his songs about unfulfilled romantic love (such as "Beautiful Dreamer," "Come Where My Love Lies Dreaming," and "Jeanie"), and his settings of poems about the Civil War were well-enough received. His minstrel songs, however, reflect the ambivalence he experienced as a member of a family with strong personal and professional ties to the political party in favor of states' rights and (at least tacit) support of slavery, and a man whose friends and in-laws supported abolition. Desiring acceptance by polite society, and unwilling to offend his family, to whom he was devoted, Foster resisted his apparent inclination to express his own abolitionist sympathies. (Foster's Civil War songs, in support of Lincoln and restoration of the Union, were published only after his parents' death.)

Yet even his early minstrel songs, while undeniably demeaning to African Americans, avoided the outrageous caricatures commonly presented onstage. One of his songs, "Uncle Ned," dealt sympathetically with the tragic figure of an elderly and terribly abused slave; another, "Nelly Was a Lady," is told in the words of a grieving slave who has been sold away from his wife, has learned that she has died, and is about to die himself from overwork and grief. The very term "lady" applied to a slave was revolutionary for the minstrel stage.

The exuberant "Oh! Susanna" (Listening Example 24) became a national hit following its performance by the Christy Minstrels in 1848, but Foster lost money on the song. Hardly the witless businessman he is often portrayed as (he kept his own account books, calculated anticipated earnings from songs, and wrote out contracts with his publishers—the earliest contracts we know of between American music publishers and an individual songwriter), Foster nevertheless made little money from his music. But this is not surprising, since he was apparently the first American to attempt to earn his living solely from the sale of his songs, and there was no organization at the time to support his efforts to collect fees owed him. If not money, his songs brought Foster lasting fame and adulation. "Oh! Susanna" soon traveled across the country, carried to the Western frontier by thousands of adventurers and homesteaders who loved her as their own.

Foster indeed was a man of paradox: His irresistible minstrel and plantation melodies set America and soon much of the world humming his tunes and

"I Dream of Jeanie with the Light Brown Hair"

Composer
Stephen Foster

CD 1
Track 23
3:17

Form
Strophic

Meter
Quadruple

Tempo
Slow

Accompaniment

A guitar accompanies the singer with simple—mostly I, IV, and V—chords, typical of the guitar or piano accompaniment Foster normally provided for his songs. The guitar also plays a brief introduction, interlude between verses, and conclusion, never competing, however, with the voice for primary attention.

Foster seems to have captured in this haunting, mostly pentatonic melody the mystic quality of Jeanie's spirit itself, "borne like a vapor on the summer air." The extreme relaxation of the tempo, called *rubato* ("robbing"—see p. 56), occurring at the end of significant phrases, enhances the romantic character of the piece, which expresses—in the romantic way—a longing destined never to be fulfilled.

Text (by Stephen Foster)

I dream of Jeanie with the light brown hair
Borne like a vapor on the summer air.
I see her tripping where the bright streams play
Happy as the daisies that dance on her way.
Many were the wild notes her merry voice would pour,
Many were the blithe birds that warbled them o'er. Oh!
I dream of Jeanie with the light brown hair
Floating like a vapor on the soft summer air.

(Second verse)
I long for Jeanie with the daydawn smile,
Radiant in gladness, warm with winning guile;
I hear her melodies, like joys gone by,
Sighing round my heart o'er the fond hopes that die:
Sighing like the night wind and sobbing like the rain,
Wailing for the lost one that comes not again;
Oh! I long for Jeanie, and my heart bows low,
Never more to find her where the bright waters flow.

"Oh! Susanna"

Composer
Stephen Foster

Form
Strophic

Meter
Duple

CD 1
Track 24
1:15

Accompaniment
Banjo

This tune indicates the internal repetition typical of Foster's songs, lending them immediate accessibility and familiarity. The music of lines 1 and 3 (**a**) is the same, and lines 2 and 4 of the verse and the second line of the chorus (**a'**) only slightly vary the ending of the identical melodic phrase. Only the first line of the chorus (**b**) introduces new material. Thus the song's melodic structure could be outlined as **a a' a a' b a'.**

Further, the phrases **a** and **a'** are pentatonic, limited to the pattern of tones represented by the five black notes on a keyboard. Only the first two tones of the **b** phrase (on "Oh! Su-") break the simple pentatonic pattern.

Neither is the rhythm complex or varied; it offers only one bit of syncopation, again in the first phrase of the chorus ("Oh! Su-san-**na**!"). Yet the song has the snap and dash of many a banjo or fiddle tune, compelling us to nod or rap along with its beat. The catchy, irresistible tune, pleasing to the ears in many times and cultures, is so strong that repetition satisfies rather than tires the listener, and "Oh! Susanna" seems destined to live forever.

Text

> I come from Alabama with my banjo on my knee.
> I'm goin' to Louisiana my true love for to see.
> It rained all night the day I left, the weather it was dry.
> The sun so hot I froze to death; Susanna don't you cry.
> Chorus: Oh, Susanna, don't you cry for me.
> I come from Alabama with my banjo on my knee.
>
> I had a dream the other night when everything was still.
> I dreamed I saw Susanna a-comin' down the hill.
> A red, red rose was in her cheek, a tear was in her eye,
> I said to her, "Susanna gal, Susanna don't you cry."
>
> (Chorus)

singing his words about a life he never experienced, for Foster was neither black nor from the South. Analysis of his best songs reveals little that is innovative or even particularly interesting in their form, rhythm, or harmony. The songs are in simple strophic form, with much repetition of the melodic phrases within each verse; there is little rhythmic variety, except for occasional syncopation, as in the **b** phrase of "Oh! Susanna!"; and most of the songs were written with simple guitar or piano accompaniments based on the three primary chords of the tonal system.

Foster wrote his songs when the sentimental parlor ballad was in vogue, and some of them may be described as such. But it is difficult to place many of Foster's songs within a particular category or genre. They are hardly art songs, because the texts are not of the quality associated with that form, but they *are* art in the sense that they are long-lived and representative of their composer's distinctive style. Foster's melodies, although folklike, are clearly composed. The songs are popular in the sense that they are enjoyed all over the world, but except for the rollicking minstrel songs, they have not been part of our usual concept of popular music.

It seems a bitter irony that a man so gifted should have been destroyed by his own inability to distinguish between genius and gentility. Unwilling even to acknowledge some of his best songs, he gave them away or allowed them to be pirated. Fearful that even the sentimental "Old Folks at Home" might offend the public sensibilities, for example, Foster asked E. P. Christy to claim its authorship, though he accepted the small royalty for each song sold. Later, as the song and indeed many minstrel songs as well gained in popularity, Foster wished to be recognized as the composer of "Old Folks at Home" and was most disappointed when Christy refused to alter their previous arrangement. It was not until the song's copyright expired in 1879 that Foster's name finally appeared as its author and composer.

Foster married in 1850, but his increasing emotional instability and heavy drinking caused his wife to leave him three years later. Stephen Foister died a pauper, alone and unrecognized, at the age of thirty-eight.

Patriotic Songs

Some of America's most enduring patriotic songs appeared between the Revolution and the Civil War and were associated with events occurring during that tumultuous time. Frequently included in theatrical entertainments then, they became and in some cases have remained widely popular.

The words to "Hail, Columbia," by Francis Hopkinson's son Joseph, were sung to the tune known as "President's March," composed by Philip Phile for the inauguration of George Washington in 1789 and commonly played when that president appeared in public. This stirring patriotic song, like many others, sometimes served political aims. For example, the 1798 war between France and England divided American allegiance, some people rallying to the side of the newly democratic French republic, whereas others felt tied to England by affection and tradition. However, the rousing words to the brand-new "Hail, Columbia," frequently performed at theatrical entertainments in that year, united emotional audiences by exalting the wonders and accomplishments of America and arousing national pride.

"Hail to the Chief," traditionally played by the United States Marine Band to announce the ceremonial entrance of the president of the United States, is generally attributed to an Englishman, James Sanderson, who possibly based his tune on an old Scottish melody. Many sets of words were added over the years, but the tune soon evolved from a popular song of the day to the march with official status that we recognize today. First performed in this country in 1812, it was sung (with a different title and text) in 1815 in honor of George Washington's birthday; in 1828 the U.S. Marine Band played it to honor President John Quincy Adams when he attended the opening of the Chesapeake and Ohio Canal.

A young lawyer, **Francis Scott Key** (1780–1843), wrote the words to "The Star Spangled Banner" under most dramatic circumstances. During the War of 1812, Key boarded a British vessel moored in Chesapeake Bay in order to plead for the release of an important American prisoner. The British agreed to release the prisoner before sailing for England, but they held both him and Key on board through the night while they attacked the city of Baltimore. In two stirring verses, the emotional young lawyer described the agony of suspense he experienced while witnessing the attack and his overwhelming pride and relief at the sight of the American flag waving high the next morning. Key set his romantic text, which he titled "The Defense of Fort McHenry," to the melody of a popular English drinking song, "To Anacreon in Heaven." (This was the theme song of an English men's club, the Anacreontic [uh-nak-ree-ON-tik] Society, dedicated to celebrating wine, music, and song.) Obviously fond of the catchy melody, Key had already used it as the setting for other poems he had written and found it suitable to express his pride, relief, and enthusiasm after the harrowing night of the attack on Baltimore. In 1813, Thomas Carr (brother of Benjamin Carr, p. 71) musically arranged the tune and rechristened it "The Star Spangled Banner."

Little did either Key or Carr suppose that many years later, during the Spanish-American War (1898), the stirring song would be designated the official anthem of the American armed forces. Still less could they imagine that, in 1931, President Herbert Hoover would sign a bill making Key's song the American national anthem. Some have suggested that the melody's wide range and large intervals ("Oh say, can you sing it?") render it more difficult to sing than is appropriate for a national anthem; but defenders stoutly respond that the dramatic nature of the melody and the effort required to sing it properly make it all the more distinctive and ideally suited for this exalted position.

"America the Beautiful"—less bellicose than "The Star Spangled Banner"; unassociated with a particular, long-ago battle; and more appreciative of the land's natural beauty—is sometimes recommended as an alternative American national anthem. A young English literature professor named Katherine Lee

Bates wrote the words to "America the Beautiful ("O beautiful for spacious skies") in 1893, after climbing to the summit of Colorado's 14,000-foot-high Pikes Peak and being awed by the view. She later revised the words, responding to suggestions from readers of her poem, which became ever more popular with the advent of radio and the patriotic fervor raised by World War I. When, in 1926, the National Federation of Music Clubs held a contest to select a musical setting for the poem, more than 900 people submitted compositions. Bates never selected a winner, but today we sing her words to "Materna," written in 1888 by a church organist and music store owner, Samuel A. Ward. (The famous song can be heard at various Web sites.) Neither Bates nor Ward ever claimed or received any royalties for this magnificent song.

Civil War Songs

In 1860, several southern states seceded from the Union, plunging the country into the Civil War. At such times of grief and turmoil, people turn to art and to music—at popular or at more serious levels—to express their anguish and ease their sorrow. Thus it is not surprising that many memorable songs concerned these particularly tragic years.

Indeed, Civil War songs appeared in a rich variety of folklike, religious, comic, and serious styles. "Dixie," as we have seen, began as a minstrel show walkaround. Some songs, lyrical and dramatic in style, suggested their composers' fondness for Italian opera. The haunting bugle call "Taps," commissioned as an elegy for Civil War casualties, evokes the same emotions today as when it was first sounded. Regional favorites, such as "Maryland, My Maryland" (which vied with "Dixie" and "The Bonnie Blue Flag" to become a Confederate national anthem), "Marching through Georgia" (a celebration of General William Tecumseh Sherman's march to the sea), and "The Yellow Rose of Texas" (originally a minstrel tune praising an African American girl as "the yellow rose of Texas" who "beats the belles of Tennessee"), stimulated patriotic fervor and became popular during the troubled period. (The Bonnie Blue Flag, the unofficial first flag of the South, flew from 1860 to 1861.)

What is surprising is how many songs inspired by the Civil War have survived more than a century to please, entertain, and move listeners of other eras who are used to other styles. Some tunes acquired new texts in the twentieth century: Thus Elvis Presley sang "Love Me Tender" to the tune of "Aura Lee," and Bob Dylan set "Blowin' in the Wind" to the tune of a slave song, "No More Auction Block for Me." Other songs survive much as they were introduced at the time of America's greatest national trauma. ("Love Me Tender," sung by Marty Robbins, is Listening Example 1.)

The stirring "Battle Hymn of the Republic" with its rousing chorus beginning "Glory, glory, hallelujah!" is set to a tune once sung as a tribute to the militant abolitionist John Brown ("John Brown's body lies a-mouldering in his grave"). Dozens of irreverent verses had been set to this simple Methodist camp meeting tune that, according to one writer, "stuck to the ears like burrs to the skirt of a blackberry girl." But upon viewing firsthand the desperate plight of

FIGURE 6.3
Julia Ward Howe.

blue-clad Union soldiers, many wounded or ill and all of them lonely and heartsick, the published poet and author Julia Ward Howe (Figure 6.3) composed her poignant poem "Battle Hymn of the Republic" to be set to the old tune; and her fervent words sung to the strong melody lifted the morale and stirred the spirits of Union troops and prisoners.

After the Civil War, the "Battle Hymn" became one of several patriotic songs (including "The Star Spangled Banner") to serve as an anthem of the re-united nation, its fervent refrain seeming to embody the very soul of American patriotism. Many people experienced profound disappointment when it, together with "America the Beautiful," lost the position of national anthem to Francis Scott Key's patriotic creation. ("Battle Hymn of the Republic" can be heard at several Web sites.)

In 1887, Julia Ward Howe wrote, "The wild echoes of the fearful struggle have long since died away, and with them all memories of unkindness between ourselves and our southern brethren. But those who once loved my hymn still sing it." And we still do.

Singing Families

Before and after the Civil War, several singing families toured the United States performing songs of many kinds. Like the twentieth-century European Trapp family portrayed in the Broadway musical and movie *The Sound of Music,* these traveling groups performed in churches, meetinghouses, and concert halls.

The most popular American singing family, the **Hutchinsons,** first came to public attention when the thirteen Hutchinson children presented a highly successful performance of religious and secular music at a New England meetinghouse in the early 1840s. Later, three Hutchinson sons formed a trio; and when, still later, their sister Abby joined them, the popular quartet toured through New England for several years. When Abby married and retired from the group, other members of the family formed various ensembles, and the Singing Hutchinsons remained famous in America and Europe for decades.

Although their music was refined, genteel, and sentimental, the texts of the Hutchinsons' songs, some of which they wrote or adapted themselves, addressed some of the most radical social causes of their day, such as temperance, women's suffrage, and the abolition of slavery. Their performances included secular, humorous songs in strophic form called **glees,** with the melody in the top voice and the other two or three voices providing chordal harmony. Glees, introduced in Europe during the eighteenth century, were originally sung by men only, but by the mid-nineteenth century many glee clubs formed in American cities included women as well as men. These popular ensembles sometimes sang more serious choral literature as well as glees and other light-hearted fare. Today's high school and college glee clubs generally are small mixed choral groups.

Concert Bands

During the Civil War, **concert bands** (Figure 6.4) played a variety of entertaining novelty pieces. The early nineteenth-century addition of valves having facilitated the playing of intricate melodies on trumpets, horns, and cornets (all previously relegated largely to adding color and harmony to band music), these instruments now assumed a prominent melodic role in marching and concert bands. During the 1850s, in fact, many bands consisted of brass instruments only, leading to criticism by some that military and concert bands of the time offered nothing but "sounding brass and tinkling cymbals," and to an expressed preference for the return of reed instruments to the band ensemble.

Bands provided an important stimulus for music publishing in America, although much of the music printed for American bands throughout the nineteenth century was written by European composers. Besides marches and dance tunes, programmatic pieces, describing in musical terms a sequence of scenes or events, were particularly popular at band concerts. "Battle" pieces featuring the sounds of gunshots, cries of the wounded, trumpet calls, and other instrumental warlike effects were especially well received.

After the Civil War, two outstanding directors—Patrick S. Gilmore and John Philip Sousa—developed the concert band into a balanced ensemble of woodwind, brass, and percussion instruments. Bands brought famous orchestral and opera music, as well as popular songs and dances, to audiences unable to attend the orchestral halls, opera houses, and popular venues of big cities, and band music became so popular that Americans gradually came to prefer its instrumental timbres to the vocal renditions they had previously favored. This

FIGURE 6.4
A concert band, circa 1875.

change in musical taste provided a firm foundation for jazz and the swing age to build on.

Patrick Sarsfield Gilmore (1829–1892) **Patrick S. Gilmore,**
one of thousands who fled Ireland's potato blights and famine to make a new life in America, considered himself American by choice. (When asked if he had been born in Ireland, he joked, "No, I was born in Boston at the age of eighteen.") He began his career as a member of a popular Boston minstrel group, in which he played the tambourine, sang in a quartet, and played cornet solos, while also acting as the group's agent. His business sense served him well as his musical career began to rise: He originated a successful series of summer concerts at the Boston Music Hall, and soon established his own professional ensemble—a new and daring business venture—known as Gilmore's Band. A virtuoso cornet player, he was appointed bandmaster of the Union army and became the most famous bandmaster of the 1860s.

When military bands broke up after the war, Gilmore formed America's first band conceived entirely as a concert ensemble. A master entertainer who organized mammoth concerts in which thousands of performers participated, he also brought outstanding European bands to perform in America. (One concert he sponsored, in New Orleans in 1864, included a band of 500 members; a chorus of over 6,000; a battery of 50 canons; 40 soldiers striking anvils; and the simultaneous ringing of all the church bells in the city.) He attracted the most prestigious performers of the day, such as the famous violinist Ole Bull, who served as concertmaster at Gilmore's colossal National Peace Jubilee of 1869.

Finally, Gilmore achieved in his Grand Boston Band the effective balance between brass and woodwind instruments we expect to hear today.

A music publisher and instrument manufacturer, the bandleader Gilmore also composed several topical songs and marches. He usually is credited with having written the popular Civil War song "When Johnny Comes Marching Home Again" (which can be heard at several Web sites), though he claimed only to have set timely lyrics to an Irish folk tune that he "happened to hear someone humming" and "taking a fancy to it, wrote it down, dressed it up, gave it a name, and rhymed it into usefulness for a special purpose suited to the times."

John Philip Sousa (1854–1932)

The year Gilmore died, a young American violinist named **John Philip Sousa** (Figure 6.5) formed a band destined to surpass in size of ensemble, variety of repertoire, and quality of performance any previous concert band, including Gilmore's. Sousa's career as a Marine began when his father learned that his

FIGURE 6.5

John Philip Sousa on a sheet music cover.

thirteen-year-old son was planning to run away from home and join a circus band. The elder Sousa promptly enlisted John Philip in the Marine Corps, where, as an apprentice in the Marine Band, he soon learned to play all the band instruments. Since the Marine Band was founded through an act of Congress signed by President John Adams in 1798, its primary mission has been to provide music for the president of the United States and the commandant of the Marine Corps. In 1801, the prestigious ensemble played for the inauguration of President Thomas Jefferson, and it has performed for every presidential inauguration since that time.

Sousa left the band at age twenty to pursue a career as violinist and conductor of theater orchestras; but five years later he became the director of the Marine Band, and in that capacity he faithfully served five presidents (Hayes, Garfield, Arthur, Cleveland, and Harrison). He brought the band to a peak of perfection, regularly astonishing audiences with incredibly soft dynamic levels and other expressive effects previously thought possible only for the symphony orchestra. Later, Sousa formed his own Sousa Band, which traveled widely and earned a worldwide reputation.

Although Sousa wrote songs, programmatic orchestral music, and especially comic operas and operettas that were widely known and popular in his time, he is best remembered today as the "march king." His marches conform in most respects to many marches by European composers, but their wealth of melodic invention and their stirring spirit render them distinctively American and irresistibly attractive. Sousa is honored not only as a great musician and composer but also as a fervent patriot. Further, as an early member and supporter of the American Society of Composers, Authors, and Publishers (ASCAP; see p. 156), Sousa made important contributions to the growth of the music business in America. He was enshrined in the Hall of Fame for Great Americans in the John F. Kennedy Center for the Performing Arts in 1976 and inducted into the Washington, DC, area Music Hall of Fame in 2002.

Marches
Although differing widely in mood and tempo, marches—be they military, funeral, patriotic, or concert pieces—normally share duple meter, with a strongly marked beat to correspond with the marching pattern LEFT-right-LEFT-right. Meter, which refers to the number of beats in a measure, may be *simple* or *compound* according to the manner in which each beat is divided.

Simple meter means that each of the beats in a measure is divided by *two*. For pieces in *simple duple meter* (for example, "Yankee Doodle" or Sousa's "The Stars and Stripes Forever"), we count the two beats in each measure as *ONE*-and-*two*-and, and so forth.

In *compound meter,* each beat is divided by *three*. For pieces in *compound duple meter* (such as "My Bonnie Lies Over the Ocean," "When Johnny Comes Marching Home," or Sousa's "Washington Post March"), we also count two beats per measure but divide them as *ONE*-and-a-*two*-and-a, or *ONE*-two-three-*four*-five-six.

A march, which may begin with a short (four- or eight-measure) introduction, consists of a series of melodic sections called **strains,** each usually sixteen or thirty-two measures long, and each repeated at least once. One of the strains, scored for fewer instruments and therefore softer in dynamic level, and also typically sweeter or more lyrical than the others, is called the **trio.** Some marches include a section called the **break**—dramatic, highly rhythmic, and often percussive in style and timbre, thus providing effective contrast to the melodic strains.

"The Stars and Stripes Forever" (Listening Example 25), designated in 1987 as the national march of the United States, conforms to this general

---

Listening Example 25

"The Stars and Stripes Forever"

Composer
John Philip Sousa

CD 1
Track 25
3:21

Meter
Duple

Key
E-flat major

Outline of the Form   A A B B C D C D C
  A = *first strain*
  B = *second strain*
  C = *trio (third strain)*
  D = *break*

After the four-measure *introduction* (counting the four measures of the short introduction will help you define the length of each strain), the *first strain* (16 measures) begins with several repeated notes. The first strain is repeated.

The *second strain* (16 measures), which has a wide range of pitches and several large leaps between tones, is played and repeated.

The *third strain*, softer and more melodic than the others and twice as long (32 measures), is the *trio*. You may sense that it is in a different key (the subdominant, A-flat major), or perhaps you will simply be aware that its character is distinct from that of the first two strains.

There is a bold, dramatic *break*.

The *trio* returns with a perky *countermelody*, a simultaneous independent melody played by the piccolo, providing intense polyphonic or *contrapuntal* interest.

There is another *break*.

The march ends with the *trio*, still in the subdominant key, accompanied by a new countermelody in the trombones.

description of a march. Sousa also wrote a text, seldom heard today, for this famous piece:

> *Hurrah for the flag of the free!*
> *May it wave as our standard forever,*
> *The gem of the land and the sea,*
> *The banner of the right.*
> *Let despots remember the day*
> *When our fathers with mighty endeavor*
> *Proclaimed as they marched to the fray*
> *That by their might and by their right it waves forever.*

Terms to Review

minstrel show   An entertainment, popular in the nineteenth century, in which white men performed music and comedy in imitation of stereotypical African Americans.

fret   A strip of material attached to the fingerboard of a string instrument, allowing players to stop the strings at specific pitches.

tambourine   A small drum with metal disks that jingle when the instrument is struck or shaken.

bones   A folk percussion instrument consisting of a pair of castanets tied together and held in one hand.

concertina   A kind of accordion or portable reed instrument. Melody and chords are achieved by depressing buttons or keys, and the wind is supplied by a folding bellows.

walkaround   A lively plantation song-and-dance routine often forming the finale of a minstrel show.

glee   A part-song with three or more lines of music, in chordal, or homophonic, texture, usually with the melody in the top voice.

concert band   An instrumental ensemble including brass, woodwind, and percussion instruments.

strain   A melodic section in a rag, march, or other vernacular form of music.

trio   A strain that is lighter in texture, softer in dynamic level, and more melodic than the other strains in the piece.

break   A dramatic, unstable, strongly rhythmic section, as in a march.

Key Figures

Thomas Dartmouth "Daddy" Rice
Daniel Decatur Emmett
Virginia Minstrels
Christy Minstrels

James A. Bland
Stephen Foster
Francis Scott Key
The Hutchinson Family

Patrick S. Gilmore
John Philip Sousa

Suggestions for Further Listening

March
John Philip Sousa, "Washington Post March"

Civil War Music
Performances by the Americus Brass Band

Suggestion for Viewing

Bamboozled (Spike Lee film concerning minstrelsy, 2000)

Critical Thinking

Discuss some of the reasons minstrelsy became so popular just at the time of rising tensions between North and South and between whites and blacks. Which does it reflect more: white people's contempt for, or their fascination with, black culture?

What might be some of the reasons that blacks performed—in blackface—on the minstrel stage after the Civil War?

Do you recognize any echoes of the minstrel tradition in contemporary American culture? In his book *Raising Cain: Blackface Performance from Jim Crow to Hip Hop*, W. T. Lhamon Jr. suggests (in a picture on the book jacket) a relationship between a minstrel performer dancing in the 1840s and M. C. Hammer performing in the 1990 hip-hop video "Hammer Time." Can you support or refute Lhamon's suggestion?

Would you choose "The Star Spangled Banner" or another patriotic song as America's national anthem? If another, which one, and why?

A young divinity student named Samuel Francis Smith set the words to one candidate for the American national anthem, "America," to a German tune, "Heil Dir im Siegerkranz," also used as the Prussian national song and the British royal anthem as well. (There had been Dutch, Danish, French, Swiss, and Austrian versions, too.) Oliver Wendell Holmes (a close friend of the poet) suggested that had the poet written "Our country" instead of "My country, 'tis of thee" the hymn would not have been "immortal." Do you agree or disagree that the choice of "My" instead of "Our" was a "master stroke"?

Go to www.mhhe.com/ferrisaml5 for a list of additional Web-based resources that relate to the content in this chapter.

Early Concert Music

Although still far less distinct than the highly subjective lines drawn today between vernacular music ("for the people") and art or concert music (for an audience viewed as somewhat select), differences between the popular and the classical worlds of music assumed more significance in the American experience as the nineteenth century progressed. While household music and religious songs retained their vital position in American life, the decades before and after the Civil War witnessed growing interest among composers, performers, and listeners in music for the concert hall.

Rise of Nationalism in Music

As discussed on pp. 78–85, Romanticism ruled the arts in nineteenth-century Western Europe and America. More specifically, German writers, artists, and especially musicians dominated their fields during this period. German composers produced long pieces with expansive melodies accompanied by full, rich harmonies. Extreme contrasts of dynamic level also characterize their music, which is often based on programmatic ideas suggesting the most intense emotional expression.

In fact, the German sound increasingly dominated music in America, where audiences preferred to hear music by the earlier German or Austrian composers George F. Handel, Joseph Haydn, Wolfgang Amadeus Mozart, and Ludwig van Beethoven, and the more modern Robert Schumann, Felix Mendelssohn, and Richard Wagner than music by composers of any other nationality, including their own. Americans also chose to study music with German teachers when possible. The great mid-century wave of German immigration to America brought this opportunity to amateur and professional musicians alike, and music students who could afford it traveled to Germany to further their music education.

The second half of the nineteenth century witnessed strong European nationalistic efforts, as certain nations not bordering directly on Germany began to assert their artistic independence and establish characteristic styles of their own.

Artists in Russia, Bohemia, Norway, and Finland soon established strong national styles, as writers, painters, and musicians drew inspiration from and based their works on the colorful folk tales, legends, and religious music of their own local experience. Suddenly the peasant became more interesting than the noble. By the later part of the century, after the ruling aristocracies of several nations had been overthrown and popular states established, **nationalism** became a significant political and cultural movement throughout western Europe.

At about the same time that American paintings began to reflect America's own natural splendors, a few intrepid composers also set out to capture the American spirit in music and promote performances of American music. These early seeds of nationalism fell on dry ground, however, largely ignored by audiences on both sides of the Atlantic. Europeans admired Americans' mechanical and industrial capabilities but considered them novices in matters of art, and many Americans concurred with that assessment. Most Americans remained hesitant to defy the established wisdom that Germans knew best how to write music. Yet a talented and highly eccentric Bohemian-American composer boldly set out to establish a genuine "American" concert repertoire.

Anthony Philip Heinrich (1781–1861)
Forced by financial reverses to leave his home and family in 1810, **Anthony Philip Heinrich** arrived in the United States, where he soon became music director of a popular theater in Philadelphia. Unable to make a good living there, however, he moved to Kentucky in 1817 and settled among the Indians of that area.

In Kentucky, Heinrich lived alone for a time in a log cabin, practicing the violin and composing programmatic pieces based on his own ideas and experiences. He also conducted what was apparently the first performance of a Beethoven symphony in this country. Profoundly struck by the beauty of the American wilderness and charmed with the music of his Native American friends, Heinrich wrote several works that expressed his appreciation and praise for America. These extravagantly titled orchestral pieces included *The War of the Elements and the Thundering of Niagara; The Columbiad, or Migration of American Wild Passenger Pigeons;* and *Pushmataha: A Venerable Chief of a Western Tribe of Indians.* Well known and admired in this country and abroad, Heinrich was acquainted with many of the outstanding figures of his age, and their influence was reflected in some of his compositions. For example, the long title of one of his pieces—*The Ornithological Combat of Kings: or, The Condor of the Andes*—reveals an interest he shared with his bird-loving friend John James Audubon.

Although Heinrich's music often quoted more or less legitimate Native American themes, he harmonized them according to Western tradition, idealizing and romanticizing the Indian experience much as James Fenimore Cooper's novels and George Catlin's paintings presented Indian life in an attractive but unrealistic light. Nevertheless, although not a great composer, Heinrich (called the "Beethoven from Kentucky") furthered the American music experience by expressing American ideas, quoting Native American themes, and enthusiastically promoting the performance of music by himself and other American composers (as he resolutely considered himself to be). His music is rarely performed today, but "Father Heinrich" is remembered and revered for his important contributions to our musical heritage.

Romantic Virtuosos

Nineteenth-century Europeans, who enjoyed expressive extremes, responded with equal enthusiasm to the sounds of a large symphony orchestra and an intimate solo recital. Americans, however, with more access to the latter than the former, attended concerts in much the same frame of mind with which they viewed a circus or minstrel show and particularly enjoyed dazzling displays of technique by solo **virtuosos.** Certainly virtuosity is among the qualities of *musicianship*—the broad combination of talents possessed by the consummate performer—which also includes sensitivity to the *style* of the music, differing from one period and one culture to another; *originality* of interpretation; and of course *accuracy*. But the spectacular performance of difficult passages of music, thrilling to see and hear, held sway in the minds and hearts of the mid-nineteenth-century American audience, where romantic glorification of the individual made virtuoso performers objects of intense hero worship.

Also, Americans then (as often now) preferred to hear familiar pieces rather than anything new or unusual. Thus a serious gap developed and slowly widened between composers, who of course sought to create something original, and listeners, who preferred something comfortably familiar. This gap affected musicians on both sides of the Atlantic, but the conspicuous lack of interest in American music on either continent further frustrated American composers.

The great nineteenth-century virtuosos, on the other hand, benefited from the American passion for their brilliant performances at the very time that Europeans had begun to tire of them. Performers flocked gratefully to America, where an adoring public eagerly applauded their showy performance techniques. Among the best-known and best-remembered of the outstanding concert artists who toured America are a Swedish singer, a Norwegian violinist, and a pianist from Louisiana.

The Swedish Nightingale
P. T. Barnum arranged a United States tour for Jenny Lind (1820–1887) (Figure 7.1) much as he promoted his famous circus acts. (He hawked her as an actual angel descended from heaven.) Although prodigiously talented, Lind wisely confined her programs in this country to the kind of repertoire she—or Barnum—knew would entertain an American audience: familiar well-loved arias (songs—see Glossary) from European operas and oratorios, with the sentimental "Home Sweet Home" (probably the most popular song of the nineteenth century, composed by the Englishman Sir Henry Bishop to a text by the American poet John Howard Payne) and songs by Stephen Foster as encores.

Jenny Lind stayed in America for about two years, traveling by steamer from New Orleans to Memphis, Nashville, and Saint Louis and visiting many

FIGURE 7.1

Jenny Lind.

other cities as well. The most successful virtuoso singer of her period, she thrilled Americans with her lovely voice, amazing vocal technique, and charming personality. "Jenny Lind fever" spread quickly, and as many people who previously had never heard or been interested in concert music became adoring admirers of "the Swedish nightingale," concert halls were built specifically to accommodate her performances, thus preparing the way for other European performers to follow.

Ole Bull   The Norwegian composer Ole Bull (1810–1880), best remembered as the outstanding violinist of his day, made five long visits to the United States, on one of them marrying an American woman. A dedicated nationalist who believed art should represent the culture that produced it, Ole Bull encouraged Americans to develop a characteristic music of their own. To this end, while managing a fledgling opera company in New York City, he offered $1,000—an impressive amount at the time—to any American composer who would write an opera on an American subject; no one, however, accepted the challenge, and the company soon collapsed.

Like Jenny Lind, Ole Bull accepted the limitations of his inexperienced American audiences and performed little serious music, entertaining them instead with his virtuosic tricks—playing on all four strings of the violin at once or producing incredibly soft *pianissimos* that romantic ears must have perceived as coming from another world. In one of his own compositions, Bull portrayed the American Revolution by alternating phrases of "Yankee Doodle" with "God Save the King," to the delight of his admiring audience. Original, flamboyant, hugely talented, and entertaining, Ole Bull added a valued dimension to nineteenth-century America's music experience. In fact, though we cannot hear Jenny Lind's or Ole Bull's performances today, reports of their professional experiences reveal much about music in America in their time.

Louis Moreau Gottschalk (1829–1869)

Among the outstanding pianists of the period was a young American who amazed and entertained audiences on both sides of the Atlantic with his virtuosic performances of his own compositions. **Louis Moreau Gottschalk** (Loo'-ee Mo-roh' Got'-shok; Figure 7.2), whose English Jewish father had been educated in Germany and whose mother was descended from a wellborn French family that had emigrated from the West Indies a generation before, was born into the brilliant cultural milieu of New Orleans. (Gottschalk's mother was called a Creole, meaning someone born in this country of a foreign family. Later the word *Creole* referred to people of mixed racial heritage, causing some to believe erroneously that Gottschalk had African American ancestors.) Gottschalk's first and strongest language was French, although he also spoke Spanish and English fluently.

New Orleans teemed with a rich variety of cultural experiences, as French, Spanish, Creoles, and African Americans mixed freely in a sophisticated atmosphere unlike that of any other city in Europe or America. From this fertile

FIGURE 7.2

Louis Moreau Gottschalk at the piano.

environment, Gottschalk absorbed the musical sounds of each culture, frequently finding inspiration for his compositions in exotic Creole tunes based on French folk and popular melodies.

Unlike Stephen Foster's Victorian family, Gottschalk's sophisticated parents had no genteel compunctions regarding professional musicians. Recognizing their son's precocious talent and the lack of educational opportunities at home, they sent him to France at the age of thirteen to study music. He stayed abroad for eleven years, becoming a great favorite of aristocratic Europeans, who admired his youthful compositions for piano and his astonishing virtuosity. Frédéric Chopin (1810–1849), the famous Polish "poet of the piano," predicted that Gottschalk would one day be the "king of pianists."

Having amazed and delighted concert audiences in Spain, France, and England, Gottschalk returned in 1853 to America, where audiences, perceiving his long stay abroad to have made him respectably foreign, responded with unbridled enthusiasm to his performances of his own melodically simple but technically demanding piano pieces. Next Gottschalk spent several years in the West Indies, whose tropical sounds and flavors he captured in some of his later compositions, returning to America in 1862 to find the country desperately at war.

Although a Southerner by birth, Gottschalk sided firmly with the North and began an exhausting concert tour across America, reaching people who had never heard concert music before and contributing most of what he earned to the Union cause. Criticized by an elite few for playing his own tuneful pieces instead of the great classical music of Beethoven, Chopin, and others, Gottschalk replied that he played what the audience wanted to hear; but he also commented late in his short life on the marked improvement he perceived in the level of American taste.

Gottschalk never married but was adored by women, who screamed and swooned and fought to grab pieces of his clothing whenever he appeared. Finally forced by a scandal (in which he probably was quite—or mostly—innocent) to leave the country in 1865, he traveled to South America, where he organized huge concerts, much like Patrick S. Gilmore's mammoth band concerts. (During one of his tours of Cuba, he produced a gigantic festival, writing three new pieces requiring a total of 650 performers, including a military band, a Caribbean drumming group, 198 choristers, 68 clarinetists, 33 tuba players, and assorted other musicians. A newspaper warned that "young ladies who are easily frightened or nervous should bring smelling salts, as we predict faintings.") Gottschalk died in South America at the age of forty. His death is usually attributed to yellow fever but actually remains a mystery—as is fitting, perhaps, for this quintessentially Romantic man.

Piano Music

Although Gottschalk composed songs, orchestral works, and even operas, he is particularly remembered for his delightful piano music. By 1800 the piano had almost displaced the harpsichord as the keyboard instrument likely to be found in homes or heard in concert. The piano constituted, in fact, the ideal Romantic instrument, providing access to every facet of emotional expression. The *damper* or "loud" pedal (to the player's right) held the tones, connecting one to another for a **legato** or smooth and lyrical melody line, or allowing the sounds to accumulate to thunderous effect. The *una corda* (one string) or "soft" pedal (on the left), by shifting the keyboard, considerably dampened the volume and altered the color of the sound. And on some large pianos, a center pedal, called the *sostenuto,* allowed the player to sustain some tones while others sounded cleanly above them.

Piano music enjoyed immense popularity in the United States, where the varied concert programs of the day often included a virtuosic piano performance by a resident or visiting concert artist. Lowell Mason's son Henry cofounded the famous Mason and Hamlin piano company in 1854; and Jonas Chickering, William Knabe, and Henry Steinway all lived in America, producing pianos unsurpassed anywhere in the world. By mid-century, the piano was widely available to middle-class homes, and much "household" piano music was available in arrangements simple enough for the average young lady to master.

Best-known among Gottschalk's piano compositions are his pieces based on popular dances and his moving **character pieces,** such as "Berceuse" ("Lullaby") and "The Banjo," that capture the mood or character of their subject in musical terms. The rhythms and forms of popular dances had long invigorated many kinds of concert music, and Gottschalk continued this tradition by writing several *waltzes* and *mazurkas* for the piano. (Concert pieces based on these and other traditional dances are intended not to be danced but rather to capture the mood, style, tempo, form, and meter of a popular step.)

Gottschalk based his stirring "Bamboula" (an Optional Listening Example) on a dance popular with whites and blacks alike in the vibrant city of his birth. He organized "Le bananier" (Listening Example 26) according to a formal design called **theme and variations:** a melody or theme recurring throughout the piece is varied, perhaps in tempo, timbre, rhythm, meter, accompaniment, ornamentation, etc., thus providing both unity and contrast. (An apt comparison may be made with the musical theme of a movie, recurring throughout the film to arouse any number of conflicting emotions according to the way it is performed.)

Orchestral Music

Musical activity increased significantly across America in the late nineteenth century. This period witnessed the establishment of some of our finest professional music schools, or **conservatories,** and several concert halls and opera houses were built. The Metropolitan Opera House, built in 1882 (Figure 7.3), and Carnegie Hall (1891) attracted enthusiastic audiences to New York City; and Americans across the country enjoyed access to more concert music of a greater variety and finer quality than ever before. Choral and chamber societies presented programs not only on the east coast but also in cities farther west such as Cincinnati and Chicago. Both serious and light operas became more and more popular, while the great vocal and instrumental virtuosos continued to attract an ever wider and more appreciative public audience.

The large orchestral ensemble, however, held little interest for the young republic. Few American orchestras existed throughout the nineteenth century,

"Le bananier"

Composer
Louis Moreau Gottschalk

CD 1
Track 26
2:48

Form
Theme and variations

Theme
The Creole melody begins with an ascending broken minor triad. Strong accents and irregular phrase lengths enhance the exotic effect of the tuneful melody.

Meter
Duple

The left hand introduces an "obstinately" repeated rhythmic and melodic pattern called an **ostinato,** which then accompanies the first section of the theme **(a),** played by the right hand. Section **a** is repeated.

The second half of the theme **(b),** higher than **a** in range, begins with three repeated and accented notes. Section **b** is repeated.

a is heard in the higher range, accompanied by a new ostinato. Repeat.

b is delicately embellished by the right hand, accompanied by chords in the left.

A variation of **a** is played in a major key, then repeated an octave higher.

A section of new material sounds improvisatory.

The major version of **a** is played by the left hand while the right hand performs dazzling runs.

Then **b** recurs briefly.

The delightful piece concludes with fragments of **a** in the left hand and rapid, virtuosic figures in the right.

although dedicated professional and amateur musicians endeavored to make the orchestral sound appealing to an American audience. In 1820, the Moravians founded a Philharmonic Society for the performance of orchestral music in Bethlehem, Pennsylvania; and in Philadelphia, American and immigrant musicians organized a Musical Fund Society, which performed symphonic music and also choral music accompanied by an orchestra. The New York Philharmonic Society, the nation's oldest orchestra still in existence today, was founded in 1842 but remained a loosely organized and rather haphazard association for many years.

Although the European orchestras playing in American generally performed European works, the first organization to give serious attention to orchestral

FIGURE 7.3

Metropolitan Opera House, circa 1900.

music by American composers was a visiting orchestra directed by the celebrated French conductor Louis-Antoine Jullien (1812–1860). A showman in the tradition of P. T. Barnum and Louis Gottschalk, Jullien wore white gloves when he conducted, from a gilt music stand, and used a jeweled baton. But however flashy he might have appeared, he led his ensemble in fine performances of great orchestral music. Jullien added American musicians to his orchestra during the year he spent in New York (1853) and, strongly prompted by the local press, included some American works in his programs. For many years, however, no one followed Jullien's brave lead.

William Henry Fry (1813–1864)
Among the struggling nationalists who benefited from Jullien's interest in American music was one of the most outspoken American nationalists of the period, **William Henry Fry.** Fry first became known as a composer of operas, including *Leonora* (1845), the first American opera to be produced in this country. He had to pay for the production himself, however, for although Italian operas presented by European

companies enjoyed immense popularity in New Orleans and New York, even those enlightened cities cared little to present an opera by an American composer. In fact, although *Leonora* was written in the familiar Italian style with lyrical melodies, attractive harmonies, and the lavish staging expected of Romantic operas, it was not very well received here; and later, while working for an American newspaper as a music correspondent in Paris (Fry was the first music critic for a major American newspaper), Fry had no success in arranging for a performance of his opera there.

Fry next ventured to offer a series of public music appreciation lectures. Complaining bitterly that the New York Philharmonic Society never commissioned and seldom performed any music by an American composer, he exhorted American musical societies to perform American works, audiences to listen to them, and critics to review them objectively. At one lecture, Fry asserted that "the American composer should not allow the name of Beethoven or Handel or Mozart to prove an eternal bugbear to him," further declaring, "It is time we had a Declaration of Independence in Art and laid the foundation of an American School of Painting, Sculpture and Music."

William Henry Fry's four symphonies and other orchestral works are rarely heard today, his music having been surpassed in quality by many other American and European compositions. Nevertheless, his experience reveals much of the struggle American composers faced until well into the twentieth century, and Fry is respectfully and rightfully remembered for his efforts in support of American music.

The individual who finally raised the level of orchestral performance and appreciation in America was a musician of German background, Theodore Thomas.

Theodore Thomas (1835–1905)

Soon after the ten-year-old **Theodore Thomas** (Figure 7.4) arrived in America from Germany, already an accomplished violinist, he became a member of the New York Philharmonic Society, playing as well for various theater and opera orchestras. (For example, in 1850 he played first violin in the orchestra that accompanied Jenny Lind.) But he intended to become an orchestral conductor and in that capacity to raise the level of Americans' appreciation for orchestral music. And so he did.

Scornful of the casual rehearsal and concert procedures of the New York Philharmonic Society, Thomas formed his own ensemble, hiring only the best musicians; rehearsing them rigorously; and, beginning in 1864, presenting public programs guaranteed to please an audience. His method was to subtly but systematically alter the balance in his concerts between light, familiar pieces and more serious, challenging works as his listeners became more experienced with orchestral fare.

Recognizing Americans' familiarity with varied and entertaining programs, Thomas invited solo virtuosos—including Gottschalk on at least one program—to dazzle the listeners, who then dutifully received perhaps one movement of a

FIGURE 7.4
Cartoon depicting Theodore
Thomas conducting in Central
Park.

more serious piece. Thomas also was careful not to plan programs that were too long. He traveled widely with his orchestra, bringing symphonic music to people who had never heard it before and extending the season's employment for his musicians; in the summer he offered outdoor "garden concerts," where refreshments were served. The quality of his performances was always superb, and America gradually developed an enthusiastic appreciation for the thrilling orchestral sound. Inevitably, German composers formed the core of Thomas's programs, although he also gave generous attention to outstanding American composers of the day.

With the support of some Chicago businessmen, in 1891 Thomas established the Theodore Thomas Orchestra, later known as the Chicago Symphony Orchestra. He conducted it until his death in 1905. By that time several other American cities had formed their own orchestras, and smaller towns had short orchestral seasons as well. During the next several decades, Americans continued to form numerous school, civic, and professional orchestras and to absorb the great symphonic literature of the world. By the mid-twentieth century public school, civic, and professional symphonies across the country rendered America a veritable nation of symphony orchestras.

Terms to Review

nationalism   The expression in art of particular cultural characteristics. The nineteenth century witnessed strong nationalistic movements in several countries.

virtuoso   A performer who possesses dazzling technical brilliance.

legato   Smooth, without perceptible interruption between notes.

character piece   A relatively short piano piece evoking a particular mood or scene.

theme and variations   An instrumental form in which a theme or melody recurs to provide unity, but in altered guises for variety.

conservatory   A professional music school.

ostinato   A repeated melodic or rhythmic pattern.

Key Figures

Anthony Philip Heinrich   William Henry Fry   Theodore Thomas
Louis Moreau Gottschalk

Optional Listening Examples

Louis Moreau Gottschalk: "Bamboula"

George Bristow: Fourth Symphony (*Arcadian*), Op. 49, third movement ("Indian War Dance")

Suggestions for Further Listening

Louis Moreau Gottschalk: "The Banjo"

William Henry Fry: excerpts from *Leonora*

Critical Thinking

Compare the effect their families and upbringing must have had on the careers of Stephen Foster and Louis Moreau Gottschalk.

Can you envision a nationalistic American music? What characteristics would you expect it to include?

Why do you suppose nineteenth-century Americans showed so little interest in concert music by American composers?

Go to www.mhhe.com/ferrisaml5 for a list of additional Web-based resources that relate to the content in this chapter.

American Concert Music Comes of Age: The Late Nineteenth Century

Although most French and Italian composers had partisans in the New World, nineteenth-century Americans who enjoyed hearing orchestral music preferred the German Romantic style to any other. Romantics (Germans and others) approached the elements of music differently from their Classical forbears. Their melodies were long and lyrical rather than short and motivic, their phrases asymmetrical rather than balanced in the classical way. Also, Romantic composers were more likely to repeat their long, songlike melodies with variation or embellishment than to develop brief intellectual melodic ideas. Chordal harmony became fuller and steadily more dissonant, as ears adapted to richer and ever more pungent combinations of sound. Adding new tones to familiar chords, Romantic composers expanded the concept of tonal harmony and achieved newly varied and colorful effects. They also treated rhythm more freely than the Classicists had, sometimes avoiding regularly recurring patterns of a certain number of beats per measure, and writing phrases of irregular length—five or seven measures, for example, instead of four or eight.

About the same time that painters began to use color for expressive rather than realistic purposes, composers began to explore the timbres, sometimes called the colors, of sounds. Thus nineteenth-century music includes increasingly rich and imaginative instrumental effects. Technological changes increasing the capabilities of woodwind and brass instruments encouraged their wider use in the symphony orchestra, and the percussion section of the orchestra also was greatly expanded, making it necessary to add more strings in order to balance the sound. Accordingly, the Romantic orchestra was not only larger than that of the Baroque or Classical period but also included a richer variety of timbres. When you attend orchestral performances today, you will probably notice that pieces written in the eighteenth century are played by a small or **chamber orchestra,** whereas Romantic pieces require a much larger ensemble.

Despite the continuing tendency among America's best-known composers to make their music sound as German as possible, a strong nationalistic urge developed among a few dedicated American musicians and listeners as the nineteenth century drew toward its close. In 1892, Mrs. Jeanette M. Thurber, one of the few Americans genuinely interested in establishing a nationalistic style of composition, invited an outstanding Bohemian nationalist composer to direct the National Conservatory of Music in New York City. While in America, the prestigious Antonín Dvořák (1841–1904) listened to the music of African Americans and Native Americans with the same fascination with which he absorbed the folk music of his own beloved homeland, expressing amazed regret that Americans seemed relatively uninterested in their "native" sounds. Dvořák did not always distinguish between genuine spirituals developed by African Americans and the derivative minstrel songs; nor did he specifically recommend that American composers quote or imitate black or Indian effects. He strongly suggested, however, that these particular musics offered unique and important sources of inspiration.

To illustrate his ideas of how American music should sound, and to express appreciation for the scenic beauty of the land he was visiting, Dvořák wrote his Symphony No. 9 (*From the New World*) and two chamber pieces. Each of these works includes melodies that seem to be based on the scales of black or Indian music as Dvořák understood them—although he harmonized the melodies and orchestrated the music according to Western custom.

After less than three years, when his homesickness compelled him to return home, Dvořák had raised very little interest in American-sounding music. This country's multiethnic population and lack of a common heritage made the concept of a nationalistic American music difficult to grasp. At least a few Americans reflected his influence, however, by using black or Indian references in their music. Among them was the distinguished African American composer Henry Thacker Burleigh (see p. 92), who inspired Dvořák's interest in spirituals.

The Second New England School

Although New York City remained the center of music performance, the intellectual atmosphere of the Boston area nurtured significant developments in music as well as in philosophy and literature, and New England produced most of the important American composers of the late nineteenth century. The Boston Symphony Orchestra, founded in 1881, loyally supported the efforts of local composers by bringing their music to public attention, often with repeated performances of a well-received work.

Members of the **Second New England School** of composers, much of whose music was comparable in quality as well as in style to that of many of their European contemporaries, shared a dedication to the principles of German music theory and a concern for careful craftsmanship leading some to dub them the "Boston classicists." They contributed to every genre of concert music. Many were church musicians and organists who included organ **transcriptions** of opera arias and symphonic music in their recitals, bringing this literature to Americans who had little access to opera or orchestral concerts. These intrepid pioneer composers also contributed strong compositions for organ and a significant body of choral music to the American music repertoire.

John Knowles Paine (1839–1906)

As a young man, **John Knowles Paine,** the oldest member and the leader of the Second New England School, made the decision—unusual for an American of his day—to become a professional musician. Having progressed in his music studies as far as possible with a German teacher in America, he traveled to Germany to polish his skills, giving organ concerts while he not only studied music theory and composition but also composed.

While in Europe, Paine wrote his Mass in D for chorus, soloists, and orchestra, reminiscent in style of a well-known mass by Beethoven. (A mass is a setting to music of the most important Roman Catholic worship service.) Although he was a Protestant, Paine took his text from the Roman Catholic liturgy, according to choral music custom. In this first large composition by an American to be performed in Europe (where it was better received than at a later American performance), Paine neither intended nor achieved a distinctively American sound.

Returning to America in 1861 to find the country at war, Paine became the organist at Harvard University, where, eager to share his newly acquired expertise, he offered free noncredit lectures in music (not considered a proper course of study at American universities) to the students. To the surprise of the university administration, Paine's lectures were very well received. Thanks to his efforts, in 1875 America's oldest college became the first to include music in its formal curriculum, and Paine became the first American professor of music.

Paine's orchestral music is far more significant than that of Heinrich and Fry, who are mainly remembered today for their valiant efforts to promote American music. His much-admired Symphony No. 1, first performed by Theodore Thomas's orchestra in 1876, was the first American symphony to be published but in Germany rather than America, and only after Paine's death. He wrote many other kinds of music as well, including songs, hymns, an opera, and several fine keyboard compositions for organ or piano, including his cheerful Fuga Giocosa (Humorous Fugue) (Listening Example 27).

Fugue

Although originally conceived as a form of European keyboard music, the highly structured **fugue** serves American composers as well. It is suited for music not only for a keyboard instrument, but for every performing medium, including the voice. A fugue is a polyphonic composition with three to five melodic lines or "voices" entering one at a time in imitation of each other, according to specific rules. (In Latin, *fuga* means flight, an effect suggested by the effect of the voices of a fugue "chasing" each other. Think of "fugitive.")

The principal theme or *subject* of a fugue enters alone. After it has been heard all the way through, it is imitated by each of the other voices in turn until each has made its entrance. The first entrance—the subject—is on the tonic; and the second voice, or *answer,* begins on the dominant. The remaining voices (usually there are a total of three or four) alternate entrances between tonic and dominant until each voice has been introduced (Figure 8.1). Whereas the

Fuga Giocosa, Op. 41, No. 3

Composer
John Knowles Paine

CD 1
Track 27
1:27

Form
Fugue

Key
G major

The subject, which is based on an old baseball song, "Over the Fence Is Out, Boys," includes a distinctive upward leap of an octave. It enters on the tonic note (G) and is soon answered at the level of the dominant (D). The third voice enters (tonic), and then the subject is tossed—like a baseball, perhaps—from one voice to another.

Paine explores several major and minor keys throughout the rest of the fugue. He sometimes treats the first four notes of the subject as a motive, repeating the bouncing figure at different levels of pitch, a technique called musical **sequence.** (Think of the first phrase of "Three Blind Mice," for example, which is repeated and then sounded at a higher level of pitch.)

Occasional large chords provide effective contrast to the polyphonic texture, and the piece becomes increasingly virtuosic and dramatic. It is never pretentious, however, and the end, like the beginning, is light and humorous.

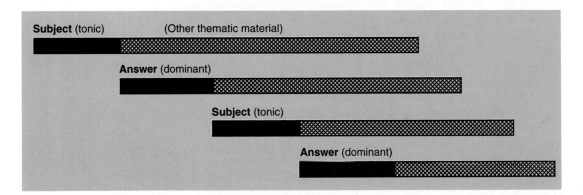

FIGURE 8.1

Exposition of a four-voice fugue.

imitation in a round or canon is literal, the melody in a sense chasing itself, the answer in a fugue begins on a different tone from the subject (dominant instead of tonic) and is only similar, rather than identical, to the subject.

This rigid structure applies only to the beginning section, or **exposition,** of a fugue, in which all the voices are introduced ("exposed"). Thereafter, each voice proceeds with independent material, referring to the subject and answer more or less frequently throughout the piece. There may be a second theme, or *countersubject,* introduced in the same manner as the subject and also recurring throughout the fugue. Thus, although intellectually conceived and tightly structured, the form is quite flexible after the exposition is completed.

Other Members of the School

A large number of capable and prolific composers, many trained in Europe, were soon active in the New England area. Most, however, found it necessary to hold academic positions in order to make a living, American audiences continuing to offer little support to American composers. Other members of the Second New England School whose names are most likely to appear today on a concert program include George Chadwick (1854–1931), whose energy and humor lend a refreshing American flavor to many of his works; and Horatio Parker (1863–1919), an organist and professor like Paine and Chadwick, widely admired for his sacred choral music as well as music for the organ and virtually every other vocal and instrumental medium.

Only recently, as enterprising contemporary musicians have performed and recorded some of their well-crafted, attractive works, have we begun to fully appreciate the music of the Second New England School. Reviewers of numerous recent recordings of symphonic works from this period have expressed both admiration for the quality of the music and regret that it has been virtually ignored for so long.

A prominent member of the Second New England School whose music is becoming increasingly well known was a woman, Amy Marcy Cheney Beach.

Amy Marcy Cheney Beach (1867–1944)

Already recognized as an outstanding pianist before her marriage at the age of eighteen to Dr. H. H. A. Beach, Amy Marcy Cheney (Figure 8.2) thereafter used her married name professionally. While not the first American woman to write music, she was the first to rank with such highly educated and sophisticated musicians as Chadwick and Parker; and she was, in fact, the first American woman to write a successful mass and a symphony. Women of her day and before simply were not afforded the education, the financial or social support, or the patronage required to succeed as professional composers.

Beach's parents and her husband recognized and encouraged her talent, although to a limited extent. She studied piano from a young age but had minimal training as a composer. She rigorously trained herself, however, translating into English important foreign treatises on instrumentation and orchestration. Before her marriage, she performed as a pianist with the Boston Symphony Orchestra and with the Theodore Thomas Orchestra; but her husband preferred that she concentrate on her compositions, a married woman's professional appearance onstage not being well accepted in her day. After her husband's death, Beach resumed her concert career, performing to great acclaim both here and in Europe.

Although her compositions were widely performed and well received on both continents, Beach could not escape references to her sex in reviews of her

FIGURE 8.2

Amy Marcy Cheney Beach.

work, reviewers sometimes criticizing her for trying to sound masculine, or praising her graceful melodies and more gentle symphonic passages as properly feminine in style. Thus, although she handled the symphonic medium very capably, it is little wonder that Amy Marcy Cheney Beach composed more art songs, including her charming "The Year's at the Spring" (an Optional Listening Example), than any other form, because her contemporaries readily accepted songs as fitting examples of feminine creativity.

In her Symphony in E minor ("Gaelic," Listening Example 28), Beach responded to Dvořák's recommendation to produce American music based on ethnic and traditional idioms. She disagreed, however, that African American or Native American music represented the influences prevalent in her society. In a letter to the Boston *Herald,* Beach wrote, "We of the North should be far more likely to be influenced by old English, Scotch or Irish songs, inherited with our literature from our ancestors." A large portion of Boston's population was Irish American, and Irish tunes had become familiar in middle-class parlors and on theater and concert stages across the country. Beach therefore chose to base her symphony on themes taken from or based on Irish tunes and to imbue the work with a Gaelic flavor. She also wrote that the symphony had a program, depicting the struggles, laments, romance, and dreams of the Irish people.

Edward MacDowell (1860–1908)

The composers of the Second New England School wrote effectively in all the symphonic, choral, and solo genres; but as we have seen, their music predominantly conformed to the sounds of their European contemporaries.

Symphony in E minor ("Gaelic"), second movement

CD 1
Track 28
8:22

Composer

Amy Marcy Cheney Beach

Form

A B A (ternary or three-part form), with a closing section, or **coda.** (In Italian, *coda* means tail.) (Although the choice of capital or lowercase letters to outline form is somewhat arbitrary, capital letters generally indicate large sections of a piece or movement, while small letters represent a small section or a phrase.)

Tempo

The first section (**A**) is slow, relaxed.

The middle section (**B**) is fast (allegro vivace).

Meter

The first section is in compound quadruple meter (12/8). We hear four slow beats per measure, each divided by three. The middle section is in simple duple meter (2/4).

A. After an orchestral introduction, the oboe, accompanied by other woodwinds, introduces the lovely theme (an Irish tune titled "The Little Field of Barley"). The tune has four phrases, the third and fourth of which are repeated.

B. Excited string figures begin the middle section (2:02). Here Beach transforms the theme, which dances through the strings lightly accompanied by the full orchestra. The theme in its new guise is repeated, and then the instruments toss the melody lightly back and forth. (Notice the tinkling sound of the triangle, which joins the fun.) Beach finds the simple tune a source of great variety, as she takes it through several keys. Then the orchestra sweeps dramatically up, and higher still, to end the section abruptly and change the mood in preparation for the return of **A.**

A. (5:29) Woodwinds return the theme to its original form. The plaintive English horn plays the melody. Then the oboe takes it over (6:04), as the orchestra gently joins in and slowly swells to a romantic climax, the strings giving their full, lush attention to the theme. Two clarinets play a rather tentative descending phrase (7:11); the oboe and English horn respond; the orchestra tapers off until suddenly the agitated **B** material returns briefly as a coda (8:01), to bring the movement to a completely satisfying end.

FIGURE 8.3
Edward MacDowell—
composer, painter, poet, and
lover of nature.

Edward MacDowell (Figure 8.3), who was too romantic to be called a classicist of any sort, and too individual to be included in a school of composers, became the first American to write concert music in a style distinctively his own.

In his teens appearing equally talented in music and art, MacDowell was
sent to Paris to study in both fields. Finally deciding to become a professional
musician, however, he traveled to Germany, where he followed the prevailing
custom of studying theory and composition. An accomplished pianist, he con-
certized widely during his long stay abroad, and some of his songs and piano
pieces, written in the accepted German style, were published in Germany
before he returned to America in 1888.

In 1896, after several years of performing, composing, and teaching in the
Boston area, MacDowell accepted the position as head of the newly established music department at Columbia University in New York City, which
afforded him the opportunity to implement his ideal of teaching music as
related to the other arts. We have already noted that Romantics often were
talented in more than one of the arts and found particular significance in relationships between music and literature. Thus MacDowell, who not only composed music and painted but also wrote poetry, believed that the arts could not

be understood in isolation from each other and established at Columbia a curriculum similar to a modern humanities program.

MacDowell professed not to espouse the nationalists' claim that quoting African American or Indian themes would establish a characteristically American music, suggesting instead that American music should seek to capture the youthful, optimistic spirit of the country. Nevertheless, he was unable to resist references to American Indian music in several of his compositions. For example, each section of his orchestral *Indian Suite* is based on Native American lore or experience, and each uses American Indian or Indian-like melodies, though the harmonies and orchestral effects are entirely European. (A **suite** is an instrumental work consisting of several sections or semi-independent pieces.) Similarly, his famous set of character pieces titled *Woodland Sketches* includes one called "From an Indian Lodge," which imitates American Indian sounds within a Western framework. (The exquisite "To a Wild Rose" from *Woodland Sketches,* is an Optional Listening Example.)

MacDowell's piano pieces, including *Woodland Sketches,* reflect his romantic love of nature, painting in musical terms idyllic scenes of woodland lakes and hills. These delicate, intimate, and modest piano miniatures capture the very essence of the sounds and moods of nature as MacDowell loved it.

His vision of music as one of the integrated arts has profoundly benefited American arts to this day, for after his death, MacDowell's widow established a summer colony on their estate at Peterboro, New Hampshire, where artists, musicians, and literary figures are invited to spend uninterrupted summers working within their chosen fields at the **MacDowell Colony.**

Arthur Farwell and the Wa-Wan Press

Arthur Farwell (1872–1952), who like so many Americans studied music in Germany, decided upon his return home that American composers should be writing something other than imitation German music. Farwell intended his music to exalt "the common inspirations of American life"—by which he meant, somewhat surprisingly, the experiences of the American Indian. To this end he imaginatively arranged some Native American tunes and composed several original pieces based on Indian melodies. Understanding that Native American music signified more than art or entertainment, Farwell attempted in his *American Indian Melodies* (1900) to reflect the essence of the myths or legends upon which the songs were based. Nevertheless, the worthy intentions of Farwell and other composers interested in Native American music were overwhelmed by their thorough indoctrination into tonal concepts. That is, they harmonized Indian melodies with tonal chords, and scored their pieces for the piano or for orchestral instruments unrelated to the Native American experience and incapable of reproducing the nuances of the melodies themselves.

Farwell's music was coolly received by audiences and routinely rejected by publishers, who gave an unfriendly reception to music by other American composers as well. So in 1901, Farwell established the famous **Wa-Wan Press** (the name is from a ceremony of the Omaha tribe), dedicated to producing

American music. Although it existed for only a decade, the Wa-Wan Press published several hundred compositions, effectively boosting the reputations and careers of several struggling American composers.

Yet the market for their music remained minimal. And few composers or listeners of the late nineteenth century showed much interest in music that *sounded* American. Although by the latter part of the nineteenth century American composers were producing impressive works in all the large instrumental and vocal forms—symphonies, concertos, sonatas, operas, and choral works—and finally were being afforded a respectful, if limited, hearing, most of them not only studied in Germany but also wrote most of their music in the firmly established German Romantic style.

Terms to Review

chamber orchestra   A small orchestra, with only a few instruments per line of music.

Second New England School   The first American composers to write significant works in all the large concert forms. Sometimes referred to as the Boston classicists.

transcription   An arrangement of a piece originally composed for a particular instrument or ensemble so that it can be played by a different instrument or combination of instruments.

fugue   A polyphonic composition in which imitative entrances of two or more voices alternate between tonic and dominant. Originally conceived for keyboard instruments, fugues now are written for other instruments and for voices as well.

sequence   The repetition of a melodic figure at different levels of pitch.

exposition   The first section of a fugue.

coda   Closing section.

suite   An instrumental work consisting of several dances or other semi-independent pieces.

MacDowell Colony   A colony for artists in every medium established on the estate of Edward MacDowell by his widow, in Peterboro, New Hampshire.

Wa-Wan Press   A publishing company established in 1901 by Arthur Farwell, dedicated to American music.

Key Figures

John Knowles Paine
George Chadwick

Horatio Parker
Amy Marcy Cheney Beach

Edward MacDowell
Arthur Farwell

Optional Listening Examples

Horatio Parker: Fugue in C Minor
Amy Marcy Cheney Beach: "The Year's at the Spring"

Edward MacDowell: "To a Wild Rose" from *Woodland Sketches*

Suggestions for Further Listening

Amy Marcy Cheney Beach: Mass in E♭, Op. 5; String Quartet (based on Eskimo tunes)

George Chadwick: "Tam O'Shanter"

John Knowles Paine: Second Symphony ("In the Spring")

Paine: Fantasie über "Ein' feste Burg"

Paine: Mass in D

Critical Thinking

How might Amy Cheney Beach's professional experience have differed had she lived half a century later?

Does Paine's Fuga Giocosa sound humorous, as its title suggests? If so, what lends it that flavor?

What do you think of the efforts by several American composers to capture an "American" sound by adapting American Indian sounds in their vocal, choral, piano, and orchestral compositions? Defend your position by referring to the elements of music. Have you heard similar adaptations in scores for films about Native Americans, and if so, were they effective?

How would you describe (perhaps using the elements of music) your concept of an American-sounding music?

Go to www.mhhe.com/ferrisaml5 for a list of additional Web-based resources that relate to the content in this chapter.

PART 2
Summary

B y the turn of the nineteenth century, Americans had become more romantic than classical in their style of expression. The romantic zeal to improve the conditions of life initiated religious and social reform movements as well as efforts to reform American music by making it sound more European. Lowell Mason, who led the movement to reform musical taste in America, wrote attractive—although quite conventional—hymns, brought music education into the public school system, and systematically attempted to raise the level of musical awareness and appreciation.

Lowell Mason's efforts notwithstanding, country folk continued to practice and enjoy their accustomed ways of reading and singing music, and singing schools remained popular in rural areas, using shape-note songbooks such as *The Sacred Harp* as teaching materials. During the Great Revival, people of all ages, both black and white, attended religious camp meetings, where they enjoyed singing rousing hymns and spirituals. Secular songs became popular, too, often reflecting the experience of everyday life. In the cities, theaters offered popular entertainment that was primarily musical. Religious songs, sentimental ballads, songs of social protest, and glees were sung in parlors and concert halls and included in the performances of well-known singing families such as the Hutchinsons.

In minstrel shows, the most popular entertainment of the period leading to the Civil War, white men blackened their skin and imitated the songs, dances, and dialect of stereotypical African Americans. Stephen Foster wrote outstanding minstrel songs of a more sensitive, less demeaning, nature than most; yet genteel society preferred his love songs, Civil War songs, and sentimental ballads about home. Concert bands directed by Patrick Gilmore and John Philip Sousa became balanced ensembles capable of performing transcriptions of orchestral and operatic literature as well as more popular pieces, and under the superb direction of Sousa, the march king, achieved the highest levels of professionalism.

Mid-nineteenth-century Americans particularly enjoyed concert music performed by virtuoso soloists, including the singer Jenny Lind and the composer and violinist Ole Bull. These European performers toured throughout the United States thrilling audiences with their dazzling virtuosic displays. America's own piano virtuoso, Louis Moreau Gottschalk, gained popularity on both sides of the Atlantic. Gottschalk introduced American audiences of the Civil War period to piano music, generally performing his own light but stirring compositions. After the Civil War, conservatories, concert halls, and opera houses were built in several American cities, as concert music grew in significance. Theodore Thomas presented orchestral programs that pleased audiences and gradually raised their level of appreciation, but primarily for European orchestral music.

The seeds of American nationalism, sown during the nineteenth century, bore fruit slowly, although several ardent nationalists, including Anthony Philip Heinrich and William Henry Fry, sought to awaken American appreciation for American-sounding music. Dvořák encouraged Americans to develop a characteristic sound of their own; but the Second New England School produced the first significant American concert music, primarily in the German Romantic style.

Edward MacDowell developed a characteristic, although not distinctively American, idiom of his own. The MacDowell Colony in Peterboro, New Hampshire, continues to invite artists in every discipline to spend summers working there.

3

The Growth of Vernacular Traditions

Music in the Vernacular: Historical and Cultural Perspective

The common, or vernacular, language of a country is the language spoken by most of its people—the language they hear and use throughout their lives. A culture's vernacular music also is commonly heard and understood, without conscious effort on the part of listeners, and with less training and experience required for its performance than for the performance of so-called classical, concert, or art music. Often the term *popular* is applied to much of the music we shall cover in this section of the text, but that term does not adequately embrace such disparate fields as jazz, folk, rap, country-western, and rock. In fact, *pop* has become a genre in its own right, distinguished from other vernacular sounds.

Walt Whitman
"I hear America singing, the varied carols I hear."

Vernacular Art and Literature
Besides music, the other arts of the post–Civil War period also captured new American flavors. The picturesque stories of Bret Harte (1836–1902), for example, brought Western local color to appreciative readers in the great cities of the East, while Mark Twain (1835–1910) made everyday scenes of his youth in the Mississippi River region internationally, and hilariously, famous. The poet Walt Whitman (1819–1892) frequently used colloquial language to express the American experience of his day in an eloquent, distinctively American, idiom. Whitman's simple, anguished words in his famous poem "O Captain! My Captain!" reached the hearts of a nation mourning the death of Abraham Lincoln.

After the turn of the twentieth century, other poets variously expressed themselves in colloquial terms. Popular culture thrived from the late 1930s through the early 1950s, when pulp novels, adventure comic books, swing music, and B movies enlivened the humdrum lives of working Americans. Some of the work of the mid-century "beat" poets, who borrowed vocabulary from jazz musicians and sprinkled their verse with obscenities in an effort to bring poetry "back to the streets," was undeniably powerful and moving.

The visual arts, too, showed a new interest in the mundane facts of everyday American life and, by the turn of the twentieth century, the robust vigor of city life replaced the idyllic rural American landscape as the subject of choice for many American artists. Ben Shahn (1898–1969), among many socially conscious painters of the period, imitated newspaper cartoons in the effort to attract large numbers of people to his paintings. By the 1950s, Jasper Johns (1930–) and Robert Rauschenberg (1925–) were introducing everyday objects (flags, numbers, street signs) into their paintings, and in the 1960s a new art, known as "pop," presented soup cans, Coke bottles, lightbulbs, comic strip characters, and movie stars in hugely glorified detail. George Segal (1924–2000) cast life-size plaster figures from live models, outfitted them in familiar commercial products, and placed them in lifelike settings, to amuse and sometimes fool the viewer's eye.

One of America's most distinguished black artists, Romare Bearden (1912–1988), worked in *collage*, a cut-and-paste technique combining objects of varying content and material to form a work of art. A member of the movement known as the Harlem Renaissance, Bearden attempted, as he said, to "establish a world through art in which the validity of my Negro experience could live and make its own logic." Bearden defied conventional rules of art, sharply cutting the human features in his stunning collages with sudden breaks and surprising repetitions that functioned for him, it has been suggested, as a visual equivalent to the jazz he loved. *Empress of the Blues* is one of his most famous works.

Vernacular Music
As we have seen, art or classical music gained favor in the New World only very slowly, over a long period of time, and much of the music already considered in this text belongs in the realm of the vernacular. Native American music never was conceived as an elite form of art; nor were Anglo-American or African American dances or songs. The hymns and psalm tunes written by self-taught amateurs formed a part of their education and recreation as well as their worship. The composer Stephen Foster had no formal music training and did not intend his music for concert performance. Spirituals and *alabados* were really religious folk songs.

However, although vernacular music has always been a significant facet of American culture, it was during the period between the Jacksonian era and the Civil War (1829–1861) that what we now call popular music emerged. Americans wrestling with rapid industrialization, economic uncertainty, slavery, westward expansion, and other overwhelming issues of social, religious, political, and economical

Empress of the Blues by Romare Bearden.

import found popular songs a helpful means through which they could cope with reality: sentimental songs on such sensitive topics as slavery, women's suffrage, or alcoholism, for example, allowed emotional release without requiring direct confrontation of the issues on a personal level.

At least until recently, vernacular music—like popular art—has evolved in an unself-conscious manner, spontaneously reflecting cultural characteristics indigenous to the region where it occurs. Thus long before art music achieved anything recognizable, however controversially, as an American sound, the young nation's vernacular music revealed strongly characteristic American traits. About the time of the Civil War, when popular culture included minstrel shows, band and circus music, the songs of Stephen Foster, and stirring performances by popular singing families, many songs, dances, and instrumental pieces acquired a new, distinctively American flavor. The rhythms, timbres, melodies, and harmonies of many songs, dances, and instrumental pieces, unfettered by conventional (European) rules, introduced new sounds suited to the pace and moods of American life and articulated in regional American accents. Some music, written down or passed along by aural tradition, was conceived to provide popular entertainment at home, in the theater, or in some other structured setting. Some tunes evolved on an open range, in a cotton field, on a chain gang, or on the field of battle, where they offered self-expression and relief to the lonely and oppressed.

Again until recently, there has been little studied attempt to preserve vernacular traditions. Favorite pieces survived from one generation to the next simply through unchanging, or slowly changing, performance practice, as we observed with the early ballad "Barbara Allen" (Listening Example 5). New sounds also gain recognition as styles, genres, or kinds of vernacular music in their own right, to be short-lived or long-lived according to the vagaries of popular acceptance and of the music business. Some very old tunes remain familiar today, whereas some highly popular songs have been largely forgotten by the fickle public who loved them a few months ago. ♪

The Rise of Popular Culture

The gap between classical and popular music widened during the last half of the nineteenth century. Of course there had always been music for everyday experience and music intended for concert performance, as there also was between religious and secular music. But such distinctions were not necessarily clear: a spiritual sung at a religious service on Sunday might provide personal pleasure on Monday, or be part of a recital on Saturday night. Classical music of the eighteenth century and the early nineteenth century offered tuneful melodies commonly hummed by Americans who perhaps never attended a concert or an opera but who heard the tunes on someone's parlor piano or in a theater performance, and soon loved and imitated them. Songwriters, in fact, often modeled their popular songs on the melodies of Austrian and Italian classical music.

But as time progressed, composers such as Frédéric Chopin, Richard Wagner, Claude Debussy, Richard Strauss, Gustav Mahler, and Arnold Schoenberg steadily increased the complexity and dissonance of their music. Meanwhile, writers of popular songs simplified their melodies and harmonies to make them more accessible, and more acceptable, to a wide audience. And so the two kinds of music grew farther apart.

The last decade of the nineteenth century witnessed two phenomenal movements in popular American music, each of which proved long-lived and influential far beyond initial intentions or expectations. These two American musics—one (ragtime) primarily instrumental and led by black musicians, the other (the songs of Tin Pan Alley) vocal and led by American Jews—aroused the immediate enthusiasm and the lasting admiration of listeners here and abroad.

Ragtime

During the rather hectic last decade of the nineteenth century, talented black pianists began to play a new, highly syncopated, and very danceable music in more or (especially) less reputable places of entertainment. Small bands,

145

too, "ragged" their arrangements, adding spicy syncopations over a steady beat. By 1897, the hot new music was being called **ragtime.**

Early ragtime pianists improvised their music, captivating audiences in nightclubs and bawdy houses with a jaunty, toe-tapping style. In the last years of the nineteenth century, however, as publishers began to show interest in the catchy new music, some ragtime players composed highly structured pieces that we now consider "classic" ragtime. This development remains controversial, some ragtime lovers insisting that writing down and publishing rags debased their essential quality as jubilant, spontaneous creations. But while the term originally had a more general meaning, normally we consider ragtime specifically a written piano music, composed for publication rather than improvised. Uprooted from their homeland and transplanted in a harsh new world, black musicians were restructuring their familiar modes of musical expression to fit their new cultural experiences. Thus in effect, ragtime was a new and essentially American music created by black musicians, based on both white European and black African traditions.

From the marches of European-influenced composers, such as Patrick S. Gilmore and John Philip Sousa, ragtime derived its march form and tonal harmony. Like a march, a rag generally begins with a brief introduction. Next we hear several strains in the order **A A B B C C D D,** each different letter representing a new strain. Usually one of the strains is a trio, often in the subdominant; and many rags, like many marches, end in this key. The pattern is not rigid, however, and certainly does not dictate the content; the first strain may return later in the piece, and many other variants of this basic march form also are possible.

Although some of the early ragtime players were self-taught, others with music training brought their knowledge of European harmony to the popular piano style. Thus, even though early rags were clearly tonal, some of them included rather complex melodies and harmonies using numerous **chromatic** tones—tones other than those of the major or minor scale on which the piece was based.

The rhythms and the "flavor" of ragtime, however—the characteristics that made it wildly popular in Europe as well as in America—derived from Africa and were practiced by singers, brass bands, and other instrumental ensembles long before ragtime was established as a piano form. Although syncopation had enlivened Western music from its beginning, the spicy nature and consistent application of syncopated rhythms were distinctive characteristics of the vigorous new vernacular music, ragtime.

Late minstrel shows constituted a strong source of inspiration for the hot new piano style: After the Civil War, as noted in Chapter 6, minstrelsy provided a lucrative source of income for black as well as white performers, and blacks formed their own lively shows in which they syncopated, or ragged, banjo tunes. The high-stepping plantation dance called a **cakewalk,** based on the syncopated figure *short-LONG-short,* became a regular feature of the **finale,** or last scene, of a minstrel show. This distinctive cakewalk rhythm also appears occasionally in the music of many composers—Gottschalk's

"Bamboula" and "The Banjo," Stephen Foster's "Oh! Susanna," and Daniel Emmett's "Dixie" to name a few. (Because *duration* implies *accent,* we hear the long note of the cakewalk rhythmic pattern as stronger than the short notes that surround it.) This pattern consistently served the ragtime pianist, whose left hand marked the regular duple meter while the right hand played a highly syncopated melody.

Outstanding ragtime pianists included **Eubie Blake,** who died at the age of one hundred in 1983; **James Scott** (1886–1938); and Ferdinand DeMenthe, known as **Jelly Roll Morton** (1890–1941)—among many others, each with his own style of writing and playing rags. Ragtime pianists recorded their performances on **piano rolls** by playing on a special piano that marked dots on a paper, which then could be punched and duplicated, making it possible for eager listeners throughout America and abroad to hear the music "live" on the new **player pianos.** A "pianist" played this novel instrument by pumping two pedals controlling a set of vacuum bellows that forced air through the holes in the paper as it wound over a tracker bar, causing the piano hammers to strike the appropriate piano strings. Player pianos brought recorded performances of the great ragtime players into people's homes before phonographs—and long before radios—became widely available. They also preserved improvised performances by many ragtime players who resisted—more, resented—the move toward "respectability" by those who published their compositions.

Scott Joplin (1868–1917) The childhood experience of **Scott Joplin** (Figure 9.1), the acknowledged king of ragtime, was rich with music, for his father, a former slave, played the violin, and there were other instruments in the Joplin home as well. The young Joplin studied piano with a German immigrant musician, who also provided him with basic studies in music theory.

FIGURE 9.1

Scott Joplin (1868–1917) was honored with a commemorative stamp by the U.S. Postal Service in 1953 as part of its Black Heritage series.

While still a teenager, Joplin left his home in Texarkana, Texas, and traveled east to Missouri, earning some money along the way by playing ragtime piano. In Sedalia and later in St. Louis—the early center of ragtime creativity—Joplin addressed both white and black music markets, playing in black bars and saloons while writing sentimental songs and arrangements in the white popular style. A shy and gentle man, he liked composing and teaching far better than playing in the rough environments where ragtime was first popular; and finally, the huge commercial success of his "Maple Leaf Rag" (Listening Example 29), published in 1899, allowed him to concentrate on the activities he preferred. This rag, previously rejected by one publisher, in 1899 finally attracted the attention of another, John Stark, who heard Joplin play it at the Maple Leaf Club. "Maple Leaf Rag" achieved enormous popularity, and Stark became Joplin's most frequent publisher for the next ten years.

Although very easy to enjoy, good rags may be quite difficult to play. Joplin's own rags reveal a change from the (relative) simplicity of such early rags as "Maple Leaf Rag" and "The Entertainer"—both irresistibly tuneful and entirely unpretentious—to some of his later rags such as "Euphonic Sounds," which sound like music more for the concert than for the dance hall. Although

"Maple Leaf Rag"

CD 1
Track 29
3:02

Composer
Scott Joplin

Meter
Duple

Key
A-flat major

Outline of the Form   A A B B A C C D D

The *first strain* (**A**) (16 measures) features the short-LONG-short cakewalk figure, which first occurs in the second half of the first measure and recurs frequently throughout the piece. The first two measures are repeated. Notice the accented chromatic notes in the next two measures and the dramatic ascending figure that follows.

The *first strain* is repeated.

The *second strain* (**B**) (16 measures), rhythmically similar to the first, is higher in pitch. It begins with a chromatically descending melodic line and is marked **staccato,** meaning that it should be played in a crisp, detached manner.

The *second strain* is repeated.

The *first strain* is played again.

Notice the rich chordal texture of the *trio* (**C**), also 16 measures, which is played and repeated. The key is the subdominant, or D-flat major.

The *fourth strain* (**D**), 16 measures, returns to the tonic and is more similar in texture to strains 1 and 2. The fourth strain is repeated.

he insisted that rags should be played as written, Joplin regularly improvised complex embellishments in his own playing—which, however, was never very fast, for Joplin knew that a dashing tempo trivialized the strength and dignity of a great rag.

Influence of Ragtime Ragtime had a striking effect on many kinds of music both in the popular and classical realms. Social dancing was strongly affected as Americans, who even before the Civil War had largely abandoned popular eighteenth-century country dances for couple dances such as the waltz and the energetic polka, after the rise of ragtime avidly adopted the **two-step,** or **fox-trot.** The frequent syncopations of the popular new dance delighted young people and the fox-trot soon replaced all other dances in popularity.

James Reese Europe (1881–1919), an African American composer and bandleader, composed some of the most popular fox-trots of his day. Flavoring his dance band music with ragtime, Reese became wildly popular in New York City. During World War I, he led an army band in Europe. The band members not only entertained troops to great acclaim but also served heroically under fire, becoming the most decorated unit in the American Army during that war.

By the early twentieth century, many forms of American popular music reflected a strong black influence, although most of the rags, blues, and jazz recordings were made by white performers. African American vocalists especially were excluded from recording, though instrumental groups, such as those led by Europe and by W. C. Handy (see pp. 202–203), were allowed to record because listeners were less likely than in vocal performances to discern the performers' race.

Soon white composers also were writing songs using ragtime rhythms, such as "Hello, My Baby!" by Joseph E. Howard, "Waiting for the Robert E. Lee" by Lewis F. Muir, and "Yessir, That's My Baby" by Gus Kahn and Walter Donaldson. In the second decade of the twentieth century, many songs with little or no syncopated rhythm and no reference to ragtime in their titles were perceived as "ragtime songs," because of the style—brash, breezy, humorous—in which they were sung and played onstage and in recordings. Their lyrics were more colloquial, closer to everyday speech, than the rather formal expressions found in other sentimental love songs of the time. In fact, though, performers capitalized on the popularity of ragtime by "ragging" (syncopating) almost any popular song of the day. Nearly all ragtime songs were written and performed by whites, who thus established a pattern to be repeated through the twentieth century, as white musicians reaped benefits from watered-down interpretations of music originating with blacks. Several European composers also reflected the influence of ragtime by writing syncopated concert pieces with "rag" or "ragtime" in their titles.

At the end of World War I, ragtime had declined in popularity. Some composers were producing rags too complex for popular appeal, and the commercial effort to reach a broad audience often diluted the very characteristics that had made early rags exciting. By then, however, jazz musicians were reflecting the strong influence of ragtime, which—while important entirely in its own right—must also be considered a precursor of that hot new American music.

Meanwhile, popular songs replaced piano music in the affections of the public, as America entered the golden age of Tin Pan Alley.

Tin Pan Alley

The popular music publishing business expanded rapidly after the Civil War, with publishing houses active in many cities, including Boston, Chicago, Philadelphia, Baltimore, and Cincinnati. Well before the turn of the twentieth century, popular music had become an important business, and songs were being written for the purpose of making money. Songs with piano accompaniment

FIGURE 9.2

Couple enjoying Tin Pan Alley
songs on piano rolls.

printed as sheet music sold in amazing quantities, made popular by variety
shows, music theater performances, and piano rolls (Figure 9.2).

In 1881, the brothers Alex and Tom Harms established a publishing firm
in New York City, achieving such commercial success that many other song-
publishing companies also based their firms in New York. This music publishing activity first centered on East 14th Street, in what was then the heart of
New York's theater district; but by the 1890s, nearly every major music publishing house was situated on or near 28th Street, soon dubbed **Tin Pan Alley,**
in reference to the sounds of many pianos playing at once, as house composers
worked out new compositions and **song pluggers** demonstrated the music by
playing and perhaps singing it for customers. Theater performers also stopped
by when in town to try out and select new songs for their shows, the primary
means by which most listeners became familiar with popular music. (In the
1920s, the new recording industry began to assume some of the responsibility
for popularizing songs; but although radio stations were playing popular
recordings in the 1930s, it was another decade before radios became widely
enough available to influence the popularity of a song.)

The Songs   Tin Pan Alley publishers produced only popular songs, and
these were nearly uniform in style, beginning with a brief piano introduction,
which might include references to the melody of the song or might simply set
the key and the tempo, and proceeding with the **verse-chorus form** that had
become standard well before the time of Tin Pan Alley. Nevertheless, the dozen
or so superb songwriters of the period developed their own styles and sounds
to produce hundreds of great songs that continue to please listeners today.

enthusiastically

The verses of a Tin Pan Alley song narrated a story or described a situation or a portrait, whereas the chorus, which was repeated after each verse, echoed or commented on the story. The songs of the 1890s often told tales of tragedy and loss, although their chorus might not reveal the sad nature of the song text: only those who sang or heard the last verse of a song, for example, might be aware that the loved one extolled in the chorus has died.

Most songs had at least two, and often several, verses, but in time the verses became less and less important, listeners clearly preferring the memorable chorus melodies and often scarcely realizing that a song also had a verse or verses. For this reason, by the 1920s Tin Pan Alley composers were writing shorter verses and fewer of them. Further, since early recordings could contain only three or four minutes of music on a record side, the verses of a song might well be omitted in recorded performances—another reason for composers not to spend precious time and effort writing them. Even when time allowed for a verse, performers often chose to repeat the familiar chorus instead, inviting an audience, if present, to sing along; and finally many Tin Pan Alley composers simply wrote songs without any verses at all.

Although largely writing songs to order, early Tin Pan Alley composers nevertheless produced many wonderful tunes still well remembered today. A large number, including "After the Ball" (1892), "The Sidewalks of New York" (1894), "Casey Would Waltz with the Strawberry Blonde" (1895), "Meet Me in St. Louis, Louis" (1904), and "Take Me Out to the Ball Game" (1908), were waltzes, reflecting the popularity of European operettas and other European music.

expressing the writer's emotions

The lyrics of many songs from this period reveal social conflicts rising from women's new position in society, as the move from agriculture to industry, from a rural to an urban setting, altered female roles in family and social life. No longer confined to the farm or to country life, better educated and more widely experienced than women of an earlier generation, the "new woman" of the period from 1890 to 1910 assumed an active, independent role, even in courtship and romance. This excerpt from "Ta-ra-ra-boom-dee-ay" (1891, attributed to Henry Sayers) suggests the flirtatious lyrics—descriptive of lightly duplicitous behavior—typical of many songs of that time:

> *I'm not extravagantly shy,*
> *And when a nice young man is nigh,*
> *For his heart I have a try,*
> *And faint away with tearful cry!*
>
> *When the good young man in haste,*
> *Will support me 'round the waist,*
> *I don't come to while thus embraced,*
> *Till of my lips he steals a taste!*

Barbershop Singing
Tin Pan Alley songs were often performed by **barbershop quartets,** a popular form of musical entertainment of that period. Four unaccompanied male voices, ranging from high to low (tenor, lead,

August 14, 1964.

Sammy Cahn (1913–1993), lyricist.
"The popular song is America's greatest ambassador."

baritone, and bass) sang popular songs in close harmony; quartets competed, in fact, to see which could make the most surprising harmonic changes in a given song "work." The lead voice nearly always sang the melody, the other voices providing harmony above and below. Barbershop singing retains an audience today, and the Society for the Preservation and Encouragement of Barbershop Quartet Singing in America has about 34,000 members in 800 chapters around the country. Women, too, usually called "Sweet Adelines" after the title of a popular song, enjoy singing in barbershop style and have their own very active organizations.

Tin Pan Alley songs lend themselves particularly well to barbershop singing: written within a modest vocal range and with simple (often clever) lyrics, they can be sung comfortably by average voices, and their simple melodies accommodate the creative harmonic changes characteristic of barbershop style, as heard in "Rose" ("A Ring to the Name of Rose") by George M. Cohan, Listening Example 30.

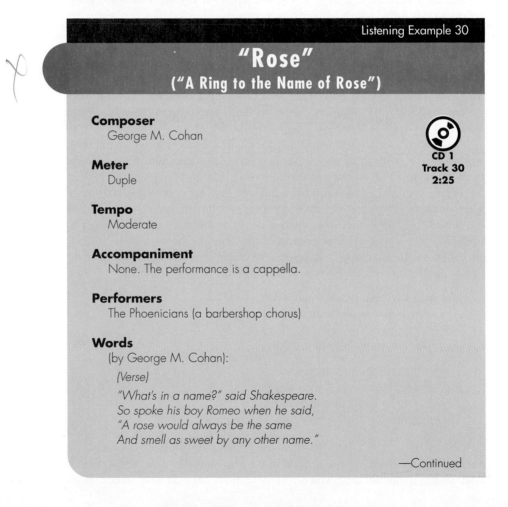

Listening Example 30

"Rose"
("A Ring to the Name of Rose")

Composer
George M. Cohan

CD 1
Track 30
2:25

Meter
Duple

Tempo
Moderate

Accompaniment
None. The performance is a cappella.

Performers
The Phoenicians (a barbershop chorus)

Words
(by George M. Cohan):

(Verse)

"What's in a name?" said Shakespeare.
So spoke his boy Romeo when he said,
"A rose would always be the same
And smell as sweet by any other name."

—Continued

"Rose"
("A Ring to the Name of Rose")

Well, I don't agree with Shakespeare,
And I'm a real Romeo.
For I'd hate to fight with Shakespeare,
But there's one thing I know. (Note the strong crescendo and the
change of harmonies on the last word of the verse.)

(Chorus)

There's a ring to the name of Rosie,
A ring, ting-a-ling, to the name of Rosie.
Other names you may say ring true,
So they do, but they ring for you.
I still cling to the name of Rosie,
'Cause there's something to the name of Rosie
That gives our hearts that ring-a-Rosie, ring-a-ling, ting-a-ling,
There's a ring to the name of Rose.

(Second half of chorus repeated.)

Cohan lends gentle emphasis to the name "Rosie" by delaying—
syncopating—the first syllable. This arrangement slightly changes Cohan's
melody, the rhythm, especially the harmony—and even the words,
adding phrases from a children's song. ("Ring around the rosy, a pocket
full of posy"—an innocent-sounding nonsense verse—has a sinister connection. Many people believe that "rosy" refers to the telltale mark on
the skin of a plague victim, "posies" to bouquets of flowers held to dis-
guise the smell of mass death, and the next, unsung, line of the verse—
ending "All fall down"—to those who have succumbed to the terrible
illness.)

Notice how flexible the rhythm is in this performance, and how effective
are the frequent, rather extreme, changes of dynamic level. Also, consider how the barbershop harmonies affect the sound of Cohan's lighthearted song.

Jewish American songwriters dominated Tin Pan Alley's years—the period
between the two world wars, or from about 1920 to about 1945. Although
forming a small percentage of the population in the early years of the United
States, Jews had been actively involved as performing musicians and music
teachers in urban areas, and had contributed significantly to the popular song
industry from its beginning. As their population in this country increased dramatically, Jewish Americans made phenomenally successful careers in various
areas of show business, including popular song.

FIGURE 9.3

Irving Berlin.

Irving Berlin (1888–1989)

The long-lived **Irving Berlin** (Figure 9.3) was born Israel Baline in western Siberia, but his only memory of his native country was of himself lying huddled in a blanket, watching from the outskirts of town as Cossacks set fire to his Jewish neighborhood. His family fled Russia and settled in 1893 in a poor tenement in New York City. There the small boy began selling newspapers on the streets and soon became fascinated with the popular songs he heard pouring through the doors of busy taverns and cafés. Singing for pennies on street corners and in saloons, and as soon as he was old enough (eighteen) becoming a singing waiter, he soaked up the sounds that later emerged in his own hugely varied body of work: barroom ballads, ethnic songs, folk songs, novelty songs, ragtime, blues, and jazz.

While working on Tin Pan Alley as a song plugger, Berlin began to write songs for vaudeville and other forms of musical entertainment. Like most Tin Pan Alley composers, Berlin felt inspired by ragtime, though, as already noted, most "ragtime songs" only approximated the mood and style of ragtime without following ragtime's systematic opposition of a syncopated melody and an unsyncopated bass.

"Alexander's Ragtime Band" (Listening Example 31), written for a vaudeville show in 1911, became Berlin's first hit song. (Alexander was the name commonly applied to the leader of a black jazz band.)

Totally immersed in American popular music and music theater, Berlin went on to become one of the best-known, most popular, and most enduring of all American songwriters. A self-taught musician, he was comfortable only

---

Listening Example 31

"Alexander's Ragtime Band"

Composer
Irving Berlin

CD 1
Track 31
2:57

Meter
Duple. The mood is that of ragtime, and the rhythm is syncopated, but not in the systematic manner of ragtime.

Singer
Bessie Smith (see p. 200)

Accompaniment
Her Band—cornet, trombone, clarinet, piano, banjo. All the instrumentalists were outstanding players, but Coleman Hawkins (clarinet) and Fletcher Henderson (piano) became particularly well-known and influential jazz musicians.

—Continued

"Alexander's Ragtime Band"

Form

Verse-chorus

Bessie Smith ("empress of the blues") and Her Band improvise freely on Berlin's happy tune, like the irrepressible jazz musicians they are (see Chapter 12). The band plays a four-measure introduction, accompanies (and competes with) Bessie Smith as she sings, and plays a full chorus alone. Listen to the cornet imitate a bugle call, for example, when the lyrics refer to it, and play all around the melody during the instrumental chorus. Also note the reference to Stephen Foster's "Old Folks at Home" ("The Swanee River").

(Verse)

Oh my honey, oh, my honey,
You better hurry and let's go down there.
Ain'tcha goin'? Ain'tcha goin'?
To that leader man, ragged meter man?
Oh honey, oh honey,
Let me take you to
Alexander's grandstand, brass band.
Ain'tcha comin' along?

(Chorus)

Come on and hear, Come on and hear,
Alexander's Ragtime Band.
Come on and hear, come on and hear,
It's the best band in the land.
They can play the bugle call like you've never heard before,
Sounds so natural that you wanna go to war.
That's the bestest band in the land, oh honey lamb.
Come on along, come on along,
Let me take you by the hand,
Up to the man, up to the man,
Who's the leader of the band.
And if you care to hear "The Swanee River"
Played in ragtime
Come on and hear, come on and hear
Alexander's Ragtime Band!

The band plays a full chorus, and Smith sings the chorus once more.

playing on the black keys of the piano, so that he was limited to playing in one key—strangely, a key (G-flat or F-sharp) many pianists consider particularly difficult. This posed a problem, since a composer must be able to write in different tonalities to match the range of a singer's voice, or to add variety to a piece of some length by **modulating** (changing systematically) from one key to another. Different keys also seem to have varied effects, some sounding warm and rich, for example, and others cool and light, making one key more suitable than another for a particular song. So Berlin had a trick piano built on which he could slide a board to change mechanically the key in which he was playing while still using primarily the black keys on the keyboard.

Besides his prodigious music talent, Berlin also had a strong business mind. In 1914, he was one of a group of prominent music creators who founded the **American Society of Composers, Authors, and Publishers (ASCAP) to** ensure that music creators would be fairly compensated for the public performance of their works. Other early members included John Philip Sousa, Victor Herbert (see p. 314), and Jerome Kern (see p. 157). Today ASCAP, with over 175,000 member-owners, protects the rights of music creators, distributing billions of dollars in royalties and licensing performances of hundreds of thousands of international creators under reciprocal agreements all over the world. Musicians in every field—hip-hop, jazz, country, Latin, symphonic music, music theater, gospel, rock, electronic—all benefit immensely from the services of ASCAP.

In 1919, Irving Berlin formed his own publishing company, while continuing to write numerous songs, many of them for the Broadway stage. In the 1930s, he moved to Hollywood to write for movie musicals. During his long career, he wrote about 1,500 songs, nearly 1,000 of which remain in print.

There seemed no limit to the range of Berlin's talent or his musical imagination. While the rollicking tunes and jolly rhythms of many Berlin songs reveal his attraction to syncopated popular dance music, others, such as "Always," "How Deep Is the Ocean?" and "The Girl That I Marry," have a warm, romantic character. "White Christmas" is the most frequently recorded song of all time. His songs have become classics of American music, as much a part of American culture as any folk song. "A good song embodies the feelings of the mob," he once said. "And a songwriter is not much more than a mirror which reflects those feelings."

Berlin's patriotic song "God Bless America" has a curious history, having sparked controversy from the time singer Kate Smith introduced it in 1938. The public received the song with wild enthusiasm, and Berlin, thrilled, donated all royalties from it in perpetuity to the Boy Scouts and Girl Scouts of America; but liberal commentators attacked it as jingoistic, flag-waving, and sentimental, whereas on the right, according to a story in *Time* magazine in 1940, the song "brought on a wave of snide anti-Semitism directed at composer Berlin"—the composer, however, of America's most popular Christmas and Easter songs, "White Christmas" and "Easter Parade." Leftists attacked the song's lack of respect for separation of church and state, and right-wingers resented a non-Christian born in another country telling God to bless America. Yet not a few Americans enthusiastically proposed replacing "The Star Spangled Banner" with "God Bless America" as the national anthem.

A painter as well as a musician, Berlin passed his last years in quiet retirement, universally acknowledged—long before the world celebrated his hundredth birthday in 1988—as the elder statesman of American popular song.

Jerome Kern (1885–1945)

Born to a prosperous New York family, **Jerome Kern,** unlike his near contemporary Irving Berlin, had a sound music education. He studied in London for a time, composing songs for the British musical stage, and absorbing something of a European sound that would affect his music always. He intended, in fact, to become a composer of classical music but found himself irresistibly drawn to the popular musical theater and began writing songs for Broadway.

Kern's first songs were simply interpolated into British shows imported to Broadway, according to the custom of that day, when songs usually were unrelated to the plot of a show and therefore could be added or substituted at will. Many composers took advantage of the opportunity to write one or more songs for a show without having to be responsible for the entire score.

Like Berlin, Kern worked as a Tin Pan Alley song plugger and a rehearsal pianist for Broadway theaters before he began writing for his own shows (see Chapter 18, p. 318). His songs often resemble those of Irving Berlin, although many include more complex harmonies and sophisticated chord changes than had been used by Berlin and other early Tin Pan Alley songwriters. Also like Berlin, Kern wrote for Hollywood sound movies, finding them a congenial medium to introduce many of his finest late songs, including "The Last Time I Saw Paris" (from *Lady Be Good,* 1941) and "Long Ago and Far Away" (from *Cover Girl,* 1944). We shall consider music for theater and films in Chapters 18 and 19, but many of Tin Pan Alley's greatest hits, written for plays or movies that have been largely forgotten, still live prominent lives quite independent of the theatrical vehicles that launched them long ago.

Cole Porter (1892–1964)

The early life of **Cole Porter** (Figure 9.4), another major contributor to the golden age of American popular song (1920s–1950s), could hardly have differed more from Irving Berlin's. Wealthy, privileged, and very highly trained (in Paris under classical musicians), Porter took his career as a composer-lyricist seriously, working every bit as hard as anyone dependent upon his job for a living. His witty, sexy, sophisticated lyrics expressed basic human emotions in clever, fresh, and subtle ways—often so risqué as to earn him the nickname "the genteel pornographer."

The film *De-Lovely* (2004), a musical biography of Cole Porter's life, movingly portrayed this gifted, privileged, yet tortured man, who suffered physical pain after his legs were crushed in a horseback-riding accident in 1937, and emotional pain as a homosexual man living a double life. He indulged in numerous affairs with men and seems to have expressed some of his conflicting feelings in tantalizingly ambiguous song lyrics—for example: "It's the wrong game, with the wrong chips; Though your lips are tempting, they're the wrong lips. They're not her lips, but they're such tempting lips, That if some night you are free, Then it's all right, yes, it's all right with me," from

FIGURE 9.4

Cole Porter (1892–1964).

"It's All Right with Me" (1952). Yet Porter remained deeply devoted to his wife, who basically accepted him as he was. One of Porter's best-known songs, "Always True to You in My Fashion," may have been addressed to her: "But I'm always true to you, darlin', in my fashion; yes, I'm always true to you, darlin', in my way."

Unlike Berlin's tuneful melodies, many of Porter's sophisticated tunes are quite difficult to sing. Often extremely chromatic, they wind their stepwise way up and down the scale, arriving just where and when they should but posing hazards to the vocalist along the way. "I've Got You Under My Skin," "In the Still of the Night," "You Do Something to Me, "All of You," "Begin the Beguine," and "Just One of Those Things" all illustrate the narrow steps and chromatic intervals typical of a Porter melody; and "Night and Day" (Listening Example 32) makes clear why many musicians prefer to listen to Cole Porter than to perform his music. (Porter is said to have referred to creating a new melody as "delicious torture," a sentiment hardly likely to have been expressed by the practical, down-to-earth Irving Berlin.)

George Gershwin (1898–1937)

Born and bred in Brooklyn, New York, **George Gershwin** (Figure 9.5) worked as a song plugger on Tin Pan Alley while still a teenager, banging out tunes for singers and dancers. Soon his own tunes began attracting the attention of Broadway publishers, and before he was twenty he became a house songwriter for the T. B. Harms publishing firm, one of the most important on the street. An excellent pianist, Gershwin was also in demand as an accompanist for professional singers.

Listening Example 32

"Night and Day"

Composer
Cole Porter

CD 1
Track 32
3:18

Singer
Frank Sinatra

Form
Verse-chorus

Meter
Quadruple

Tempo
Moderately slow

Sinatra chose not to sing the verse here, but Fred Astaire can be heard singing the complete song on the Web. The verse, which says that "the beat, beat, beat of the tom-toms / when the jungle shadows fall" and "the tick-tick-tock of the stately clock / as it stands again the wall" remind the singer of "you, you, you," repeats one note thirty-three times and another note, a half-step higher, twenty-nine consecutive times, in a kind of sophisticated "word painting"—that is, musically expressing a verbal concept.

Fred Astaire introduced "Night and Day" in Porter's musical *Gay Divorcé* (1932), and despite the severely compressed vocal range and the tortuously chromatic melody, it was a sensation from the start. Here, the lush orchestral introduction and accompaniment, and Sinatra's dreamy mood, project the romantic atmosphere of the beautiful song. Yet Sinatra slightly alters the difficult melody—to accommodate musical taste or vocal limitations? If possible, listen to Fred Astaire's version, which is much closer to the song as Porter wrote it, and compare the two performances.

An early Gershwin song, "Swanee," written for a Broadway *revue* (a variety show—see p. 311) when he was twenty-one, received little attention until the popular singer Al Jolson (1888–1950) adopted it as a regular part of his performances. Jolson's dramatic, full-voiced singing style and impassioned delivery made the song an instant hit—the biggest hit song of his career—and brought Gershwin into great demand to write songs for the musical theater. During his short lifetime he wrote the scores for some 30 musicals and composed over 600 songs, many of which, including "Someone to Watch Over Me," "'S Wonderful," and "I Got Rhythm," were defined not only by Gershwin's beautiful melodies and complex harmonies, but also by clever lyrics written by George's brother

FIGURE 9.5
George Gershwin
(1898–1937). "True music
must repeat the thought and
inspirations of the people and
the time. My people are
Americans and my time is
today." (1925)

Ira. Ira Gershwin (1896–1983) wrote the words to one of George Gershwin's most beautiful melodies after his brother's death from a brain tumor at age thirty-nine. He titled this moving tribute to a beloved brother, which has become one of the Gershwins' best-known songs, "Our Love Is Here to Stay." The youngest Gershwin brother, Arthur, was also a songwriter, although he never became very well known.

Gershwin, like Berlin, Kern, and Porter, also wrote for Hollywood movies, bringing to them the same sophisticated skills he had honed on Broadway. But unlike the other great Tin Pan Alley songwriters, Gershwin had strong, even compelling interest in classical music and jazz. Although he was not a jazz musician himself, his musical language has the sounds and the flavor of jazz, and his songs lend themselves particularly well to jazz interpretations. (We will study jazz in Chapters 12, 13, and 14.) Gershwin's richly dissonant harmonies include sometimes humorous, sometimes plaintive turns and embellishments, making his music absolutely recognizable as his own; and his hauntingly beautiful melodies render his songs as meaningful and as well loved today as ever.

Decline of Tin Pan Alley

Several factors contributed to the gradual lessening of the influence of Tin Pan Alley on American popular music. Inevitably, popular taste began to change after half a century of domination by one powerful system. Sentimental songs that retained significance through the years of World War II became less relevant after the war was won, the troops were home, the economy boomed, and youthful tastes came to the fore. Humorous, nonsensical "novelty" songs accommodated the lightened mood;

Latin rhythms attracted wide audiences; songs from the country and from the West joined and in some cases replaced the urban song style that had dominated American popular music for so long.

Coincidentally, in 1940 ASCAP enforced a strike against the major radio networks, which would not meet ASCAP's demands for fees significantly higher than those currently paid. For over a year, pending settlement of the strike, radio stations could play no new recordings of Tin Pan Alley music. Desperate for new music to program, the stations readily accepted music offered by a newly formed organization, **Broadcast Music Incorporated (BMI),** whose members were generally younger than and largely unaffected by the professionals of Tin Pan Alley, and whose music reflected varied regional tastes.

The tide was about to turn, bringing a wave—many waves—of new sounds in popular music.

Terms to Review

ragtime   A written piano music, duple in meter, moderate in tempo. The left hand marks the beat while the right hand plays a syncopated melody.

chromaticism (chromatic, adj.)   Use of tones not belonging in a particular major or minor scale.

cakewalk   A plantation dance with syncopated melodies, including the *short-LONG-short* figure that became characteristic of ragtime.

finale   In music theater, the final scene of an act or of the show.

piano roll   A perforated paper roll on which pianists of the late nineteenth and early twentieth centuries recorded their performances.

player piano   An instrument for playing piano rolls by pumping pedals to force air through the holes in a piano roll as it wound over a tracker bar.

staccato   Short, detached.

two-step or **fox-trot**   A popular American dance derived from ragtime. The meter is duple, the rhythm syncopated, the tempo moderate.

Tin Pan Alley   The name for the popular-music publishing industry from the late nineteenth century through the first half of the twentieth. Also, the streets in New York City where the publishing houses were located.

song plugger   A music store employee who demonstrated popular music for customers by playing it on the piano and sometimes by singing it as well.

verse-chorus form   A common song form in which verses relating the song's story alternate with a tuneful chorus, or refrain.

barbershop style   Unaccompanied (traditionally male) voices singing popular songs in close harmony.

modulate   To change systematically from one key to another, usually by using one or more tones common to each key as a pivot.

American Society of Composers, Authors, and Publishers (ASCAP)   Organization formed in 1914 to ensure that music creators would receive fair compensation for public performance of their works.

Broadcast Music Incorporated (BMI)   A performing rights licensing agency formed in 1940 to represent a broader range of popular and alternative music than ASCAP seemed to serve.

Key Figures

Eubie Blake
James Scott
Jelly Roll Morton

Scott Joplin
James Reese Europe
Irving Berlin

Jerome Kern
Cole Porter
George Gershwin

Suggestions for Further Listening

Recordings of Tin Pan Alley songs performed by
    Joan Morris and William Bolcom, Frank Sinatra, Bing
    Crosby, Billie Holiday, or Ella Fitzgerald.

Suggestions for Viewing

De-Lovely, 2004. Metro-Goldwyn-Mayer film on the life
    of Cole Porter.

Critical Thinking

Do you think that Scott Joplin improved or damaged
ragtime by turning it from an improvised style to a written
piano music?

Discuss the reasons for the rise, and then the decline, of
Tin Pan Alley.

How do ASCAP and BMI affect the popular music
consumer today?

Go to www.mhhe.com/ferrisaml5 for a list of additional Web-based resources that relate to the content in this chapter.

Country Music

As various vernacular musics evolved in America's urban and rural environments throughout the nineteenth century, people living in certain remote areas of the eastern hills continued to sing and play their traditional music much as it had been performed in the countries and in the times of their ancestors. Relatively isolated from mainstream popular music and largely unaffected by modern trends, they passed the old tunes and performing customs from one generation to the next by oral tradition, thus faithfully preserving many early folk ballads—especially those, like "Barbara Allen" (Listening Example 5), brought to America from the British Isles.

After the Civil War, however, new influences invaded even isolated mountain areas, inevitably affecting the music as well as every other aspect of life. Migrant workers seeking jobs laying railroad lines, mining coal, or working for the textile mills being established in remote hill areas where tough union rules could safely be ignored brought new kinds of music and new musical instruments with them into the hills. Of particular significance was the five-string banjo, on which one string played a constant or repeated pitch, or **drone,** ideal for accompanying hill or country music (Figure 10.1).

Conversely, mountain people began to take temporary jobs in the cities, from which they brought home new subjects for songs and new musical sounds. Soon new "folk" songs evolved, similar to the traditional ballads but characteristically American in subject and style. Sometimes people lost track of the origin of a song, so that one included in the "folk" repertoire might actually have been composed rather than improvised, memorized, and passed down in the traditional way.

From Country to City

In the early 1920s, commercial recording companies began to send talent scouts into the hill country both to search for folk singers and instrumentalists with a distinctive sound and to entice country musicians to come to the cities, where the market for recordings of "old time" music was increasing. In 1925,

163

FIGURE 10.1

A musician playing a five-string banjo.

four musicians from Virginia recording under the name Hill Billies gave rise to the term **hillbilly music,** somewhat scornfully applied to the music of country fiddlers, harmonica players, and singers of traditional country ballads. For a time, "old-time," "hillbilly," and "country" all referred to the rich store of traditional music coming down from the hills.

Hill musicians traveled with tent shows, medicine shows, and vaudeville shows (see p. 309). They amazed audiences with their virtuosic performances at fiddlers' contests; and at country fairs they sang songs concerning the elemental subjects of human experiences—love, work, family life, death—in a semidetached, impersonal manner that made their music all the more moving. City listeners soon perceived the wealth of beauty and entertainment this unfamiliar style offered, and the audience for country music continued to expand.

As commercial radio evolved, hillbilly music proved widely popular, and "barn dance" radio shows sprang up not only in the South, but through the Midwest as well. The most famous of these shows, the **Grand Ole Opry,** which debuted on a station in Nashville, Tennessee, in 1924 and had much to do with the establishment of Nashville as a base for the country music industry, remains a vital country music institution today.

The trend toward popularity and commercialization, however, inevitably signaled the end of the old way—the oral tradition—of preserving original folk songs and performance practices. The commercial market required a constant supply of new pieces, and professional country musicians adapted to this demand by writing new songs and learning to perform them in a manner acceptable to a city audience. Story songs, or ballads, were particularly well received, and many were about dramatic topics of the day: a coal mine disaster, a murder, a hanging, the sinking of a famous ship. By the mid-1920s, as recordings of country music became widely available and brought the country sound to an ever wider audience, even hill people themselves began to lose track of which folk songs were traditional and which were created by modern professionals.

In 1927, two different strains of hillbilly music reached the public: one introduced by a soloist from the Deep South, and the other made popular by a singing family from the mountains of Virginia.

Jimmie Rodgers (1897–1933)

Jimmie Rodgers (Figure 10.2) came from Mississippi but wandered through several states in the course of his brief career. He had little formal training but many creative ideas, and he was willing to try anything suggested by the record producers who promoted him. Although accompanied on his recordings by various and unusual combinations of instruments, Rodgers probably was most effective when he accompanied himself on the guitar, providing appropriately simple support for his clear, pleasant tenor voice, which he sometimes used in the falsetto range. He also had a natural **yodel**—a rapid alternation between full voice and falsetto—later

FIGURE 10.2

Jimmie Rodgers and the Carter Family, pictured during a recording trip to Victor Studios in New Jersey.

imitated by many country singers. The thirteen songs called "blue yodels" for which Rodgers was particularly famous had the form and harmonies of the twelve-bar blues (see pp. 197–198), with his distinctive yodel added at the end of each verse, as in "Blue Yodel No. 9," Listening Example 33.

Known as the "singing brakeman," Rodgers drew on his experiences as a former railroad man for some of his songs. Others concerned love gone wrong, cowboys, the Southern home he missed, and country folk whom his listeners either recognized or idealized. While country songs more commonly paid homage to mother than to dad, Rodgers, whose mother died when he was only six, paid sentimental tribute to the father who raised him in "Daddy and Home" (an Optional Listening Example).

Although Rodgers performed professionally only for about six years, dying of tuberculosis at the age of thirty-six, he became extremely popular during his short career, during which he established the solo song as an important part of hillbilly music. He had the honor of becoming the first person elected to the Country Music Hall of Fame, established in Nashville, Tennessee, in 1961.

The Carter Family

The **Carter Family** (Figure 10.2) represented a different tradition from that of Jimmie Rodgers: Whereas he typified the hard-living solo wanderer, they symbolized the close, conservative family. Rodgers's relaxed, bluesy voice made the solo country song popular, while the Carters performed as a group, their harmony close and their voices tense.

Alvin Pleasant Delaney (A. P.) Carter (1891–1960), his wife Sara, and his sister-in-law (Sara's cousin) Maybelle, who came from the mountains of Virginia, sang traditional songs, ballads, and hymns in the rather pinched, nasal voices and the close, tight harmony characteristic of mountain people. They often favored the rhythms of ragtime and early jazz and even spiked their songs and their instrumental music with a zesty **backbeat** (accents on beats *two* and *four* instead of the usual *one* and *three*). Their varied song repertoire included topical ballads describing train wrecks and other notable disasters, and sentimental songs praising mountain flowers, simple country churches, and lovely pale maidens, as well as hymns and joyful camp meeting spirituals, such as "There'll Be Joy, Joy, Joy" (Listening Example 18).

The Carters accompanied themselves with guitar, on which Maybelle Carter developed considerable virtuosity; and with autoharp, a simple folk instrument whose strings are strummed or plucked with one hand while the other hand depresses buttons to form chords. Many of their recordings include fine instrumental breaks between the verses of a song, but "Chinese Breakdown" (Listening Example 34) is a rare example of a purely instrumental piece recorded by Maybelle and Sara Carter. Here Maybelle Carter demonstrates the now widely used "Carter scratch," a country guitar technique of picking a melody on the bass strings.

During the 1920s and 1930s, members of the Carter family collected, arranged, and recorded hundreds of American traditional songs, spirituals, and

Listening Example 33

Blue Yodel No. 9

Composer/Performer
Jimmie Rodgers

CD 2
Track 1
2:37

Form
Strophic, with a comfortably irregular number of bars per line and lines per stanza

Tempo
Moderately slow, "bluesy," relaxed

Accompaniment
Trumpet (Louis Armstrong) and piano (Lil Hardin, Louis Armstrong's first wife). The piano provides steady accompaniment, while the trumpet responds to and interacts with the voice.

After the six-measure trumpet and piano introduction, Jimmie Rodgers sings the first stanza, accompanied by the piano. Notice that the trumpet enters, usually just past the halfway point of a line, to offer instrumental response and commentary. The trumpet also answers Rodgers's yodel, interspersed between stanzas.

Standin' on the corner, I didn't mean no harm.
Along come a po'-lice, he took me by the arm.
It was down in Memphis, corner of Beale and Main.
He says, "Big boy, you'll have to tell me your name."

(Yodel)

The second stanza has three lines: one of six bars and two of four bars each. Again, the trumpet enters midway and completes the lines.

I said, "You'll find my name on the tail of my shirt; I'm a Tennessee
*   hustler, and I don't have to wait.*
Listen, all you rounders, you better leave my women alone,
'Cause I'll take my special and run all you rounders home."

After Rodgers's yodel, the trumpet takes a three-line twelve-bar verse, accompanied by the piano. The last stanza has four lines:

My good gal loves me, everybody knows.
And she paid one hundred cash dollars just for me a suit of clothes
She come to the joint, a forty-four in her hand.
She said, "Stand aside, all you women and men, 'cause I'm lookin' for
*   my man."*

Rodgers's yodel, then the expressive horn and steady piano, conclude the song.

Listening Example 34

"Chinese Breakdown"

Composers
The Carter Family

Meter
Duple

Style
Mountain music

CD 2
Track 2
1:02

This is the music bluegrass was based on: good-natured, virtuosic string playing, steady in tempo, happy in mood. Notice the marked backbeat (accents on *two* and *four*) in Sara Carter's autoharp, which accompanies Maybelle Carter's melody cleanly picked on the bass strings of the deeper, more mellow guitar.

folk songs, thereby laying the foundation for modern country music. Bluegrass, honky-tonk, Western swing, and rockabilly—all discussed in this chapter—are among the Carter Family's direct heirs. Further, several generations of Carters have continued to perform country music professionally. June Carter (1929–2003) became widely known in her own right as a singer who delivered great country songs, earthy or spiritual, with the plaintive wail of a mountain girl. Appearing regularly on Nashville's Grand Ole Opry in 1950, she befriended Elvis Presley and Hank Williams (she was godmother to Hank Williams, Jr., as well as to Roy Orbison's sons) and met **Johnny Cash** (1932–2003), who would become, in 1968, her third husband.

Johnny Cash, the "man in black" (who said in a song of that name in 1971 that he wore black to remind himself and his audiences of society's injustices), was never part of the country music establishment. With strong ties to rockabilly, in 1992 he was inducted into the Rock and Roll Hall of Fame, and he recorded his own versions of songs made famous by rap and heavy metal artists. But his best-known songs, including "I Walk the Line" and "The Green, Green Grass of Home," always sounded like country music. Cash, devoutly religious and strongly allied with many social movements and causes, can also be seen as country music's first protest singer, relating in his deep, virile, bass tones grievous injustices against prisoners, Indians, and innocents caught up in war. (Johnny Cash sings "The Ballad of Casey Jones," Listening Example 35.)

June Carter and Johnny Cash's daughter Roseanne Cash has been a major country music performer since the 1980s. She is a master at mixing country, folk, pop, and rock influences in her Grammy-winning music. Roseanne's stepsister Carlene, who kept the Carter name, carried her country music to England, where she recorded with assorted rockers. Today she continues to combine the sounds of rock and country in her own distinctive way.

Styles of Country Music

By the late 1920s, most Americans had radios, which brought hillbilly or old-time music and (white) religious country music, called **gospel** into homes across the country. (Black gospel music evolved in Northern urban African-American churches, where poor blacks, having migrated from the South, developed a new kind of religious songs and a way of singing them. Black gospel music acquired secular as well as religious association and richly affected black—and white—popular music; see p. 271.) Spiritual songs, well-loved from camp meeting days, found a new identity as part of the country music family. Thus the typical radio program of the 1920s included sentimental parlor songs (such as "I Dream of Jeanie with the Light Brown Hair," Listening Example 23), old English and American ballads (such as "Barbara Allen," Listening Example 5), work songs, and gospel hymns, performed by country singers, usually accompanied by a fiddle or banjo and sometimes by a guitar. String bands, consisting of several fiddles, one or more banjos and guitars, and sometimes a string bass, played rollicking dance tunes. Popular radio shows also included "dance songs," in which string bands alternated verses with a solo voice.

Country and folk musicians seem gifted with the ability to absorb and reflect in their music various eclectic influences and life experiences, thereby developing characteristic sounds, country in flavor but distinctive in style. Many kinds of rural music have evolved across America, reflecting local experience and preferences, thus producing a great body of modern country and folk musics of seemingly endless variety and charm. Some of this music reflects country people's perception of and reaction to the urban developments that change the country way of life: The opening of mines in the hill country, the building of highways through country fields, economic depressions, and the commercialization and urbanization of modern life, all spurred folk expression. Thus country music evolved as an urban, commercial expression of rural folk culture.

American Folk Ballads

Topical songs—personal stories relating current political or social events—have always had a place in American folk music, but their topical nature discouraged their survival beyond memories of the events they described, and few of those we remember today are much more than 100 years old. About the turn of the twentieth century, however, the growth in the trade union movement and passionate interest in numerous social causes produced a large number of topical songs, most of them aimed at city audiences rather than rural audiences, and most with a decidedly leftist bent. Throughout the early years of that century, railroads, representing progress and the future, acquired a sheen of glamour and proved a popular subject for ballads, including the very familiar "Wabash Cannon Ball," written and recorded by Roy Acuff in 1936. Although composed, written down, and commercially disseminated, such ballads had much of the flavor and appeal of the traditional folk ballads discussed in Chapter 2 and are reminiscent of the broadside ballads on topics relevant to an earlier age.

One of the most popular and enduring American ballads, "Casey Jones" (Listening Example 35), describes a train wreck that actually occurred in 1900—although not exactly as the song relates the tale. The famous ballad has an uncertain history: A laborer named Wallace Saunders (or Wallis Sanders), who had known and liked the engineer Casey Jones, seems to have set the story of the wreck to an old railroad song called "Jimmie Jones," altering the events, however, to advance the drama, thereby making Casey Jones a folk hero.

Saunders, who was black, never received a penny for the song, which white entertainers made into a grassroots hit and which in time acquired a catchy chorus, repeated after each verse. Today, a century after the famous crash occurred, this early American song lets us relive the heroic last moments of a flawed but courageous man, whose legend survives today.

Bluegrass

In the 1930s and 1940s, **Bill Monroe** (William Smith Monroe, 1911–1996) blended old-time string band music with the holler of the blues and the improvisation of jazz to create a music called (since the 1950s) **blue-grass,** a virtuosic instrumental style rooted in mountain music such as The Carter Family performed. This revival of a traditional music took its name from Monroe's string band, called the Blue Grass Boys (Figure 10.3), named for his home state of Kentucky, whose music on the radio and in recordings soon became widely popular and commercially important.

Bluegrass is unique among country musics, which consist mostly of song, in being primarily an instrumental concept. The bluegrass ensemble includes a fiddle, a guitar, a string bass, a five-string banjo, and often a mandolin—a popular Italian instrument that produces a delicate yet vibrant sound when its strings are plucked. The **acoustic,** or natural, instruments of a bluegrass band make the characteristic timbres light, but the fast tempos and virtuosic playing provide plenty of excitement.

Besides being a virtuoso performer on the mandolin, Monroe also set a new vocal standard with his haunting calls and high-pitched harmonies (the high

FIGURE 10.3

Bill Monroe playing the mandolin with his Blue Grass Boys at the Nightstage in Boston, MA.

"Casey Jones"

Words
Wallace Saunders

Tune
Anonymous

CD 2
Track 3
3:00

Singer
Johnny Cash

Accompaniment
Banjo, background
choral harmonies

Form
Verse-chorus

Meter
Four beats to the bar

Tempo
Fast

The engineer John Luther Jones, nicknamed Casey for his hometown—Cayce, Kentucky—had safely delivered the fast passenger express known as the Cannonball to Memphis, Tennessee. Tired from his long run from Canton, Mississippi, Jones intended to rest for the night; but learning that the engineer scheduled to run the Cannonball south was ill, Jones agreed to take over the run, which finally began an hour and a half late. Proud of his record for meeting schedules, Jones determined to make up the lost time and nearly succeeded in doing so by running his train at more than 100 miles an hour at a time when speeds of 70 or 80 miles an hour were considered highly daring for passenger trains. But his reckless speed caused him to miss signals warning that several cars of a derailed freight train lay sprawled across the tracks straight ahead of him. Had he slowed as he properly should have, approaching the end of his run, a collision could have been averted; but Jones saw the danger too late, commanded his fireman to save himself by jumping off the train, and stayed in the cab himself to meet certain death. Desperately squeezing the throttle and brakes to slow the train to less than 50 miles an hour before it finally slammed into the train ahead, he spared his passengers injury, and all escaped unharmed.

A mournful train whistle, followed by a percussion instrument's rhythmic "chugging," introduces the ballad. The banjo sets the beat, and Johnny Cash sings the first verse. A small group of singers provide background harmonies and sing the first phrase ("Casey Jones") of the chorus.

The banjo plays brief interludes between each chorus and the next verse, emphasizing the stirring backbeat.

Notice the rise in key level for the second half of the second verse, with a corresponding rise in emotional tension. (Chorus.)

In the third verse, Cash momentarily abandons the melody to dramatize his tale with a kind of dramatic declamation. (Chorus.)

The last verse features another rise in key. We hear the chorus, and the train whistle returns to end the ballad as it began.

lonesome sound) based on hymn-singing techniques learned in his youth, as heard in "It's Mighty Dark to Travel" (an Optional Listening Example). However, even with bluegrass ballads, sung in the high tones and with the close mountain harmony introduced to urban music by the Carters, the emphasis is on important instrumental interludes or breaks. No less than other country musics, bluegrass has absorbed varied influences and adapted its sound to suit evolving tastes. The verse-chorus form of bluegrass ballads reflects the style of Tin Pan Alley; the virtuosic instrumental playing owes homage to jazz; the manner in which Monroe and his musicians sometimes took turns playing lead and making virtuoso displays suggests the inspiration of western swing (see p. 176).

The virtuosic performances in Listening Example 36 ("Earl's Breakdown") reveal the reasons bluegrass remains among the most appreciated styles of country music today. The musicians **Lester Flatt** (guitar) and **Earl Scruggs** (banjo), who left Bill Monroe's Blue Grass Boys in 1948 to form their own

Listening Example 36

"Earl's Breakdown"

Composer
Earl Scruggs

CD 2
Track 4
3:00

Instruments
Guitar (Lester Flatt), banjo (Earl Scruggs), mandolin, fiddle, bass

Form
Variations on a tune

1. The banjo presents the tune, which has two parts, acompanied by the other instruments. In the second part (beginning at 0:15), Scruggs uses a tuner to bend the pitches expressively.
2. (0:29) The fiddle offers virtuosic variations on both parts of the tune.
3. (0:58) Scruggs takes the tune back, with chromatic variations, again bending the strings in his distinctive style.
4. (1:26) The fiddle ranges ever more widely in pitch, treating only the first half of the tune.
5. (1:41) The banjo takes another turn, introducing a new picking style.

As the instruments continue to treat the versatile tune in a creative, virtuosic manner, listen attentively to all of them, including those playing stimulating accompaniment to the exciting solo performances. A good bluegrass musician knows when to shine as the performing star, and when to enhance a colleague's playing by providing creative and appropriate backup; and a good bluegrass listener appreciates every line of music.

group (the Foggy Mountain Boys), developed a distinctive style of bluegrass, and greatly popularized this stimulating country music: The smooth vocal harmony of Flatt and Scruggs's band, as well as Scruggs's dazzling banjo technique and Flatt's guitar trick called the Lester Flatt G-run, in which the guitar concludes another instrument's solo break with a strong bass figure, all attracted a wider audience to classic bluegrass. Monroe strongly resented the success of Flatt and Scruggs, but during the folk revival of the early 1960s (see p. 187), he accepted the title they and other young musicians bestowed on him: "father of bluegrass." Monroe continued to perform at the Grand Ole Opry until shortly before he died.

During the 1960s, the vibrant sound of the acoustic string instruments and the brilliant playing of the instrumentalists made bluegrass particularly popular on college campuses, in coffeehouses, and at folk festivals around the country. Bluegrass has flavored television shows—*Beverly Hillbillies* (theme song by Flatt and Scruggs), *Petticoat Junction, Green Acres*—and films: *Bonnie and Clyde,* and the famous "Dueling Banjos" of *Deliverance,* for example. In 1954, Elvis Presley recorded a revved-up rockabilly version of Monroe's song "Blue Moon of Kentucky." More recent references to bluegrass include Steve Wariner's "Domino Theory" (1990), sung in the high-pitched tones of mountain music and accompanied by mandolin, steel guitar, and fiddles. The title cut of Vince Gill's album *High Lonesome Sound* (1996) beautifully updated the traditional bluegrass sound. In 1995, the songwriter-singer-instrumentalist Steve Earle accompanied "Train a-Comin'" with unamplified instruments only, and his CD *The Mountain* (1999), on which he played his songs accompanied by the Del McCoury Band (mandolins, banjos, guitars, fiddles, and upright basses) became a standard-bearer of contemporary bluegrass.

The film "O Brother, Where Art Thou?" (2000) and its soundtrack brought bluegrass, gospel, and other "old-time" music to large numbers of new enthusiasts, providing a market for the music of young and middle-age musicians who like to perform traditional music. Today's performers in bluegrass style include Alison Krauss and Emmylou Harris, among many others. Alison Krauss, a fiddle virtuoso from Illinois, sings with a silvery voice that lacks the regional accent and twang distasteful to many younger listeners; Emmylou Harris has had a long and varied career as a folk and country music revivalist.

Recently several bands, including one from New England called Northern Lights, have gained national attention playing tight instrumentals and close-knit harmonies in so-called *newgrass* style. The movement began in the early 1970s, when some rock and jazz musicians began to share the instrumental techniques of bluegrass music. Combining some of the rhythmic and harmonic complexities of jazz (Chapter 12) and classical music with lyrical melodies and often a good dose of humor, such versatile musicians as John Prine, Lyle Lovett, and Jerry Garcia may be said to have made newgrass their common sound. The singer, songwriter, and multi-instrumentalist John Hartford, one of the architects of the newgrass movement (but best known for his hit song "Gentle on My Mind" and his appearance in *O Brother, Where Art*

Thou?), chose to make what he knew would be his last album (*Hamilton Ironworks,* 2001) a collection of traditional fiddle tunes played in bluegrass style. (Hartford died later in 2001.)

Today's best-known bluegrass singer and band, Alison Krauss and Union Station, have won many awards and maintain a seemingly nonstop schedule of performances. The outstanding solo musicians in this band include Jerry Douglas, a virtuoso performer on the **Dobro**—a wood-body resonator guitar with a metal cover plate over the sound hole and an aluminum cone for amplification. An accomplished composer as well as a gifted performer, Douglas has become known all over the world, and the Gibson guitar company has named a Dobro model after him.

And so the old style, rooted in rural traditions, enjoys new life in various versions today. The passionate fans who gather each summer at bluegrass festivals around the country burn with a zeal approaching that of the faithful attending old-fashioned religious camp meetings.

Country Pop and the Nashville Sound

Country music achieved wide popularity in the 1940s. During the war years, Northern GIs at Southern training camps had their first exposure to hillbilly music, and many were captivated by the sound; and soldiers from various regions of this country stationed together in Europe often found country music their favorite. The war also caused an exodus of Southern whites, who took their music with them to new work and living sites in the North and West. In 1947 the Grand Ole Opry staged a two-night performance at Carnegie Hall in New York City with astounding success.

However, when rock and roll exploded on the popular music scene in the early 1950s (Chapter 16), the country music industry faced imminent disaster. Country singers did not immediately abandon traditional styles, of course, but recording executives and performers soon realized that two new audiences needed to be addressed: youngsters excited by the new sounds of rock and roll, and urban adults uncomfortable with the raw sounds of traditional country music. Both audiences resisted country music instrumentation—the hillbilly fiddle and the wailing steel guitar—but accepted country songs if accompanied by an electric guitar and drums (for young people) or piano and strings (for adults).

After World War II, teenagers, white and black alike, preferred to invest their spending money in the new music inspired by the music young blacks enjoyed—rhythm and blues (see pp. 271–272). As rock and roll increasingly dominated the popular music market, the audience for traditional country music fell away: record sales decreased and radio listeners vanished. **Rockabilly,** the style in which the exciting new singing sensation Elvis Presley performed, responded to the new threat by combining country themes with the rhythms and instrumentation of rock and roll.

When RCA records opened independent studios in Nashville in the late 1950s, **Chet (Chester Burton) Atkins** (1924–2001), one of the most admired and influential guitarists in the world, was appointed head of the Nashville division and set out to change the sound of country music. The unexpected but undeniable commercial success of Patti Page's recording of "Tennessee Waltz" (1950, a song inspired by the popularity of Bill Monroe's recording of "Kentucky Waltz" in 1948) moved Atkins to acknowledge the advisability of obscuring the boundaries between country and pop and producing songs that would score on both the popular and the country music charts. Intending to establish an "easy-listening" country sound, Atkins toned down rhythm sections and added background voices to soften the harsh effect of traditional country music. The sophisticated, polished sound he achieved became known as the **Nashville sound.**

Nashville had been the preeminent center of the country music business since 1942, when Roy Acuff (1903–1992)–a mountain boy from east Tennessee who symbolized the link between old-time early-morning radio, medicine shows, and hotel-room recording sessions on the one hand and modern commercial country music on the other—founded the first modern music publishing company there. Now Nashville met the threat of rock and roll by combining country themes with pop instrumentation. Nashville soloists singing of traditional country topics jived up their rhythms and often added a background chorus of voices singing not in the close mountain harmony of the Carters but in a trained professional style, much like the doo-wop singers of Motown rock and roll (pp. 277–278). Chet Atkins sang country songs and played his guitar in a style close to that of Tin Pan Alley.

Thus some country musicians modified their twang and polished their performances, presenting country-style songs in a pop format in order to survive as commercial entertainers. Soon **cover recordings** of country hits, made by Tony Bennett, Frankie Laine, and other popular singers, appeared on the popular music charts. The smooth voices and polished styles of Eddy Arnold and Jim Reeves, often accompanied by a string orchestra, also represented country pop.

As the strong rhythm and lively instrumentation of recordings by Johnny Cash attracted members of the rock and roll audience, and Tennessee Ernie Ford's recording of "Sixteen Tons" (written by the brilliant country guitarist Merle Travis) soared rapidly to the top of the best-selling charts, other country artists felt compelled to modify their styles by adopting techniques of rock and roll. Some Nashville soloists substituted a "hot" guitar for their banjos and mandolins. Their instruments now included electric guitars, drums, and electric bass as well.

By the early 1960s, the success of Chet Atkins's Nashville sound and of country pop in general caused Nashville to become, with New York City and Hollywood, a recording capital of popular music. Country's flirtation with rock and roll faded in the 1960s, but country pop has flourished in the early years of the twenty-first century. Faith Hill, Shania Twain, Tim McGraw, Randy Travis, George Strait, and Garth Brooks—among others—enjoy huge popular and financial success in the field today.

Country Goes Western

Even before bluegrass and the Nashville sound established their popularity in the Eastern United States, country music moved west, where it developed further distinctive styles. In the 1930s, people displaced from their jobs by the economic turmoil of the Great Depression, or forced to abandon farms located in the drought-stricken Dust Bowl, left their accustomed environments and roamed west, carrying with them their traditional music customs, if little else. This kind of forced migration continued in the 1940s, during World War II, as people leaving familiar rural areas to find jobs in the cities brought along their taste for country music. Young people in the armed services had an unprecedented opportunity to associate with others from diverse backgrounds, and many from the city discovered they liked the country music sound.

As the Western states welcomed and absorbed country music, they added distinctive flavors of their own. Texans reflected the *mariachi* sounds of Mexico, the Cajun music of Louisiana, the Hawaiian steel guitar, and the songs of lonesome cowboys in their own versions of country music, which may properly be called **country-western.**

Western Swing Whereas country music in the Eastern United States generally reflected the conservative mood and morality of the Christian home, the Western country flavor was closer to that of the dance hall. Texans responded to the big band craze of the 1930s and 1940s (see pp. 213–214) with a dance band style of their own, called **western swing:** To the piano, sax, brasses, and jazz rhythm section of the Eastern big band, Texans added fiddles and the steel guitar, while their singers added yodeling in the style of Jimmie Rodgers. Fast tempos, hot rhythms, and wonderfully virtuosic instrumental solos also indicated a strong jazz influence on western swing.

Bob Wills (1905–1973, Figure 10.4), the major figure in the development of western swing, performed country fiddle tunes, Hispanic folk music, African American folk blues, jazz—and more. His band, the Texas Playboys, fluctuated in membership and in numbers over the years but always featured musicians of talent and accomplishment. Wills, who played fiddle and mandolin, punctuated the band's performances with jive talking, falsetto asides, and cries of "ah-ha!" as heard in "New San Antonio Rose" (Listening Example 37), his signature tune. Wills's innovative combination of horns, fiddles, and steel guitar grabbed the public's ear, and "New San Antonio Rose" became a huge national success in the 1940s.

Bob Wills and the Texas Playboys played straight fiddle tunes, cowboy numbers, hit parade songs, jazz instrumentals, blues numbers, Mexican music, and more. Mixing all these styles together presaged the tendency of today's popular musicians to achieve an eclectic mix of various musics—including western swing. Today the wildly exciting Hot Club of Cowtown, for example, combines Bob Wills's western swing with the hot stylings of a French jazz violinist (Stephane Grappelli) to produce a swinging music suited for dance and fun.

FIGURE 10.4
Bob Wills.

Listening Example 37

"New San Antonio Rose"

Composer
Bob Wills

Performers
Bob Wills and His Texas Playboys

CD 2
Track 5
2:33

Meter
Four beats per measure

Form
A series of strains (**A, B,** and **C**) in the order **ABABCACA.**

After a four-measure introduction by the horns, typical of swing dance band music, the horns play **A** in a relaxed fox-trot style (16 measures).

The horns play **B;** then **A** returns (0:22)/(0:43), sung this time, with saxophone accompaniment. The vocal continues with **B** ("It was there I found beside the Alamo . . .")

(1:20) A new strain, **C** ("Moon in all your splendor"), is sung, accompanied by trumpets, adding a *mariachi* (Mexican) flavor to the sound.

(1:38) The vocal continues with **A** ("Broken song, empty words I know . . ."), accompanied by saxes and percussion.

(1:56) The *mariachi* trumpets play **C,** then **A** (2:14), and a concluding measure.

Honky-Tonk While Texas dance halls rang with the sounds of western swing bands, another country-western style developed in the intimate Texas bars and clubs called honky-tonks. The patrons in these small crowded rooms were more interested in listening than dancing to the **honky-tonk** songs, which addressed in the frankest terms harsh subjects relevant to the experience of returning servicemen and uprooted or separated families: infidelity, divorce, alcohol, home sickness, separation, loneliness, prison. Singers delivered the rough, realistic lyrics in an earthy, matter-of-fact manner typical of the country style.

Accompanying bands, if any, had a distinctive instrumentation borrowed from the blues, jazz, or Hawaiian ensembles, but electrified in order to be heard in the noisy honky-tonks. An amplified piano, loud enough to carry above the noise of rough drinking crowds, often provided the sole accompaniment. Electrification, in fact, proved essential to honky-tonk music, and nearly all the instruments—even the fiddle—were likely to be electrified in the honky-tonk band.

Historically, the stars of honky-tonk were white men from the Southwest, including Ernest Tubb, Lefty Frizzell, Buck Owens, Merle Haggard, George Jones, and George Strait. However, Charley Pride, the only black country music performer to have a long and distinguished career, has found honky-tonk a congenial medium, as have the Hispanic singers Freddie Fender and Johnny Rodriguez. Greatest of all honky-tonk stars was probably **Hank Williams, Sr.** (1923–1953), though Williams cannot be confined to one style: Blending blues, gospel, mountain music, and honky-tonk, he became a legendary figure in country music, as influential as Jimmie Rodgers and as passionately admired. At the time of his early death, Williams was the best-known and most financially successful country singer.

For a time, honky-tonk shied away from the wrenching honesty that, like the blues (pp. 196–203), helped its listeners confront hard times and even death. But recent honky-tonk responds to the new public frankness on subjects such as sex, drugs, and violence with strong new lyrics, often delivered by female singers.

Cowboy Songs From the time of the earliest talking pictures, Americans flocked to western films, and by the mid-1930s the craze for westerns was full-blown. Films portrayed the West as Hollywood envisioned it: full of wide-open spaces, dramatic scenery, beautiful and virtuous women, and despicable villains, invariably vanquished by brave and handsome cowboys—many of whom sang romantic cowboy songs.

Some of the Hollywood singing cowboys actually were from the West. Gene Autry, born near Tioga, Texas, in 1907, was working as a telegraph operator when, one night in 1927, the great humorist Will Rogers overheard him singing and strumming his guitar and encouraged him to try his luck in New York. Unsuccessful in New York, Autry got a job with a radio station in Tulsa, where he was known as "Oklahoma's yodelin' cowboy," a tribute to the "singing (and yodeling) brakeman" Jimmie Rodgers. A good businessman as well as a highly talented musician, Autry started his own publishing company and film production company and became the first movie star to get into television. Today the Autry Western Heritage Museum in Los Angeles, California, presents a multiethnic history of the American West and its impact on pop culture.

Tex Ritter, another famous singing cowboy, also came from Texas; but many of the songs he, Autry, and other "cowboys" sang were written by Tin Pan Alley professionals. Among the most famous of these were "Tumbling Tumbleweeds" (featured as a tremulous harmonica solo in the film *City Slickers* in 1991) and "Cool Water," both written by Bob Nolan, a founding member of a famous singing trio called the Sons of the Pioneers. Most of the songs sung by Roy Rogers, who, like Autry, starred in about 100 western films, were also written by Nolan. Of course there were real cowboy songs as well, many of them with lilting Irish tunes to which nineteenth-century immigrant Irish cowboys set new words describing life on the American range. These, together with the songs composed for western films, became part of the country-western repertoire.

By the late 1940s, cowboy songs had largely faded in popularity. Gene Autry, who earlier had recorded songs from the African American blues tradition ("Black Bottom Blues," "Wild Cat Mama," and "Traveling Blues," for example), went on to sing songs in the popular rather than the western vein. (He is best known today for "Here Comes Santa Claus," which he cowrote with Oakley Haldeman; and "Rudolph, the Red-Nosed Reindeer," written by Johnny Marks.) Tex Ritter's biggest hit, "High Noon" (written by Dimitri Tiomkin), was high on the pop charts rather than the roll of country-western hits.

The western sound that Autry helped popularize has experienced something of a revival, however, partly spurred by movies such as *Sleepless in Seattle* (1993), which included "Back in the Saddle" (cowritten by Ray Whitley and Gene Autry) on its multiplatinum soundtrack, and *The Horse Whisperer* (1998). The simple melodies and straightforward lyrics of country-western songs often appeal to listeners who are less comfortable with the electronics and indecipherable words of some popular musics.

Women in Country

The road life, honky-tonk settings, and all-male bands typical of country music did not encourage participation by women, at least during the first half of the twentieth century, when women's seemly, or proper, place in American society was quite rigidly defined. Most of the women who made early successful careers in country music were heavily influenced by pop stars and may be seen as crossover artists bridging country and pop: Thus **Patsy Cline** (1932–1963), who came from a country background and had a strident, powerful country sound, gained high positions on both pop and country charts. Kitty Wells, known as the "queen of country music" through the 1950s, faced strong competition from a number of great female singers in the succeeding decade.

Loretta Lynn, who also favored honky-tonk instrumentation, and who appealed to beleaguered housewives with such songs as "The Pill," perhaps had the strongest claim to inherit Wells's title.

In the 1990s, women established a commanding, even dominant, presence in country music, both as writers and as singers of "new country." Mary Chapin Carpenter and Reba McIntyre, among others, broke new ground by singing country-style songs about contemporary city people. Mixing old-fashioned values and country instrumentation with frank sexuality and samplings of other vernacular sounds, women, including Shania Twain, LeAnn Rimes, Deana Carter, and Mindy McCready, have reigned securely at the top of the country charts. For much of the summer of 2000, Lee Ann Womack's single "I Hope You Dance" (on an album of the same name) was the top country single.

Harmony singing, too, has shown a new strong female influence. Close, tight country music harmonies between a man and a woman, as in the duets of George Jones and the late Tammy Wynette, or Porter Wagoner and Dolly Parton, constituted a kind of musical dialogue, the combination of enormously different but compatible voices implying sexual tension, resolved or not. But even more characteristic of country harmonizing are same-sex combinations, in which the blending of voices is tantalizingly close. The somewhat unlikely collaboration of Dolly Parton, Emmylou Harris, and Linda Ronstadt put three enormously talented but strikingly different country singers together in an amazingly successful sound. Growing up, **Dolly Parton** sang traditional ballads and gospel songs with her eleven brothers and sisters. Besides her pure, clean soprano voice, she also has a genuine talent for songwriting. **Emmylou Harris**'s background is more diversified, but she now sings country songs with a rare combination of strength and fragility. **Linda Ronstadt,** from the Southwest, has a background in Mexican and Spanish music and began her career singing rock and roll. A true crossover artist, she has sung operetta and classical songs, but since the 1970s seems to have settled on country. All three women have a wide range of emotional expression, and their combined vocal talents are impressive indeed. Their first album, *Trio,* released in 1987 (including "To Know Him Is to Love Him" by Phil Spector), is an outstanding example of traditional harmony singing. As a point of interest, one song on another album, "After the Gold Rush," is accompanied by synthesizer, strings, and a glass harmonica (see p. 69).

Recent Country

More sophisticated in performance and broader in scope than ever, country music continues to hold a wide audience, as "new country" vies with "traditional country" on radio stations and in the hearts of country music lovers. Successful releases by Dwight Yoakam, George Strait, and other popular country singers have come out of California, which competes with Nashville for influence in the country market, as country music faces a veritable identity crisis, challenged by traditionalists (mostly in Nashville) on one hand and modernists (many in California) on the other. In 2000, at the Academy of

Country Music Awards (based on the West Coast), George Strait and Alan Jackson performed "Murder on Music Row" (Music Row refers to Nashville, where the Country Music Association presents its own annual awards), a stinging indictment of all that West Coast people find wrong with country radio today: "The steel guitars no longer cry and the fiddles barely play, but drums and rock-and-roll guitar are mixed up in your face." Songs such as the Kentucky Headhunters' hit "Rock 'n' Roll Angel" illustrate a new confidence that allowed country musicians in the 1990s to refer good-humoredly to their formerly dreaded competition. Yoakam and others regularly give the hillbilly twang a happy rock-and-roll spin.

A new activism appears in the music of some country stars: the Dixie Chicks famously criticized the president of the United States, and in 2002 Toby Keith expressed the opposing point of view with his song "Courtesy of the Red, White, and Blue." (The musicians paid for their frankly expressed views with lost performance opportunities.)

A new traditionalism leads other country stars to replace synthesizers, string sections, and pop drumbeats with acoustic guitars and fiddles, and some seek to recapture the friction and grit of original honky-tonk. Fiddling and banjo contests regularly draw huge crowds to folk festivals and state fairs. The catch in the throat, the plink of a mandolin, the woozy swoop of a steel guitar, even a modest mountain twang have returned to current country; and western swing, and—especially—bluegrass have a strong presence in country music today. The bluegrass influence is apparent in the music of many outstanding country musicians who combine various styles of their choice to create music of their own. We have already mentioned Alison Krauss, who blends bluegrass, jazz, rock, and folk; and Jerry Douglas, who performs bluegrass, rock and roll, jazz, blues, and classical music on his Dobro. Bela Fleck does amazing things with bluegrass, jazz, classical, and rock on his five-string banjo. The virtuoso fiddler Mark O'Connor blends bluegrass with funk and jazz. All these current musicians can be found on the Web, often with clips of their music available at the click of a mouse.

Here, it is time for you to leave the textbook and, using the names offered above as starting points, explore country music in your world today.

Terms to Review

drone   A single tone, sounded continuously or repeated many times.

hillbilly music   A term applied to early country music.

Grand Ole Opry   The world's longest-running radio show, which began as a barn-dance radio program in Nashville, Tennessee, in 1925 and continues to present country music's top performers.

yodel   A singing technique that involves changing rapidly back and forth between the normal and falsetto voices.

backbeat   A heavy accent on the normally weak second and fourth beats of a measure in quadruple meter.

gospel   A folklike religious music. White gospel includes camp meeting spirituals; black gospel has had far more influence on popular music.

bluegrass   A commercial instrumental style, for acoustic instruments, derived from mountain music.

acoustic   A natural, as opposed to electric, instrument.

Dobro   A wood-body guitar with a metal resonator and an aluminum cone for amplification.

rockabilly   A close amalgamation of country music and rock and roll.

Nashville sound   Country music's commercial response to rock and roll, with country themes, pop instrumentation, and a heavy beat.

cover recording (cover)   A rerecording of a popular record, sometimes intended to appeal to a broader audience than the original recording addressed.

country-western   Western music with a country flavor.

western swing   The Texas swing band style, influenced by Mexican and Hawaiian sounds and by jazz.

honky-tonk   A Texas vocal style, featuring harsh, honest lyrics.

Key Figures

Jimmie Rodgers
The Carter Family
Johnny Cash
Bill Monroe
Lester Flatt

Earl Scruggs
Chet Atkins
Bob Wills
Hank Williams
Patsy Cline

Loretta Lynn
Dolly Parton
Emmylon Harris
Linda Ronstadt

Optional Listening Examples

Jimmie Rodgers: "Daddy and Home"

Bill Monroe: "It's Mighty Dark to Travel" (early bluegrass)

Suggestions for Further Listening

The Smithsonian Collection of Classic Country Music
The Unbroken Circle: The Musical Heritage of the Carter Family (Dualtone, 2004)
O Brother, Where Art Thou (2000, soundtrack of the film)

Albums by Hot Club of Cowtown (western swing)
Albums by Mark O'Connor (fiddle)
  Bela Fleck (banjo)
  Jerry Douglas (Dobro)
  Alison Krauss and Union Station

Suggestion for Viewing

DVD: *O Brother, Where Art Thou?* (2000)

Suggestion for Reading

Mark Zoonitzer with Charles Hirschberg, *Will You Miss Me When I'm Gone: The Carter Family and Their Legacy in American Music* (Simon & Schuster, 2001).

Critical Thinking

What do you think has caused many country musicians to seek to "return to the roots" of country music?

Do you prefer traditional country or modern interpretations? Why?

Do you prefer acoustic (bluegrass) music or electrified (honky-tonk) style? Why?

Why does country seem to lend itself to describing life's most elemental feelings and experiences? Is it the instrumentation? Regional accent? Rhythm? Delivery style? Something else?

Go to www.mhhe.com/ferrisaml5 for a list of additional Web-based resources that relate to the content in this chapter.

Ethnic Traditions and the Urban Folk Revival

Country music characteristically absorbs ethnic and regional styles, adapting them to become a part of the country sound. Thus as people in the Western states welcomed country music, they naturally added distinctive flavors derived from their own experience. Hawaiian music, for example, reached the Western states and eventually moved east across the mainland, becoming an important component of country-western music. Texans' country music also reflected sounds from their neighbors to the south and east: the *mariachis* of Mexico and Louisiana's Cajun music and zydeco.

Hawaiian Music

Hawaiian music, rooted in old religious chants and hymns, absorbed rhythms, sounds, and instruments brought to Hawaii by missionaries, tourists, and settlers from many other lands. Particularly, Hawaiians enjoyed the guitar, brought by Mexican cowboys in the mid-1800s, adapting the instrument, however, to accompany hula and Hawaiian songs and hymns. By loosening (slackening) the strings, Hawaiians invented the **slack key guitar,** giving the instrument a characteristic resonance and allowing new styles of fingering and picking. Charles Philip "Gabby" Pahinui (1921–1980), the acknowledged master of the slack key guitar, acquired fans around the world for his virtuosic style of Hawaiian music.

The Hawaiian **steel guitar** is even better known and has had more influence on various country musics. This instrument, with metal strings raised above the fret board, is held horizontally in the lap. The player presses a steel bar against the strings, rather than pressing them to the fret board with the fingers as on a traditional guitar; and by sliding the metal bar along the strings with the left hand, the player achieves a gentle slide, suggestive of and congenial to a country twang. Invented and popularized in Hawaii around the turn of the twentieth century, the steel guitar caused a sensation at the Panama-Pacific International Exposition of 1915 in San Francisco, and from there it spread throughout the United States, exerting a profound and lingering influence on country music. By the end of the 1930s, the Hawaiian steel guitar—electrified or acoustic—

FIGURE 11.1
A ukulele.

was well established in Southwestern country bands and was becoming a part of Southeastern country music as well.

The **ukulele,** a small guitar with four strings, also attracted much enthusiasm at the Panama-Pacific Exposition, where the Hawaiian Pavilion featured Hawaiian songs, hula, and instrumental music. Portuguese immigrants brought the ukulele to Hawaii in 1879, and according to one legend, Hawaiians, enchanted at the way fingers flew over the strange new instrument, called it "ukulele," meaning "jumping fleas." By the 1920s, as Hawaiian music became hugely popular on the mainland, Tin Pan Alley performers accompanied many of their songs with a ukulele. Interest waned for a time, but recent years have seen ukulele festivals sprout up not only in Hawaii, but on the mainland as well: the Northern California Ukulele Festival and the Uke Festival in Massachusetts draw large crowds every year.

Hawaiian music, popular in its own right, also has profoundly affected mainland country music (and pop). Songs such as "Hawaiian Wedding Song" and "Blue Hawaii" wooed a receptive audience, and the steel guitar, slack key guitar, and ukulele have played a more subtle but vital role in promoting country music.

Cajun Music

Evicted by the British from their homeland in Acadia (Nova Scotia) in the mid-eighteenth century, the French Acadians (later called Cajuns) sought asylum in the bayous of Southwest Louisiana, finally settling in a remote area south of New Orleans. There, relatively isolated from most of American society, they continued to speak French, slowly evolving a *patois,* or mixed language, of their own.

The success of hillbilly recordings in the 1920s sent record companies' talent scouts to Louisiana searching for additional regional styles to record, and soon outstanding Cajun musicians were attracting an enthusiastic listening public. In 1932, as national record companies actively promoted commercial recordings of regional music, a folklorist named **John Lomax** (1867–1948) also traveled to Louisiana, where he recorded genuine traditional Cajun music for the Library of Congress. Meanwhile, however, radio brought new musical influences, such as blues and hillbilly, to Cajun regions, and Cajun musicians began to follow the example of Jimmie Rodgers, the Carter Family, and later Bob Wills, often translating popular country and country-western songs into French. Thus the Texas-Cajun influence was in fact a two-way affair.

Although the sensitive listener may detect a hint of tragedy in **Cajun music,** the sound is prevailingly lighthearted, with dance rhythms and catchy melodies dominated by the wonderfully raucous sound of the accordion. The Cajun accordion, with ten melody buttons (instead of piano keys) on one side and two bass accompaniment buttons on the other, produces a loud, vibrant sound requiring singers to produce a high, strained tenor voice that will carry over the roaring accordion and droning fiddles. Often one hears shouts ("Oh, ya, yaie!") reminiscent of bluegrass sounds.

Cajuns particularly enjoy waltzes and other dances, such as the two-step in Listening Example 38, which they perform with rhythms and timbres as spicy as their highly seasoned food.

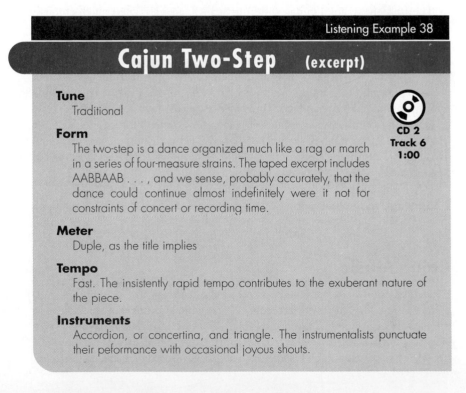

Listening Example 38

Cajun Two-Step (excerpt)

CD 2
Track 6
1:00

Tune
Traditional

Form
The two-step is a dance organized much like a rag or march in a series of four-measure strains. The taped excerpt includes AABBAAB . . . , and we sense, probably accurately, that the dance could continue almost indefinitely were it not for constraints of concert or recording time.

Meter
Duple, as the title implies

Tempo
Fast. The insistently rapid tempo contributes to the exuberant nature of the piece.

Instruments
Accordion, or concertina, and triangle. The instrumentalists punctuate their peformance with occasional joyous shouts.

Zydeco

A more recent accordion-based music, **zydeco** (zy-deh-COH), distinguished by spicy-hot Caribbean and Latin rhythms, is the music of southern Louisiana's Creoles—a term of various meaning (see p. 121) but here applying to *gens de couleur libre* ("free persons of color"). A revolution in Santo Domingo toward the end of the eighteenth century sent huge numbers of French citizens, both black and white, fleeing north to join the French-speaking communities in Louisiana. The black refugees brought with them their Caribbean rhythms, religious practices, and spicy cuisine, and like the Cajuns, they developed a distinct French dialect or patois.

The term "zydeco" is a corruption of the first two words of the French phrase *les haricots sont pas salés,* meaning "the snap beans aren't salted," a traditional indicator of hard times. But there is no misery to the rich zydeco sounds of accordion and harmonica, accompanied by a tambourine and sometimes by a *frottoir,* or a rub board (a washboard-like instrument that the musicians may strap to their chests for ready access—Figure 11.2) marking the hotly syncopated rhythms. An electric guitar and bass, drums, and sometimes even a saxophone enliven the sound. Heard mainly along the Gulf Coast, where a blend of African American French Creole traditions has created a rich gumbo of musical flavors, contemporary zydeco bands combine the energy and amplification of the hottest rock groups with the exotic melodies and dialect of the Cajuns to produce their own intoxicating music.

Mainstream artists, too, show the influence of the compelling Cajun and zydeco musics. Paul Simon's tribute to zydeco and its late "king," Clifton Chenier—"That Was Your Mother"—was one of the highlights of Simon's multimillion-selling album *Graceland,* for example. (Clifton Chenier performs in Listening Example 39.) When asked what drew her to Cajun, country singer Mary Chapin Carpenter (who won a Grammy in 1992 for her Cajun-flavored "Down at the Twist and Shout") replied, "In no particular order: percussion, fiddle, spices, waltzes, Acadian accordion, the tempo, lyrics of love and spirit, gumbo, wails, Highway 10, darkness, dance halls."

Urban Folk Music

While bluegrass musicians specifically sought to perpetuate traditional country music values, urban folk musicians instead performed folklike music in a polished, suave manner designed to appeal to fans of popular music. Some set new words to traditional tunes; others composed new songs in the folk or country style. Increasingly, singers used folk music as a forum for the expression of their political beliefs.

The **urban folk revival** evolved during the 1950s and early 1960s into a very popular movement, attracting huge crowds of mostly young, often socially conscious, and sometimes politically active young people. These urban folk enthusiasts drew inspiration from the stirring music of a singing hobo, **Woody Guthrie,** one of many songwriters provoked by the Great Depression to write movingly of injustice and inequality in American society.

FIGURE 11.2

Zydeco musicians. Left to right:
Robert Clemon, accordion;
Clifton Edmond, rub board;
and Albert Chevalier,
accordion.

Woody Guthrie (1914–1967) The singer-songwriter Woodrow

Wilson "Woody" Guthrie (Figure 11.3) evolved from a simple hillbilly singer
into a sophisticated composer and performer of protest songs while surviving
the Great Depression as a hobo riding the rails or thumbing rides on the highways of America. Having seen his own family devastated by forces beyond
their control (dust storms, fire, bank failures, illness), Guthrie determined that
only by banding together—in trade unions and otherwise—could common
people survive. He expressed this belief poignantly in his songs, many set to
traditional folk and religious tunes.

In the winter of 1940, while barely recovering from the trauma of the Great
Depression and witnessing the suffering of others, Guthrie came to despise
Irving Berlin's stirring patriotic ballad "God Bless America" (p. 156). Guthrie
protested against what he considered the cloying sentiment and overblown
sophistication of Berlin's song by composing the ballad we know as "This
Land Is Your Land," which Guthrie originally called "God Blessed America
for Me." To Berlin's romantic pastoral imagery ("From the mountains / To the

Listening Example 39

"Tu le ton son ton"
("Every Now and Then")

**CD 2
Track 7
3:42**

Form
Twelve-bar blues (see page 197. There are several three-line verses, with four bars in each line)

Meter
Quadruple

Tempo
Moderately fast

The famous zydeco vocalist and accordion player Clifton Chenier (1925–1988) performs here, accompanied by electric bass, drums, and washboard (sometimes called a rub board). The song, probably improvised by Chenier, begins with an instrumental three-line twelve-bar verse. Some of the succeeding verses are sung; others are performed by the instruments accompanied by encouraging shouts from Chenier.

Notice the steady walking bass and the rasping rhythms of the washboard. Generally the performance suggests the influence of rock, or rhythm and blues, more than the country effect of white Cajun music.

prairies / To the oceans, white with foam"), Guthrie retorted with six verses of his own, beginning, "This land is your land, this land is my land, / From California to the New York island, / From the redwood forest to the Gulf Stream waters; / God blessed America for me." But Guthrie's song continued with a far more complete depiction of America's ills as well as its beauties, as in this verse: "One bright sunny morning in the shadow of the steeple / By the relief office I saw my people— / As they stood hungry, I stood there wondering if / God blessed America for me." Guthrie set his moving verses to a tune perhaps derived from a Baptist hymn, "Oh My Lovin' Brother," though scholars dispute that derivation.

Little realizing the popular potential of his song, Guthrie did not publish it until 1944, during the late period of World War II, by which time he had changed the title to "This Land Is Your Land" and the refrain (the line repeated at the end of each verse) to "This land was made for you and me." He continued to change the song, substituting new verses of pungent social commentary even as he slowly succumbed to Huntington's disease, which eventually killed him. In his last years, Guthrie expressed frustration that his song had become widely known and popular—but without its protest verses.

Protest was not a traditional characteristic of country music, but social commentary was, and Guthrie's stirring poems and songs on a variety of topics

FIGURE 11.3
Woody Guthrie.

inspired the folk revivalists of the late 1950s and the succeeding socially turbulent decade. Many people consider Woody Guthrie America's greatest folk poet.

The Movement Evolves Among those inspired by Woody Guthrie was **Pete Seeger** (b. 1919), the son of a famous musicologist specializing in American folk music (Charles Seeger). Pete Seeger left college to collect folk songs, learned to play the banjo, and traveled with Guthrie in the years before World War II. Later the younger Seeger formed the Weavers (so named to reflect "the qualities of rhythm and work"), a folk group dedicated to preserving the tradition of political-activist protest songs. The Weavers' first great hit, "Goodnight Irene," was first popularized by **Huddie Ledbetter (Leadbelly**, 1885–1949), a gifted black blues singer and songwriter. Leadbelly was discovered, while serving a term in jail for assault with intent to murder, by the musicologist John Lomax and his even more influential son **Alan Lomax** (1915–2002). Not a traditional folk song, "Goodnight Irene" was written and published in 1886 by a black railroad porter, Gussie Lord Davis; but Leadbelly had learned it in a much altered version. Impressed with the song (as Leadbelly performed it) and with Leadbelly's talents, the Lomaxes helped to secure the talented blues musician's early release from prison and to launch him on a performing and recording career. Leadbelly's fervor for civil rights led him to join Pete Seeger, Woody Guthrie, and others prominent in the urban folk revival movement.

The Weavers' popularity would seem to have rendered them impervious to attacks from the increasingly suspicious political right; but the cold war and the McCarthy era's Red Scare hysteria forced them, temporarily, to restrict their appearances to union halls, civil rights and peace benefits, and college campuses. Finally, in 1955, Pete Seeger faced censure by Congress. Hauled before a subcommittee investigating supposed subversive influences in entertainment, Seeger refused to cooperate and was blacklisted from television for his leftist leanings. His fortunes soared, however, at the end of the decade, when he left the Weavers and forged a highly successful solo career. Ironically, perhaps, in the late 1990s he was inducted into the Rock and Roll Hall of Fame.

As popular attention was diverted to the Kingston Trio's recording of "Tom Dooley" (1958)—a murder ballad innocent of political overtones—the urban folk revival came into full bloom, forming an important tie between country music and mainstream pop. The Kingston Trio and other suburban, collegiate, clean-cut groups, including the Limelighters, the New Christy Minstrels, and (especially) Peter, Paul and Mary, joined such city-bred singers of protest songs as Joan Baez, Bob Dylan, and of course Pete Seeger to produce commercial music for a sophisticated urban audience. Performing in coffeehouses, in city nightclubs, and on college campuses, they also effectively revived interest in early folk music—at least among themselves. The Kingston Trio's "Tom Dooley" (a song discovered, like "Goodnight Irene," by Alan Lomax) had first been recorded in the 1920s by a blind fiddler descended from the sheriff who had arrested the murderer Tom Dula; the version by the Kingston Trio sold 4 million records. In 1963, the Weavers recorded an adaptation by Bob Dylan of an old slave song, "No More Auction Block for Me," now titled "Blowin' in the Wind." Joan Baez made serious studies of folk and country music, learning traditional songs and performance customs and bringing them to a receptive modern audience. Baez's recordings of the Carter Family's songs, for instance, introduced them to a new audience and also to musicians who composed original "folk" songs modeled on such country classics.

Bob Dylan (b.1941)

Bob Dylan (Figure 11.4), born Robert Zimmerman in Duluth, Minnesota, followed his idol Woody Guthrie to New York. There Dylan began performing in clubs and recording his original folk-like protest songs while learning as much as possible from Guthrie. Dylan's singing voice was harsh and his guitar self-accompaniments were unsophisticated; but the passion in his voice and the stirring messages of his texts—written by himself, some on intensely personal issues—made him the favorite figure of the folk revival. For a time he had a close relationship with the singer Joan Baez, who rose to folk stardom before he became known and who generously supported his early performances. But within a few years, Dylan abandoned Baez and took his own independent path.

FIGURE 11.4

Bob Dylan performing at the 2002 Newport Folk Festival.

Having linked country music with mainstream pop by presenting folklike music in a pop atmosphere, the urban folk revival now initiated another significant change in the popular music industry, inspired by the songs of Bob Dylan. Before Dylan, the folk revivalists, like performers in the Tin Pan Alley tradition, had mostly performed songs composed or handed down by others; but Dylan's original songs inspired others in the folk revival movement also to write their own material. Thus, rather than performing new arrangements of traditional tunes, the folk revivalists now produced original "folk" songs. Dylan was soon to connect with rock as well, not only in the sense that early rock performers wrote most of their own material, but—surprisingly—by making a transition from leader of urban folk to electric rock performer.

Newport Folk Festival. In the early 1960s, the Newport Folk Festival was the central annual event for those who loved folk music. Guitar pickers, blues singers, old-time fiddlers, and banjo players from all over the country joined gospel singers, Cajun bands, bluegrass groups, and folk stars like Joan Baez and Pete Seeger for several days of concerts, workshops, and jam sessions. Most saw folk music as a tool for social change, and by 1963 they revered Bob Dylan, whose songs—including "With God on Our Side" and "Blowin' in the Wind"—movingly addressed social issues of the day.

But Dylan responded to the catastrophic events of 1963–1965 (the assassination of President John Kennedy and of Malcolm X, the killing of civil rights workers in the South, the growing involvement of American troops in Vietnam, and the doubling of the draft quota) by starkly altering his message and his style. His subject matter changed from protest to songs about personal relationships, often expressed in complex imagist poetry. His look changed, too, from casually scruffy attire to leather jackets, Cuban-heel boots, and sunglasses. His fans, expecting to hear the old Bob Dylan perform at the Newport Folk Festival in 1965, were outraged when he appeared wearing a black leather jacket and played an electric guitar backed by a rock rhythm band with the sound system cranked up to an ear-splitting level (see p. 284).

Yet by the 1990s, Dylan seemed to have come full circle, recording albums of traditional folk and blues material ("Good as I Been to You," "World Gone Wrong," and "Time Out of Mind"). His album "Love and Theft" (2001) also includes the sounds of blues, jazz, folk, and rockabilly. Today his poetry is attracting acclaim in its own right: Great Britain's poet laureate has referred to Dylan as one of the greatest artists of the twentieth century; and the American composer John Corigliano—who wrote the music for the film *The Red Violin* (1999)—has set Dylan's words to his own music in a song cycle (a group of songs usually on works by a single poet) titled *Mr. Tambourine Man: Seven Poems of Bob Dylan*.

(We will meet Bob Dylan again in Chapter 16, in the discussion of folk rock.)

A New Romance

Though Dylan shocked his fans by approaching rock and roll in 1965, rock and country now meet on increasingly congenial ground. Flirtation between the two genres began even earlier: Johnny Cash jammed with rockers Elvis Presley, Jerry Lee Lewis, and Carl Perkins in the mid-1950s, and a decade later the Beatles recorded country singer Buck Owens's "Act Naturally" as the B side of their single "Yesterday." Queried recently about his reaction to appearing in the Rock and Roll Hall of Fame, Seeger replied, "Rock is what future centuries will probably say was the twentieth-century folk music."

Since the 1990s, **alternative country** has attracted a small but dedicated group of enthusiasts dedicated to rivaling the polished, professional sounds of mainstream country music coming from Nashville by blending punk (see pp. 294–296) and rock and roll effects with country sounds. Alternative country defies closer definition: Its own magazine, *No Depression* (named after the Carter Family's song "No Depression in Heaven") declares that it covers "alternative country music (whatever that is)."

Today both rock and country audiences seem willing to accept elements of each other's music. In the summer of 2004, the rocker Matt (Uncle Kracker) Shafer toured successfully with the country music star Kenny Chesney and the country trio Rascal Flatts. Country and rock merge as well on modern country radio and in some of Nashville's videos, as audiences simply looking for a good time enjoy the two-way love affair.

Country music, after all, is one of the roots of rock and roll, as we shall see in Chapter 16.

Terms to Review

slack key guitar   Hawaiian guitar with loosened strings, having a characteristic resonant sound.

steel guitar   Guitar with metal strings, held horizontally on the lap, played by sliding a metal bar along the strings with the left hand while plucking the strings with the right hand.

ukulele   Small Hawaiian guitar-like instrument with four strings.

Cajun music   An accordion-based country music of the Cajun people, vibrant, lighthearted, often with a strong dance beat.

zydeco   Rock-flavored black Cajun style of country music.

urban folk revival   Socially conscious movement popular in the 1960s, relating country music and mainstream pop.

alternative country   Variously defined style, blending punk and rock-and-roll effects with country sounds.

Key Figures

John Lomax	Pete Seeger	Alan Lomax
Woody Guthrie	Huddie Ledbetter (Leadbelly)	Bob Dylan

Suggestions for Further Listening

Gabby Pahinui with The Sons of Hawaii (slack key guitar).

Cajun music: "Fais pa ça" ("Don't Do That").

Zydeco albums by Clifton Chenier or by Queen Ida and the Bon Ton Zydeco Band.

Suggestion for Viewing

The Big Easy (1987, film featuring Cajun performers).

Critical Thinking

If you have access to examples of music performed on an acoustic guitar, a slack key guitar, and a steel guitar, how do you differentiate between the sounds of those instruments? What kinds of music does each instrument best serve?

How would you compare the sounds of white Cajun music and black zydeco?

Do you think Irving Berlin's "God Bless America" or Woody Guthrie's "This Land Is Your Land" better expresses the American experience today?

Do you think Bob Dylan will be best remembered in the future for his music or for his poetry?

Go to www.mhhe.com/ferrisaml5 for a list of additional Web-based resources that relate to the content in this chapter.

The Jazz Age

As Americans danced into the beginning of the twentieth century, saloons and dance halls rang with the sounds of ragtime, the two-step, and various Latin dances (see p. 254) soon to become even more popular. Fast tempos, syncopated rhythms, and dance band timbres replaced the sedate ballroom dances played by the string orchestras of an earlier time. (See Figure 12.1.) As dance rhythms became more complex, solo instrumental lines more independent, and instrumental timbres more varied, Americans discovered that listening to the new music was just as exciting as dancing to it. By 1917, they were calling it **jazz.**

The popular writer F. Scott Fitzgerald dubbed the 1920s—the decade of dance marathons, speakeasies, a stock market boom, Babe Ruth, Greta Garbo, and Rudolph Valentino—the "jazz age," and so that period is often called today. Of course the roots of jazz lie far earlier, and jazz was not the only music popular in the "roaring twenties," but that was when the new music came to wide public attention through the performances and recordings of a large number of tremendously talented musicians who would dominate the field for decades to come.

The roots of jazz, rich and varied, include white European marches, hymns, and various popular dances; Creole and Caribbean influences; and of course and most significantly the stirring, hot rhythms, dramatic percussive effects, and distinctive vocal and instrumental performance techniques derived from black Africa. Ragtime, which already embodied characteristics derived from white and black music, profoundly influenced the evolving style. It is not surprising, then, that jazz styles vary widely—in mood, instrumentation, tempo, and even artistic intent, although generally jazz is regular in meter, involves so-called *blue notes,* and is improvised to a greater or lesser extent, depending on the performers' inclinations and abilities. Although rooted in folk and popular styles, jazz rarely entered the popular music mainstream. It reached an enthusiastic segment of the popular music audience, of course, but it belongs to America's art music tradition as well.

FIGURE 12.1

Blues, Archibald Motley. The syncopated rhythms of Motley's swaying musicians and dancing couples superbly evoke and reflect the influence of the music of the jazz age.

Blues

The foundations of jazz, primarily an instrumental music, lie in the **blues,** a vocal form whose origins, although stubbornly obscure, derive from African American traditions and date from sometime in the nineteenth century (Figure 12.2). Just when the blues emerged is the subject of dispute, but certainly after the Civil War intimations of what we call the blues were heard from slaves and from newly emancipated blacks, who often found their lives more rather than less difficult after they received their freedom. Away from their familiar plantation environment, lonely and in desperate need of money, some became migrants, some went to prison, and others held backbreaking, unrewarding jobs such as digging ditches or laying railroad lines. In their new distress, they sometimes expanded field hollers into simple solo songs, laden with emotional content and highly expressive of their loneliness and pain. In effect, they were singing the blues.

Country or Rural Blues This new kind of solo song, introduced by blacks, was folklike in sound but highly distinctive in character and form. The texts of the early, **rural** or **country blues** addressed every aspect of life, but most concerned work or, sometimes, love—unrequited, betrayed, or gone wrong. Blues singers expressed their troubles in an unaffected, straightforward

FIGURE 12.2
The origin of the blues.

manner, without sentimentality and often with a wry or whimsical humor that lessened the sadness while increasing the poignancy of their tale of woe.

They could hardly have guessed the inestimable influence their simple music would have upon the development of every genre of American music.

Form. The earliest blues stanzas probably consisted of one line of text sung three times to a familiar or improvised melody. But in time it became customary to sing the first line twice and add a conclusion or response, in the form **AAB** (statement, repeat, response). Because each stanza had three lines, and each line had four measures or bars, the form is called the **twelve-bar blues**. It is the only purely American contribution to musical form.

> *Hard times here, worse times down the road.*
> *Hard times here, worse times down the road.*
> *Wish my man was here to share the load.*

Melodic Characteristics. Blues singers and later instrumentalists adopted the African custom of treating the third, seventh, sometimes fifth, and less often sixth degrees of the scale as neutral or ambiguous tones, the wonderfully flexible blue notes the jazz musician "bends" (lowers or slightly raises) to produce gracefully fluid, emotionally expressive melodic lines. Besides these "bent," "tired," or "worried" notes, vocal and instrumental scoops and slides or glissandos, also derived from black African singing, further colored the performance of early blues melodies.

Blues Harmony. In time, a simple harmonic pattern emerged in which the tonic, subdominant, and dominant chords occurred in unorthodox order, providing a strong, simple, and distinctive harmonic framework for the blues musicians to improvise around.

> *Line 1: stays tonic*
> *Line 2: IV goes to I*
> *Line 3: V goes to IV goes to I*

It is in the third line that the distinctive harmonic irregularity occurs, as V—which implies a movement toward tonic—surprisingly "regresses" to IV. The verbal explanation sounds technical—all the more interesting, when one considers that the distinctive chord pattern evolved from simple custom.

Improvisation. This asymmetrical, strictly tonal, textually simple form beautifully served the improvising musician in several ways. Vocal and instrumental timbres were limited only by a performer's imagination and the availability of musical instruments, and possibilities abounded for subtle rhythmic adjustments over the solidly steady beat. Each of the characteristics of text, form, melody, and harmony described previously further supported the musician's improvisational efforts:

1. Each line of text took about 2½ bars to complete, leaving 1½ measures of thinking time to be filled with half-spoken, half-sung nonsense syllables, later called **scatting** or **scat singing,** or by improvisation on accompanying instruments.
2. Repetition of the first line of text gave the singer additional thinking time to plan the response.
3. Melodies could be embellished and colored by scoops, slides, blue notes, and other creative and expressive effects.
4. The basic harmonic pattern allowed ample harmonic variety, the simple chords supporting without getting in the way of creative ideas.

Soon the rural blues evolved from intensely personal introspection to a form of shared entertainment, sung around campfires or in the poorest living quarters to ease spirits when the labor of the day was done. Any available instrument might accompany the voice, perhaps answering the singer and filling out a line with its own melodic interest. This call-and-response effect is among the African traditions essential to the blues; others include the deeply personal expression and various expressive manners of vocal embellishment. While the chords and structured regularity of the blues reflect white customs, these always remain subject to a performer's individual interpretation and never govern or limit a musician's creativity. Thus in his performance of "Hellhound on My Trail" (Listening Example 40), the famous early blues singer **Robert Johnson** (1911–1938) handles the form casually, adding a measure here or there as it suits him.

Classic Blues

Blues conceived primarily as entertainment, performed in theaters and clubs and on commercially distributed recordings, is called **classic blues.** Whereas country singers accompanied themselves, usually on guitar or banjo, classic blues performers often had a band backing them up, and the piano assumed increasing importance. More professional, more stylized, more universal than the earlier primitive or rural blues, classic blues found a wide audience among white as well as black Americans.

Listening Example 40

"Hellhound on My Trail"

Composer/Performer
Robert Johnson (1911–1938), one of the great country blues singers, accompanying himself on his guitar

CD 2
Track 8
2:34

Meter
Quadruple

Tempo
Slow

Form
Twelve-bar blues

The bluesy mood fits the impassioned nature of the text, and the varying length of the lines indicates the informality and improvisatory nature of country blues. Notice, too, the manner in which Johnson fills out each line with repetitions of fragments of the text and with eloquent commentary on his guitar. The frequent blue notes and intricate melodic embellishments add to the individuality and the passion of Johnson's performance.

I got to keep movin'. Blues fallin' down like hail.
I got to keep movin'. Blues fallin' down like hail.
And I can't keep no money with a hellhound on my trail.

If today was Christmas Eve, and tomorrow Christmas Day,
If today was Christmas Eve, and tomorrow Christmas Day,
I would need my little sweet rider [lover] just to pass the time away.

You sprinkled hot-foot powder [a voodoo spell?] all around my door.
You sprinkled hot-foot powder all around my door.
It keeps me with a ramblin' mind, Rider, every old place I go.

I can tell the wind is risin', the leaves tremblin' on the tree.
I can tell the wind is risin', the leaves tremblin' on the tree.
All I need is my little sweet woman to keep me company.

Whereas the outstanding singers of rural blues were men, famously including Huddie Ledbetter (see pp. 190–191) and Blind Lemon Jefferson among many others, the early classic blues singers were mostly women, and nearly all of the great blues lyrics are written from a woman's point of view. Again in contrast to folk or country blues, which embraced a wide range of topics, most classic blues lyrics concern love—especially "love gone wrong." By the 1920s, theatrical performance was becoming recognized as an acceptable profession for women (white or black), and the field offered many unprecedented social and economic opportunities.

FIGURE 12.3

The American blues singer
and songwriter Bessie Smith.

Gertrude **"Ma" Rainey** (born Gertrude Pridgett, 1886–1939), one of the most imitated and influential classic blues singers and composers, established something of a link between early rural blues and sophisticated blues performances recorded for commercial distribution. Having performed in both styles, Ma Rainey, sometimes called Madame Rainey and the mother or the queen of the blues, taught **Bessie Smith** (1894–1937), who became perhaps the most famous of all classic blues singers (Figure 12.3). Bessie Smith is remembered today for the intense personal feeling with which she imbued her performances, embellishing melodies and bending tones—as in Listening Example 41, "Lost Your Head Blues"—to communicate the deepest emotions to her rapt and sympathetic audiences.

Ma Rainey, Bessie Smith ("empress of the blues"), and a number of other great classic blues singers brought a new professionalism and theatrical polish to blues, which soon became a highly profitable medium of entertainment. Of the great classic blues recordings, Bessie Smith's earned the most money for her recording company, but although Columbia Records paid her well, she never received any royalties for her efforts, and she died, after an automobile accident, nearly penniless.

"Lost Your Head Blues"

Composer
Probably Bessie Smith

CD 2
Track 9
2:54

Performers
Bessie Smith, vocalist, with trumpet and piano accompaniment

Form
Twelve-bar blues

Harmony
The harmony is entirely based on the I, IV, and V chords. Bessie Smith weaves her flexible vocal line over and around this solid support.

Meter
Quadruple

Tempo
Moderately slow

The trumpet and piano play a four-bar introduction.

There are five three-line verses. To each line of each verse sung by Bessie Smith, the trumpet responds, in turn answering, mocking, and encouraging the singer.

Lightly dissonant piano chords lope along throughout the performance, supporting both voice and trumpet while remaining uninvolved in the dialogue between them.

The melody remains fairly constant for each verse, although always subject to Smith's supple vocal manipulations. Especially in verses 3 and 5, Smith ranges slightly afield, but never far from the original melodic line.

Notice the slight slowing in tempo at the end of the last line, signaling the conclusion of the song.

Lyrics
I was with you, baby, when you didn't have a dime.
I was with you, baby, when you didn't have a dime.
Now since you got plenty money, you have throwed your good gal down.

Once ain't for always, two ain't for twice.
Once ain't for always, two ain't for twice.
When you get a good gal, you'd better treat her nice.

—Continued

"Lost Your Head Blues"

When you were lonesome, I tried to treat you kind.
When you were lonesome, I tried to treat you kind.
But since you've got money, it done changed your mind.

I'm goin' to leave, baby, ain't gonna say goodbye.
I'm goin' to leave, baby, ain't gonna say goodbye
But I'll write you and tell you the reason why.

Days are lonesome, nights are long.
Days are lonesome, nights are so long.
I'm a good ole gal, but I just been treated wrong.

The performance seems tightly organized and professionally delivered, yet both voice and trumpet suggest literally endless possibilities for interpretation of this famous blues piece. The straightforward delivery of complaint, unburdened by sentimentality, and relieved by slight, wry humor, is characteristic of the blues. Listen for expressive slides and blue notes throughout the piece in both trumpet and voice.

Urban Blues

It was only a matter of time before the professional publishing and recording industries recognized the commercial potential of the blues, and blues pieces began to be published as sheet music. White composers started to write blues, and the word "blues" appeared in the titles of many pieces, including some that were not blues at all. Published blues first appeared about 1912, and by the 1920s so-called blues **race records** (the unfortunate industry term for recordings intended for an African American audience) were being mass-produced.

As the blues entered the popular music stream, blues composers adapted the twelve-bar form in a manner they supposed would better appeal to a mainstream (white) audience. Intended for performance by professional musicians, the so-called **urban blues** could be more complex in form and more sophisticated in harmony than the earlier rural blues; and although some or even most of the stanzas of urban blues retained the three-line form, one or more verses had the conventional four- or eight-line (sixteen- or thirty-two-bar) form. Soon urban blues, recorded by professional blues singers, was being disseminated to a wide and increasingly appreciative public. As the great blues singers made some of their finest recordings with the outstanding jazz musicians of their day, close connections were established between instrumental jazz and urban blues, which shared a folk or popular heritage, a regular beat, subtle rhythmic variations, versatile blue notes, and fluent improvisation.

Although **William Christopher** (**W. C.**) **Handy** (1873–1958), the African American bandleader and composer who called himself "father of the blues,"

FIGURE 12.4
W. C. Handy (at left) with Duke Ellington.

hardly invented the form, he certainly led it into the world of commercial popular music. As a young man, Handy (Figure 12.4) learned to play a cornet and (to his Methodist father's dismay) joined a minstrel troupe. He then formed his own dance band, which played in Memphis for a while before moving to Chicago and finally to New York. There Handy began writing and publishing urban blues, including the best-known example, the beautiful "St. Louis Blues" (Listening Example 42). Notice how complex the formal arrangement of this blues piece has become in contrast to the improvised twelve-bar country blues: Here we have an extremely sophisticated vocal and instrumental performance of a published composition in which the verses vary in melodic content and even in number of lines per verse.

New Orleans Jazz

As musical instruments left over from Civil War military bands became readily and cheaply available, black musicians began playing them in their own manner, improvising freely on favorite familiar tunes. In New Orleans, small brass bands played for parades, concerts, and even funerals, developing a famous tradition that survives today. Having performed solemn music to accompany the funeral party both to the cemetery and—for a dignified interval—on the way back to town, the band breaks into joyous music whose familiar tunes and hot rhythms virtually compel the mourners' healthy return to everyday life.

In time, the bands' instrumental techniques became more individual, the tempos faster, and the mood more high-powered and intense. Although some

"St. Louis Blues"

Composer
W. C. Handy (words and music)

CD 2
Track 10
3:09

Form
Modified twelve-bar blues

Verses 1 and 2 follow the twelve-bar form.

Verse 3 has four lines; the first two rhyme, as do the last two.

The song ends with a fourth stanza, in twelve-bar form, but with a
melody different from verses 1 and 2.

Meter
Quadruple

Tempo
Slow

Performers
Bessie Smith, accompanied by Fred Longshaw on reed organ (see
picture on page 80) and by Louis Armstrong (see p. 206) on trumpet.
Although the reed pump organ suggests the rustic flavor of country
blues, the young Louis Armstrong already reveals his mastery as a jazz
musician, competing with Bessie Smith for virtuosity and emotional
expression.

Lyrics
I hate to see the ev'nin' sun go down.
I hate to see the ev'nin' sun go down,
Makes me think I'm on my last go-'round.

Feelin' tomorrow like I feel today,
Feelin' tomorrow like I feel today,
I'll pack my grip and make my getaway.

St. Louis woman wears her diamond rings,
Pulls a man around by her apron strong.
'T'wan't for powder and this store-bought hair,
The man I love wouldn't go nowhere—nowhere.

I got the St. Louis blues, just as blue as I can be.
He's got a heart like a rock cast in the sea,
Or else he wouldn't have gone so far from me.

Notice the rhythmic freedom with which Bessie Smith delivers the words
in her big, robust voice and the manner in which she bends pitches, as
on "sun" in the first phrase of the song, with Armstrong echoing her effects on his trumpet.

FIGURE 12.5
Members of a jazz combo.

of the musicians read music, most did not and simply improvised freely on familiar tunes. In a word, they were playing jazz. Soon small bands or **combos** (Figure 12.5) of black musicians were providing indoor entertainment, their hot new dance music combining the steady beat and stirring tempo of European march and dance tunes with the subtle and complex syncopations of black African and Caribbean effects.

As already noted (see p. 121), New Orleans, which had alternately been under French and Spanish rule and to which many Afro-Latin people had fled from Caribbean settlements such as Haiti and Cuba, offered a rich cultural climate. Its music included popular French, Spanish, Creole, and black tunes; serious and comic opera; and airs from marching, dance, and concert bands. The city generously nourished the exciting new vernacular sound, with the notorious Storyville red-light district of gambling saloons, bordellos, and dance halls offering ample job opportunities for jazz musicians. Thus it is not surprising that New Orleans produced a large number of astonishingly talented

FIGURE 12.6

Louis Armstrong.

jazz musicians who soon attracted others to their city, making it the first important center of jazz.

Most **New Orleans jazz** combos consisted of three to eight people playing clarinet, cornet or trumpet, and trombone, with a rhythm section including banjo, tuba, and drums. Later, combos playing indoors rather than on the streets added a piano and sometimes replaced the tuba with a string bass. Having selected a hymn, rag, march, popular song, or blues and agreed upon the harmonic patterns to be repeated throughout, the musicians began improvising around the tune: The cornet handled the melody; the clarinet wove counter-melodies around it; the trombone provided supporting harmonies; and the rhythm section marked the beat, a straight four-to-the-bar, with an accent on *ONE* and a secondary accent on *three*. Early New Orleans performances were basically collective improvisations played in this manner, the soloists taking turns improvising complex variations on given (known) melodies while the other musicians provided rhythmic and harmonic support.

Louis Armstrong (1900–1971)
Louis Armstrong (Figure 12.6) survived a violent childhood in New Orleans to become a gentle, kindly, good-natured man and an incredibly talented musician. He played the cornet in King Oliver's band as a boy, and in the early 1920s followed Oliver to Chicago, where Armstrong formed his own band (the Hot Five, later the Hot Seven) and began making important jazz recordings, including the performance of his wife's composition "Hotter Than That" heard in Listening Example 43. Switching to the trumpet, Armstrong developed previously inconceivable virtuosic techniques for that instrument, producing pure, clarion tones that had never been heard before.

Even more significant than his virtuosity, however, were Armstrong's original and highly creative solo improvisations, as beautifully expressive as they were technically brilliant. The extraordinarily wide emotional range of his playing greatly expanded musicians' and listeners' concept of what jazz was all about, leading the great bebop trumpet player Dizzy Gillespie (see p. 223) to express the feeling of many musicians when he said of Armstrong, "No him, no me."

Armstrong also sang (in a manner of speaking), scatting in an amazingly creative, often humorous, always expressive way. Finding sadness or humor or elation in a song, he let it issue forth as a purely natural, purely human statement. In this and in every way, he personalized his performances as no one had before, taking the music and making it his own.

Chicago Jazz

In the 1920s, after the authorities shut down New Orleans's lucrative Storyville district, many outstanding jazz artists moved to Chicago, which then became the new performing and recording center for jazz. Chicago's large population, thriving speakeasies, and fledgling recording opportunities—as well as a

"Hotter Than That" (excerpt)

**CD 2
Track 11
1:31**

Composer

Lillian Hardin Armstrong (1898–1971)

Lil Hardin, an outstanding jazz pianist who became Louis Armstrong's second wife, performed regularly with the Hot Five, the group that recorded this piece and many other early Armstrong hits.

Meter

Quadruple

Tempo

Fast

Instruments

Cornet, trombone, clarinet, piano, banjo, guitar

The cornet, trombone, and clarinet take turns improvising while the other instruments provide a rhythmic accompaniment. Armstrong's cornet solos dominate, of course. And in his scat singing he "plays" his voice like another instrument, revealing a seemingly limitless range of creative and expressive techniques.

plentiful supply of jobs in the railroads, stockyards, and mills—soon attracted jazz musicians from all over the country.

In Chicago, many young white musicians became enamored of the sounds of the New Orleans combos and, in the sincerest form of flattery, set out to imitate them. **Dixieland,** the term for this white imitation of New Orleans jazz, in time came to be applied to all early jazz, although musicians distinguished between New Orleans Dixieland and Chicago Dixieland. The Chicago combos usually added a saxophone to the New Orleans instrumentation and replaced the banjo with a guitar; further, big-city tension and drive characterized Chicago jazz, which often began and ended with more complex improvisations than New Orleans musicians used, and which emphasized the role of soloists to a greater degree. A marked backbeat often enhanced the excitement of the newer style. It has been suggested—but one can never know—that the white musicians actually strove to outdo their models (see Figure 12.7).

Before the end of the roaring twenties, the heart of jazz shifted again, this time to New York City, where numerous combos and many jazz pianists continued to evolve distinctive sounds. Another important regional style—Kansas City jazz—was already evolving but reached its peak in the next decade, the 1930s, which we will cover in Chapter 13.

Jazz Piano

Jazz pianists, whose instrument sounded its own harmonies and who could practice independently of other musicians, enjoyed greater opportunity than other jazz instrumentalists to maximize their individuality; and indeed a number of jazz pianists developed distinctive styles extremely influential in the transition from ragtime to jazz. **Jelly Roll Morton,** mentioned in Chapter 9 as an outstanding ragtime player, combined ragtime and *boogie-woogie* techniques to produce his own inimitable jazz piano style, with rhythms looser and melodies less embellished than those of ragtime. (Morton is often also spoken of as the first jazz composer. Certainly he was the most innovative "hot tune writer," to use his expression, until Duke Ellington began composing in the 1930s.) Earl Hines (1903–1983) played with a swinging, flexible style usually associated with band instruments rather than with the piano. And Art Tatum (1910–1956), one of the most admired pianists in jazz history, combined his gifts for complex and ingenious harmonic changes and incredibly powerful technique with elements of the piano style called *stride*.

Boogie-Woogie   As accompanying instruments assumed ever more significant roles in performing the blues, the next logical step was adapting blues to instrumental forms. Thus before 1920, certain ragtime pianists carried the twelve-bar structure, and often the characteristic harmonic progressions of the blues as well, to the piano.

Unlike the written ragtime pieces, **boogie-woogie** or **piano blues** was freely improvised, the new jazz pianists accompanying a syncopated melody in the right hand with a characteristic highly rhythmic left-hand ostinato. This **eight-to-the-bar** accompanying pattern (subdividing the four beats of a measure into eight pulses, usually in the pattern *LONG-short-LONG-short-LONG-short-LONG-short*) resulted in complex cross rhythms, which—combined with a brisk tempo and a new driving intensity—quickly made boogie a music popular to dance and listen to (Listening Example 44).

Listening Example 44

"Shout for Joy"

CD 2
Track 12
2:23

Composer and Performer
Albert Ammons (1907–1949)

Meter
Duple

Form
Twelve-bar blues. After a four-bar introduction reminiscent of the familiar "Westminster Chimes," we hear eight three-line verses. (The easiest way to count phrases is to tap your foot on each beat: Eight beats constitute one line or phrase; each verse contains three lines.)

Accompaniment
The jumping "eight-to-the-bar" left-hand ostinato nearly compels a rhythmic response from the listener—as well as a probable happy smile.

Melody
Over the pounding beat, the pianist's right hand plays joyous melodic improvisations.

Verse 1: After two bars introduce the ostinato, a lighthearted melody enters in the right hand, occasionally embellished with a kind of "shake" between tones.

Verse 2: Dissonant chords mischievously accent the space between beats.

Verse 3: A three-note pattern (da-DA-dum) recurs throughout this verse.

Verse 4: This verse begins with a slightly higher-pitched four-note pattern. The "shake" returns.

Verse 5: A rising pattern, lower in pitch, with longer note values, is enhanced by the characteristic boogie "shake" for a shimmering effect.

Verse 6: Happy new melodic ideas play over the relentless, compelling ostinato.

Verse 7: This verse is colored by the "shake" and by distinctive chromatic harmonies.

Verse 8: Highest in pitch of all the variations, this one involves intricate fingerwork in the right hand. The final phrase tapers down to a quiet, unassuming end.

Stride Piano
Stride piano retained the regular left-hand metrical pattern of ragtime, alternating low bass notes on *one* and *three* with midrange chords on *two* and *four* under an improvised melody in the right hand. **James P. Johnson** (1894–1955), the "father of stride piano," certainly furthered the transition from ragtime to jazz, with playing that was more dissonant, more

loosely structured, more strictly improvisational, and more highly syncopated than other jazz piano music of the 1920s. Although Johnson composed other kinds of music as well, including "The Charleston," which flappers joyously danced through the roaring twenties, he is best remembered for his great stride compositions such as "Carolina Shout" (Listening Example 45).

Fats Waller (1904–1943), who studied with James P. Johnson, developed his own legendary jazz piano style, more driving, intense, and virtuosic than his mentor's. Although Waller went on to become one of the great jazz entertainers and a composer of hundreds of tunes, he never surpassed the beauty of Johnson's technically demanding stride pieces. And although Waller's stride piano playing was a direct descendant of ragtime, Waller rarely wrote out his pieces in full, generally writing only a simple melody line and the most fragmentary additional notations. (All that was required to copyright an original tune was a melody and a title.) Some of his compositions were published as sheet music during his lifetime, and he did record some piano rolls, but neither form is considered representative of the performances Waller would have realized from the same pieces.

Listening Example 45

"Carolina Shout"

Composer
James P. Johnson

CD 2
Track 13
2:45

A shout was a form of religious dance popular on plantations through the nineteenth century in which slaves expressed according to African custom their new Christian fervor (see pp. 43–44).

Meter
Duple

After a four-measure introduction, the first phrase of the first strain begins its deceptively lazy descent, accompanied by the left hand, which ingeniously shifts the accents back and forth from *one* to *two*, or to the "and" between beats.

0:25 The first strain is repeated.

0:45 The second strain, lower in pitch, further varies the rhythms, rocking the beat from hand to hand.

1:04 The harmonic complexity increases with the third strain, implying a quickened pace—though the tempo actually holds steady—as chords in the left hand *respond* to the high-pitched *calls* of the right hand.

Shorter, more fragmented phrases further intensify the last two strains, as the vigorously striding left hand offers ever-new variations on the beat.

A cascading four-bar **coda,** or ending section, brings the stunning piece to a satisfying close.

Sweet Jazz

Throughout the 1920s, as the center of jazz innovation and performance shifted from New Orleans to other cities, especially Chicago and New York, a tame but attractive music that came to be known as **sweet jazz** reached a wide audience through the sophisticated, classically tinged performances of the **Paul Whiteman** Orchestra, the most popular dance band of its day. Whiteman, a (white) classically trained violinist who adored jazz, but lacked the gift to create the uninhibited improvisations of the jazz musicians he admired, formed his band in the early 1920s to play jazzy arrangements of popular and even classical melodies.

Although Whiteman was known for a time as the "king of jazz," his music bore only a marginal relationship to real jazz. Most of the notes were written out for his musicians, who did not indulge in creative flights of improvisational fancy; but their jazzy timbres and syncopated rhythms suggested to listeners the flavor of jazz. Most significantly, sweet jazz introduced the art of the arranger, which was to become even more important in the era of the big bands.

As sweet jazz soothed troubled audiences during the Great Depression, *real* jazz—hot, and mostly black—went underground. But during the 1930s jazz finally found a popular audience, as big band music came into its own. Now Americans were ready to swing!

Paul Whiteman
"Jazz came to America three hundred years ago in chains."

Terms to Review

jazz   A means of performing music. There are many moods and styles, but improvisation is an inherent characteristic of jazz.

blues   A black vocal music.

rural or **country blues**   Folklike vocal blues.

twelve-bar blues   The standard form of the blues, consisting of three-line stanzas with four bars, or measures, in each line.

scatting, scat singing   Vocal improvisation on neutral syllables.

classic blues   Professional, stylized blues, conceived for performance in theaters and clubs and for commercial recordings.

race records   Term used before 1949 by the popular music industry for recordings intended for an African American audience. (Later called rhythm and blues.)

urban blues   Blues pieces written for publication and professional performance, often slightly altered from the standard twelve-bar form.

combo   Small jazz ensemble.

New Orleans jazz   Virtuosic improvisation by members of a jazz combo on a given (already known) melody.

Dixieland   A white imitation of New Orleans jazz, faster and more intense than the original style. Dixieland was introduced in Chicago.

piano blues or **boogie-woogie**   A popular piano style with the form and harmony of the twelve-bar blues, but faster in tempo and with a dance beat.

eight-to-the-bar   The ostinato accompanying a boogie, dividing each of the four counts in a measure into a long and a short beat.

stride piano   A jazz piano style in which the left hand alternates low bass notes on *one* and *three* with midrange chords on *two* and *four*.

coda   A closing section.

sweet jazz   Music with the sound and flavor of jazz, but arranged so as to require little improvisation.

Key Figures

Robert Johnson   W. C. Handy   James P. Johnson
Gertrude "Ma" Rainey   Louis Armstrong   Fats Waller
Bessie Smith   Jelly Roll Morton   Paul Whiteman

Optional Listening Examples

George Gershwin: *Rhapsody in Blue*   George Gershwin: Concerto in F

Suggestions for Further Listening

Examples of blues, boogie, and Dixieland included in
The Smithsonian Collection of Classic Jazz

Suggestion for Viewing

Lightning in a Bottle (blues documentary, 2004)

Critical Thinking

What characteristics do country blues, classic blues, and urban blues share? In what ways do they differ?

What characteristics do vocal blues and piano blues (boogie-woogie) share? How do they differ?

Why do you think the outstanding rural blues singers were men and the great classic blues singers women?

How would you compare *sweet* jazz with *real* jazz? Why do you suppose Paul Whiteman was called the king of jazz? What audience would his music have most appealed to?

Go to www.mhhe.com/ferrisaml5 for a list of additional Web-based resources that relate to the content in this chapter.

Jazz 1930–1960

J azz reached a peak of popularity in the mid-1930s, a relatively optimistic period when the Great Depression gradually receded and America's involvement in World War II lay ahead. Recordings and radio programs having made the sounds of sweet jazz widely familiar by then, multitudes of people—both white and black—craved more adventurous listening, and with Prohibition ended, real jazz came to be performed in an atmosphere more congenial to the general public than the small, illegal speakeasies of the 1920s. Crowds flocked to hear the big bands play, and by 1935 **big band** music resounded from radios, recordings, juke boxes, and dance halls all over the country.

Big Band Swing

While sweet jazz soothed more timid listeners, black jazz musicians added instruments to their small combos and developed the vibrant sound that came to be known as big band jazz, or **swing.** The new sound was of such huge appeal to whites and blacks of virtually every stratum in society that jazz and popular music came together for a time, and swing constituted *the* popular music of the 1930s.

Both "big band" and "swing" need clarification. The earliest big bands actually had only five or six members, but the standard soon became twelve to eighteen players, in three sections of instruments:

1. Brass (trumpets, trombones).
2. Woodwinds, called **reeds,** in which the player causes small flexible pieces of cane to vibrate (saxophones, sometimes also a clarinet).
3. Rhythm (a guitar and/or double bass, piano, drums).

"Swing," like many terms in art, has several meanings, some rather technical. For example, *swing eighths* are strings of eighth notes performed in uneven rhythm, alternating long and short notes of subjective rather than measured length. This contributes to the flexible give-and-take, or expressive

213

rubato, within the steady jazz beat. But "swing" also refers to a mood, a lilt, a magical effect that great jazz achieves and that sympathetic listeners recognize and respond to. When all elements of a jazz performance come together and work, the music swings.

Eventually the big, or swing, bands experienced the stimulating interaction between black and white musicians characteristic of many developments of jazz, for although the makers of recordings and the managers of commercial radio stations still severely segregated popular music intended for blacks or whites, African American music inevitably became more familiar to and popular with a greatly widening audience. White people often traveled to Harlem, a black neighborhood in uptown New York City, where they could hear the finest jazz musicians in the world collectively improvise, or **jam.** And even people who hardly understood the complex new music found themselves intoxicated with its nearly indefinable trait called *swing.*

Art of Arranging
Whereas early jazz combos functioned well with free improvisation, the larger groups of players needed to follow some kind of structured plan, relying upon arrangements that were either written down or thoroughly worked out in rehearsals. Because many such arrangements were based on New Orleans originals, listeners perceived much the same music as New Orleans and Dixieland jazz; but the larger combos, more sensuous orchestration, and more structured atmosphere made the new sound more intelligible to a wide audience. Because most of the big band musicians had more formal music training than most of the jazz pioneers, big band harmonies were more adventurous and their pieces more highly structured than those of early jazz. Solo improvisations, still hot, were brief, the band playing together much of the time.

The great ragtime and jazz pianist Jelly Roll Morton was one of the first bandleaders to provide arrangements for his band, beginning in the mid-1920s. Even more influential for later jazz bands, however, were the arrangements of **Fletcher Henderson** (1897–1952), who made large groups *sound* as if they were improvising and in fact left room for improvisation, within limits. A fine pianist with a degree in chemistry, Henderson in effect transformed the large "sweet" dance band into a jazz band, skillfully alternating the independent use of each section (trumpets, trombones, saxophones, rhythm) with outstanding solos. So successful were his innovations that they were copied by nearly every dance band of the big band era and in fact remain standard for many high school and college jazz bands today.

Count (Bill) Basie (1904–1984), who defined jazz as "music you can pat your foot to," became one of the most popular of all big band arrangers and leaders. The music of this quiet, unobtrusive pianist and leader dominated the **Kansas City jazz** scene. Musicians coming from Chicago, New York, New Orleans, and elsewhere found Kansas City a hospitable environment for gradually developing a distinct style of jazz, a pared-down, lighter, more relaxed music than jazz created in either New Orleans or Chicago. Instead of interweaving musical lines in the complex web of sound characteristic of

Listening Example 46

"Taxi War Dance" (excerpt)

Composers and Arrangers
Count Basie, Lester Young

Instruments

CD 2
Track 14
1:50

Four trumpets, three trombones, three saxophones, piano (Basie), guitar, double bass, drums

Basie introduces a rolling figure in the lower piano range, which continues as trumpets make brief, emphatic comments, accompanied by trombones and drums.

0:09 Lester Young begins his relaxed, swinging saxophone improvisation, which he extends and develops.

0:44 The trumpet figure and rolling piano riff return, and we hear a trombone solo accompanied by the rhythm section.

1:22 The trombones play a four-note motive (a distinctive rise, then a fall, in pitch), answered by the trumpets. This figure recurs several times, interspersed between solo passages for the other instruments, as the piece continues.

New Orleans combos, Kansas City arrangements were based on simple musical phrases, called **riffs,** which were repeated over and over again. The music had a light, airy feel—less dense and more spacious than other styles.

With his refined "less is more" style of piano playing, Basie proved that *space,* or *silence,* is as important to music as *sound.* He chose his notes—whether as pianist or arranger—meticulously, giving each utmost significance. Basie's band was particularly admired for its rhythm section, in which guitar, bass, and drums were so closely integrated as to produce a perfectly balanced sound. And Basie's unique style of piano playing gave further reason for some to consider his ensemble the best swing band of all.

The brilliant tenor saxophonist **Lester Young** (1909–1959) seemed uniquely comfortable with Basie's style. In "Taxi War Dance" (Listening Example 46), we hear Young answering Basie's spare, rolling piano figures with his own light, elegant melodic saxophone phrases.

The white clarinetist and bandleader **Benny Goodman** (1909–1986; Figure 13.1) brought big band music to national attention through his many recordings and radio programs. Although Goodman's unprecedented inclusion of outstanding African American soloists in his band was warmly appreciated, his exploitation of the contributions of black musicians sometimes caused resentment. Many of the Goodman band's best arrangements, for example, were by Fletcher Henderson, but although the band made Henderson's arrangements extremely popular, Henderson never earned the money that Benny Goodman and his band accrued. Both Goodman and Henderson had received classical music training; both insisted on disciplined musicianship from their band members; and the fact that Goodman's band became more popular than Henderson's was a source of some bitterness by the end of the decade.

Goodman later divided his playing and recording between big bands and various smaller ensembles, for while big bands remained highly popular well into the 1940s, the range of jazz styles expanded greatly during that decade, offering musicians and listeners alike a wealth of exciting new musics.

Most popular of all the big bands, and probably the easiest to recognize, was the **Glenn Miller** band. Alton Glenn Miller (1904–1944; he detested and dropped his first name) knew he had limited talent as a trombone player and devoted his attention to arranging, at which he clearly excelled. In 1940, for example, he recorded forty-five songs that made it onto the top-seller charts—a figure neither Elvis Presley nor the Beatles ever matched. He developed a distinctive sound—a clarinet lead supported by four saxophones—rich, sensuous, and nearly irresistible.

At the height of his popularity, Miller, age thirty-eight, enlisted in the Army Air Corps and, as leader of the Army Air Forces Band, made it his mission to update military music to a style that the World War II troops would enjoy. Miller disappeared in a small military plane flying from England to recently liberated France, possibly the victim of "friendly fire." Yet his music, including the classics "Moonlight Serenade," "String of Pearls," and "In the Mood" among too many others to mention, endures as the musical symbol of an entire generation, and today—sixty years after his death—there are "Glenn Miller bands" and Glenn Miller fans all over the world.

FIGURE 13.2

The jazz musician and composer Mary Lou Williams.

Mary Lou Williams (Mary Elfrieda Scruggs, 1910–1981), another noted arranger for big bands, was a rare exception in the developing world of jazz— a highly successful woman instrumental soloist (Figure 13.2). Having played the piano in public since the age of six, she married a carnival band member, and when her husband left the band to join another she hired a replacement for him and ran the group herself. Later she worked as a freelance arranger for several bands, including Benny Goodman's, and became a staff arranger for Duke Ellington (see below), producing highly original and distinctive arrangements while also performing as a pianist both here and in Europe.

Having contributed to all the evolving styles of popular piano music, from ragtime to bebop and beyond, Williams performed fluently in all of them. After arranging and composing for Duke Ellington for many years, she became his close friend in later life and played at his funeral; and in 1996, she was honored with the first of an annual series of Mary Lou Williams Women in Jazz festivals at the Kennedy Center in Washington. A street in Kansas City is named after her.

Edward Kennedy "Duke" Ellington (1899–1974)

In 1922, **Duke Ellington** (Figure 13.3) moved from his hometown, Washington, D.C., to New York City, where he formed his own small dance band. By 1927 he had transformed the ensemble into the ten-member Duke Ellington Orchestra, playing hot New Orleans jazz at the popular Cotton Club in Harlem. The talking brass instruments, wailing clarinets, ritualistic drumbeats, beautiful melodies, and precise orchestration of the Ellington sound astonished black and white listeners alike. Ellington hired the best musicians available and deftly exploited the unique sounds of each in his gifted orchestrations, writing for specific musicians to capitalize on special talents they sometimes didn't know they had. Although he was already famous as a great jazz pianist, Ellington is said to have used the jazz band as his real "instrument," exploring its entire range of sounds with unprecedented imagination and creativity. By

FIGURE 13.3
Duke Ellington.

juxtaposing instruments in nontraditional combinations and using them in the extreme limits of their range, he transformed their sound, sometimes effectively obscuring their identification.

Far more than an arranger, Ellington is recognized as a serious composer, producing symphonic works such as "Black, Brown, and Beige" (1943), international pieces such as "Latin American Suite" (1968), and large-scale sacred works incorporating dancers, choruses, and gospel singers together with his own band, as well as the lovely songs to which generations have danced and romanced. Drawing from many seemingly irreconcilable American musics, including field hollers, Shaker hymns, fiddlers' dance tunes, minstrel songs, ragtime, Tin Pan Alley, New Orleans jazz, and—especially—the blues, Ellington created a particular American tapestry of mood and style.

Listening Example 47 presents "Mood Indigo," a haunting tune Ellington composed in 1930 and arranged innumerable times for many combinations of

Listening Example 47

"Mood Indigo"

Composer
Duke Ellington

CD 2
Track 15
3:03

Performers
Duke Ellington and His Orchestra

Tempo
Rather slow and bluesy. Although the performance is of a quality and style suitable for intense listening, it is also eminently danceable.

Instruments
This big band arrangement includes five trumpets, three trombones, five saxophones (two tenor, two alto, one baritone), two clarinets, bass, drums, and Duke Ellington at the piano.

After a brief piano introduction, a muted sax, accompanied by a **walking bass,** improvises on the famous melody, barely suggesting fragments of the tune. The trumpets finally introduce the lovely theme (1:54), playing in a style appropriately warm and mellow rather than brilliant or virtuosic as in standard dance pieces. The bass continues to provide steady support as the muted saxophone delicately embellishes the highly chromatic melody.

Even in this brief rendition, the colors of the sounds change continuously, rendering the timbres endlessly interesting in their own right. Listening to other versions of "Mood Indigo" provides further insight into Ellington's incredibly versatile and imaginative approach to orchestration.

instruments. The chromatic melodies, *bitonal* harmonics (juxtaposing one key over another), and dreamy mood made "Mood Indigo" music to listen to, as well as dance to; and lyrics added later rendered the piece a popular song of lasting appeal.

During the early days of rock and roll, Ellington's jazz was heard less often, but at the 1956 Newport Jazz Festival his orchestra made a tremendous hit, leading to a best-selling album, *Ellington at Newport,* and to prestigious new concert dates. From then Duke Ellington's fame soared to unprecedented heights. We will meet him again in the discussion of concert jazz.

Women in Jazz

Besides the internationally known big bands of Duke Ellington, Count Basie, Benny Goodman, Fletcher Henderson, Glenn Miller, and three or four other outstanding men, from 1937 to 1948 there was also an all-female band that can only be described as a blazingly hot jazz force. Women wishing to play jazz in those days faced nearly insurmountable odds: it was widely assumed that they didn't have the strength, temperament, or talent to measure up to the men.

Nevertheless, during World War II, all-woman bands (all-girl bands, as they were called then) flourished as men went off to war, and people grew accustomed to seeing women in various nontraditional roles. Well-known all-white female bands included one led by Phil Spitalny (note the male leader) and another led by Ina Ray Hutton. Most impressive of all, however, were the **International Sweethearts of Rhythm.** Predominantly black, with Chinese, Indian, Hawaiian, and white representation as well, they were also all-female and thus were largely ignored by white audiences, films, and print media, who would not take a bunch of women seriously as jazz musicians. Yet at Harlem's Apollo Theater and Savoy Ballroom—drawing probably the most demanding jazz audiences in the land—they made a tremendous, and a lasting, hit.

Reactions against Big Band Music

A new generation of young Americans unfamiliar with early jazz danced to the happy sounds of big band music through the 1940s. Many older people enjoyed the music as well, finding the repertoire familiar because the big bands, like the earlier combos, based their music upon marches, hymns, and the made-to-order songs of Tin Pan Alley, whose formula had altered only slightly since the 1890s.

Reactions against big band music began to set in, however, even while crowds continued dancing to its swinging beat, as increasingly complex band arrangements, emphasizing rhythm and swing rather than melody, sometimes rendered the source tune unidentifiable. Though the repetition of riffs held arrangements together while effectively heightening the intensity of the mood, the swing crowd began to resist challenging instrumental arrangements in favor of simple songs.

Although primarily an instrumental concept, early jazz had important reciprocal relationships with popular song: Early combos improvised on the melodies or harmonies of popular songs, and many songs of the 1920s and 1930s were jazz-flavored. The big bands played arrangements of old and new songs from Tin Pan Alley. Thus it is not surprising that at some point in the 1930s, big bands began to work closely with vocalists. Slowly the style of big band music changed as bands assumed the role of accompaniment and as great instrumental soloists vied for popularity with outstanding vocalists, regularly alternating instrumental and vocal choruses. Ella Fitzgerald (1918–1996) became famous for her scat singing, and crooners such as Rudy Vallee and Bing Crosby became increasingly popular as the technology of microphones and recording engineers allowed their more intimate personal styles to be projected to an audience. In time, crowds came not so much to dance as to hear Crosby, Frank Sinatra, and other popular singers, for whom the bands provided support. A lush string sound returned to favor, replacing the brassier sound of big band jazz; and by the mid-1940s singers accompanied by orchestral ensembles supplanted the big swing bands in the affections of the white public.

Billie Holiday (1915–1959)

Billie Holiday (born Eleanora Fagan) trod softly between the worlds of jazz and pop, although her interpretations of many great blues songs were undeniably those of a great jazz singer. Jazz scholar Nat Hentoff said that Lady Day, as she was respectfully known, could simply say hello, and the sound and rhythm of that one word became the very definition of jazz. Among her most striking innovations was her way of "microphonizing" her voice—using the microphone, at that time a new enhancement, not only to amplify but to alter her voice and add expressive effects.

A tragic figure who died possessed of just seventy cents despite having earned a lot of money during her career as singing and recording artist, she once recorded an unforgettable ballad, "Strange Fruit," concerning lynching. The words of the ballad—devastating to hear or read—have a strange history of their own. They were written not by a black but by a first-generation Jewish American whose parents had come to the United States from Russia. Abel Meeropol (1903–1987), whose pen name was Lewis Allen (and who later adopted the two children of Ethel and Julius Rosenberg, whom he had never met, after their parents' execution in 1953), was inspired by a picture of a lynching to write the poem and to set it to music. (The words to "Strange Fruit" can be found at several Web sites.)

Bebop

In the early 1940s an angry new style emerged, largely unnoticed at first but destined to exert great influence on the future of jazz. The new music, called **bebop** or **bop,** began as a revolt by a few virtuosic black musicians against the domestication of jazz by the swing bands of the 1930s. Bebop musicians reacted against the polished performances of written, rehearsed "jazz"; they resented limitation to the short stylized solos of big band music, the dependence on written arrangements, and the lack of freedom to improvise. They further resented the disproportionate financial rewards granted to white musicians less creative and less innovative than many underrecognized blacks. The tight, difficult, virtuosic music they conceived as a return to the ideals of early jazz (improvisation, virtuosity, and close interaction between soloist and combo) is generally considered the first truly modern jazz.

Like much of the concert music of the 1940s and later, bebop was performed by a small ensemble of virtuoso musicians. The music consisted of stark, clear, technically demanding instrumental lines. The angular melodies moved by large unpredictable leaps instead of narrow steps, and the solos were so rapid-fire that they were too fast to dance to—and almost too fast to listen to. Rather than following prearranged or familiar harmonic progressions, bop musicians challenged each other to chart new harmonic paths and make them work. Their chords, large and richly dissonant, startled ears accustomed to tame, consistently pleasant sounds. Further, they sometimes improvised on the *harmony* of a famous tune rather than on the *melody,* which remained obscure to puzzled listeners. The best bebop musicians in fact achieved a revolutionary sound that effectively changed the course of jazz.

The typical bebop combo consisted of trumpet and saxophone, double bass, piano, and percussion. The melody instruments (trumpet and sax) sometimes began a composition by playing a pop, blues, or original melody in unison, then alternating with increasingly complex improvisations while supported by the other players. The double bass, which marked the beat, sometimes took melodic responsibility as well in a pattern inherited from the swing era called the walking bass, while the piano and percussion supplied unexpected, irregular accents.

A saxophonist who died young and a trumpet player who remained active until shortly before his death at seventy-six were among the innovators and outstanding exponents of bebop.

Charlie "Bird" Parker (1920–1955)

As a youngster in Kansas City, Missouri, **Charlie Parker** (Figure 13.4) absorbed the sounds of Lester Young, Count Basie, and other outstanding jazz musicians active there. Later Parker moved to New York City, where he jammed in Harlem's clubs with pianist **Thelonious Monk** (1920–1982) and trumpeter Dizzy Gillespie (see pp. 223–225), inspiring and inspired by them to develop the complex new music.

Not only was Charlie "Bird" Parker an amazing saxophone virtuoso, his sax tone dry and biting and his melodies highly jagged in contour, but he also introduced new rhythmic, melodic, and improvisational techniques that lifted jazz to a different plane. A knowledgeable musician, he sometimes quoted fragments of popular and classical compositions, moving rapidly from such familiar phrases to soaring flights of melodic virtuosity. Parker often performed with a fiercely rapid tempo and an unrelenting emotional intensity that left the weak behind but offered adventurous listeners glorious new insights to jazz.

Addicted to drugs and alcohol and ill for much of his short life, Parker—whom some consider the most influential of all jazz musicians—died when he

FIGURE 13.4
Charlie Parker.

FIGURE 13.5

Dizzy Gillespie.

was only thirty-four. In 1988, the movie *Bird* brought the story of Charlie Parker to popular attention; but among serious jazz afficionados, his memory and influence have never faded.

John Birks "Dizzy" Gillespie (1917–1993) **Dizzy Gillespie**

(Figure 13.5) improvised rhythms of a complexity unprecedented in Western culture, reached notes no one knew the trumpet could play, and devised harmonic changes defying the accepted rules of harmony. But even more important, his music touched the human spirit with passion and beauty.

Gillespie enjoyed African Cuban rhythms and sounds, which he included in such pieces as his big band number "Manteca," among the earliest pieces to bring Latin American sounds to modern jazz. (See Chapter 15.) Less zealous than Parker and apparently comfortable with a variety of jazz styles and techniques, Gillespie remained an active performer until shortly before his death, his famous balloon cheeks highly visible on television programs and in concerts around the world.

Parker and Gillespie's performance of "KoKo" (Listening Example 48) demonstrates the incredible virtuosity, musicianship, and compatibility of these outstanding musicians.

Although popularity was never a primary goal of the bebop musicians, their style might have attracted a wider audience had the public been able to

"KoKo"

Performers

Charlie Parker (alto saxophone), Dizzie Gillespie (trumpet, piano), Max Roach (drums), Curley Russell (bass)

CD 2
Track 16
2:53

Tempo

Extremely rapid

At a session intended to record a swing standard titled "Cherokee," by Ray Noble, Parker and Gillespie improvised halfheartedly on the tune until Parker, tired of the familiar melody, decided to improvise instead on the *chords*. Therefore, instead of beginning as usual with the "head," or reference to the standard tune, Parker used bits of his own melodic material, skillfully weaving them over and through the rather unusual chord changes of "Cherokee." The resulting historic recording—one of Parker's greatest solos—is based on no prewritten melody at all (incidentally requiring Parker's recording company to make no royalty payment for "Cherokee," because chords, unlike melodies, did not bear a copyright). Neither is Parker's "KoKo" related to Duke Ellington's earlier composition of the same name.

Introduction: The alto sax and muted trumpet begin the elaborate, rather eerie, introduction, playing in unison, accompanied by lightly brushed drums.

We hear a brief muted trumpet solo (0:10), an alto sax solo (0:15), and the sax and muted trumpet playing in parallel harmony (0:20), all accompanied by complex accents on the drums.

Parker plays the first chorus (0:27), accompanied by drums, a fast walking bass, and (soon) sparse piano chords, played by Gillespie, who has put down his trumpet and moved to the keyboard. Technically, the chorus is in **AABA** form, the bridge (**B**) beginning about 53 seconds into the piece.

Parker maintains his extremely brisk tempo and astonishing virtuosity throughout the second chorus (beginning at about 1:15).

An intricate drum solo (2:10) varies the texture and sonority—and gives Gillespie time to return to his trumpet.

The alto sax and muted trumpet play in unison (2:31), accompanied by brushes on the cymbals.

We hear a muted trumpet solo, then an alto sax solo, both backed up by cymbals.

The parallel harmony of alto sax and muted trumpet heard in the introduction return to round out and conclude this remarkable piece.

experience its evolution. At the very time Parker and Gillespie were leading the bebop revolution, however, a recording artists' strike caused a ban on commercial recordings of popular music that lasted for about two years (see p. 161). Thus even the devoted jazz audience was largely nonplussed by the sophistication and complexity of the first bebop recordings produced when the strike finally ended. One tends not to like what one does not understand, and there were many who did not understand bebop.

But bebop is an important music, which not only challenged and stimulated talented musicians and conscientious listeners but also ushered in the age of modern jazz. Meant for listening more than dancing, bebop had significant implications for musicians interested in establishing relationships between concert music and jazz.

Jazz as Concert Music

A number of Americans writing music in the vernacular tradition have applied their knowledge of classical techniques to popular pieces; and many composers have simply refused to distinguish between classical and popular musics in terms of either quality or preference. Among those we have studied, John Philip Sousa, the march king, also composed operettas and symphonic works; Scott Joplin, the king of ragtime, wrote operas; and George Gershwin wrote one opera and several symphonic pieces as well as the many Broadway show tunes we still hear and romance to today.

Thus during the 1940s, as jazz steadily grew more serious, dissonant, intellectual, and complex, some jazz musicians absorbed influences from contemporary classical music, reversing the process by which classical musicians had borrowed jazz techniques for their own purposes. No longer music for dancing and entertainment alone but for serious listening as well, jazz had become, in fact, a kind of classical or concert music in its own right. By the early 1950s, jazz was performed frequently in concert, especially on college campuses and at huge jazz festivals. Both black and white jazz musicians, and their listeners as well, took a more intellectual approach to jazz than had earlier been customary, and jazz criticism became a recognized field. Today, as we shall see in Chapter 14, certain jazz composers collaborate with poets, choreographers, and classical musicians to produce serious concert works.

Jazz Composition Because the essence of jazz is improvisation, musicians wishing to combine classical and jazz techniques faced a new challenge: They had to create a balance between what was written, what was improvised by the soloists, and what an ensemble achieved collectively. Certainly there were precedents for requiring performers in the classical tradition to improvise:

1. During the Baroque period (1600–1750), composers wrote the melody and bass lines of a composition, leaving the harmonies to be filled in by a lute or keyboard player.
2. In the early Classical period (1750–1825), soloists improvised one or more cadenzas in performing a solo concerto.

3. Church organists often are expected to improvise music that connects one part of a service, or one verse of a hymn, to another.

In all these cases, however, musicians improvised within established guidelines appropriate for a given style of music. Jazz as classical music was a *new* concept, and musicians involved in its evolution faced new situations. The symphonic jazz of the 1920s, such as George Gershwin's *Rhapsody in Blue,* was simply concert music with some of the flavors of jazz; and the big band arrangements approached the concept of composed music but were hardly original compositions. By the 1940s, however, jazz composers were doing more than arranging familiar tunes—they were writing original jazz compositions, and at that point jazz entered the world of art music. Some will question whether concert jazz is jazz at all; but the question remains unimportant if we value each style and each piece of music according to its merits, no matter what label it carries.

Duke Ellington, whom we have already met as an outstanding big band leader and as the composer of "Mood Indigo," also wrote serious concert, or classical, music. His scope, in fact, was enormous: In addition to his beautiful ballads and inspired band arrangements, he composed tone poems, ballet suites, concerto-like miniatures for star sidemen, sacred music, topical revues, film scores, and extended jazz works; and at the time of his death he was writing a comic opera, *Queenie Pie,* intended for public television. Finally staged in Philadelphia and Boston in 1986, *Queenie Pie* has received occasional performances in other cities since.

Ellington has, in fact, been referred to as America's most prolific composer of the twentieth century, in both number of pieces (almost 2,000) and variety of forms. In title and content, his serious compositions often reflected the black experience in America with extraordinary depth, wit, tenderness, and strength. Among his best-known symphonic works, for example, *Black, Brown, and Beige,* subtitled "A Tone Parallel to the History of the Negro in America," premiered by Duke Ellington and his orchestra at Carnegie Hall in 1943, has been played by many other major orchestras since. Ellington returned to Carnegie Hall on a near-annual basis until 1948; and when the nation mourned the death of President Franklin D. Roosevelt in 1945, Ellington's orchestra was the only dance band selected to pay tribute in a memorial radio broadcast.

Ellington wrote "Concerto for Cootie" (Listening Example 49), one of his most beautiful compositions, to feature the trumpeter Charles "Cootie" Williams. A **concerto** is defined as a multimovement composition for orchestra and one or more soloists—that is, a piece consisting of several semi-independent sections, or *movements.* (See the Prelude, p. 9.) Ellington chose, however, to write a one-movement piece.

Progressive Jazz

In 1949, pianist-arranger **Stan Kenton** (1912–1979) led a twenty-piece orchestra in a jazz concert at Carnegie Hall, where his tightly organized and beautifully balanced ensemble played with elegance and precision. Kenton's name for this music, **progressive jazz,** became the name of a new jazz movement. Kenton also

"Concerto for Cootie"

Composer
Duke Ellington

**CD 2
Track 17
3:19**

Form
ABA

Meter
Four beats to the bar

Tempo
Relaxed

Instruments

Saxophones, clarinet, trumpets, trombones, bass, drum

Although not written in the Classical concerto form, which has three movements, this piece retains the masterful interplay between soloist and orchestra characteristic of the Classical form.

The trumpet (Cootie Williams) begins the piece on the downbeat with a phrase later adapted to begin Ellington's popular standard "Do Nothin' Till You Hear from Me."

Williams presents the beautiful **A** theme in several ways, skillfully altering the timbre of his instrument by using various mutes and playing techniques. The accompaniment also changes each time the theme recurs, producing rich and varied sonorities.

(1:56) The dramatic **B** theme differs from **A** in key and timbre. Williams plays it with the open horn, creatively extending and elaborating upon the melody.

(2:37) **A** returns, and the piece ends with a brief coda.

made other important contributions to modern jazz, including serious exploration of Latin American drums and rhythms in his big band jazz. (See p. 257.)

While Kenton and Woody Herman promoted progressive jazz in the East, **Dave Brubeck** (b. 1910) was in the forefront of progressive jazz on the West Coast, where performances such as that in "Take Five" (Listening Example 50) brought his quartet increasing fame and prestige. Brubeck, a pianist and composer who played with Dixieland and swing bands as a youngster, majored in music in college and then studied composition with the French composer Darius Milhaud (1892–1974; this name is pronounced mee-OH), one of several important European composers who sought to escape the horrors of World War II by living and teaching in America, profoundly affecting the course of our music history. Milhaud, who was particularly interested in jazz and had

Listening Example 50

"Take Five"   (excerpt)

Composer
Paul Desmond (saxophonist)

CD 2
Track 18
1:57

Performers
Dave Brubeck Quartet (piano, sax, bass, drums).

Meter
Quintuple, or five beats per measure. The beats are divided in the pattern *one*-two-three-*four*-five.

The piano marks the beginning of each measure with a low accented pitch, while the sax and drum solos weave intricate patterns over the steady five-beat accompanying figure.

written several symphonic pieces with jazzy rhythms and timbres, encouraged Brubeck to apply jazz techniques to his concert compositions.

But Brubeck also absorbed ideas from European art music. For example, intrigued by the manner in which Baroque keyboard players improvised chords over a given bass line, he produced polyphony reminiscent of the Baroque style. Brubeck's harmonies, however, are those of his own century, including effects that are **atonal** (without a tonic) and **polytonal** (with two or more tonics); and his rhythms are the complex rhythms and sometimes polyrhythms of modern jazz. He frequently uses **irregular meters**—five or seven beats per measure instead of the usual two, three, or four.

Dave Brubeck's Quartet (Brubeck as pianist, Paul Desmond on alto saxophone, Joe Morello as drummer, and David Wright on bass) achieved unprecedented popularity and sales for a jazz recording with Desmond's engaging piece "Take Five."

Cool Jazz

At the same time that Desmond, Brubeck, and Charles Mingus (see pp. 233–234) were evolving their "progressive" ideas, other jazz musicians were developing a style they called **cool,** closely related to and sometimes indistinguishable from progressive jazz. In reaction to the complexity and exclusive nature of bebop, they organized larger bands that included the sensuous sounds of symphonic instruments such as the French horn and oboe. More elegant and less hot than bebop, cool jazz clearly reflected the influence of European concert music—especially the Impressionistic harmonies of Claude Debussy and the sharp dissonances of Russian composer Igor Stravinsky.

FIGURE 13.6
Miles Davis.

The important musicians involved in cool jazz included **Miles Davis** (1926–1991, Figure 13.6), who in 1949–1950 led the nine-piece orchestra (nonet) that recorded the album later titled *Birth of the Cool*. Not much noticed at the time, the album later made a major impact on jazz musicians and fans. The project was Davis's; he organized the recording sessions, directed, called rehearsals, hired the halls, and wrote or cowrote some of the music.

"Boplicity" (Listening Example 51) demonstrates this more cerebral, less impassioned way of playing jazz.

But cool jazz was only one of the many styles Miles Davis explored, as he continued to make important contributions to jazz over the years. He became particularly interested in expanding the melodic possibilities of jazz by basing melodies on modes rather than on the major, minor, or blues scales. The music on Davis's album *Kind of Blue,* largely modal (see Prelude, p. 5), had a strong influence on many jazz musicians of varied tastes. A virtuoso trumpet player, Davis was also an outstanding bandleader, composer, and innovator who continued throughout his life to experiment with creative ideas in jazz.

Hard Bop

In the late 1950s, certain black musicians reacting against the detached, intellectual, "white" sounds of West Coast cool jazz combined driving rock-related rhythms with the "amen chords" of gospel to produce **hard bop.** Earthy, emotionally exuberant, intensely physical in concept, hard bop derives from the blues and embodies strong rhythms and bluesy phrasing. Melodies are straightforward, harmonies are simplified, and the rigid beat is punctuated with strong backbeats. Whereas bebop musicians generally improvised around the structure—although not the melody—of a popular or familiar tune, the less cerebral, aggressive hard bop often worked around new, unknown melodies.

"Boplicity"

CD 2
Track 19
3:00

Composers

Miles Davis and Gil Evans. "Boplicity" was cowritten by Davis and Evans and arranged by Evans. Davis wrote the melody, and Evans scored the written ensembles, adding horns and tuba to provide new timbres to the jazz ensemble.

Performers

The Miles Davis Nonet (nine-member ensemble) included trumpet, trombone, alto and baritone saxes, French horn, and tuba, bass, drums, and piano. The members of the nonet varied, but the musicians involved in this recording included Gerry Mulligan on baritone saxophone, and John Lewis on piano. Listen for the trumpet and alto on top, the baritone sax and tuba on the bottom, and the horn and trombone in the center. The rhythm instruments basically accompany the others.

"Boplicity" demonstrates Miles Davis's self-restraint and dramatic timing. He clearly appreciates the importance of silence as well as notes. The diminished use of **vibrato** (a discreet variation in pitch that adds warmth and intensity to vocal and instrumental sounds) produced a drier, "cool" sound compared with the hot effects of bebop. A piece of smooth, easy listening, "Boplicity" projects more simplicity than bop, while yet respecting the basic premises of the music it purports to challenge. Slower-paced, less emotional, more cerebral, and quieter than the impassioned sounds of bebop, "Boplicity" integrates many characteristics of bebop with the taming effects of arrangement, combining orchestral colors with the freedom of a small band.

The drummer **Art Blakey** (1919–1990), who worked with many of the biggest names in jazz, formed his own hard bop group, the Jazz Messengers, in the late 1940s and retained the name for other groups active in 1950s-style music. His 1955 recording of Horace Silver's "The Preacher," a funky blues piece with elements of gospel, clearly reflected the increasing influence of rhythm and blues (see p. 271–272) and gospel on jazz.

Ever more varied, increasingly sophisticated, jazz acknowledged at the end of the 1950s—as it does today—continuing awareness and appreciation of its roots.

Terms to Review

big bands Popular dance ensembles of the 1930s and 1940s, consisting of from twelve to eighteen players.

swing A term with many meanings, including (*a*) a mood of lilting spontaneity; (*b*) a danceable music played by the big bands in the 1930s and 1940s.

reeds Wind instruments in which the player causes small, flexible pieces of material called reeds to vibrate. Clarinets and saxophones are single-reed instruments; oboes and bassoons have double reeds.

jam   To improvise together with other members of an ensemble.

Kansas City jazz   A light, spacious, relaxed style based on melodic riffs.

riff   A repeated melodic or rhythmic pattern that provides unity in a jazz composition.

walking bass   A steadily moving pattern in the plucked string bass, having melodic as well as rhythmic implications.

bebop   A complex, highly improvised jazz style, largely developed by Charlie Parker and Dizzy Gillespie.

concerto   A multimovement work for orchestra plus solo instrument.

progressive jazz   A symphonic approach to jazz, introduced by Stan Kenton.

atonal   With no tonic note and no tonal relationships.

polytonal   In two or more keys at the same time.

irregular meters   Meters other than duple, triple, or quadruple. (Usually five or seven beats to the bar.)

cool   A jazz style introduced about 1950 for large bands including some symphonic instruments.

vibrato   A slight variation in pitch adding warmth and intensity to vocal or instrumental sounds.

hard bop   A style combining rock-related rhythms with gospel.

Key Figures

Fletcher Henderson
Count Basie
Lester Young
Benny Goodman
Glenn Miller
Mary Lou Williams

Duke Ellington
International Sweethearts
   of Rhythm
Charlie Parker
Thelonious Monk

Dizzy Gillespie
Stan Kenton
Dave Brubeck
Miles Davis
Art Blakey

Optional Listening Example

Dizzy Gillespie: "Shaw 'Nuff"

Suggestions for Further Listening

Thelonious Monk: "'Round Midnight"
Miles Davis: *Birth of the Cool*
Art Blakey: "The Preacher"

Duke Ellington: Various versions of *Mood Indigo*
Ellington: Soundtrack of the film *Anatomy of a Murder*
Abel Meeropol, "Strange Fruit," sung by Billie Holiday

Suggestions for Viewing

Lady Sings the Blues (1972, a film about Billie Holiday)
Bird (1988, a film about Charlie "Bird" Parker)

The Terminal (2004, a film about jazz musicians, featuring Benny Golman, a former member of the Jazz Messengers)

Critical Thinking

Discuss the relationship between Fletcher Henderson and Benny Goodman. Is Goodman to be praised for having hired Henderson as an arranger, or criticized for having exploited the black musician's talents?

Have opportunities improved significantly in recent years for women in jazz? If so, how?

Of the styles studied in this chapter, which do you prefer and why? Which are likely to have the most influence on future musicians?

Go to www.mhhe.com/ferrisaml5 for a list of additional Web-based resources that relate to the content in this chapter.

Jazz since 1960

A s emerging new styles joined without replacing established trends in jazz, the jazz experience increased in complexity and sophistication, although hardly in popularity. From the time bebop entered the fray— well before rock and roll swept the popular music industry off its feet— jazz has belonged as much to the classical as to the popular music world. Jazz pianist, composer, and scholar Billy Taylor refers to jazz, in fact, as America's classical music.

Throughout the 1960s, jazz musicians explored relationships between classical and popular music, placing less emphasis on outstanding solo performances accompanied by players who obligingly yielded the spotlight until their turn came to take it, and favoring instead collective improvisation by several, or even by all, ensemble members at the same time.

Charles Mingus (1922–1979)

Charles Mingus (Figure 14.1), a double bass player intimately involved with progressive jazz in the 1950s, made important contributions to jazz history both as a bass player and as a composer with unprecedented ideas of jazz composition. Mingus made the bass line significantly more interesting and important than it had been in early or traditional jazz styles, his magnificent bass solos sometimes imitating saxophone or piano lines.

During the 1960s, his ideas concerning jazz composition made Mingus an extremely controversial, although ultimately influential, figure. Perhaps more than any other jazz musician, Mingus explored the complex relationships between jazz composition and improvisation, for which purpose he established the Charles Mingus Jazz Workshop in New York in 1955. Although he prescribed a formal framework for each composition, Mingus encouraged individual freedom and creativity within that framework, disapproving, for that reason, of a written score.

Mingus's "unwritten compositions," in the tradition of progressive jazz, were rhythmically very complex. His rhythmic pulse was flexible, and he liked

233

FIGURE 14.1

The American jazz musician
Charles Mingus.

to accelerate tempos, often calling out instructions to the players. Further, he changed meters frequently. His sometimes modal bass lines precluded the use of traditional chord changes, requiring musicians to improvise new kinds of melody lines instead of those based on given tunes. In short, Mingus revolutionized the concept of jazz as well as of jazz composition.

Free Jazz

The innovations of Charles Mingus and others during the 1950s encouraged a number of jazz musicians to seek new approaches to improvisation, which remained at the core of the concept of jazz. Some shared with Mingus the conviction that jazz was not necessarily—or primarily—about individual solos, but about rhythm and interplay best expressed by the **collective improvisation** of several or all members of the ensemble. In 1960, **Ornette Coleman** (b. 1930) introduced free collective improvisation in an album titled *Free Jazz,* which defied the perception of jazz as generally accessible to the ordinary listener, for **free jazz** was a difficult music, challenging to performers and listeners alike, with no familiar chord changes, no references to popular songs or blues, and no steady beat. In free jazz, each musician improvised independently, aware of and responsive to the other players but bound by no preset obligations. Even the initial phrases of a composition, played by the ensemble's soloists together, were not necessarily in unison.

Free jazz further released musicians from the strictures of tonality, of recurring rhythmic patterns or a fixed pulse, and of predetermined themes. (They did, however, have short melodic motives—riffs—that they could insert in the improvisation and that others could join in on.) It has been suggested that free jazz expressed in musical terms the same sorts of freedom African Americans were demanding and finally achieving in many areas of life during that turbulent decade. And the new assertive independence free jazz offered rhythm

FIGURE 14.2

The album cover for Ornette
Coleman's *Free Jazz*, with art
by Jackson Pollock.

instruments might be compared to the respected positions African Americans
were now assuming in life. The new music also bore a relationship to chance
music (discussed in Chapter 23), and Coleman stated that he thought his playing had some rapport with abstract expressionist art. The cover of Coleman's
recording *Free Jazz* features, in fact, a reproduction of a Jackson Pollock painting (Figure 14.2).

Free jazz also reflects an interest in non-Western music, which intrigued
many twentieth-century composers of classical music. Having no chord
changes to play relieved free jazz ensembles of the need to include a piano,
with its restrictive keyboard limited to the tones of the black and white keys.
This in turn freed musicians to explore non-Western scales and encouraged
them to include instruments from other cultures in their ensembles and to play
Western instruments in nontraditional ways. The use of *microtones* (lying between the tones of a piano keyboard) and certain rhythmic techniques derived
from the music of India heighten the emotional effect and intellectual challenge of Coleman's performances.

The jazz saxophonist and composer **John Coltrane** (1926–1967, Figure 14.3) became in a sense the spiritual leader of free jazz during the last years
of his short life. Coltrane's free spirit, however, caused him to change his stylistic preferences throughout his career. Early known for producing "sheets of
sound," because he played so many notes at rapid-fire tempos (as on *Giant
Steps,* 1959), he explored other areas of interest in later works. For example,
having worked with Miles Davis on the influential album *Kind of Blue*,
Coltrane furthered his interest in modal music, and also reflected the hypnotic
pulsating quality of Indian music, in *My Favorite Things* (1960).

Widely known and admired for the beautiful tone and the variety of effects
he achieved on his tenor and soprano saxophones, Coltrane countered Ornette

FIGURE 14.3

John Coltrane.

Coleman's concept of collective improvisation by playing individual solos of unprecedented length, most famously in "Chasin' the Trane" (1961). Generally dissonant and complex, Coltrane's music features frequent harmonic changes and some polytonal passages.

In 1964 Coltrane produced the very spiritual, emotional album *A Love Supreme*. Here he seemed to identify with rebellious youth of the 1960s seeking new cultural and spiritual identities based on non-Western traditions. Effectively combining religious ecstasy with tranquillity and meditation, this hypnotic mixture of music and chanting became one of the best-selling and best-loved jazz albums of all time. We hear an excerpt from Part I of *A Love Supreme* in Listening Example 52.

Third Stream

Third stream *combines* jazz and classical music in a manner that—unlike the *blending* of classical and jazz effects in symphonic, cool, and progressive jazz—allows each style to retain its characteristic qualities. The composer who first attracted attention to this new idea, which had not yet been named, was **John Lewis** (1920–2001), a classically trained African American pianist interested in the forms of European art music, especially of the Renaissance and Baroque periods. Lewis founded the Modern Jazz Quartet (MJQ) in 1952 (Figure 14.4) and wrote many compositions for that ensemble, often using forms—such as *canon, fugue,* or *variations*—of the earlier periods he admired. Some of Lewis's compositions were to be performed by the MJQ with a symphony orchestra or with another classical music organization, the members of the jazz quartet improvising some of their music while the classical ensemble played what was written. Thus each group remained true to its traditions, and the collaboration formed a new style of music combining classical forms with jazz improvisation and the feel of swing.

The term for the new style was introduced in 1957 by **Gunther Schuller** (b. 1925), who, for a time at least, believed that jazz and classical music should

A Love Supreme, Part I,
"Acknowledgment" (excerpt)

CD 2
Track 20
4:33

Composer

John Coltrane. Coltrane conceived the themes and the style, mood, and philosophy of the piece; but his quartet seemingly drew inspiration from Coltrane's mind (heart, soul), for there was no written score.

Performers

John Coltrane Quartet (Coltrane's tenor saxophone plus piano, bass, drums)

Meter

After the freely improvised introduction, the meter is basically quadruple. The meter is free and flexible, however, changing as the piece progresses. Listen too for complex polyrhythms skillfully performed by each of the instruments throughout the piece.

Form

"Acknowledgment" is the first of four sections, which make up a suite. The other three parts are "Resolution," "Pursuance," and "Psalm."

A gong begins the rhythmically free introduction. Coltrane's sax, in a meditative mood, explores several rhapsodic phrases, quietly accompanied by dissonant piano chords and shimmering metallic sounds. The introduction tapers off with a few breathy sax notes and gentle rolls on the piano. Notice the variety of richly sensuous timbres in this brief opening passage.

The bass introduces the four-note main theme, based on the words "a love supreme," and the quartet continues the spiritual quest, alternately meditative, contemplative, passionate, ecstatic, and at peace. The very simple bass lines would seem inadequate to support the complexity of all that is built upon them, yet everything holds together beautifully.

Our excerpt tapers off, due to time constraints; but you may find the complete movement at several sites on the Web. Listening to the remainder of the piece, notice that before abandoning his sax to chant the phrase "a love supreme," Coltrane plays the strangely moving four-note motive in each of the twelve keys—perhaps to suggest the complete availability of the love supreme. His chanting lends a mystic, hypnotic flavor to this emotionally varied piece, which gradually lessens in intensity of emotion and ends quietly.

FIGURE 14.4

The Modern Jazz Quartet (MJQ). Drums, Connie Kay; piano and director, John Lewis; bass, Percy Heath; vibraphone, Milt Jackson.

be treated as separate but congenial entities. In 1957 he referred famously to classical music as the "first stream" of music and jazz as the "second stream," calling their combination in a manner allowing each to retain its characteristic qualities *third stream* music.

Third stream music as Schuller conceived it remained in vogue for only a short time; but the collision—or cooperation—it represents between classically trained musicians, who depend on fixed ideas of standard Western notation, and jazz musicians, who predicate their art on pliability and invention, persists. Ornette Coleman, who remains interested to this day in the concept that used to be called third stream, has been writing classical music since the 1950s, when he produced several string quartets; and in the 1960s he combined jazz and classical concepts much as John Lewis and Gunther Schuller were doing. His piece for symphony orchestra and solo jazz improvisers titled "Skies of America," written in the mid-1960s, gives the conductor something of an improvisatory role as well: choosing between an array of notated inserts to be cued to the orchestra by means of hand signals. Of course the piece poses quandaries for classically trained orchestral musicians accustomed to relying on a straightforward interpretation of the notes printed in a score: thus when Coleman suggested at a rehearsal of the piece by the New York Philharmonic in 1997 that the musicians might choose to play notes *other* than those he had written, a violinist complained that this concept was very hard to understand, to which Coleman replied, smiling, "Just because it's hard to understand doesn't mean it's not true."

The 1970s

Before 1970, it is possible to define a dominant, though hardly exclusive, style characteristic of each decade: we may see the 1920s as the jazz age, the 1930s as the era of swing, the 1940s reacting to bebop, the 1950s staying cool, and the

1960s exploring relationships between jazz and classical music. Although no one style reigned exclusively at any time, and all existed concurrently with other important kinds of jazz, each of those decades is associated with a particular approach to jazz distinguishing it from other such periods. It is even possible to discern an alternation between *classically* cool and *romantically* emotional music decade by decade: the emotional intensity of the roaring twenties, followed by the soothing sounds of big band music, succeeded by the challenge of bebop, countered by *The Birth of the Cool,* to which the 1960s offered the intellectually rigorous free jazz.

From 1970 to 1980 several important movements not only coexisted but seem to have had relatively comparable influences on the jazz of succeeding periods. The decade experienced a comeback of *swing,* which remains strong today; European *chamber music–style combos* appealed to many musicians and listeners; and *bebop* made a powerful and lasting return. But two other movements vied for attention during the 1970s: *world music* and—especially—*fusion.*

Fusion (Jazz-Rock)

Jazz and rock, which came from the same roots (blues, gospel, work songs), both faced crises as the 1970s began. Jazz seemed to have lost its identity, foundering somewhere between classical and foreign ethnic musics; and rockers, mourning the deaths of some of their greatest stars, struggled to find the means to address the tragic social and political events of the day (see p. 290).

Miles Davis's ensemble incorporated rock rhythms in some of their music beginning in the mid-1960s; and early in the new decade numerous other jazz musicians, who after all had grown up to the sounds of rock and roll, also began to invigorate their music with the rhythms of what had become the most compellingly popular music in history. Introduced in Great Britain in 1963, the movement sprang to life here with Miles Davis's recording of *Bitches Brew* (1969). Davis fanned the flames begun by *Bitches Brew* with *On the Corner* (1972), referred to by some critics as "antijazz." The album features an amazing array of instruments, including an Indian sitar, and a rock (funky) drumbeat shocking to some listeners, thrilling to others. (The dense textures and complex rhythms derived from rhythm and blues gave rise to the term *funk* or *funky* in its 1970s connotation.)

Jazz-rock, or **fusion,** or **jazz-rock-fusion,** as it is variously called, melds rock rhythms and the use of electronic instruments with collective improvisation, extreme ranges of volume (from very loud to whisper-soft), and rapid shifts in meter, tempo, and mood that are uncharacteristic of rock. Further, fusion is an instrumental music, without the vocals generally inherent to rock. But the use of bass guitar or electric bass instead of jazzers' traditional stand-up bass allowed fusion groups to play faster and to alter their sounds with electronic effects; and the manner in which snare drums and bass drums replaced the rhythmic effects previous jazz ensembles had assigned to piano and cymbals raised the rhythmic section to a position of dominance unprecedented in the history of jazz.

By the mid-1970s, some jazz ensembles included electronic organs and other keyboards, on which many jazz pianists enjoyed working, as well as a variety of synthesizers. Electroacoustic instruments—those on which sound is mechanically generated and then electronically amplified and altered—were often included as well. (Electric instruments belonging to the second category include piano, clarinets, guitars, saxophones, trumpets, and drums.) These ideas were not new: Benny Goodman's sextet featured an electric guitar in 1939, the electric organ first gained popularity in black rhythm and blues, and the multi-talented singer pianist Ray Charles (see pp. 280–281) played an electric piano for "What'd I Say" in 1959. But electric instruments affected jazz to a new degree in the 1970s. Recording technology also acquired unprecedented importance for jazz musicians, rendering the sound engineer an artist as well as a technician, responsible for manipulating the musicians' sounds to best advantage.

Weather Report, an outstanding fusion band of the 1970s and 1980s, was formed by two musicians (Joe Zawinul and Wayne Shorter) who had worked with Miles Davis on *Bitches Brew*. The band stunningly presents the virtuosity and rhythmic complexity associated with jazz-rock fusion. One of the earliest and most influential jazz-rock groups, Weather Report remained active for over fifteen years. (Song samples from Weather Report's album *Night Passage,* 1980, can be heard at Amazon.com.)

Two influential jazz pianists, each of whom—like so many jazz innovators of the 1970s and later—had also worked with Miles Davis, became particularly prominent in fusion. **Herbie Hancock** (b. 1940) found inspiration from and achieved huge success with electronic instruments. His album *Headhunters* (1973) became the first jazz album to be certified gold and remained for a time the best-selling of all jazz albums. The electric bass and keyboards and synthesizers on this album gave jazz a radical new sound, sometimes called *funk* (to be discussed in Chapter 16). *Headhunters* attracted a sizable international following for its creator, but Hancock has continued to explore acoustic jazz, jazz-rock, funk, "space music" (which sounds like background music for a science fiction film), and other sounds and styles that interest and challenge him.

The other pianist formerly associated with Miles Davis who became prominent in fusion was **Chick Corea** (b. 1941, Figure 14.5). In 1970 Corea formed a popular and influential fusion group, Return to Forever. A highly accomplished acoustic piano player, Corea turned more and more to a wide variety of electronic keyboard instruments during the 1970s. He also reflected the other major movement of that period, interest in world music, incorporating the influence of Latin American rhythms in his compositions and performances. (See p. 263 for Corea and the *bossa nova*.)

Stretch It, Part I (Listening Example 53), from Corea's album *Inside Out* (1990), illustrates the virtuosity and the rhythmic sophistication of fusion, which remains a vital jazz style today. (Amazon.com offers samples of Corea's music from various periods of his career.)

Integration of Foreign Sounds

Fusion, which implies a bringing together, also brought about serious schisms within the world of jazz, as musicians chose between acoustic and electronic instruments, between the flexible rhythms of free jazz and a soul- or gospel-influenced steady beat, and among a huge variety of concepts of music from foreign cultures. In the late 1960s,

FIGURE 14.5
Pianist Chick Corea onstage at the San Sebastian Jazz Festival, Spain, July 25, 1998.

Listening Example 53

Stretch It, Part I

Composer
Chick Corea

CD 2
Track 21
0:51

Performers
Chick Corea Elektric Band, consisting of piano and synthesizer (Chick Corea), sax, guitar, electric bass, and drums

Tempo
Fast

Meter
Duple—but listen for rhythmic complexities and changing meters as the piece progresses.

The piano begins with a carefree upward thrust, which the band furthers, setting the happy mood of the little piece. A recurring bouncy two-note motive enhances the good humor. Despite melodic as well as rhythmic intricacies, with phrases rising and falling in turn, the piece leaves us with a feeling of uplift, ending as it began with a joyously soaring phrase.

John Coltrane sparked interest in bringing characteristics of many foreign ethnic musics into jazz, and after his death this became a compelling concept for a number of outstanding jazz musicians, who integrated music from India, Brazil, Arabia, Bali, Japan, China, various African cultures, and many other cultures into their own distinctive performances. European concert music also attracted many jazz musicians, some of whom moved to Europe, where they lived for several years.

One such musician was **Don Cherry** (1936–1995), who worked with Ornette Coleman and John Coltrane and performed and recorded in Europe and in New York during the 1960s. Having traveled extensively in Asia and Africa as well, Cherry settled in Sweden in the early 1970s and became active there in music education and performance. Referring to himself as a "world musician," Cherry played many ethnic instruments from Tibet, China, India, Bali, and other countries besides the trumpet for which he first became known. In 1978 he and two colleagues—a Brazilian percussionist and an American who played sitar, tabla, and percussion—formed a trio, Codona, that performed a seemingly boundless array of ethnic musics for schoolchildren, enthusiastic adult audiences, and recordings.

The 1980s

For jazz musicians, the 1980s proved a fragmented period of enormous diversity, exploration, and discovery. New information about other music traditions, together with sophisticated new technology, greatly extended the range of jazz identity. World music remained important. Electronic techniques expanded their applications. In many cases, a single musician or group participated in a number of kinds of jazz, establishing no definitive identity with any one.

Among the great diversity of jazz styles, however, two fields of interest seem particularly characteristic of the 1980s: crossover jazz, or the blending of jazz and various other musics; and a strong revival of interest in traditional styles.

Crossover Music The blending of jazz and classical music, defined as third stream by Gunther Schuller, has faded into and out of favor over the years. John Lewis's Modern Jazz Quartet, for example, seen as a black response to the intellectualism of the Dave Brubeck Quartet, and as New York's answer to West Coast cool jazz, gained popularity and stirred up controversy, and the group played their "Last Concert," as they titled the performance and its subsequent album, in New York in 1974. Sensing a change of sensibilities in 1981, however, the Modern Jazz Quartet regrouped for a tour of Japan, which was so well received that they resumed touring. In 1984 they returned to the studio to resume their recording career as well.

Fusion, another form of crossover, remained strong in the 1980s, though not as popular as it had been in the 1970s. Herbie Hancock shocked and inspired listeners with his album *Future Shock* (1983), including the astonishing "Rockit," a fusion of jazz, funk, and electronics that became a massive hit and inspired an early MTV video.

A major artist of the period, who remains important today, is the jazz guitarist **Pat Metheny** (b. 1954). He initiated a rock band format that produced album after album of melodious jazz-rock. Metheny, like so many great jazz artists, has a seemingly inexhaustible range of interests and talents. In 1985, he composed the score for the movie *The Falcon and the Snowman,* which led to his recording "This Is Not America"—a Top 40 hit—with David Bowie. Having explored the musical possibilities of the twelve-string guitar and the guitar synthesizer, or *synclavier,* Metheny continues to move between pure jazz and pop jazz, to high acclaim.

Traditionalism Throughout the 1980s, as some jazz musicians blended jazz with rock, folk, pop, and foreign sounds, others resisted such combinations and the white European concert sounds of much crossover music, returning instead to earlier styles, variously updated to modern tastes. In 1982, the jazz trumpet player Wynton Marsalis (see pp. 245–246) founded a quintet that seemed to mark the beginning of this neoconservative trend in jazz. The traditionalists favored a return to pre-fusion acoustic values and to the disciplined, though elastic, harmonies and rhythms of earlier styles.

New Orleans, Chicago, and Dixieland jazz acquired a new generation of fans, while the dancing public enjoyed popular swing hits such as Glenn Miller's "In the Mood" and "String of Pearls." Never widely popular, bop and so-called post-bop offered traditionalists of the 1980s a structured yet progressive sound—daring, but not too new. The return to the steady beat associated with swing and other traditional jazz was likely to be tempered, however, with freely flowing, flexible rhythms and meters. These are indigenous to much music in Africa, but applying them to the music we call jazz was new.

The 1990s and Beyond

The 1990s became the first decade in the history of jazz to have no defining movement. Relationships to rock loomed ever more important as the twentieth century drew to a close, and soul, funk, world music, and crossover remained strong as a new fusion—jazz-rap—evolved. Fusion, in fact, becomes ever more complex, as musicians explore and expand styles, techniques, and technology. For example, when the British jazz group Us3 released their album *Cantaloop 2004,* updating their sampling of Herbie Hancock's 1994 recording "Cantaloupe Island," a press release described the new recording as "jazz-influenced urban sounds leaning heavily on a Latino R&B vibe" with vocals by a Brooklyn rapper and a singer who had been born in South Africa and was then based in London.

A new style, called *no wave* or *noise* evolved alongside all the others. According to the reed player, composer, and jazz scholar **John Zorn,** no wave seeks the emancipation of noise. Pieces in this style are extremely brief, very fast, and loud. Some people have described this music as a collage of very short, isolated sound events.

Zorn is among an impressive number of contemporary jazz musicians who are following Duke Elllington's lead in finding ways to integrate composition and improvisation. Although no one has yet attained the renown or adulation accorded to Ellington during his lifetime, or accomplished Ellington's seemingly effortless negotiation between popular culture and the fine arts, several visionary composers are attracting the attention and admiration of critics and fans of jazz. Many of them are masterful improvisers; several are scholars; all seem interested in putting to their own various uses many or all of the various ethnic, technological, traditional, and experimental resources offered in the early years of the twenty-first century.

The few well-recognized names in contemporary jazz introduced here are among those most likely to appear in reviews of concerts and recordings in newspaper and journals, and to be heard on outstanding jazz radio programs. The following brief paragraphs will indicate the wide range of sounds included in the realm of jazz today and perhaps will tempt you to explore these sounds at local libraries, on your radio, or on the Web.

Henry Threadgill (b. 1944)

Henry Threadgill, who plays saxophone and flute, has traveled with gospel musicians and blues bands. In the early 1960s, he became associated with a highly influential collective called the Association for the Advancement of Creative Music (AACM), formed to help Chicago musicians present their new, commercially unacceptable, music. In the 1970s he formed the group Air, a trio that explored African music, ragtime, and assorted other traditional musics; and since 1980 he has formed a number of groups using unusual instrumentation, such as the Very Very Circus, which uses trombone, two tubas, two guitars, and drums. This probably unique combination of instruments fuses the music of avant-garde jazz, funk, salsa, and East European marches into a highly original and distinctive sound. Besides a rigorous composing and recording schedule, Threadgill performs annually at leading jazz festivals throughout North America. (Samples of Threadgill's music can be heard on the Web.)

Anthony Braxton (b. 1945)

Anthony Braxton, also a former member of AACM, reached a milestone in jazz history by recording a double album of solo alto saxophone music, *For Alto,* released in 1971. Soon other alto sax players followed his lead by making their own solo recordings. In the 1980s Braxton toured in Europe, but recently his attention has been at least as much on composing as on improvising, although he is a master improviser.

Braxton, endlessly exploring and restlessly seeking creative new means of expression, has written for everything from the solo saxophone to huge orchestral ensembles and opera. A highly intellectual composer, he has devised systems for composing music, some based on mathematical relationships, diagrams, or formulas as a means of generating improvisation within the framework of an orchestral composition. In some of his pieces, parts can be played by different instruments, depending on what is available or desired for a particular performance. Some of his compositions can be played together, in a concept related to the ideas of John Cage and chance music (see pp. 378–384).

Anthony Davis (b. 1951)

Anthony Davis, sometimes referred to as a crossover musician, frequently blends jazz and classical styles in his compositions. A fine pianist and improviser, he prefers to write out most of his own music, having said that he considers improvisation just one compositional tool within the framework of a piece. His compositions draw on classical and Eastern musics, and his avant-garde jazz ensemble Episteme has been involved in some third stream–style performances with traditional, or classical, performers.

Davis's first opera, *The Life and Times of Malcolm X* (1986), was the first of several American operas based on a contemporary political subject (see p. 356). His fourth opera, *Amistad,* about a shipboard uprising by slaves and their subsequent trial, premiered in 1997. Meanwhile, in 1993, Davis made his Broadway debut, composing the music for Tony Kushner's prizewinning play (actually two plays) *Angels in America.* Davis's symphonic, choral, and chamber works, in which he deftly combines jazz and classical concepts, also are internationally admired. His orchestral music, organized according to clear formal designs, often includes improvisatory passages, and his recent Violin Concerto and the orchestral piece *Notes from the Underground* have effective jazz undertones. Davis has been a professor at the University of California at San Diego since 1998. In 2003–2004 he served as an artistic adviser and composer in residence for Improvise!—the American Composers Orchestra's festival and conference exploring improvisation in orchestral music.

Wynton Marsalis (b. 1961)

Wynton Marsalis (Figure 14.6) is a classicist who believes that bebop is the foundation of modern jazz and who continually defends, updates, and modernizes early jazz styles in his own compositions. A Juilliard-trained trumpet virtuoso who achieves an extremely beautiful quality of sound, Marsalis is also known as an educator and composer and, since

FIGURE 14.6
Wynton Marsalis, 2004.

1992, as the artistic director of jazz at Lincoln Center in New York. Having toured for a time with Art Blakey's Jazz Messengers, Marsalis took time off to steep himself in the roots of the tradition he so admired, and his deep study of blues, gospel, work songs, and the work of Louis Armstrong and Duke Ellington brought to his playing and to his composing new passion, depth, and technical brilliance.

Having voiced his concern with restoring "respect and seriousness" to jazz, Marsalis also believes the future of jazz holds more emphasis on composition than on soloing, and like many other jazz composers today, he writes music intended to last. Indeed, jazz recordings in general are turning toward more closely arranged projects than were undertaken in earlier times, when outstanding soloists reigned supreme.

In 1994, Marsalis's book *Sweet Swing Blues on the Road* received high praise. In 1998, Marsalis received the Pulitzer Prize for music for his extended composition "Blood on the Fields." However, this recipient of numerous national and international awards remains a controversial figure among jazz fans and musicians, some of whom consider him too intellectual and too narrow-minded as to what constitutes "real jazz." Nevertheless, his inspired trumpet playing, gifted teaching, tireless proselytizing for jazz, and impressive compositions suggest that his will continue to be a significant name in jazz.

Jazz Today and Tomorrow

The important American music we call jazz continues to evolve, offering performers and listeners a full range of creative experience. Tradition and innovation variously inspire today's jazz musicians and fans.

The blues, for example, was the subject of a special celebration during 2003, declared, by Congressional Proclamation, the Year of the Blues. This was a commemoration of W. C. Handy's first hearing, in 1903, a man playing slide guitar with a knife and singing a plaintive blues. As a result of this life-changing experience, Handy later began publishing commercial blues, establishing the relationship between blues and the music business. Today we recognize the blues as a basic structure (which, however, the greatest blues musicians often ignore), a feeling, an attitude, an exacting discipline—a virtually indefinable and seemingly indestructible American music.

Important to the jazz business today are the numerous collectives organized to support jazz musicians. Since the early days of jazz, collective organizations have helped musicians make a living, creating jobs (gigs) and, beginning in the 1960s, new compositions; but now they play a stronger role than ever. The most significant collective today, the Jazz Composers Collective, founded in 1992, finds grant money for commissioning compositions and recordings, sponsors concerts, and builds audiences for new jazz music.

Jazz instrumentation continues to evolve, as musicians explore new technology and world sounds. The electric organ, for example, which played a small role in early jazz, has become increasingly relevant in jazz (and in other popular musics as well) today. Thomas (Fats) Waller played jazz on a giant pipe organ in the 1920s, and in the 1940s and 1950s jazz organ trios consisting of electric organ, guitar, and drums (sometimes augmented by a tenor saxophone) imitated an orchestral sound. Now synthesizers and portable digital organs make the instrument's sound readily available, and the commercial success of the recent sampling of organ-heavy soul jazz recordings from the 1960s has created a new audience for the Hammond (electric) organ itself. Particularly influential is the playing of (Wild) Bill Davis, considered the creator of the modern jazz organ.

The arranging impulse largely dropped out of jazz performance from the 1960s through the 1980s, but now, stimulated by such musicians as Henry Threadgill and Wynton Marsalis, it is back. As already mentioned, while great jazz soloists still stir up frenzied enthusiasm among their fans, there appears to be a trend to move away from emphasis on virtuosic solos to a collective endeavor, in which the focus within an ensemble is controlled by the bandleader and shifts from one musician to another. Thus performances today often seem to be more about rhythm and interplay than about solos or even melodies.

A prominent chamber ensemble, the Turtle Island String Quartet, adventurously fuses the classical string quartet with popular contemporary American styles, including bluegrass, swing, and bebop, as well as funk, rhythm and blues, hip-hop, salsa, and others. The quartet also explores classical Indian music, creating entirely new sounds with a blend of classical, world, folk, jazz, and pop music. (Examples of the music of this quartet can be heard on the Web.)

As of 2005, innumerable jazz festivals around the country and around the world celebrated local and international talent, often presenting several days of concerts, workshops, demonstrations, dance parties, parades, and jazz camaraderie. Students and professionals offer their music and hear the music of others, teaching and learning together in a concentrated and stimulating atmosphere, as musicians and fans steep themselves in the sounds and flavors of today's jazz. Virtually any day of the year will find a jazz festival—or several festivals—joyously under way.

Since John Lewis and Gunther Schuller began integrating jazz and the classics into a third stream; since John Coltrane and others began improvising on scales from India and rhythms from Africa; since Miles Davis sanctioned the use of rock and funk riffs in *Bitches Brew*—it has become increasingly unrealistic to confine jazz to narrow definitions. Composed or improvised, conceived to entertain or to challenge the intellect, jazz in its various, changing guises continues to be a vital feature of the American musical landscape.

Terms to Review

collective improvisation   Simultaneous improvisation by some or all members of a combo.

free jazz   A style of free improvisation introduced by Ornette Coleman in 1960.

third stream   A term coined by Gunther Schuller referring to the combination, but not the blending, of jazz and classical music. Today the term is loosely used in reference to avant-garde jazz styles.

jazz-rock, fusion, jazz-rock-fusion   A jazz style melding rock rhythms and the use of electronic instruments with collective improvisation, extreme ranges of volume, and rapid shifts in meter, tempo, and mood.

Key Figures

Charles Mingus	Herbie Hancock	Henry Threadgill
Ornette Coleman	Chick Corea	Anthony Braxton
John Coltrane	Don Cherry	Anthony Davis
John Lewis	Pat Metheny	Wynton Marsalis
Gunther Schuller	John Zorn	

Optional Listening Example

Anthony Braxton: *92 + [30, 32, 139] + [108c, 108d] for Creative Orchestra*

Suggestions for Further Listening

Gunther Schuller: *Transformation* (for an eleven-piece ensemble)
Charles Mingus: *Better Git It in Your Soul*
Coleman Hawkins: *Body and Soul*

Ornette Coleman: *The Shape of Jazz to Come*
John Coltrane: *Giant Steps*
Chick Corea: *Now He Sings, Now He Sobs*
Don Cherry: *Mu (The Complete Session)*

Critical Thinking

Discuss the seeming oxymoron "jazz composition." How do jazz composers meld composition and improvisation? Are you familiar with the music of any other periods where these concepts were joined (improvised keyboard parts during the Baroque and improvised cadenzas in Classical concertos are examples).

Why do you think jazz musicians today seem more interested in collective performance than in solo virtuosity? Which is more interesting to you?

Why do you think foreign (world) music has affected the music of more jazz musicians than rock, country, or pop musicians?

Does jazz today relate to the nearly hundred-year-old jazz tradition?

Does jazz relate to today's experience?

Go to www.mhhe.com/ferrisaml5 for a list of additional Web-based resources that relate to the content in this chapter.

PART 3
Summary

The form of John Philip Sousa's marches—a series of melodic strains—was also the form of ragtime, a written piano music combining black rhythmic effects with European harmony and form. Ragtime pianists play syncopated melodies in the right hand accompanied by a simple duple pattern in the left. By the time of World War I, rags were being widely published by Tin Pan Alley, as the popular music industry was known, and many popular Tin Pan Alley songs had the sound and spirit of ragtime. The great popular songwriters included Irving Berlin, Cole Porter, and George Gershwin, each of whom wrote for Broadway musicals as well as for Tin Pan Alley.

Country music, rooted in rural and mountain folk traditions, became commercial when Jimmie Rodgers popularized hillbilly songs and the Original Carter Family brought mountain harmony to the city. Recordings, and later radio shows, spread country music to an ever wider audience. Country musicians absorbed many influences as they moved to different states, and soon new styles evolved. Texans danced to western swing and listened to honky tonk, and the cowboy songs of western films joined the hillbilly repertoire to produce a new genre, country-western music. With the exception of bluegrass, an instrumentally dominated revival of mountain folk music, country music consists primarily of song.

When black musicians combined the forms, harmonies, and timbres of white popular musics with Creole, Caribbean, and black African rhythmic and melodic techniques, they produced a hot new music for dancing and later for listening called jazz. The blues, an early manifestation of jazz, began as a black folk song style but evolved to a sophisticated and influential form of popular music. Boogie-woogie transferred the form and harmonic structure of the blues to the piano.

New Orleans nurtured the first important black combos, in which soloists improvised on a given tune while other combo members backed them up. Later, in Chicago, white Dixieland bands imitated the New Orleans sound. White as well as black teenagers and young adults danced to early jazz, but the white middle-age public preferred sweet jazz during the turbulent Depression years. Although not technically jazz at all, these genres introduced the art of the arranger and helped prepare America to swing with the big bands of the 1930s.

In the mid-1930s, jazz reached its peak of popularity, which lasted for about a decade. Big bands played arranged rather than improvised versions of blues and pop tunes, their harmonies more adventurous and their pieces more structured than in earlier jazz styles. Charlie Parker and Dizzy Gillespie led a musicians' rebellion against the commercialism and popularity of big band swing, establishing bebop, a music for listening, not dancing, which ushered in the age of modern jazz. And in the 1940s, the interest of the general audience and many serious jazz musicians turned away from big bands as singers replaced them in popularity.

Since 1950, jazz musicians have formed alliances with the world of concert music, producing symphonic works with jazzy flavors, jazz pieces in classical forms, and third stream pieces in which jazz and classical music meet, yet retain their independent qualities. Among the individuals particularly influential in concert jazz, Duke Ellington, considered one of America's greatest composers, wrote music for both the concert hall and the church; Dave Brubeck extended the rhythmic concepts of jazz pieces by using unusual meters; and Charles Mingus explored techniques of jazz composition, providing a formal framework but no written score for a piece.

Progressive jazz introduced a symphonic concept, and cool jazz added a sensuous element to jazz. Free jazz declared independence from most of the preconceived notions about jazz, allowing collective improvisation by the members of a jazz band. Fusion melds jazz and rock, and jazz musicians have found many ways to integrate foreign sounds into their music. Seemingly threatened with extinction for a time, as rock became ever more popular, jazz composition is now among the most important fields of American music.

PART

A Diversity of Popular Musics

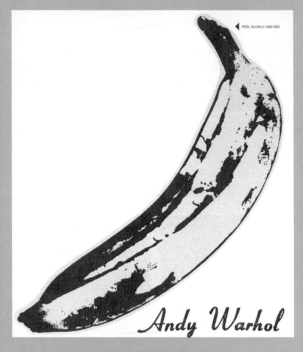

Andy Warhol's cover for the album *The Velvet Underground and Nico*.
(© 2001 Andy Warhol Foundation for the Visual Arts/Artists Rights Society [ARS], New York.)

With the coming of rock and roll, American popular music diversified as never before. Pop and country-western struggled to hold their own against the powerful new music; but in time various styles, including disco, new wave, gospel, rap, jazz, and innumerable regional and ethnic musics, found audiences and vied for popularity with rock and among themselves.

Vernacular Art

The 1950s spawned the *beat generation,* a term invented by Jack Kerouac and originally represented by a small group of excessively talented friends who provided some of the twentieth century's most inspired poetry and prose. Allen Ginsberg, William Burroughs, Jack Kerouac, and their like-minded friends and colleagues stood for nonconformity, a concept in vogue in Europe as well (think of England's angry young men and Jean-Paul Sartre's existentialists). James Dean in the movies and Chuck Berry and Elvis Presley on the radio gave vent to the same spirit motivating the literary beats, who also, however, tempered their expression with an Eastern (specifically Buddhist) philosophy.

The visual arts, too, found new means of expression and established new artistic ideals. The famous Pop artist Andy Warhol (1928–1987) puzzled and intrigued his contemporaries, and he continues to compel our attention today. Working with silk-screen prints made from images taken from newspaper and magazine photos, Warhol ran colors through the screen directly onto his canvas, achieving surprising—some said audacious—new color harmonies. His finest pictures are "serial" paintings, multiple repetitions of the same image on a single canvas. For subjects he chose ubiquitous objects of popular American culture: movie stars, advertising logos, political figures, and popular musicians, many of whom he counted among his personal friends. It has been said that art and music are separate mirrors that reflect some of the same things, and certainly Warhol identified closely with some vernacular musicians of his day. In 1965, the punk rock group Velvet Underground accompanied the showing of one of Warhol's artworks, and the next year he painted a banana for the cover of their first album (*The Velvet Underground and Nico,* released in 1967; see photo on p. 252).

Vernacular Music

During the twentieth century, popular or vernacular music became a significant cultural concept and an important business, as it remains today. Recent decades have produced an unprecedented variety of popular music, including grunge, hip-hop, alternative rock, women in rock, new country, teenybop, Latin pop, and rave, all of which have not replaced but rather joined rhythm and blues, classic rock, light pop, and all the other musics that belong to and express our popular culture.

The 1990s proved to be one of pop's most experimental periods, when experimentation was aided by technological advances that brought down the costs of recording, and by computerized inventories that allowed stores to carry more stock. In the early years of the twenty-first century, the downloading of music has changed the nature of the pop marketplace, challenging major labels to find new ways to make money in what may soon be the post-CD era.

And so we are in the midst of a prodigiously productive period, richer than any earlier time, and richer than any other contemporary culture, in the variety, quantity, and quality of our vernacular music. ♪

Latin Popular Musics

Music from Latin America, having enriched the popular and concert music of the United States for at least a century and a half, is of more significance to North American popular music today than ever before. In the Southwest, where venerable Spanish traditions remain strong, traditional dance music is played much as it has been for many generations. In other parts of the country, Latin American dance music has strongly affected North American pop and jazz. And today "Latin pop" is a category in its own right—a strong one—on the *Billboard* trade magazine popular music charts.

Early in the twentieth century, Latin popular dances took the United States by storm, first as exotic curiosities, next as fads, and finally entering the mainstream of American popular music. The first of the Latin rhythms to affect American pop was the Argentinean **tango,** a graceful yet torrid dance aptly described as "a vertical expression of a horizontal desire." Sedate in tempo but highly sensuous in performance, the tango was introduced to Broadway audiences in 1911 and was made widely popular as danced by Irene and Vernon Castle in a 1913 musical (see pp. 319–320). The tango represents a sophisticated fusion of European and African ingredients.

Lyrical tango *melodies* often suggest the influence of Argentina's large Italian population. The basic tango *rhythm* is that of an older Cuban dance, the **habanera** (named for Havana, Cuba), which subdivides eight eighth-notes (four beats) into 3 + 3 + 2. The habanera beat has been of enormous significance to popular music in the United States; for example, in the mid-nineteenth century Louis Moreau Gottschalk used the rhythm in several of his popular piano pieces (see pp. 121–123); Jelly Roll Morton claimed that New Orleans ragtime players often applied the "Spanish tinge," as he called this beat, to their left-hand accompaniments; and in 1914, W. C. Handy used the rhythm in the four-line verse—the "tango section"—interspersed between the blues stanzas of "St. Louis Blues" (Listening Example 42). Since those early days, the habanera beat has been heard as the basic rhythm of numerous pop styles.

In the 1930s several Latin dances entered American pop through big band music, especially that of the popular bandleader **Xavier Cugat** (Figure 15.1), who was born in Spain but raised in Cuba. Several renowned Latin performers,

FIGURE 15.1

Xavier Cugat and Carmen Miranda, stars of Latin music in concerts and film musicals of the 1930s and 1940s.

including Desi Arnaz and Carmen Miranda (Figure 15.1), began their careers at about that time, appearing in popular stage shows in the 1930s and later in film musicals.

Three Latin areas—the Caribbean, Brazil, and Mexico—have particularly influenced the popular, classical, and religious music of North America.

The Caribbean

The slave trade bringing blacks to North America carried many slaves to the Caribbean islands (and even more to Brazil). Slaves in these Latin American areas managed better than their northern counterparts to preserve their cultural traditions, partly because the traditional drumming largely forbidden in the North was tolerated south of the border, and also because the African tribal religions blended far better with the Christian Catholicism prevalent in Latin America than with the Protestantism characteristic of the North.

Since 1898, when Puerto Rico became a protectorate of the United States, a steady influx of Puerto Ricans have arrived to settle primarily in New York City. Cubans, too, have come to New York in some numbers, although far more have settled closer to home and to where they land by boat, in Florida. Chicago and Los Angeles also have sizable populations of Caribbean peoples, including those from Haiti, Trinidad, and other areas of the West Indies. Both Cubans and Puerto Ricans brought numbers of African-derived musical and dance forms to the United States; but because Spanish colonizers transported far more African slaves to Cuba than to Puerto Rico, the black Cuban population is sizable and the African influence on its culture particularly strong.

Santeria: The Way of the Saints

The traditional rhythms of Cuban *batá* drums accompany the most sacred and complex rituals of Santeria, a religion created in the New World by slaves brought from West Africa to work on Caribbean sugar plantations. (Batá are double-headed, hourglass-shaped drums, generally thought to be in the shape of the thunder ax of the god they represent. Both heads of the drums are sounded with the hands.) Nominally converted to Catholicism, slaves often fused their traditional beliefs and rituals—vital connectors to their past—with elements of their new religion. In this way in Cuba, the religious practice called Santeria evolved.

In the United States, Santeria has attracted not only members of the Cuban and Puerto Rican communities but many African Americans and a growing number of Anglo-Americans as well. Santeria songs, each associated with a particular deity, normally are sung without harmony in call-and-response fashion between leader and group, the leader often improvising phrases in an open, relaxed vocal style characteristic of some African practice. The rhythms of the accompanying batá drums also have specific ritual significance, each rhythm constituting a musical prayer that honors and represents a specific god. Because batá drumming is an oral tradition, living in the minds of performers rather than on a printed page, batá ensembles continue to evolve their own individual performance style and technique, always rooted, however, in ancient African tradition.

Bomba

Among the first Latin dances to become popular north of the border was the **bomba,** a distinctive African-derived Puerto Rican couple dance allowing the man great flexibility and freedom to display his dancing skills while his female partner performs relatively fixed steps. They dance to a song whose text—performed in call-and-response fashion—usually concerns everyday or topical events, accompanied by drums plus optional maracas, *guiro* (a notched gourd, open at one end, scraped with a stick or with metal wires), and cowbell. A pair of sticks strikes a fixed rhythmic pattern on the side of a drum or other hard resonant surface, as the male dancer and lead drummer respond to and compete with each other in rhythms of increasing complexity.

Rumba

Rumba is actually a generic term for a group of Afro-Cuban musical and dance forms. Couples dancing a rumba hold each other slightly apart, shoulders level, while moving their hips provocatively from side to side. The basic rhythm of two or four beats to the measure is divided according to the *clave* rhythm, tapped out by cylindrical sticks called *claves,* which underlies all Cuban dance music: The first of two measures is in habanera rhythm, and the second measure sounds on beats two and three (see Figure 15.2). The tempo varies but is never very rapid.

FIGURE 15.2

The subtle, syncopated clave rhythm.

CLAVE RHYTHM

Rumba is the style at the deepest roots of Cuban music, having arrived in Cuba with African slaves. Soon African languages were replaced by Spanish, and the melody lines adapted scales and figures from Spanish songs. This synthesis seeded virtually all the Cuban music that followed, including son, chachacha, conga, mambo, even salsa, as well as cabaret music, pop songs, and Cuban classical compositions. Around the world rumba reached into rhythm and blues, disco, Spanish flamenco-pop, and African guitar-rock. As vital today as at its beginning, rumba continues to evolve: younger musicians with conservatory training emphasize their instrumental technique; jazz flourishes sometimes infiltrate the drumming; elements of rap are moving into the vocals.

Traditional Cuban instruments add to the exotic flavor of the rumba: *Bongos* are pairs of drums of different size, held between the knees and usually played with the fingers and hand, sometimes with a stick. *Conga* drums, largest of the Latin instruments, also often are played in pairs, the sound produced by their muleskin head varying according to whether it is struck by the heel, palm, or fingers of the hand. Pairs of metal drums called *timbales* are mounted on a stand and struck with a stick. *Maracas* are pairs of gourds filled with pebbles or seeds and shaken or rotated by handles attached to one end.

While Cuban and Puerto Rican musicians performed rumbas during the 1930s in New York's uptown Latin district known as El Barrio, Xavier Cugat and other bandleaders entertained downtown ballroom crowds with a rhythmically simplified hybrid Latin and American version of the dance. Soon the rumba's extreme popularity led Tin Pan Alley songwriters to join the Latin bandwagon, producing such wonderful songs as Irving Berlin's "Heat Wave" and Cole Porter's "Begin the Beguine." (The *beguine* is a native dance of the West Indies.)

Cu-Bop

By the 1940s, Cuban instruments and instrumentalists were strongly affecting jazz. Among the most popular influences was that of yet another dance, the **conga,** performed in a line or chain essentially as a march but with a heavy accent every fourth beat emphasized by a side kick by the dancers. Having added a great Cuban conga drummer to his Afro-Cuban jazz orchestra, Dizzie Gillespie, in a bebop concert at Carnegie Hall in 1947, introduced **cu-bop,** merging Latin rhythms with his bebop style.

From then on, Gillespie, Duke Ellington, Stan Kenton, and other U.S. musicians flavored much of their music with Brazilian, Cuban, and other Latin influences. At the heart of Cuban (and African) drumming is the superimposition of rhythmic patterns: over a constant underlying pulse, other pulses are layered and then varied, creating rhythmic expectation through repetition and then subverting it. This is also a large part of what a jazz soloist does, and jazz musicians readily adapted such techniques to their performances. Stan Kenton's band greatly increased the intensity and excitement of some of their music by employing a typical Latin rhythmic effect called *double-timing,* which subdivides the beat (as into eighths instead of quarters), implying a faster tempo without actually increasing the rate of speed, because the musicians play twice the number of notes per beat.

Mambo

Tito Puente (1923–2000), born in New York City to Puerto Rican parents, became known as the mambo king for his sophisticated "downtown" versions of yet another Latin dance craze, the **mambo.** A bandleader of Afro-Cuban music and a percussionist, Puente had studied at Juilliard and other professional music conservatories and tempered his Latin rhythms with cooler European harmonies, timbres, and tempos. He was influenced by swing and by his religion, Santeria, reflected in his album *Top Percussion* (1957).

Hot or cool, the mambo, developed in this country by Latin and Latin-influenced musicians, merged Afro-Cuban sounds with those of big band jazz. Couples danced the mambo moving forward and back, either holding each other in rumba fashion, touching one hand only, or not touching at all. The slower, simpler **chachacha,** popular in the 1950s, is closely related to or even a form of the mambo, adding a double step between the fourth (last) and first beats. The mambo's influence proved farther-reaching than its originators or even the mambo king might have envisioned. Having merged with big band jazz and having inspired many Tin Pan Alley songs recorded by such popular singers as Perry Como and Nat "King" Cole, the mambo also strongly affected rhythm and blues in the 1950s and introduced Latin rhythms into early rock. Bo Diddley, Ray Charles, and James Brown number among the many musicians who absorbed the Latin percussion sounds and rhythms into their own unique musics.

Salsa By the late 1970s, a Cuban music that had been considered a substyle of popular music for decades emerged as a major ingredient in virtually every vernacular field, receiving with its new status a new name as well—**salsa.** The word, meaning sauce, had long been applied to peppy Cuban sounds, but the young people who coined it as a name seemed to think of the music it defined as something new. In fact, as its popularity spread, salsa drew from a wider range of Latin sounds than before while yet remaining closer to Cuban music than any other Latin style. Today the term *salsa* is sometimes used generically to denote all African-Latin popular musics.

Salsa indeed was dance band music, but with instrumentation, rhythms, and a general flavor quite unlike the swing band sound. Its timbres were primarily those of voices and trumpets or, alternatively, flutes and violins; and its complex rhythms continually absorbed varied Puerto Rican and South American elements, which sophisticated jazz musicians enthusiastically incorporated into their highly virtuosic performances (see Listening Example 54).

By the 1980s and 1990s, as a younger generation of Puerto Ricans born in New York turned away from traditional salsa toward rhythm and blues and hip-hop, the sounds of salsa changed, acquiring a distinct African American inflection. The match of young freestyle singers with classic salsa rhythms has proved powerful indeed, as revealed by the brisk sales of recordings by two popular young salsa artists, Marc Anthony (Marco Antonio Muñiz) and India (Lindabel Caballero).

Reggae **Reggae** fused elements of North American rock and African Jamaican music to form a kind of "acculturated rock" popular in England in the 1960s and in the United States a decade later. **Bob Marley** (1945–1981),

"Ojos"   ("Eyes," 1978)

**CD 2
Track 22
4:50**

Performers
Rubén Blades (vocal), Willie Colón (trombone)

Rhythm
Clave rhythm

Instrumentation
Brass (with trombone playing the lead lines instead of salsa's traditional trumpets or flutes); percussion, including conga drum, timbales, bongos, maracas, and claves. A piano plays repetitive syncopated patterns.

Form
Two-part: *canto* (narrative) and *montuno* (rhythmic, more instrumental than vocal in concept).

This performance of "Ojos" exemplifies how salsa musicians absorb varied influences and apply them to this basically Cuban style. The trombonist, composer, and bandleader Willie Colón, born in New York City but of Puerto Rican heritage, replaces the traditional trumpets or flutes of salsa with trombone, and blends jazz harmonies and jazz-style soloing into his salsa performances. Thus the brass instruments in this performance sound much like those of big band jazz. The Panamanian Rubén Blades (whose mother was Cuban, and who often is referred to as the Latin Bruce Springsteen) adds a showman's flair to his vocals. (Blades, a four-time Grammy winner who has recorded in both English and Spanish and has collaborated with Lou Reed, Elvis Costello, and Sting, has acted in and written songs for a number of movies and recently performed on Broadway in Paul Simon's musical *The Capeman*.)

Canto   After a brass introduction, the first section, much like the verse of a Tin Pan Alley song, presents the narrative content of the song, accompanied by the band.

Montuno (1:11)   The second section alternates instrumental and vocal performances. During the vocal solo, a chorus of male voices intersperses calls of "Ojos." Later the vocalist encourages the instrumentalists with improvised phrases. Notice that the intensity and rhythmic complexity of the piece increase as the performance proceeds. Listen for intricately woven and highly syncopated rhythmic patterns governed by the clave rhythm—which has, however, been too thoroughly internalized by these sophisticated musicians to be readily identified by the casual listener. Try to follow one or more independent instrumental lines at a time, noticing the manner in which their accents fall on, or between, different beats. Hear the strong ostinatos played by the piano. Notice, too, how the vocal line becomes rhythmically and melodically freer and more complex toward the end of the piece.

a leading Jamaican reggae performer, became very well known and highly revered in North America.

Reggae comes in several styles, all roughly related to rhythm and blues, although reggae's African polyrhythms are more complex, the bass lines stronger and the tempos more relaxed than those of R&B. Reggae combos consist of electric guitars, electric organ, electric bass guitar, and drums, with electronic studio techniques sometimes making significant contributions as well. A technique developed by Jamaican disc jockeys of rapid patter talking over the sound of spinning records, called **toasting** or **dubbing,** was destined to have far-reaching effects on the development of rap music in the 1970s and 1980s (pp. 297–298).

Reggae—a vernacular music (rock) borrowed and transformed by a culture (Jamaican) other than the one that introduced it (African American) to form yet a new style—reveals the possible complexity and enrichment afforded by such wide acculturation. Reggae also exemplifies a *popular* music with strong *religious* connotations, for it is closely associated with a black religious movement called Rastafarianism. In addition, many reggae songs have urgent *political* content, promoting the "back to Africa" movement that emerged in the 1960s. In the 1970s, Marley sang of equality, unity, and love, all with an underlying threat of revolutionary violence, and today's hard-core reggae fans still favor the searing political indictments that infused much of his music. **Buju Banton** (Mark Anthony Myrie) evokes Marley's spirit in his album *Unchained Spirit* (2000). Another of Marley's spiritual descendants, **Luciano,** on his album *Ultimate Collection* (2003), sings of moral chastisement and spiritual uplift.

Calypso

Calypso, a song style of Trinidad also popular in Jamaica and elsewhere in the Caribbean, began as a form of communication between African slaves forbidden to talk with each other. Their satirically humorous song lyrics, often sung in a French-Creole dialect, or patois, mocked their masters; many songs were politically charged, many frankly risqué.

Calypso singer-composers often take grandiose names, the most famous including Lord Executor, Atilla the Hun, and Mighty Sparrow. When the Andrews Sisters, in 1944, did a cover version of Lord Invader's "Rum and Coca-Cola," calypso immediately found a wide North American audience. A decade later, Harry Belafonte's album *Calypso* (1956) included "Banana Boat Song" ("Day-O"), probably the calypso song best-known internationally.

The favorite accompanying instrument for calypso is the **steel drum,** developed in Trinidad in the 1940s—the only new acoustic instrument of the twentieth century. The steel drum, or pan, is made by pounding the bottom of a 55-gallon drum into a concave dish and chiseling grooves of various sizes to produce various tones. Each note area is painstakingly tuned by further pounding, giving the resulting instrument a distinctive ringing quality.

As calypso declined in popularity in the 1970s, succumbing to competition from other musics (reggae, disco, rock), a more up-tempo, less socially conscious, party music version of calypso called *soca* arose. *Rapso,* with calypso-style lyrics, and with rhythms influenced by hip-hop, also became popular. Yet calypso retains significant numbers of devoted fans today and seems to face a bright future.

Brazil

It seems logical to relate the relaxed, easy pace of Brazilian music to the sounds and inflections of the Portuguese language spoken in Brazil. In any case, Brazilian dances—gentler, slower, and less intense than the exiciting Cuban and Puerto Rican musics—achieved their own popularity in the United States, though never to the degree of the hot Caribbean sounds.

Samba and Bossa Nova

The Afro-Brazilian **samba,** sometimes called the national dance of Brazil, arrived in New York around 1949 and quickly became popular as sung and danced by the glamorous Carmen Miranda. The word *samba* has various religious connotations, and samba has been the main dance at Rio's Carnival, wildly celebrated before Lent each year.

Bossa nova emerged in the 1960s at least in part as a reaction among the youth of Rio's middle and privileged classes against the perceived commercialism of samba. Derived from, or a variation of, samba, it was sometimes called jazz samba, since it fused elements of cool and progressive jazz with sophisticated Brazilian rhythms.

Less vibrant and more melancholy than Cuban-flavored music, the bossa nova adapted beautifully to the world of jazz, where its flexible rhythms and colorful instrumentation continue to stimulate sophisticated musicians. But much like bebop in the United States, the subtle bossa nova met initial resistance from traditionalists who did not understand its elusive flavors and new sounds. Also like bebop, it is a music primarily for listening. In fact, unlike the rumba, the samba, and other Latin musics popular north of the border, bossa nova is not a dance but a rhythm—rather, a number of subtle, flexible polyrhythms. Whereas samba featured exotic stars singing and dancing in front of a flashy band, bossa nova performers sang softly, accompanied by a single guitar or at most a four-man band. The style was intimate and very sophisticated.

The term *bossa nova* first emerged in the lyrics of a song by **Antônio Carlos Jobim** (1927–1994), a leading figure of the bossa nova movement. *Bossa* was slang for something particularly distinctive; *nova* means "new." The song that introduced the phrase was "Desafinado" (Listening Example 55), meaning "Off Key," and the lyrics say that by singing "off key" the singer was trying to attract the attention of his beloved. (Most familiar of all to a general audience in the United States was another bossa nova by Jobim, the lovely and very popular "Girl from Ipanema" (with vocalist João Gilberto).

In the early 1970s, several important groups and individuals adopted the quietly sensuous rhythms and melodies of bossa nova to flavor their own distinctive music. Weather Report famously added Brazilian percussionists to the ensemble. Brazilian singer Flora Purim, who appeared equally comfortable

"Desafinado"   ("Off Key")

CD 2
Track 23
4:10

Composer
Antônio Carlos Jobim

Lyricist
Newton Mendonça

Performers
João Gilberto (vocalist, guitarist) and Stan Getz (jazz tenor saxophonist)

Meter
Four beats to the bar

Tempo
Slow, relaxed

Form
Strophic

Gilberto's calm voice seems uniquely suited to present the long, sinuous, chromatic melodic line, accompanied by subtle but insistent rhythms in the drums, bass, piano, and guitar. Everything about the performance seems gentle; the softly dissonant harmonies, lightly syncopated rhythms, and even the Portuguese language all fall easily on the ear. However, Jobim conceived some harmonies to make the singer seem "off key." Further, the syncopated melody (deemphasized by Gilberto's half-sung, half-spoken delivery) is set against competing guitar rhythms, leaving the listener uncertain where to locate the main beats. In other words, this song that sounds so easy to sing demands performers with an extremely acute sense of pitch and rhythm.

After Gilberto sings four four-line stanzas, with a fifth line added to his last verse, Stan Getz gives an instrumental version of the piece, similarly accompanied by drums, bass, piano, guitar, and—at the very end—Gilberto's soft syllables in the background. The muted tenor sax, like Gilberto's singing voice, has the warmth and subtlety of a sultry tropical night.

Se você disser que	*If you say that*
eu desafino, amor	*I sing out of tune, love,*
Saiba que isso em mim	*I want you to know that this*
provoca imensa dor	*causes me great pain.*
Só privilegiados têm ouvido	*Only the priviledged have ears*
igual ao seu	*as good as yours.*
Eu possuo apenas	*I only possess*
o que Deus me deu	*what God gave me.*

—Continued

Listening Example 55—Concluded

"Desafinado" ("Off Key")

Se você insisted em classificar	If you insist in classifying
meu comportamento de antimusical	my behavior as antimusical
Eu mesmo mentindo	I myself lying
Devo argumentar	should argue
Que isto é bossa nova	that this is bossa nova,
Que isto é muito natural	that this is very natural.
O que você não sabe	What you don't know
nem sequer pressente	or even suspect
é que os desafinados	is that those that are out of tune
também têm um coração	also have a heart.
Fotografei você	I photographed you
na minha Rolleyflex	with my Rolleiflex.
Revelou-se a sua	It exposed your
enorme ingratidão	enormous ingratitude.
Só não poderá falar	Only you will not be able to speak
assim do meu amor	like this of my love.
Este é o maior	This is better
que você pode encontrar	than you are able to find.
Você com a sua música	You with your music
esqueceu o principal	forgot the main thing
é que no peito	is that in the chest
dos desafinados	of those out of tune
No fundo do peito	Deep within the chest
bate calado	beating quietly
Que no peito	That in the chest
dos desafinados	of those out of tune
também bate um coração.	a heart also beats.

performing both jazz and Brazilian music, sang first with Stan Getz, (Figure 15.3), next with Gil Evans, and finally with avant-garde pianist Chick Corea and his group Return to Forever. Purim's husband, percussionist Airto Moreira, also joined Corea's group, enhancing their sounds with the Latin bells, rattles, and shakers he had used earlier when performing with Miles Davis. And through the 1980s, the subtlety and flexibility of bossa nova had strong appeal for Pat Metheny's jazz-rock groups, free jazz musicians, and bop.

Mexico

The southwestern states of Texas, New Mexico, Arizona, and California absorbed many sounds from nearby Mexico, where folk music and popular music strongly reflect the songs and dances of African slaves. The country music of

FIGURE 15.3

Stan Getz playing tenor sax.

the Southwest naturally shows the Mexican influence. Woody Guthrie, who began playing music in Texas in the late 1920s (see pp. 187–190), sometimes adapted Mexican topical ballads, or *corridos,* to his own inimitable style; and the Mexican *ranchera* (ranch song) "El Rancho Grande" became a standard of western swing bands. It has even been suggested that the "blue yodel" of Jimmie Rodgers and others may have been stimulated by Mexican singing styles.

Any number of dances also traveled back and forth between Spain and Mexico, acquiring changes in name, instrumentation, and performance style as they continued to develop. *El Cutilio* (Listening Example 4) is a traditional Spanish social dance, or *baile,* that was popular in the Southwest before and after the Civil War and remains so in that region today. Unlike the religious *alabados,* rarely heard today, *bailes* continue to delight people of every age and social situation. Performed now as then to celebrate engagements, weddings, birthdays, and other joyful events, these rollicking dance tunes lighten the hearts of those who hear them—although few remember how to dance the intricate steps popular more than 100 years ago.

Tejano and Norteño Music

In the mid-nineteenth century, Europeans from Germany, Poland, and what is now the Czech Republic migrated in large numbers to Texas and northern Mexico, affecting the language, literature, art, and cuisine as well as the music of those regions. Among the effects their strong influence brought about were the addition of the accordion to popular bands and the oom-pah-pah beat of polkas to Spanish songs and dances. The distinctive music tradition that evolved from this blend of styles is known as **norteño** in northern Mexico and **tejano** in south Texas.

By the 1950s, Tejanos were singing in Tex-Mex rather than traditional Spanish; during the 1960s and 1970s an orchestral sound infiltrated many tejano bands; and by the 1980s keyboards were included as well. The murder in 1995 of a shining young star, **Selena Quintanilla-Pérez,** brought tejano music to national attention, and the sound has become more familiar and more popular as it continues to evolve. The accordion still dominates some ensembles, but more and more tejano groups are mixing salsa, meringue, techno, and pop in their sound.

Tejanos were closely involved in the development of corridos and another accordion-based music, conjunto.

Corridos

Storytelling songs, with roots in both Mexico and parts of the southwestern and western United States, **corridos** relate the unofficial history of Mexican communities and their heroes. Powerful meditations on honor and bravery, corridos focus more on the story they tell than the music. Their subjects change with time. During the nineteenth-century Mexican war of independence and the twentieth-century Mexican revolution, corridos informed the people of newsworthy events. More recent corridos have celebrated famous leaders; delivered moral messages; related tales of everyday life and love, immigration, and the drug trade; and expressed nostalgia for Mexico.

Traditionally sung by a solo vocalist accompanied by a guitar, corridos have in modern times been performed, and made more complex, by popular music groups. Los Tigres del Norte, a highly popular Mexican band, includes at least one or two corridos on each CD it produces.

Conjunto

During the late nineteenth century, as Mexican Americans spread not only throughout the southwestern United States but also well to the north and east, they carried with them their traditional norteño music. Their **conjunto** ensembles, usually including besides the accordion a guitar and sometimes a double bass and drums, played polkas, waltzes, and other European dances popular in Mexico and along both sides of the border. By the 1950s they also accompanied the singing of rancheras, corridos, and other traditional Mexican songs. During the mid-twentieth century, conjuntos (Figure 15.4) entertained in cantinas through the Southwest, sometimes adding a saxophone to further color their distinctive sound.

FIGURE 15.4

The 1950s was a peak period for Mexican American music, and among the leading norteño groups was Los Alegres de Teran.

FIGURE 15.5

Strolling mariachis entertain passersby.

In recent years, some conjunto musicians have resisted the traditional polka sounds, blending other musical styles, including jazz, into their performances. Besides saxophones, some have added keyboards and synthesizers to their ensembles, creating *conjuntos orquestales*. Through these and other effective means, such as traveling widely, teaming up with other musicians, and adding conjunto beat to other popular musics, conjunto musicians have attracted enthusiastic new audiences to their *música alegre* ("happy music").

Mariachis By the late 1970s, folk, country, and rock rhythms and instrumentation increasingly reflected vibrant Mexican traditions, including the sounds of strolling **mariachis** (Figure 15.5). They perform an important Mexican folk music frequently heard in the southwestern United States. Originally a string ensemble, mariachis now add one to three trumpets to the violins, guitar, and perhaps *guitarron* or bass guitar (the instrumentation is quite flexible) making up the traditional ensemble. It is thought that because their joyous music was so often played at weddings, they may have derived their name from a corruption of the French word for marriage, *mariage*.

In Listening Example 56, "Jarabe Tapatío" ("Mexican Hat Dance"), we hear the mariachi sound—the musical symbol of Mexico. This dance, with its colorfully costumed performers, tells a story of love and courtship: a *charro* gallops on his horse to see his girlfriend; they flirt in several of the figures; he throws his hat onto the ground and dances around it and the girl; she picks up the hat, in acceptance, and places it on her head. Together they dance in joy and triumph.

Latin Music Today

Once an exotic flavoring added to light classical or early popular music, Latin music has become a vital force of great complexity, variety, and significance in the music of the United States, signified by the current popularity of such stars as Gloria Estefan, Ricky Martin, Jennifer Lopez, Christina Aguilera, and Shakira.

"Jarabe Tapatío"

CD 2
Track 24
1:54

Origin

Traditional

The *jarabe* is a medley of dances from various regions of Mexico, and *tapatío* means "from the city of Guadalajara." *Jarabe* translates as "sweet syrup," perhaps suggesting the mixture of meters within one section of a *jarabe*, though no one knows the meaning for sure. (Compare the term *jarabe* with *salsa*.)

Meter

Duple

Texture

Mostly chordal

Form

A series of strains, each composed of eight-bar phrases (labeled **A, B, C,** and **D**).

After a brief rhythmic introduction, the brass instruments, punctuated by percussion, play the first phrase of the first strain (**A**), which begins with three upward leaps. The phrase is repeated. The answering phrase (**B**), beginning with a downward inflection, features twin trumpets. This phrase, too, is repeated.

The second strain includes the same phrases (**A, A, B, B**), a half step higher in pitch. Notice the accordion countermelody in the repeat of **A.** The twin trumpets again play **B.**

The third strain, another half step higher, responds to **A** with a new melody, **C** (**A, A, C, C**). The twin trumpets play the repetition of the new phrase.

After an eight-bar percussion interlude (starting at 1:25), we hear the fourth strain, beginning with a more frenzied presentation of **C,** followed by a new melody, **D,** which is repeated (**C, D, D**). Increased activity in the accompanying instruments adds to the excitement as the piece draws to its rousing finish.

Cuban band music, brought to popular attention through the success of the audio CD and film *Buena Vista Social Club* can be heard performed in an up-to-date style by the big band Cubanismo, which fuses Cuban traditional music with more modern arrangements and suggestions of music from other countries. North of the Mexican border, Latin rock is making an impact reminiscent of the influence of rock and roll south of the border years ago. In fact, *rock en español* embraces everything from Mexican rappers to Argentinean melodic singer-songwriters, all making an imprint on the American market.

The band Santana having ruled the Grammy awards in 2000 (they won eight), the National Academy of Recording Arts and Sciences created a new Latin branch, which presented the first Latin Grammy Awards later that year. The fifth annual Latin Grammy Awards (2004) celebrated the richness and diversity of Latin music, with tributes to tradition as well as to hard-rocking contemporary performances: the awards categories included pop, rock, tropical, regional, traditional, jazz, Brazilian, children's, classical, production, and video—among others.

Terms to Review

tango   A graceful, sensuous Argentinian dance, the first of the Latin rhythms to become popular in the United States.

habanera   A Cuban dance, whose rhythm is the basis of the tango.

bomba   A Puerto Rican couple dance derived from Africa.

rumba   A group of Afro-Cuban musical and dance forms, with many variants.

conga   A Cuban carnival dance-march: the dancers, having formed a chain, mark every fourth beat with a heavy kick.

cu-bop   Dizzy Gillespie's fusion of Latin rhythms with bebop.

mambo   An Afro-Cuban form of big band dance music.

chachacha   A slower version of the mambo, with a double beat added between the last and first beats of each measure.

salsa   Popular Cuban dance band music with rhythms derived from African-American dances.

reggae   A blend of rock and African-Jamaican styles.

toasting or **dubbing**   A technique developed by Jamaican disc jockeys of rapid patter talking over the sound of spinning records.

calypso   Caribbean song style with humorously satirical topical texts.

steel drum or **pan**   Percussion instrument made by pounding the bottom of an oil drum into a concave shape and hammering grooves for the notes.

samba   The most famous Brazilian song-dance; duple meter.

bossa nova   Brazilian rhythm, slower and more subtle than Cuban dances, reflecting the influence of cool and progressive jazz.

norteño   A distinctive, European-influenced music of northern Mexico.

tejano   The Texas version of norteño music.

corrido   Storytelling song, with roots in Mexico and the southwestern and western United States.

conjunto   An ensemble accompanying dance and song in norteño music, north and south of the Mexico-Texas border.

mariachis   Mexican groups of strolling musicians playing string instruments and often led by one or more trumpets.

Key Figures

Xavier Cugat
Tito Puente
Bob Marley

Buju Banton
Luciano

Antônio Carlos Jobim
Selena

Suggestions for Further Listening

Duke Ellington, "Conga Brava"
Miles Davis and Gil Evans, "Sketches of Spain"
Chano Pozo: El Tambor de Cuba (a three-CD set featuring Luciano Pozo, the Cuban drummer hired by Dizzy Gillespie in 1947)
Tito Puente, "Top Percussion" (Santeria music with sacred batá drums)

Buena Vista Social Club (audio CD, Cuban son music)
Bossa nova: *Getz-Gilberto* (Stan Getz and the Brazilian composer-singer-guitarist João Gilberto)
Reggae: *This Is Reggae Music* (various artists)
Salsa: *Machacha* (features Clare Fisher and Salsa Picante)
Calypso Awakening: from the Emory Cook Collection

Suggestions for Viewing

The Buena Vista Social Club (documentary film on traditional Cuban music)
Songs of the Homeland (documentary of tejano music)
Movies with tango scenes:
    Scent of a Woman (1992)
    The Tango Lesson (1997)

Moulin Rouge (2001)
Ássassination Tango (2002)
Selena (1997. The story of Selena Quintanilla.)

Critical Thinking

Do you think the radio stations in your area give adequate air time to Latin popular music?

Of the three influential areas covered here—the Caribbean, Brazil, and Mexico—which has most affected the music with which you are most familiar?

Which do you think will be the strongest trend in the future: Latin pop influenced by music from the United States, or "Latin-tinged" U.S. popular music? Why?

Go to www.mhhe.com/ferrisaml5 for a list of additional Web-based resources that relate to the content in this chapter.

Rock and Roll

The baby boom of World War II produced, in the 1950s, a teen boom of unprecedented numbers, wealth, and influence. Little interested in the sentimental popular music of the Depression and war years, these numerous young people craved excitement and a music expressive of their own frustrations and needs, a music to which they could dance. And for the first time in American history, the teenage population had money enough to command the attention of the popular music industry.

The Generation Gap

Several postwar conditions fostered an unprecedented sense of independence and even rebellion among American youth. Many failed to understand in such prosperous times the frugal ways of their parents, who had survived but not forgotten the Great Depression and years of wartime austerity. Military families experienced frequent relocation, particularly unsettling to children and teens. Young people in more stable conditions often had mothers working outside the home, filling jobs vacated by men still in the military, or continuing jobs to which they had become accustomed during the war or upon whose income they felt dependent. These and numerous other social and economic conditions caused a serious, unprecedented gap in communication and understanding between adolescents and their parents.

The spirit of rebellion also waxed strong among young African Americans returning from war to find the equality they had experienced on the battlefield bluntly denied them in the domestic workforce. Spurred by the injustice of social discrimination, the civil rights movement steadily gained momentum, and black power became a force to be reckoned with.

Meanwhile, popular music after World War II became increasingly diversified, generally moving away from instrumental music back to song. This young generation perceived swing bands as too polished, the performers' dress too formal, and the shows too structured to please them. The sentimental ballads of mainstream pop, suitable for the slow dances popular among young adults, could not satisfy the restless teenage audience, and the complexity of modern jazz—primarily instrumental, often dissonant, intended more for listening than for dancing—simply antagonized them. More and more young white people preferred the vital, stirring sounds of black *gospel* music and *rhythm and blues* to the music their parents had enjoyed.

Gospel

Gospel music, also called religious blues, descends from the religious spirituals developed by the slave culture, celebrated later in camp meetings and later yet in concert environments. *Gospel* actually refers to a family of religious musics, white and black, including the white spirituals discussed in Chapter 5; however, only black gospel music has profoundly affected popular music, becoming in effect a branch of rhythm and blues and contributing vitally to both jazz and rock.

The line between sacred and secular is often thin, and gospel generally refuses to draw that line, simply combining religious expression with techniques generally associated with secular music. **Thomas A. Dorsey** (1899–1993), generally considered the father of gospel music, was moved by personal tragedy (the death of his wife and infant son in childbirth) to turn from his career as a blues pianist and composer to writing gospel blues. More personal, sentimental, and emotional than spirituals, gospel songs compel participation. By the mid-twentieth century, performers were punctuating their singing with slides, growls, dips, shouts, blue notes, and falsetto, heightening individual expression and raising the emotional level to extremes.

Whereas Dorsey's music and the performances of numerous early male gospel quartets could be described as *blues-flavored gospel,* in 1955 Ray Charles (1930–2004) added highly secular lyrics to an old spiritual, producing a *gospel-flavored blues* hit, "I Got a Woman." (The lyrics can be found on the Web.) Charles's fusion of gospel and blues scored high on the rhythm and blues charts, and soon some gospel male quartets (sometimes quintets or sextets) turned to the denser, more driving hard soul gospel sound. Shouting with a raucous call-and-response fervor, they became a vital part of the American entertainment business after World War II. While some gospel singers (Mehalia Jackson, for example) continued singing religious gospel songs, others (Sam Cooke, Aretha Franklin) turned from sacred to secular music.

All the elements of black gospel music, including a steady beat underlying strong rhythmic complexity, hand clapping, percussive accompaniment, call-and-response, melodic improvisation, and enthusiastic unrestrained body movements and dancing, found their way into the music called **rhythm and blues (R&B).**

Rhythm and Blues

For many years, the popular music recording industry, as mentioned previously, applied the term *race records* to popular musics, ranging from country and urban blues to jazz, white-style ballads, and gospel, performed by and marketed primarily for blacks. Much black popular music was based on the form and harmonic pattern of the blues; most of it was in quadruple meter, with strong backbeats on the normally weak second and fourth beats of the measure; and most of it was danceable. Religious or secular, it generally involved syncopated rhythmic improvisation, call-and-response between a leader and a group or congregation, and vocalizations utilizing African techniques—extremely high and low ranges, falsetto, numerous blue notes, and expressive vocal catches strengthening the emotional character of the music.

Although performed in an idiom deemed unacceptable for mainstream markets, black popular music steadily developed an enthusiastic audience among young white listeners. Finally, in 1949, the industry trade journal *Billboard* abandoned the offensive term *race records,* grouping all the popular music intended for a black audience under the term *rhythm and blues,* and for several years that was the phrase generally applied to black popular music.

Rhythm and blues ensembles, whether swing-style bands or small combos, were loud, usually featuring an electric guitar and sometimes other electrified instruments as well. The music had a strong vocal orientation, with at least one singer and often an all-male vocal group involved, the need for singers to shout or scream to be heard above the instrumentalists contributing to the emotional intensity of the music. The lyrics of most R&B songs—though frankly, unselfconsciously, and even blatantly sexual—remained primarily good-natured. **Joe Turner** ("boss of the blues," 1911–1985) and **Willie Mae "Big Mama" Thornton** (1926–1984) were among the best-known and most admired R&B performers.

Although white listeners readily accepted the soothing music of certain black male ensembles, they did not yet accept black music per se: The performances of such **doo-wop** ensembles as the Mills Brothers and the Ink Spots, featuring high falsetto voices, smooth harmonies, and subtle rhythmic backgrounds sung to nonsense syllables, were relatively white in style. The Platters' doo-wop recordings "Only You" and "My Prayer" are other well-known examples of early doo-wop music. The black soloists Lena Horne, Nat "King" Cole, and Ella Fitzgerald also had hits on the pop charts in the late 1940s and early 1950s, but most of their repertoire was from Tin Pan Alley, and their performances, too, generally conformed to white practice. But black listeners tended to prefer rhythm and blues, and by 1950, increasing numbers of young whites did, too.

Finally, the unexpected but quite congenial blending of rhythm and blues with another non-mainstream music—country-western—invigorated and in fact revolutionized American popular music.

Country Music Meets R&B

Black rhythm and blues and white country-western shared a number of important characteristics. Both lay outside the popular mainstream; both were rooted in the South; both were danceable; both consistently involved the guitar (acoustic, electric, or amplified); both featured frank lyrics and earthy delivery styles; and both were sung in dialects different from that of the standard white urban population.

Thus it is not surprising, given the restless climate of young listeners hungry for something hot and new, that in the early 1950s these two dissident styles met and fused to produce the most widely and most wildly hailed popular music the world has known: rock and roll.

signal, greet enthusiastically

Birth of Rock and Roll

Convinced that white listeners would reject the raucous sound, producers and directors generally refused to program rhythm-and-blues hits on mainstream radio. But a disc jockey in Cleveland, Ohio, named **Alan Freed** soon realized that many white teens preferred R&B hits to mainstream popular music, and beginning in 1951 he played increasing numbers of rhythm-and-blues records on his radio programs, which reached a broad general audience. Freed also promoted live stage performances of music in R&B style, with both blacks and whites present on the stage and in the audience.

Then two young white country singers with black delivery styles entered and forever altered the popular music picture. The terms *rock* and *roll* had long been familiar, and sexually suggestive, in black popular music; but Alan Freed is credited with coining the term **rock and roll** for the new style with which Bill Haley and Elvis Presley revolutionized the popular music world.

Bill Haley (1925–1981)
When **Bill Haley and His Comets,** initially a country-western group, began to combine white western swing with elements of black rhythm and blues, they seemed temporarily displaced musicians—at home in neither popular music camp. They didn't know it then, but they were playing a brand-new music—rock and roll, soon to replace all others in popularity. In 1954, their cover recording of Joe Turner's R&B hit "Shake, Rattle, and Roll"—widely played by radio stations that would not have touched the R&B version—quickly soared to the top of the popular music charts. And the next year, the Comets' recording of "Rock around the Clock," used as the theme for the movie *Blackboard Jungle,* became the first international rock-and-roll hit.

Elvis Presley (1935–1977)
Elvis Presley (Figure 16.1), another country boy, followed much the same course from country to rock and roll, but the astonishing degree of popularity he achieved was unprecedented then and, for a solo singer, remains unsurpassed. Through a combination of talent, persistence, and luck, Presley achieved a recording contract and soared to the top of his profession with dizzying speed.

Presley's early **rockabilly** or country rock records actually found more favor with blacks than whites, but his appeal soon became interracial and international. The term *rockabilly,* suggesting a hybrid of rock and hillbilly, was first printed in a trade journal in 1956, the year that Presley made a cover recording of "Hound Dog," recorded earlier by Big Mama Thornton. Whereas her record was not played on any but "race" radio stations, Presley's was widely heard and soon reached the top of first the black and then the white pop charts.

FIGURE 16.1
Elvis Presley.

Elvis, almost entirely self-taught, played little more than simple chords on his guitar; but he had a beautiful and amazingly versatile voice to which he added warmth and intensity by the use of vibrato. Another early recording, "Heartbreak Hotel" (also 1956), proved the range of his expressive gifts, from wild and raucous to wrenchingly warm and tender.

Early Characteristics
loud, harsh—sanding

African Americans migrating north to Chicago after World War II found a wealth of music happening there as jazz musicians, country and urban blues musicians, boogie-woogie pianists, and others played for self-entertainment, for commercial clubs, and for the recording studios. Some of the new arrivals began to develop their own distinctive kinds of rock and roll, more closely related to rhythm and blues than was Presley's, which was rooted in country-western music. Their accompanying instruments included one or more amplified guitars, a saxophone, and sometimes a trumpet, over which a singer screamed or shouted. The meter was quadruple, with strong backbeats, and the tempo danceable. Bo Diddley (Otha Ellas Bates, later known as Ellas McDaniel, whose nickname is assigned various and conflicting origins though it probably comes from the single-string instrument called a diddley bow) played his electric guitar with terrific rhythmic vitality, achieving an extreme range of sounds in an age before technology made such effects commonplace. Little Richard (Richard Penniman) thumped his piano and screamed his lyrics, sacred or profane, with equal fervor.

Chuck Berry (b. 1926, Figure 16.2), among the most talented early black stars of rock and roll, fused with rhythm and blues more country-western elements than had other outstanding black musicians of the mid-1950s. A great guitarist and a talented songwriter who wrote most of the material he performed, Berry was also an effective singer, shouting protest and rebellion in a high, clear tenor voice over his highly amplified guitar. Berry became as

FIGURE 16.2
Chuck Berry.

famous for his "duckwalk" across the stage—knees bent, head thrusting forward and back as he played his guitar—as Elvis was for his pelvic gyrations; but more significantly, Berry's music strongly influenced both the Beatles and the Rolling Stones, who later sang his songs and imitated his distinctive style. Berry's many hit recordings included "School Day" (1957, Listening Example 57).

End of the First Era

The end of the 1950s proved a dark time generally for the promising new music, rock and roll: Elvis Presley had been drafted into the army; Little Richard walked away from rock and roll (temporarily, for religious reasons, returning after several years to resume his highly successful career); Buddy Holly died in a plane crash. Scandal plagued several stars, notably Jerry Lee Lewis, who had married his very young third cousin; and Chuck Berry, who had been arrested for taking a minor across state lines.

White performers, seeing their profits slip away to the R&B market, began to make tame, toned-down cover versions of R&B songs, with sexual references less blatant and rhythms less hot; and radio stations that had never programmed "black music" willingly played the "whitened" cover recordings, which they considered more suitable for the general audience. The popular television program *American Bandstand,* hosted by Dick Clark, featured white teen idols such as Paul Anka, Bobby Darin, Fabian, and Frankie Avalon singing respectable, urban versions of rhythm-and-blues hits.

The **payola** investigations of 1959 to 1960, which revealed that disc jockeys were routinely accepting money and gifts for playing (plugging) certain records, tarnished even the popular Dick Clark and virtually destroyed Alan Freed: convicted of "commercial bribery," Freed received a fine and a suspended sentence;

"School Day"

CD 2
Track 25
2:34

Composer/Performer
Chuck Berry

Meter
Four beats to the bar

Form
Twelve-bar blues

Tempo
Brisk

The fast-paced lyrics describe the routine of a typical 1950s high school student, who follows a school day of torments from the person sitting behind, little time for lunch, and a mean-looking teacher, with a far more meaningful afternoon—listening to the latest hits on a jukebox.

The form is the blues, but the mood is light and the energy level high. Berry does not follow the text repetition within each three-line verse typical of the classic blues.

Of the seven verses, all but the fifth—which is a guitar solo—involve call-and-response between the singer and the guitar, which often imitates the vocal line it follows.

Throughout the song, the uneven subdivisions of the strongly accented beats that lend the rhythm a "shuffle" effect nearly compel a physical or, at least, an emotional response from the listener.

was blackballed by the music industry; and died, penniless, of the effects of alcoholism, at age forty-three.

As rock and roll lost its hard edge and energy, pop became more bland than ever, sending the 1960s off to a slow, unpromising start.

Surfing Music

Social unrest and violence reached unprecedented heights during the early 1960s, as the civil rights movement made dramatic breakthroughs, often at tragic cost, and President Kennedy spoke movingly of a new frontier, challenging young people to make heroic sacrifices in order to realize high ideals. But to warm, relaxed, materialistic youths living in sunny southern California, Kennedy's challenge sounded remote and unreal. Their ideal existence consisted of sun, fun, and—essentially—the beach. And **surfing songs** describing the relaxed California life also provided vicarious pleasure to young whites living in less idyllic parts of the troubled country.

The Beach Boys, formed in the early 1960s by **Brian Wilson** (b. 1942), included two of his brothers, a cousin, and a friend. Wilson, who led the group and wrote some of the songs, had a pleasant falsetto voice, and the Beach Boys sang their simple songs with smooth and soothing harmony.

But soon the Beach Boys evolved into sophisticated concert and studio musicians, effectively articulating such teen concerns as school spirit and fast cars besides the (supposedly) comfortable California surfing life. Temporarily sidelined by a nervous breakdown, Brian Wilson poured his talent into songwriting to produce, in 1966, *Pet Sounds,* which became an influential theme album in a market whose albums primarily had consisted of single, unrelated songs. Later the same year, the Beach Boys released their best-selling single, "Good Vibrations," accompanied by such nontraditional rock music sounds as sleigh bells and the electronic *theremin* (see p. 341).

(see p. 341)

After 1966, the Beach Boys changed both their leader and their image, growing long hair and beards and adding sophisticated electronic effects to their music, now darkened by protest songs. In the 1980s, the Beach Boys enjoyed something of a comeback, but in 1983 Dennis Wilson drowned, and the later Beach Boys' albums made limited impact on the volatile rock market. Their lasting fame and influence seemed fated to reside in their songs of sun, sand, and surf. Yet in 2004, the man who on *Pet Sounds* poignantly sang "I just wasn't made for these times" achieved a triumphant return with the release of *Smile,* an album left unfinished in 1967. Long known as "the greatest album that never was," it has brought Brian Wilson acclaim as one of America's finest songwriters.

Motown

Surfing music meant little to young African Americans facing challenges of a more serious kind. Angered to see white performers reaping huge profits from covers of black hits and from bland surfing songs, some black musicians set out to earn a higher share of the wealth. Most notably, in 1959, a young black songwriter named **Berry Gordy, Jr.,** formed a company called **Motown** for the purpose of marketing black rock and roll as aggressively and as lucratively as the products of white musicians.

Motown was established in the "motor town," Detroit, which became to rock and roll what Nashville was to country. Under Gordy's guidance, the new company turned out hit records as efficiently as assembly lines turned out cars, each one technically perfect, efficiently marketed, and of broad crossover appeal. Gordy custom-designed his singers, carefully supervising their repertoire and requiring them to take classes in diction, grooming, stage presence, and choreography. Thus the Motown sound was lighter, smoother, and less sexy than other, blacker, rock and roll. Motown groups like the Supremes, the Temptations, and the Miracles drew on rhythm and blues and gospel, but they also drew on the pop conventions of Tin Pan Alley, designed to appeal to young whites as well as (or more than) blacks in order to draw a mass audience. There was usually a lead singer and a background vocal doo-wop group,

FIGURE 16.3
The Supremes.

who enriched the sonority by singing nonsense syllables in pleasant harmony. Whereas early Motown records used very simple instrumentation, strings and other orchestral instruments accompanied later performances.

The outstanding Motown group was the female trio the Supremes (Figure 16.3), with their famous lead singer Diana Ross (Listening Example 58). Well-known male vocal groups sponsored by Motown included the Four Tops and the Temptations. Michael Jackson was only five years old when Motown discovered him and his brothers, a family group—the Jacksons—perfectly illustrating both the virtues and the liabilities of Motown, for the conformity and uniformity Gordy demanded left his stars little room for individual development. Stevie Wonder, who also recorded for Motown, became the first member of the group to achieve artistic independence and gain control over his own recordings.

Although Motown made a lot of money for black singers, the music they produced was actually more popular with white than with black listeners, and by the mid-1960s, black musicians were effectively asserting themselves with their own new music, *soul.* First, however, an invasion from abroad revitalized the fading American rock and roll.

The British Invasion

The remarkable group that came to be known as the **Beatles** (in punning reference to Buddy Holly's Crickets, whom they greatly admired, and "beat" music) began as a Liverpool gang more interested in finding trouble than in changing the course of rock and roll. John Lennon formed the group, which included Paul McCartney and soon George Harrison.

Listening Example 58

"Stop! In the Name of Love"

Composers
Brian Holland, Tamont Dozier, and Eddie Holland, Motown's
premier songwriter/production team, known as H-D-H.

CD 2
Track 26
2:52

Performers
The Supremes

Form
Modified verse-chorus

Meter
Four beats to the bar

Tempo
Moderate

Here the chorus, or refrain, serves as the "hook," a catchy four-measure
phrase that begins the song and recurs after each sixteen-measure (four-
line) verse.

Refrain: Sung by the Supremes (four measures). Using a portion of the refrain as introduction was characteristic of the Motown sound.

Instrumental phrase: Four measures.

Verse: Sung by Diana Ross (sixteen measures). We hear the Supremes
in the background, and toward the end of the verse, the Supremes
sing a brief phrase ("Think it o-o-ver") that serves as a further unifying
factor—besides the refrain—throughout the song.

Refrain: The Supremes sing it twice, adding the motto "Think it o-o-ver,"
also twice.

Verse: Diana Ross, with the Supremes in the background. As Ross sings
the fourth line of the verse, the Supremes join her, repeating "Think
it o-o-ver."

Refrain: As before.

Verse: Diana Ross sings just two lines of the verse, and all bring the song
to an end with repetitions of the refrain and the unifying motto.

Notice the constant steady pulse, with accents applied about equally
between downbeat and backbeat throughout the song, with no hint of
the sophisticated cross-rhythms and polyrhythms of African music.

In 1962, having replaced their early drummer Pete Best with the already
popular Ringo Starr, the Beatles shared a London performance with Little
Richard, recently returned to rock and roll, and became an overnight sensation.
They attracted a producer, quickly became famous in England, and very soon
were rocking the musical world with their own brand of rock and roll.

Impressed with the growing fame of the young rock and rollers, whose records by 1963 were hugely popular in America, television host Ed Sullivan invited the Beatles to perform on his popular show in 1964—little anticipating the riot of enthusiasm their arrival in America would cause. Their clothes, hairstyles, and foreign accent made a terrific impression on American teens, who screamed and swooned with adulation. The Beatles' lighthearted, good-natured songs with their catchy melodies and quite innocent lyrics ("I Want to Hold Your Hand") lifted the spirits of American youth, inaugurating Beatlemania.

But at the end of just a decade, the Beatles separated, each wishing—needing—to satisfy his own creative needs. The Who evolved later in the 1960s, an unlikely combination of talented but disparate individuals. Although each member of the group performed in a style unlike the others, somehow their brand of chaos worked, and they became quite popular in the United States. The Rolling Stones, another hugely influential English group, also began to perform in the early 1960s; but because their style and influence belong to the next decade, we will discuss them in Chapter 17.

Back to Black Rock

The relationship between black and white rock and roll has been and remains curious and complex. With roots in both cultures, rock was primarily a black concept; yet white country singers who sounded black made the style popular, and the Beatles gave it the shot of energy that rescued it from early death. American blacks, however, soon sought to regain the initiative they had temporarily lost to English groups and soloists.

By the mid-1960s, "black power" and "black is beautiful" were potent slogans in the United States, where blacks generally had less interest in integrating with whites than in establishing their own cultural identity. Many, resentful of the basically white flavor of the Motown sound, began to perform a kind of updated rhythm and blues, which they named *soul,* a post-1950s term for black pride and the term with which the music trade magazine *Billboard,* in 1964, replaced rhythm and blues.

Soul   At first, **soul** evolved as a new blues, sung by small vocal groups with harsh voices and a rough delivery style, accompanied by small combos, usually including a saxophone. The added intensity of conviction, passion, and sincerity characteristic of the new black music, blending secular lyrics and gospel energy, remained inherent even in the broader stream of music to which the term *soul* came to be applied.

Aretha Franklin (Figure 16.4), known as "Lady Soul," began her music experience singing in church and, like many soul singers, transferred the emotional gospel style to popular and rhythm-and-blues songs. The "father of soul," **Ray Charles** (Ray Charles Robinson, 1930–2004), received excellent music training in his teens, though blind from glaucoma from the age of seven. A fine pianist and singer, who also played the saxophone, Charles was among the first blacks to become technically expert with studio recording technology, thereby enhancing the quality of recordings by himself and other blacks. He

FIGURE 16.4

American blues, gospel, soul, pop, and jazz singer Aretha Franklin.

also had a great gift for involving an audience in his performances, singing secular songs with the abandon of gospel music and using call-and-response to capture listeners' attention and participation. A knowledgeable and complex musician who continued to work year-round until shortly before his death, Charles blended the improvisation of jazz, the beat of rhythm and blues, and the emotional fervor of gospel in his own infectious, inimitable style.

In 1965, **James Brown** (b. 1933), the "godfather of soul," also known as "Mr. Dynamite," recorded "Papa's Got a Brand New Bag" (Listening Example 59), pointing soul in a fiery new direction. Like Ray Charles, James Brown became a good businessman, who financed his own highly successful album *Live at the Apollo* (1963) when his record company failed to back him. Brown, however, never enjoyed the commercial success Charles achieved. The African roots of soul are apparent in his harsh, intensely emotional singing, and by the 1970s, he had redefined soul and gospel into a new style, *funk*.

Funk **Funk** began as a new expression of black consciousness, rooted in soul, often with lyrics referring specifically to interracial issues. When a number of white musicians responded to the lure of funk by copying it, funk formed in a sense a bridge between sympathetic whites and blacks.

Although related to the blues in mood and instrumentation, funk follows no prescribed harmonic pattern as guitars, keyboards, or both fill in simple, repetitive harmonies above a strong bass-guitar line. Rhythms, often highly complex, are punctuated by an intriguing variety of drums. All four beats to a measure may be accented evenly, in striking difference from the strong backbeats characteristic of much rock music.

"Papa's Got a Brand New Bag"

CD 2
Track 27
2:06

Composer, Lyricist, Singer
James Brown

Meter
Four beats to the bar

Form
Twelve-bar blues

After a brief instrumental introduction—announcement, really—Brown sings six verses, praising "Papa's brand new 'bag'" and the way she dances. Brown generally conforms to the form and harmonic changes of twelve-bar blues; however, the second line of text in each verse is original, rather than a repeat of the first line as in classic blues. Notice, too, that the third verse consists of only eight bars instead of twelve.

The accompanying instruments (bass, horns, drums, guitar) play overlapping, independent rhythmic patterns (*polyrhythms*), punctuating the vocal line and adding rhythmic as well as timbral interest. We do not hear the competition or interaction between voice and instruments typical of classic blues performances.

Come here, sister. Papa's in the swing.
He ain't too hip about that new breed babe.
He ain't no drag. Papa's got a brand new bag.

Come here, mama, and dig this crazy scene.
He's not too fancy, but his line is pretty clean.
He ain't no drag. Papa's got a brand new bag.

He's doin' the Jerk. He's doin' the Fly.
Don't play him cheap, 'cause you know he ain't shy.
He's doin' the Monkey, the Mashed Potatoes.
Jump back, Jack, see you later alligator.

Come here, sister. Papa's in the swing.
He ain't too hip now, but I can dig the new breed babe.
He ain't no drag. He's got a brand new bag.

Oh papa! He's doin' the Jerk. Papa, he's doing the Jerk.
He's doin' the Twist, just like this. He's doin' the Fly ev'ry day and
*   ev'ry night.*
The thing's like the Boomerang.

Hey, come on. Hey! Hey! Come on.
Hey! Hey! He's up tight, out of sight.
Come on. See what you know . . .

FIGURE 16.5

American rock, soul, and funk group Sly and the Family Stone.

The recording of "Thank You (Falettinme Be Mice Elf Agin, 1970)" by Sly Stone (Figure 16.5) introduced the bizarre spellings imitated by some later funk musicians. George Clinton, leader of the group called Funkadelic, is considered a rigorously pure funk musician, but many other groups participate in funk with less consistency and dedication. Thus Earth, Wind, and Fire is considered a jazz-funk group, whereas the Commodores are a smooth funk band with crossover appeal to the disco audience (see pp. 292–293). The funk music of Kool and the Gang includes their recording "Funky Stuff" (1970) and, from later in the 1970s, "Celebration."

From Rock and Roll to Rock

Ominous, often tragic, social events of the mid- to late-1960s, including riots in the ghettos of Harlem and Watts in 1965, further race riots in 1967, and the murder of Martin Luther King, Jr., in 1968, again changed the mood and the music of youth. As students held sit-ins at colleges across the land protesting against discrimination, authoritarianism, and eventually the war in Vietnam, popular music closely reflected the new mood. The vivid new music replacing the carefree early rock and roll was collectively called **rock,** of which many and diverse branches or brands evolved.

Folk Rock   The mood of protest having strengthened, rock crowds demanded more than entertainment, and by 1965 urban folk singers who included protest songs in their performances at colleges and in night clubs were addressing rock audiences as well, reflecting the serious new mood by blending light rock effects with tuneful melodies and protest lyrics in what became known as **folk rock.** Mellow groups such as Peter, Paul and Mary, unable or unwilling to update their lyrics and their style, quickly became less relevant and less popular.

On the other hand, the urban folk singer Joan Baez (Figure 16.6) was among those who intensified the emotional content of their songs and addressed topics

FIGURE 16.6

Joan Baez performing
at Big Sur.

of current controversy and concern. Drawing upon her examples and those of Woody Guthrie and Pete Seeger, other folk musicians also began adding elements of rock to their performances, thereby reaching a wider audience.

To the confusion of some fans, Bob Dylan switched from urban folk to folk rock in 1965, replacing the acoustic instruments of his early days with an electric guitar and a rock rhythm section. And when Dylan began to sing of personal rather than social or universal problems, he antagonized many previously loyal listeners. Some think today, however, that the powerful messages of protest and reform in Dylan's moving poetry are destined to survive his music.

Several groups joined the folk rock movement: the Mamas and the Papas added a light rock flavor to their familiar style of folk music; Crosby, Stills, Nash, and Young also updated their sound by adding light rock effects; Simon and Garfunkel and the Fifth Dimension performed in folk rock style as well. But the Byrds, even more strongly affected by Bob Dylan's new approach, became the group most closely allied to the folk rock style, using the amplification and distortion of instrument sounds for expressive effect. Their recorded versions of Dylan's "Mr. Tambourine Man" (Listening Example 60) and Pete Seeger's "Turn! Turn! Turn!" made a very strong and lasting impact on a wide audience.

Acid Rock
"Psychedelic" or **acid rock** began, in San Francisco, about 1965 as an attempt to reproduce the sensations experienced by someone under the influence of LSD ("acid" in street slang). Because the music was to be felt as well as heard, the sound was amplified to unprecedented levels, the extremely—even excruciatingly—loud volume and heavy distortion of sounds causing emotional, psychological, indeed psychedelic effects in the listener. Improved amplification systems and other technical advances made stadiums

"Mr. Tambourine Man"

**CD 2
Track 28
2:29**

Composer
Bob Dylan

Performers
The Byrds

Meter
Four beats to the bar

Tempo
Slow, relaxed

Form
Verse and refrain

During the four-bar instrumental introduction, the drums and tambourine punctuate the sounds of the twelve-string electric guitar, electric bass, and other instruments with a strong backbeat.

The Byrds sing the song's familiar two-line refrain (eight bars in each line) in their close, country-style harmony, the main melody sometimes lying below a higher melodic line, or countermelody, as often occurs in country music. Their simple chords occur in slightly surprising order compared with the harmony of earlier popular music.

The soloist—singer-guitarist Roger (Jim) McGuinn—sings two verses of irregular length: fourteen lines in the first (beginning at 0:42), ten in the second (beginning at 1:10). (Such irregularity of phrase length and stanza lines is reminiscent of the traditional manner of performing folk songs such as "Barbara Allen," Listening Example 5.) Perhaps the several other verses Dylan wrote for the song, expressing loneliness and the desire to find relief in the sound of the tambourine, seemed too personal for group performance; in any case, the Byrds' performance is less than half the length of Dylan's recording of "Mr. Tambourine Man."

The Byrds sing the refrain once more, and the guitar and bass gently fade away.

and large arenas the ideal venue for huge concerts, perfectly suited to the acid rock experience. During performances, which often were extremely long (time being meaningless to someone in a psychedelic trance), dramatic light shows, emissions from smoke and fog machines, and other special effects produced their own psychedelic aura, rendering such concerts theatrical events in which music constituted only one of the entertainment elements, and in which the audience was expected to be totally involved. References to drugs, sometimes expressed in code to avoid censorship, became more and more overt:

"White Rabbit," performed by Jefferson Airplane, never pretended to be about anything else.

Yet while some acid rock groups, such as the Doors, sang of sex and death and self-destruction, the Grateful Dead, associated with the same movement, remained relatively mild (or at least less violent) in performance. Their members earned credibility by living for a time in the Haight-Ashbury district of San Francisco, sharing the hippie experience they related in their music, and even today these solid rock and blues musicians retain a devoted following.

Psychedelic Blues

Two blazingly gifted stars, one a singer, one a guitarist, changed the concept of musical sound and experience in their astonishing performances of psychedelic blues. When Janis Joplin passionately sang of her sad and hopeless life, or Jimi Hendrix set fire to his guitars onstage, the audience literally felt the performers' pain.

Janis Joplin (1943–1970, Figure 16.7), a white woman inspired by Bessie Smith and Willie Mae "Big Mama" Thornton, imbued every song she sang with the passion and sincerity of the blues. With a voice sometimes described as coarse sandpaper, Joplin became the most powerful female performer of the rock era, expressing with eloquence, but never overcoming, the agony of her sad and hopeless life.

An impoverished half African American, half Native American left-handed guitarist from Seattle, **Jimi Hendrix** (1942–1970, Figure 16.8) captured the spirit of despair and frustration of American (and British) youth in the late 1960s with his scorching electric guitar. Indulging freely in the drugs he believed

Handwritten margin note: inspire: stimulate to creative activity animate w/ a feeling

FIGURE 16.7

Janis Joplin, July 29, 1968. Acid rock was a means of expressing frustration with the values of an older generation.

FIGURE 16.8

The American musician Jimi Hendrix.

enhanced his passion and performance skills, he delivered all the anger and violence of the era in his thunderous electric blues, famously dousing his guitar with lighter fluid and setting it on fire at the Monterey Pop Festival in 1967.

Gifted beyond verbal description, Hendrix used his enormous talent to develop guitar techniques beyond the imagination, and the ability, of fellow guitarists. Although solidly rooted in the blues, which Hendrix played to masterful effect, his music forged a new world of previously unheard sounds. To the extreme electronic feedback and distortion being used by other likeminded guitarists, Hendrix added his own distinctive vocabulary of riffs, bent notes, scales, and electronic effects, making his music truly personal and in fact inimitable.

Heavy Metal The late 1960s produced several American groups inspired by the wild, frenzied performances and distorted guitar sounds of the British Led Zeppelin (which developed a huge and nearly fanatical following in the United States) and by the explosive innovations of Jimi Hendrix, whose style became identified as **heavy metal.** The new sound, extremely loud and often electronically distorted, achieved American identity through Blue Cheer, formed in 1966, and Iron Butterfly, whose recording of "In-A-Gadda-Da-Vida" ("In a Garden of Eden"?) added distorted guitar to the sound of an electric organ. Early metal, with ensembles consisting of drums, bass, and one or two guitars, catered to young, white, working-class, often alienated males seeking realization of their fantasies of power and aggression. Economic crises, political corruption, the scaling back of social services, and perceptions of changing gender roles and family structure all fed the aggressive new music.

In time the style matured and to some degree diversified; but the essence of early metal was male and powerful.

Alice Cooper, as both the musician Vincent Furnier and his band were known, delivered overtly sexual heavy-metal rock theatrics. Their sensational tactics (Furnier often donned a boa snake) won further acclaim in the early 1970s, when theatricality dominated rock performances.

A Future Unassured

Toward the end of its second decade, rock was being celebrated at major rock festivals across the country, the most notable of which, held at Woodstock, New York, in August of 1969, was attended by more than 400,000 people. But some such festivals spawned violence and tragedy: four people died at Altamount Speedway near San Francisco, and three were killed at the "Celebration of Life" on the banks of Louisiana's Atchafalaya River. Rockers hardly seemed to know how to celebrate their hard-won recognition; and although rock music had grown strong and varied, its future seemed insecure as the 1970s began.

Terms to Review

rhythm and blues (R&B)   Broadly, black popular music of the 1950s. More specifically, a black popular style in quadruple meter, with strong backbeats and a danceable tempo.

doo-wop   The name given to background vocal ensembles accompanying Motown singers, often by singing neutral or nonsense syllables.

rock and roll   A popular music of the mid-1950s to mid-1960s combining characteristics of rhythm and blues and country-western music.

rockabilly   A close amalgamation of country music and rock and roll.

payola   The acceptance by disc jockeys of money and gifts in return for plugging recordings.

surfing songs   Songs by the Beach Boys and other groups reflecting the easy California lifestyle.

Motown   A highly successful black company that recorded, published, and sponsored black popular music.

soul   A fervent, emotional black style rooted in gospel and the blues.

funk   Rock music rooted in soul but with lyrics expressing interracial concerns.

rock   A collective term encompassing many styles of popular music that evolved from and succeeded rock and roll.

folk rock   The addition of light rock effects to urban folk music.

acid rock   Sometimes called psychedelic rock. Music that attempts to evoke the sensations experienced by a person under the influence of LSD.

heavy metal   A rock style, extremely loud and often electronically distorted, introduced by Jimi Hendrix.

Key Figures

Thomas A. Dorsey
Joe Turner
Willie Mae "Big Mama" Thornton
Alan Freed
Bill Haley and His Comets
Elvis Presley

Chuck Berry
Brian Wilson
Berry Gordy, Jr.
Beatles
Aretha Franklin
Ray Charles

James Brown
Janis Joplin
Jimi Hendrix
Alice Cooper

Suggestions for Further Listening

Atlantic Rhythm and Blues, vols. 1–7
Bill Haley: *Golden Hits*
   Greatest Hits
Elvis Presley: *Golden,* vols. 1–4
Chuck Berry: *Greatest Hits*
Beach Boys: *The Best of the Beach Boys*

Bob Dylan: *Times They Are a-Changin'*
Ray Charles: *Rock Begins,* vol. 1
"Shake, Rattle, and Roll," performed by Joe Turner; performed by Bill Haley and the Comets
"Tutti Frutti," performed by Little Richard; performed by Pat Boone

Suggestion for Viewing

Ray (2004; film about Ray Charles)

Suggestion for Reading

David Hajdu: *Positively Fourth Street: The Lives and Times of Joan Baez, Bob Dylan, Mimi Baez Farina, and Richard Farina.*

Critical Thinking

What is your view of cover recordings of rhythm-and-blues hits (such as "Tutti Frutti") by white singers (such as Pat Boone)? Why were the covers successful? How did their success affect black performers? How did the quality, and the style, of the white performance compare with the R&B recordings? Do you see moral implications of this practice? Business implications?

How does the popular music market today compare with the youthful market of the 1950s? Do young people have the same impact—or more, or less? How do those who were teenagers in the 1950s affect the popular music market today?

Where do you think Bob Dylan has found his most congenial medium, and where do you think his legacy lies: folk music, rock, poetry, other?

In what ways do you think Motown served black musicians? In what ways might Motown have damaged them?

Go to www.mhhe.com/ferrisaml5 for a list of additional Web-based resources that relate to the content in this chapter.

Popular Music since 1970

During 1970, a year of devastating social and political significance in the United States, frustrated protesters against the war in Vietnam, most notably on college campuses around the country, provoked hostility throughout other strata of society. When National Guard troops at Kent State University shot at student protesters, killing four and wounding at least nine, student riots broke out but soon succumbed to a despairing sense of demoralization and helplessness. Meanwhile other groups, including women, Native Americans, Chicanos, and gays, inspired by the civil rights movement of the 1960s against the conservative "silent majority" caused further unrest in American society.

Rockers were deeply affected by the mood of the time, further darkened by the deaths of several prominent rock figures—Jimi Hendrix (1970) from an overdose of sleeping pills, Janis Joplin (1970) from an overdose of heroin, and Jim Morrison of the Doors (1971) from a heart attack. Musical innovation temporarily lessened as rockers absorbed these shocks and looked ahead; and some groups, for whom the sound engineer had become an essential partner in performance, abandoned live performance entirely.

As the British invasion continued, the Rolling Stones became enormously popular in America, covering American blues and soul recordings at first, then diversifying to become a highly eclectic band. The American rock and pop scenes, too, diversified, producing new styles and branches of styles, as musicians struggled to express and affect their troubled times.

Nevertheless, solo singers, many of whom wrote their own songs, acquired significance as the new decade began.

Singer-Songwriters

"The Boss," **Bruce Springsteen,** probably the most successful rock star of the late 1970s, pointed rock in a new direction in 1982, with his album *Born in the U.S.A.* (whose title song was a bitter indictment of the treatment veterans received upon returning home from Vietnam). Springsteen further revitalized music in the mid-1980s with his stirring songs on socially relevant topics, whose messages were further implemented by Springsteen and other like-minded rock stars in the rock-sponsored benefits for starving masses in Ethiopia, "We Are the World" and "Live Aid." In 1995, Springsteen commanded new attention and respect with his profoundly moving songs in the film *Philadelphia*. (Song samples and lyrics from Springsteen's albums are readily available on the Web.)

Women singer-songwriters often have had to fight the record industry, which has a long tradition of making over its female artists. Much like Diana Ross of the Supremes in the early days of Motown, today's female singers may endure studio scripting, sculpturing, and choreographing to an extreme degree. Yet Carole King, Mary Chapin Carpenter, Sheryl Crow, Lucinda Williams, and Emmylou Harris, among many others, became and remained successful. (Tracks from some of their recordings can be heard at their Web sites.)

Among those resisting dominance—by studios, by men, even by customary chord progressions or lyrics—**Joni Mitchell** has used the conventions of blues, rock, and folk to write unconventional songs about her own most personal experiences. Her style and her voice have changed over the decades, as her interests ranged from nature to narrative to political indignation.

Art Rock

Rockers and jazzers increasingly collaborated among themselves while also incorporating effects of the music of other cultures. **Blood, Sweat, and Tears,** a rock quartet with a brass section and later with a saxophone as well, produced a sound closer to jazz than to rock, and the even more popular group **Chicago** included rock musicians who incorporated in their music some elements of jazz. Although rock and classical music seem a less likely combination than vernacular rock and jazz, the interest in fusion also encouraged collaborative experiments among musicians in those fields, with varying degrees of success. The superficial quoting of themes from familiar classics, as in the Dutch rock group Ekseption's "The Fifth," based on themes of Beethoven, seems musically insignificant, and most arrangements of classical pieces that use rock instrumentation and rhythms have not proved of much or of lasting interest.

Some ensembles, however—several if not most of them British—have achieved an effective blend of serious concert music and rock, called **art rock.** (The term *art rock* does not imply that other rock styles lack artistic qualities: it is simply a convenient way to describe the combination of rock with concepts of "classical," "concert," or "art" music. Each of those terms is flawed as well, and the conscientious musician uses them with qualification.)

Emerson, Lake & Palmer related rock to classical music in several intriguing pieces. The Moody Blues produced an art rock album with the London Festival Orchestra in 1967 and Genesis, King Crimson, Pink Floyd, and Yes are among other English groups who have explored the concept of art rock. A Dutch group, Focus, and a New York ensemble, Ars Nova, also have experimented with this combined style.

Disco

Disco, which began as *discothèque* in France after World War II, may be seen as the result of a romance or a clash between the popular cultures of Europe and America, and between the social elite and the cultural underworld. It is a difficult music to place, having begun in French jazz clubs, turned to rock music in the United States in the 1960s, and topped the pop charts in 1975.

Swing and jazz clubs in France, banned by the Germans in wartime because of their American, black, and Jewish associations, became symbols of dissent in the French underground, enhancing their aura of illicit excitement and thrill. The first American discothèque, which opened on New Year's Eve 1960, catered to a desire among wealthy jet-setters for an entertainment atmosphere less staid than New York's famous Stork Club and El Morocco. Soon more clubs opened, in New York and in other American cities, all however retaining highly exclusive requirements, including expensive membership dues.

By the mid-1960s, the discothèque had spawned a multitude of dance crazes, including the Twist, the Jerk, and the Watusi among many others, and the role of the disc jockey evolved from the anonymous one of simply playing records to sensing and directing the mood of a crowd throughout the evening. Discothèques of the late 1960s offered enormous dance floors, multiple rock bands playing live music (instead of records), huge rotating mirrored light balls, and extreme sonic overload, all inducing virtual hallucinogenic states. But as the role of discothèque attendees altered from frenzied dancer to passive observer, the discothèque phenomenon seemed about to fade away.

In the 1970s, however, it was dramatically reanimated by gay men, blacks, Hispanics, and other urban contingents suppressed during the 1960s and reveling in their newly liberated position. Thus relaunched, and rechristened *disco,* the popular dance phenomenon maintained a highly visible presence throughout the new decade (Figure 17.1). Much of the disco culture concerned drugs and sex, and the hedonistic philosophy that nothing is wrong if it feels right (or as Mae West once said, "Too much of a good thing may be a great thing"), remained at the core of disco culture; but this philosophy also produced the first distinctive disco music. Dissatisfied with short rock singles not primarily intended for dancing, disco deejays and dancers of the 1970s sought extended pieces with continuous danceable rhythms based on the black R&B roots of pop music. The early 1970s produced several hit disco songs, and in 1975 Van McCoy and "The Hustle" went to the top of the pop charts, signifying the mainstreaming of a culture that had prided itself on various kinds of exclusivity, from the wealthy elite to black and gay men.

FIGURE 17.1

Overhead view of the crowd dancing at Studio 54 in New York City, October 31, 1981.

The new crowds attending Studio 54, which opened in New York in 1977, still had to pass the "entrance requirements" of the club's owners; but at the end of that year, the astounding success of the film *Saturday Night Fever* further buoyed disco's rising fortunes. The movie's double-album soundtrack eventually became the biggest-selling record of all time (later replaced by Michael Jackson's *Thriller*), and by 1978 40 percent of all the music on *Billboard*'s Hot 100 was disco. The songs of the Bee Gees, biggest of all mainstream disco stars, had traditional pop music themes with no relationship to the hedonistic, highly sexualized culture of most early disco.

For a time, rock fans felt threatened by disco, which they viewed as synthetic, aristocratic, and fake; but in the end disco provided the common enemy against which rock fans rallied. The Disco Demolition Rally at Chicago's Comiskey Park stadium in July 1979 blasted out of control, as rock fans broke up mountains of disco records as well as much of the stadium itself, giving Comiskey much the same role in defeating disco that the bloody Altamont concert had played in ending the counterculture of the 1960s. After Comiskey Park, the disco market crashed, doomed as well by a wave of political conservatism and the fear of AIDS.

Punk

In the 1970s **punk** evolved from the raw, raucous garage band music of the 1960s and from the New York City avant-garde scene. While teenagers banged out their emotions and frustrations on whatever instruments—sometimes including garbage can lids—they could get hold of, slightly older and more sophisticated musicians, poets, and artists in New York also were expressing anger and disillusionment with the social and cultural conditions of their day. The imminent threats of war, nuclear disaster, economic turmoil, and out-of-control technology fed their anger and despair; and the hippies' preaching of love to all, the sophisticated arty sounds of art rock, heavy metal's pyrotechnical displays of instrumental virtuosity, and the synthetic sounds of disco fueled their fury. Like the beats of the 1950s (notably including Jack Kerouac, Allen Ginsberg, and William Burroughs) and earlier the Dadaists—a group of European artists protesting against the horrors of World War I—New York's avant-garde musicians of the 1970s turned to irony and anti-art to vent their frustration. Recordings of the simple, repetitious, angry garage band music stimulated their conception of the rebellious new music, which contended that nothing sort of overturning society could improve the sorry state of the world.

Punk was born in a small New York bar called CBGB (full name, CBGB & OMFUG, for Country, Blue Grass, Blues, and Other Music for Urban Gourmets), where five men calling themselves the **New York Dolls** (see Figure 17.2) began performing in 1971. The musical elements associated with punk include a rigid eighth-note rhythmic throb and a vocal range so narrow as to approach a drone; but ultimately of more interest, perhaps, is punk's association with the art world. A significant number of punk musicians attended art school and brought to their music modern art concepts of shock value, performance as art, and fashion, which profoundly affected the music they performed and how they performed it.

To the alienated attitude, the repetitious unemotional delivery, the pessimistic subject matter (drugs, prostitution, sado-masochism), and the angry

FIGURE 17.2

The influential American glam rock band, the New York Dolls.

new sound of the garage bands, the New York Dolls added glitter (they wore lipstick, heavy eye makeup, and high heels) and a lighter touch. Heavy guitar distortion and a pounding beat contributed to the wild excitement of their audiences. Commercial success largely eluded them, however, as other bands, including Television, the Patti Smith Group, and the Ramones, continued their movement.

Avant-garde art particularly influenced **Television,** a punk band strongly attracted to Andy Warhol and the Velvet Underground (see p. 253) and to the free jazz improvisation of John Coltrane. One member of Television, Tom Verlaine (Tom Miller), took his stage name from the French Symbolist poet Paul Verlaine (1844–1896), who represented meanings in his delicate, sensitive verse by the imaginative use of words for their sensuous effects. Although punk was by definition anti-intellectual, Television added to their music a degree of complexity and an aesthetic dimension unique among punk bands.

Patti Smith, a professional writer of poetry, plays, and articles, took her group to CBGB's in 1975, singing angry, gutsy vocals with lyrics and a delivery style calculated to shock her audience. The Patti Smith Group attracted a great deal of attention; but better-known and ultimately more influential were the **Ramones,** who modeled their image on the New York Dolls and took their name from "Paul Ramon," an early stage name of Paul McCartney. (Each member of the band, formed in 1974, assumed the last name Ramone.) Uninterested in art, free jazz, or literature, the Ramones projected raw energy, spirit, emotion, and fun; and their short, simple, fast, hard-driving songs stayed high on the charts into the early 1980s.

In the mid 1970s, Malcolm McLaren, the British owner of an antifashion London clothing store and sometime manager of the New York Dolls, brought the pessimistic, anarchic punk sound to England, where British young people, experiencing far more serious social and economic conditions than their peers in the United States, took the angry new music to their hearts. McLaren's British band, the Sex Pistols, became wildly successful at home and influential in the United States. Soon American society was avidly imitating punk fashion, as models spiked their hair and ostentatiously fastened gaping holes in their trendy clothes with flashy—sometimes gold—safety pins. The striking visual effects of punk dress, hair, and makeup strongly influenced art and fashion around the world.

In the 1990s, several California punk-rock bands, including the Offspring, Rancid, and Green Day, made punk no longer the music of a righteous minority. Singing of alienation, resentment, and self-destruction to very short, catchy tunes accompanied by speed-strummed guitars and walloping drums, they brought the humor and tuneful adrenaline of punk to a mass public. The female punk trio Sleater-Kinney, formed in 1994 in Olympia, Washington, vehemently expressed a sense of exclusion and marginalization from a woman's point of view. Meanwhile, the punk look—leather, studded dog collars, and razor-shredded clothing—evolved to include body piercing and punk hairstyles spiked up to seven inches long and vividly colored in unlikely hues such as purple, pink, or green. Yet punk lives today, as it began in the 1970s, through live shows in small places such as bars and pubs, rather than through huge arena concerts or commercial recordings on major labels. In the society of punk, personal interaction between a band and its audience remains essential.

Grunge

Teenagers of the 1990s, called generation X by the press, continued to find rock a congenial medium in which to release their fears and frustrations brought about by economic uncertainty; family instability; violence on television, on the movie screen, and in the streets; gangs; racial warfare; and social injustice. Some craved an angry, harsh, aggressive sound reflecting their own disturbed feelings, much as baby boomers had turned to early rock and roll.

In the Northwest, **grunge,** sometimes called the Seattle sound, combined the aggression of heavy metal with a melodic element reminiscent of the Beatles. The pacesetter grunge band **Nirvana,** led by **Kurt Cobain,** achieved a hybrid of pop, metal, and punk that became a national phenomenon. Pearl Jam followed Nirvana to the top of the chart in 1991; and in 1993, the early grunge band Soundgarden hit the top with *Superunknown*. The despair of the post–baby boomers was heightened by the deaths, from drug overdoses, of some grunge soloists, and especially by the shotgun suicide of Kurt Cobain, probably the most important figure in the movement.

New Wave

The term **new wave** was loosely applied to several sounds of the mid-1980s, some of which reflected certain characteristics of earlier styles. Neither angry nor political, new wave groups defused punk by imitating its manner but not its substance. That is, adopting punk's unconventional dress and bizarre stage movements, new wave musicians criticized society without resorting to shock tactics.

Although it contained some of the elements of punk, new wave was far broader in concept, constituting more a philosophy of life expressed through music than a distinctive musical style. Much of the music of one outstanding American new wave group, **Talking Heads,** is based on the simple harmonies and complex rhythms of some African musics; but the music of other well-known new wave bands, including **B-52s, Cars,** and especially **Police,** responds to different sources of inspiration. The term always referred to new or progressive music, conceived with the aid of modern studio and electronic techniques.

Electronic Dance Music

By the mid-1980s, popularity had shifted away from new wave, as many bands and several individuals with distinctive sounds became rich and famous. Prince (known then as "the artist formerly known as Prince"), Michael Jackson, Lionel Richie, Madonna, Cyndi Lauper, and Sting (formerly of Police), among the best-known names of mainstream rock in the 1980s, maintained various degrees of popularity through the 1990s. Synthesizers and other electronic instruments increasingly varied the sonorities of live and recorded performance, and concerts and recordings achieved new levels of sophistication.

The first years of the new century experienced a return of interest in the popular culture of the 1980s, which was a source of nostalgia for older rockers and was stimulating to youngsters curious about their parents' youthful experience. Thus in 2001, disco and new wave underwent a dance-floor revival, as electronic producers mimicked the pop songs they had grown up loving, to produce a new abstract (without lyrics) dance music as easy to hear as to dance to. Electronic timbres devised by classical composers (to be considered in Chapter 21) once seemed unearthly and unacceptable to pop and classical audiences alike, but now merely reflect the everyday reality of touch-tone phones, cash machines, car alarms, and innumerable electronic and digital tones our ears take for granted. Today some producers use the Jamaican-born technique of dubbing, in which a producer remixes a popular song by removing virtually everything (melody, harmony, vocals, etc.) except the beat and the bass line, thereby creating a new composition.

Rock and electronic music evolved together, both depending on instruments that plugged in, both addressing disembodied audiences through radio and records. As rockers started to hear music as signals and processing, and quickly took to distortion and feedback as desired ends to be attained, the techniques of cutting, mixing, sampling, looping, layering, and sequencing soon became commonplace in rock. Melodically, rhythmically, and harmonically simpler than electronic music devised by the classical electronic avant-garde, dance music produced by synthesizers, samplers, computers, and drum machines has been increasing in popularity year by year. Often surreal and hypnotic, and in variably loud, the music is designed to make people dance, to take them from reality to another place. Variously called *house, techno, electro, nu new wave,* and other names as well, electronic dance music forms an important part of America's landscape in the early twenty-first century.

Hip-Hop and Rap

Rap, which began as a means of black self-expression in the mid-1970s, has raised perennial questions about relationships among art, politics, and public morality. Rap grew out of the **hip-hop** movement, a popular new dance style, conveying a sense of urban unrest, which developed in New York in the 1970s. The dancing could generate intense excitement, whether it was done by youngsters on the street or in commercial dance halls. As part of the entertainment at hip-hop dance parties, disc jockeys (DJs) mastered complex turntable techniques based on Jamaican *toasting,* humorous syncopated patter delivered over remixed instrumental versions of popular records; *backspinning,* playing one record while turning a second one backward, repeating phrases and beats; and *scratching,* moving a record in both directions under the needle. Fascinated with the turntable show, people often stopped dancing to watch, whereupon DJs, to stir up the action on the dance floor, hired MCs (this term may, or may not, stand for "mike controllers") to fire up the crowd with shouts of "Get up!" "Jam to the beat!" and so on. When the MCs began speaking to the rhythm of the music and trading rhymes with each other and with the DJ, rap was born.

Rap draws from African, Afro-Caribbean, and African-American rhythmic styles; from urban street jive; from black radio DJs from the 1950s through the 1970s; from the heavyweight champion boxer Muhammad Ali; and from a rich assortment of other historical and cultural influences. In black music, vocal timbres, rhythms, and vocal inflections all convey meaning, and MCs exploit the entire range of tonal semantics in their delivery styles.

The question whether hip-hop is a culture or a craft arose as immensely successful white rappers, such as Vanilla Ice, the Beastie Boys, and later Eminem, among others, claimed that hip-hop is a craft, something one can learn to do regardless of one's cultural or ethnic heritage. These rappers emphasize clever, rapid-fire lyrics supported by music strictly designed to show off the complicated rhythms of the words. Certain black hip-hop musicians counter that hip-hop is a culture one is born into, which cannot be limited by the specific sounds produced. Thus Missy Elliott, who sings as much as she raps, and the Roots, an eight-piece hip-hop band using traditional instruments in place of turntables and samples, consider themselves full-fledged hip-hop artists born and bred: they simply prefer a more musical style of hip-hop.

Social Concerns
In the 1980s, rappers began writing socially conscious lyrics, addressing ghetto conditions and economic inequalities in the United States, which they delivered in their individual "flow" styles—their manner of combining rhythmic play, rhyme scheme, phrasing, accents, timbres, and pitch inflection. Although rap began as a predominantly male activity, Missy Elliott is among several successful female rappers today. While many male rappers extol men's domination over women, Sister Souljah's lyrics have addressed drug abuse, black-on-black violence, and national politics; and Queen Latifah's album *Black Rain* is packed with socially responsible messages about safe sex, relationships, and love. **Salt–N–Pepa** (see Figure 17.3) have offered stinging criticism of male promiscuity and spoken of female self-empowerment—though their third album, *Very Necessary* (1993), rhymed the praises of men.

The more brutal "gangsta rap" of the late 1980s, often praising misogyny and violence, had devoted listeners, both black and white, but drew condemnation from courts and law enforcers. Tupac Shakur, murdered in 1996 at age twenty-four, rapped about violence, social realism, fate, and pain. Moments of tenderness and compassion in his songs are overwhelmed with fierce black-against-black anger and brutality, and he followed expressions of respectful praise for women with harangues about "bitches" and "ho's." The white rapper Eminem (Marshall Mathers), a master of gallows and gross-out humor, gleefully aims cruel gibes at gays, women (including his mother and his wife), and assorted real people in public life; yet many admire his ingenious wordplay, inventive beats, daring candor, and wicked humor. The language with which Ice-T, Ice Cube, and the Geto Boys, for example, rap about gang warfare and

FIGURE 17.3
Salt–N–Pepa.

drive-by shootings is offensive to many, but the situations they so blazingly describe certainly exist.

Back to the Roots Some rappers, of course, produce lighthearted, playful songs, and in the 1990s rap-based cartoons appeared on television. Rap soon joined mainstream popular culture on television (Will Smith in *The Fresh Prince of Bel-Air*) and in Hollywood films (with the rappers Ice-T, Queen Latifah, Will Smith, and Eminem, among others). Ice Cube (O'Shea Jackson), having become a successful actor, screenwriter, and movie producer, worked simultaneously in the summer of 2003 on the family-friendly movie *Barbershop 2: Back in Business* (as actor and executive producer) and on the angry album *Terrorist Threats,* full of socially charged rage.

Today sophisticated northern urban rappers tap the rich resources of earlier black music: some, for example, play versions of the music enjoyed by black field workers in the Deep South more than fifty years ago. The song "Shake Ya Tailfeather," performed by Sean Combs (P. Diddy) in the movie *Bad Boys II,* derives its title from "Shake Your Moneymaker," written by slide-guitar master Elmore James about 1960. In those days, of course, royalties went to publishers and record companies instead of to blues artists, who often suffered severe economic deprivation. Today's rappers, in contrast, demand professional deals that allow them to own their works and get rich.

Contemporary Black Gospel

Today's black gospel, although derived from early traditions, sounds very little like the spirituals sung, shouted, and danced in camp meetings over a century ago. Recently, perhaps for the first time, the secular elements of gospel have stirred significant controversy. Electric bass, keyboards, and even a hip-hop flavor bring gospel to rock mainstream airwaves, to the joy of some and the dismay of traditional gospel fans, who see the trend as leaning more toward making money than saving souls.

Certainly the money is rolling in: recently contemporary, or crossover, gospel became America's fifth-largest musical genre, trailing only R&B, alternative, rap, and country on the charts. Gospel's virtuoso instrumentalists blend jazz, rock, country, funk, and hip-hop gestures; and gospel choral singing, full-throated and dramatic, is a thrilling sound. Soloists ignite audiences with the power and range of their voices and with their intricate melodic invention rivaling the improvisations of jazz. Of course the recordings have never sounded better, because of higher production standards.

Kirk Franklin skillfully melds hip-hop and traditional gospel conventions in performances such as his popular hit "Stomp," a collaboration with the group God's Property, featuring the rhythm track to the Funkadelic's funk anthem "One Nation under a Groove" and a guest rap by Salt (Cheryl James) of Salt–N–Pepa. Franklin's explosive vocal presentation has been compared to that of James Brown or Ray Charles—both of whom were criticized for blending sacred and secular effects.

Traditional gospel continues to thrive as well, most notably perhaps in the person of **Shirley Caesar,** who began her gospel career in the 1950s and was featured on the soundtrack of the Disney film *The Prince of Egypt* in 1998. The crossover trend may be a cyclical phenomenon or simply a natural consequence of the manner in which this important, stimulating sacred-secular music has evolved.

The Future Is Here

New technology makes possible an array of sophisticated effects, as synthesizers and other electronic instruments increasingly vary the sonorities of live and recorded performance, and concerts and recordings achieve new levels of sophistication. Collaborations involving dead artists—Lauryn Hill with Bob Marley and Celine Dion with Frank Sinatra, for example—sell well. Acculturation, too, becomes ever more significant, as improved communication and expanded travel bring fascinating new sounds to the western vernacular music experience.

In the election year 2004, politics seemed to play a stronger role than pop music had experienced since the controversies over civil rights and the Vietnam war in the 1960s and early 1970s. At that time, artists such as Bob Dylan (*The Times They Are a-Changin'*), Buffalo Springfield (*For What It's Worth*), and Marvin Gaye (*What's Goin' On?*) were heard widely on pop and rock radio stations. Today's mainstream music (consider Avril Lavigne's *My Happy Ending*) seems more concerned with having a good time than changing the world, but in 2004 folkies, punks, rappers, and indie rockers took musical political stands. Eminem released a strong political video (*Mosh*), and John Fogerty, Dan Bern, and Missy Elliott were among many other musicians who urged people to vote. Songs supporting American troops abroad have been well received, especially on country radio. Today's radio stations are tightly controlled, playing the songs record companies pay them to play, with little leeway to make independent programming decisions; but personal computers offer unprecedented opportunities to the interested public to hear popular music produced by independent labels, here and abroad.

While social consciousness stirs rockers' emotions and stimulates their talents, many rock musicians have returned to their roots, producing rhythm and blues, rockabilly, soul, and psychedelic music, as a new generation, representing many cultures, races, and experiences, carries forward the remarkably varied and durable music we call rock. In the first decade of the new century, **electro** or **nu-wave** performers like Adult and Fischerspooner look back to the synthesizers, sequencers, and drum machines that transformed the sound of mainstream pop and underground pop music of the 1980s. Preferring old-fashioned "human" sounds to the cold tones and stiff beats of modern digital technology, they gravitate to spectacles influenced by performance art, to witty lyrics, and to extravagant amounts of profanity. **Techno,** on the other hand, involves sounds for which real instruments may or may not exist—sounds which can be played at speeds and in note combinations possible only with the aid of electronics. While electro is full of flamboyant personalities, techno values anonymity.

DJs have much to do with what music is played and how it is heard, and *scratch DJs,* or *turntablists,* have become artists in their own right. The turntable, in fact, may be the most important musical instrument of the current era. Several schools offer professional instruction in turntable techniques. The music heard in dance clubs today—called drum-and-bass, house, or trip-hop, among other names—is usually sample-based and electronically composed, and is therefore a DJ's creation. There is even a system now to notate the scratches making up DJs' compositions, allowing top scratch DJs to publish and copyright their compositions and aspiring DJs to see and learn the music.

Music Business

Music Business The business of music has changed more drastically, and more rapidly, in recent years than ever before. Musicians are easily replaced by electronic synthesizers; singers can lip-sync before high-paying live audiences; and internet pirates make illegal sharing of music relatively easy, threatening the music industry—any industry, in fact, that trades in intellectual property.

Further, perfectly legal Internet plans now make CDs cheaply, quickly, and readily available, putting significant numbers of music stores and companies out of business. Those that survive will need to address issues, both ethical and practical, that did not previously exist but that have become part of the business of music today.

Thanks to technology, to multiculturalism, and to the accomplishments of previous generations of pop musicians, the pop scene today is richer and more varied than ever before. Recycling and retrospection vie with the spirit of futurism to stimulate creativity in the world of pop.

Terms to Review

art rock   A blend of rock and symphonic or concert styles.

disco   Commercial dance music popular in the 1970s.

punk   A British reaction to flagrantly commercial rock and roll.

grunge   The Seattle sound, a hybrid of pop, heavy metal, and punk.

new wave   A term encompassing several styles, all conceived within the context of modern studio and electronic techniques.

rap   Rapidly spoken patter derived from reggae performance practices, accompanied by funk-style rhythms.

hip-hop   Sounds accompanying rapped lyrics.

electro or **nu-wave**   Machinelike sounds, revived from the 1980s.

techno   Futuristic electronic music featuring hard, driving sounds and rhythms.

Key Figures

Individuals:
Bruce Springsteen
Joni Mitchell
Patti Smith
Kurt Cobain
Kirk Franklin
Shirley Caesar

Groups:
Blood, Sweat, and Tears
Chicago
New York Dolls
Television
Ramones
Nirvana

Talking Heads
B-52s
Cars
Police
Salt–N–Pepa

Suggestions for Listening

New York Dolls: "Personality Crisis"
Patti Smith: *Horses; Dream of Life*
Ramones: *Ramones*
Talking Heads: *Stop Making Sense*

Chicago: *Chicago V*
Eminem: Soundtrack to *8 Mile* (2002 feature film)
Much of the music discussed in this chapter can be heard on the Web.

Critical Thinking

Does your personal music collection include albums by any of the performers discussed in this chapter? What does your collection reveal about your preference for one or more particular styles of popular music? Has your preference changed significantly over the last five years? If so, how? Do you find the music being produced today more or less interesting than other popular musics (country, jazz, rock, pop) covered in this chapter and in earlier chapters of this text?

Do you consider hip-hop a craft (that can be learned) or a culture (that must be experienced from birth)?

How do you view duets between live and dead performers? Are these duets still the work of the original artist? Do they confuse or weaken the original artist's intentions? Does it matter? Are the duets comparable to sampling a lick from another artist's recording?

Why would people pay for music when they can get it free? Should musicians own the rights to their work? Should the companies that produce them, or that record them, own the rights? If a singer makes a cover recording of an earlier record, who should own the rights and make the profits from the new product: the first or second singer? The first or second record company? The composer? Other?

Go to www.mhhe.com/ferrisaml5 for a list of additional Web-based resources that relate to the content in this chapter.

PART 4
Summary

Latin dances invigorated the American pop music scene beginning in the 1930s, when big bands popularized several dances from the Caribbean, Brazil, and Mexico. The tango, bomba, rumba, and other Latin dances soon became a seemingly inherent part of the North American popular experience. Brazil's samba and bossa nova offered quietly sensuous rhythms and melodies to North Americans groups, and Mexican mariachis became an inherent component of southwestern music.

In the 1950s, white country-western music combined with elements of black rhythm and blues to produce rock and roll, as the popular music industry responded to the desires and the dollars of American teens. Bill Haley and Elvis Presley, white country singers with a black style of delivery, made the new music widely popular, and soon cover recordings of rhythm-and-blues hits were earning significant money. Rebelling against the whites' windfall from the genius of black music, Motown produced records that pleased whites but earned money for black performers, while soul brought music of a new intensity and sincerity to rock and roll.

The British invasion begun by the Beatles continued with the Rolling Stones, who came from comfortable English backgrounds but whose music reflected the experiences of poor black Americans. In the 1970s, punk evolved from garage-band music and the New York City avant-garde art and music scene. Punk music varied from angry to good-natured, while punk dress, hair, and makeup influenced art and fashion around the world.

New wave music, like punk, criticized society, but without the anger and intensity of punk. Progressive in intent, new wave relied on the aid of modern studio and electronic techniques. Grunge, or the Seattle sound, expressed but hardly relieved the anxieties of generation X, much as early rock and roll had served baby boomers; but the untimely deaths of several grunge artists lessened the influence of the style. Prince, Michael Jackson, Lionel Richie, Madonna, Cyndi Lauper, and Sting, among other individuals, maintained various degrees of popularity during the 1990s. Meanwhile, synthesizers and other electronic instruments increasingly varied the sonorities of live and recorded performances.

Electronic dance music, popular in the 1980s, experienced a strong revival in the early years of the twenty-first century. Disco and new wave returned, and electro and techno styles vied for popularity. Rap, growing out of the hip-hop movement in the 1970s, reached a mainstream audience before the turn of the new century through television programs, Saturday morning cartoons, and commercial films. Today black and white male and female rappers compete to produce the cleverist lyrics, the most outrageous rhymes, the most effective "flow," and sometimes the greatest shock, accompanied by various styles of hip-hop music. Black gospel retains a strong and devoted audience and stays high on the popular music charts.

Recently DJs, who traditionally played music they were paid to spin, have become artists in their own right, using the turntable as an instrument on which they can develop refined scratching techniques. Old and new music, and new techniques applied to old music, all have their place in today's pop scene.

PART 5

Music for Theater and Film

Music and Theater: Historical and Cultural Perspective

Music and drama seem meant for each other, each medium transforming and enhancing the other to form a perfect union immeasurably greater than the sum of its parts. In fact, a close relationship between the two arts dates back in Western history at least as far as the ancient Greeks, who claimed to have achieved the ideal mating of words and music in their magnificent theatrical choruses. Since that time, many have disagreed as to what the Greeks considered this ideal to be, and whether they found the music or the text the most important element in performances combining these arts. But the mutual attraction of music and drama remains as strong and as intriguing to most of the world's cultures today as it was in ancient times.

Musical Theater in America
America's earliest professional musical performances (see pp. 71, 73–74), mostly imported from England, proved highly popular in cities large enough and settled enough to indulge in extravagant entertainment. In the nineteenth century, Italian operas drew large and enthusiastic audiences in several Southern cities and even in Boston—although

**Alan Jay Lerner,
lyricist**
"We are not an aria
country. We are a song
country."

the Bostonians' puritanical reservations caused nearly every theater there to be known as "Museum" or "Athenaeum." French light operas and—especially—the British Gilbert and Sullivan's hilarious operettas aroused tremendous enthusiasm among crowds of Americans, who returned again and again to see these shows.

Early American productions included some based on British ballad operas, incorporating popular songs into melodramatic stage presentations. The first notable American musical, *The Black Crook,* which appeared on Broadway right after the Civil War (1866), was a 5½-hour spectacle of song and ballet. Although so successful as to make its creator (Charles M. Barras) comfortable for life, the show spawned few imitations, and minstrel shows constituted the primary native contributions to the musical stage for the last half of the nineteenth century. The first American musical comedy is generally considered to be George M. Cohan's *Little Johnny Jones,* produced in 1904 (p. 316).

Broadway Musicals

Much as art and literature reflect the mores and tastes of the era that produces them, Broadway musicals also review and critique the standards of their time. The severe Protestant ethic instilled by the Puritans and practiced in much of American society through the nineteenth century appeared to be crumbling by the turn of the twentieth century, when a looser morality prevailed at least in the large cities. Increased knowledge of sexual hygiene lessened fears of infection; the automobile provided opportunities for courtship away from family observation; movies pictured situations previously unimaginable but highly attractive to the young and inexperienced. As we have seen, provocative Latin dances surpassed the sedate waltz in popularity. Women's dresses became shorter and their underwear less constrictive. And liquor prohibited was certainly more exciting than legal brew.

The Broadway musical stage reflected all of these and other characteristics of American life as well. George Gershwin's *Of Thee I Sing* (1931) was a sidesplitting musical satire on American politics, and his opera *Porgy and Bess* (written for the Broadway theater—not the opera house) offered a sympathetic view of Negro life in Charleston. Social commentary pervaded important shows, notably Jerome Kern's *Show Boat* (1927), and the revue *Pins and Needles* (1922).

Yet, though the Broadway musical today is the source of admiration and imitation in the very countries that inspired it, the medium is indeed grounded in foreign traditions, and the latter years of the twentieth century experienced a British invasion of the musical stage akin to, perhaps even surpassing, that of pop music in the 1960s and beyond. Thus perhaps it is not surprising that although the musical shows of a given period reflect certain styles and mores of their time, the American musical stage cannot be relied upon to provide a cultural snapshot of society. Broadway has been traditionally white and mainstream: jazz, rock, hip-hop, rap, and Latin music have made token appearances, but the overall picture is largely monochromatic.

For economic as well as cultural reasons, the strongest trend in recent years has been to stage revivals of safe (that is, formerly popular) shows: in the 1999–2000 season, only three new shows with an original book and score opened on Broadway, and no season since has been notably richer. The staggering expense of staging a new musical, and the perceived preference of the contemporary audience for nonchallenging entertainment, have had a profound effect upon the development of the Broadway musical.

Opera

Although the line between musical theater and opera used to be recognizable, if difficult to define, today's musicals and operas are almost interchangeable. Following the example of nineteenth-century European "realistic" (*verismo*) operas, such as Giacomo Puccini's *La Bohème* and *Madama Butterfly,* many American opera composers have based their works on stories of American life or legend (Douglas Moore's *The Ballad of Baby Doe*), or even, more recently, on relatively current events (John Adams's *Nixon in China,* for example). It remains to be seen whether these—as well as recent musicals based on popular Italian operas, such as *Rent* (by Jonathan Larson, based on *La Bohème*) and *Miss Saigon* (by the English composer Andrew Lloyd Webber, based on *Madama Butterfly*)—will attract the long-lasting devotion of their Italian forebears.

Today, in fact, musicals and operas have drawn so close as to render differences between them not only obscure but largely meaningless. For example, Broadway shows addressed to the children's market, including such mammoth Disney productions as *Beauty and the Beast* and *The Lion King* are largely sung throughout, with little or no spoken dialogue, in the tradition of classical opera.

Films

When sound came to Hollywood films, music became indispensable to this new form of dramatic entertainment as well. Not only did music evoke emotional responses in movies of a dramatic nature; several outstanding Broadway composers took their talents to Hollywood and adapted old musicals or wrote new musicals for film.

Music continues to play a major role in the allure of movies, and we—the audience—readily succumb to its effects. Even movie musicals, out of favor with the filmgoing public for some time, seem to be making a strong comeback. Several movie musicals were released, scheduled for release, or in the planning stages during 2005.

Despite the glut of alternative entertainment available on video, computers, television, and a multiplicity of home entertainment systems, audiences continue to fill theaters and movie houses and to buy albums of theater music. This part of our text explores the relationship between music and drama, the history of American musical theater, and the effects music achieves on screen, in the opera house, and on the Broadway stage. ♪

Musical Theater

aried songs by European and American composers, including selections from popular English ballad operas and tuneful melodies from the Italian opera repertory, occasional art songs, sentimental ballads, and patriotic tunes, enriched early nineteenth-century theatrical performances in America. Although composers had begun to distinguish between music intended for professional performance and music to be sung and played at home, for the general public the differences between popular and classical, or formal and informal, music remained much less distinct than we find them today.

Variety Shows

As prosperity returned after the turbulent Civil War years, theater—especially musical theater—became increasingly popular in America. Then, as now, theater activity centered in New York City, and by the turn of the twentieth century several kinds of musical shows vied to appeal to the Broadway audience. Full-length musical performances imported from abroad became popular and received critical acclaim, but most American musical shows between the Civil War and World War I had a variety format with little, if any, plot.

Most popular by far of all the musical shows representative of the period leading up to and succeeding the Civil War were minstrel shows, but before the turn of the century *vaudeville* rivaled minstrelsy in popularity.

Vaudeville   Tony (Antonio) Pastor (1837–1908), the acknowledged inventor of **vaudeville,** worked in minstrel shows, for the circus, and as a comic singer before forming his own theater and touring companies. His family-friendly variety shows, eventually known as vaudeville, quickly attracted the middle classes.

Vaudeville closely resembled minstrel shows and often included blackface acts; but whereas the members of a minstrel troupe remained onstage throughout a performance, each act of a vaudeville show involved different performers. Vaudeville also featured a much wider variety of entertainment than minstrelsy. Circus stunts, jugglers, dog acts, comedy teams, songs, dances—virtually

FIGURE 18.1
Edward Harrigan and
Tony Hart in a comic
scene from a vaudeville show.

anything conceived to amaze and delight an eager but unsophisticated audience
occurred on the vaudeville stage.

Among the most popular performers of the post–Civil War period, or indeed
of any period, was the zany comedy and song team of Edward Harrigan and
Tony Hart. Depicting scenes of everyday American life, including "ethnic" comedy sketches of Irish and German urban immigrants, Harrigan and Hart (see Figure 18.1) captured the devotion of New York City's vaudeville audiences, who
readily related to the topical humor of their shows. (In 1985, a musicalization of
the lives of Harrigan and Hart was highly *un*successful on Broadway.)

The musical *Chicago* (1975), with score by John Kander and lyrics by
Fred Ebb, gloriously, and hilariously, revived and celebrated the vaudeville tradition in American musical comedy; in fact, its authors originally subtitled the
show *A Musical Vaudeville*. Quite unlike the distant, sentimental, and exotic
worlds of many shows of the 1950s and 1960s, *Chicago* brought peppy tunes,
raunchy lyrics, and brassy dances to the Broadway stage. The story—about a
married chorus girl who shoots her lover, is put on trial, learns how to capitalize
on the sentiment of the public, becomes a celebrity, goes free, and ends up as a
popular performer—evoked the snap and crackle of Chicago in the 1920s but also
struck a familiar chord when revived in 1996 for an audience highly conscious of
media-savvy lawyers and of links between crime, celebrity, and money. Every
song and dance is staged as a kind of number performed on the vaudeville circuit
stage, and the audience members come to feel like the very public to whom the
girl plays, and pleads for her life. The film *Chicago* (2002) made the show available to anyone with access to a movie theater or a video or DVD player.

In 2004 and 2005, a revival of old-time show business in New York City,
with echoes nationwide, further evidenced the lingering appeal of vaudeville.
Featured acts included the Bindlestiff Family Cirkus, whose show on a given
night might include a ukulele duo, a yo-yo master, a trapeze artist, a whip act,

and a sword swallower. New or postmodern vaudevillians are younger than were the original performers, their shows are often longer and more thoughtful, and ample audience participation is a hallmark of their acts.

Burlesque

Burlesque, another kind of variety show popular in the last half of the nineteenth century, is a form of satire which ridicules something important or, conversely, treats something inane or ridiculous with mock dignity for humorous effect. Mid-nineteenth-century burlesque shows featured strings of comic scenes of this type. Later, as striptease performances inserted between the acts drew more applause than the comedy scenes themselves, burlesque gradually degenerated from a rather risqué entertainment to a fairly crude—although immensely popular—form of theater. But the true legacy of burlesque is comedy. Although vaudevillians looked down on burlesque as an inferior kind of entertainment, many vaudeville stars enhanced their incomes on the burlesque stage, where they perfected their own style of comedy, heavily weighted toward physical humor: pies in the face, seltzer in the pants, etc. Jackie Gleason, Bert Lahr, W. C. Fields, Red Skelton, Phil Silvers, and Bob Hope, among many great comedians, learned their craft through burlesque.

By the 1920s, burlesque had largely degenerated to strip shows, and crackdowns by law enforcers closed many burlesque houses. By the 1960s, with hard-core pornography readily available, burlesque no longer held much interest. Yet the comic legacy remains strong. In 1979 *Sugar Babies,* a rollicking remembrance of the best in burlesque, opened on Broadway starring Mickey Rooney and Ann Miller, who sang and danced their way through an uproarious evening of nonsense that delighted Broadway audiences for more than 1,000 performances and then toured until mid-1986.

Saturday Night Live and the *Jerry Springer Show* offer versions of burlesque on television—skewering politicians and titillating audiences to various degrees. And big-screen spoofs such as *Young Frankenstein, Spaceballs,* and the *Austin Powers* films—even *Shrek 2* (2004)—carry on the comic tradition of burlesque. Today's burlesque performers often come from the world of modern dance and use their dance background to give burlesque an experimental edge, and sets and design are becoming as important to a burlesque show as inventive movement. Once a fading form, burlesque has reclaimed its place in the varied world of music theater.

Revues

A common theme rather than a plot relates the scenes of a **revue,** still another form of musical variety show. Songs by the same composer or lyricist may be selected from several different shows, or each scene of a revue may address the same topic—such as love through women's eyes, or relations between the sexes, or married life—with music selected from various sources. In Irving Berlin's *As Thousands Cheer* (1933, successfully revived on Broadway in 1998), for example, each sketch or song was supposedly torn from a recent newspaper headline.

Lavishly staged revues of the early twentieth century featured lovely costumes, extravagant sets, and—especially—beautiful young women. Such spectacles, titled "Follies" or "Scandals" or "Vanities," staged every year from the early 1900s to the 1930s, provided generous job opportunities for composers, singers, dancers, stage and costume designers, and orchestra musicians.

Most popular of all revues were the Ziegfeld Follies, staged by **Florenz Ziegfeld** (1869–1932) nearly every year between 1907 and his death (with three more Ziegfeld Follies produced after that). With extravagant staging and costumes, these shows, whose theme (popular at the time) was the glorification of the American girl, included wonderful songs, such as "Shine On, Harvest Moon" (Listening Example 61) from the *Follies* of 1908 and "A Pretty Girl Is Like a Melody," written by Irving Berlin for the *Follies* of 1919. (A musical

---

Listening Example 61

"Shine On, Harvest Moon"

Composers
Jack Norworth and Nora Bayes

Form
(Modified) verse-chorus

CD 2
Track 29
2:45

Meter
Four beats to the bar

Tempo
Moderate

Chorus: In lieu of an introduction, the orchestra plays the first two lines (eight bars) of the chorus, its timbres characteristic of big band music of the 1930s. A violin plays a *countermelody* above the muted trumpet's main melody line, accompanied by a guitar gently strumming each beat and slightly marking the backbeat. The vocalist (Ruth Etting, very well known in the 1930s) sings the last two lines of the chorus, lightly accompanied by the orchestra.

Verse: (0:42) As Etting sings the verse, which places more emphasis on the text than on the tune, the muted trumpet responds good-naturedly to her lament and her plea.

Chorus: (1:23) Accompanied by the orchestra and a countermelody in the muted trumpet, Etting sings the chorus again in her own expressive manner.

Chorus: (2:04) With her silky, supple voice, Etting sings improvised embellishments of and alterations to the melody, bringing the song to a simple close with a slight relaxation in tempo (*ritardando*).

Notice that the verse-chorus form is slightly altered here, beginning with the chorus instead of the verse, and giving the first two lines of the first chorus to the orchestra.

biography of Florenz Ziegfeld, titled *Ziegfeld,* opened on Broadway in 1988 but was not very well received.)

During the Great Depression of the 1930s, when soaring budgets made the elaborate Ziegfeld-type spectacles too risky to produce, more intimate revues took over the popular theater. By then social and political commentary was accepted even in the format of a revue. Thus *Pins and Needles,* a very successful musical entertainment sponsored by the Garment Workers Union and created and performed by amateurs, was basically a propaganda forum for that union, but it included some great songs and became a hit on Broadway.

Since then revues have existed in all sizes and shapes, a glorious grab bag kind of theater, brainier than vaudeville or burlesque; consisting of sketches, songs, and dances; and often addressing a common theme with a humorously skeptical point of view. Many recent revues have been based on the music of one composer, such as *Side by Side by Sondheim* (1977); *Eubie!* (1978), a collection of the rag- and jazz-based songs of Eubie Blake; *Ain't Misbehavin'* (1978), with songs by Fats Waller; and *Sophisticated Ladies* (1981), a dance extravaganza based on the music of Duke Ellington. The all-black revue *Bubbling Brown Sugar* (1976) featured songs by several great African American writers, including Eubie Blake, Fats Waller, and Duke Ellington.

Operetta

Unlike variety shows, musical **book shows** have an integrated plot—a story told in song, in spoken dialogue, or in some combination of the two. One example of such a show, the European **operetta,** became immensely popular on Broadway before the turn of the twentieth century, providing a vital stimulus for the development of the American musical stage.

An operetta (sometimes called a **light opera**) is a musical play integrating the songs, dances, and instrumental pieces with a story. Although the music of the great operettas is of a quality and a level of difficulty suitable for trained singers, no effort or experience is required of the audience, who may expect to be thoroughly entertained.

Gilbert and Sullivan

The delightful operettas of William S. Gilbert and Arthur Sullivan have been immensely popular in America from the time they first appeared in this country to today. Gilbert's **patter songs** ridiculed politics, manners, society—any subject was fair game—in rhyming multisyllabic words that delight audiences and stimulate imitation in every kind of humorous musical entertainment. Sullivan, poking musical fun at opera, religious music, virtuosic singing, and every other serious aspect of music, wrote delightful tunes with simple harmonies and attractive orchestration. Even today, **Gilbert and Sullivan operettas** provide virtually irresistible entertainment. (See Figure 18.2.)

American Operettas

John Philip Sousa, his success as bandmaster and march king notwithstanding, hoped to become an American counterpart of Gilbert and Sullivan and in this quest composed fifteen operettas. The most

FIGURE 18.2

A scene from Gilbert and
Sullivan's *H. M. S. Pinafore.*

famous, *El Capitan* (1896), a comic portrayal of the Spanish administration in
colonial Peru, was highly successful in New York and then on a coast-to-coast
tour. (The *El Capitan* march, based on two melodies from the operetta, appeared in arrangements for piano, banjo, guitar, mandolin, zither, and various
combinations of each of these instruments and remains one of Sousa's best-
known marches.) However, Sousa's lyrics were never as inspired as Gilbert's,
and he never found a librettist who might have collaborated with him as successfully as Gilbert did with Sullivan. By the turn of the twentieth century, his
theater works began to be eclipsed by European operettas and by a fledgling
new form, musical comedy. Sousa's operettas are seldom performed today, but
the New York City Opera produced his *Glass Blowers*—described by one reviewer as "a European-style operetta with a hard, bright American edge"—as
recently as 2002.

   In the early years of the twentieth century, several Viennese musicians recently arrived from Europe composed American operettas based on European
traditions. Also, the music of such born-and-bred European composers as
the Irishman Victor Herbert, the Bohemian Rudolf Friml, and the Hungarian
Sigmund Romberg was conceived for an American audience and is valued as a
vital part of our American heritage. Highly influential upon the development of
American musical theater, these beautiful shows, more romantic than comical,
featured exotic settings that lifted the audience from the everyday world to
heights of delightful fantasy. The music, too, was romantic in style, with
memorable melodies, rich harmonies, and attractive orchestration; and the

complicated love stories, no matter how unlikely or contrived, nearly always ended happily.

Musical Comedies

Blessed with a wealth of European and American operettas as well as variety shows ranging from crude burlesques to extravagant revues, the early twentieth-century Broadway audience hardly felt the need for a new form of musical theater. Yet despite early resistance, an exciting new genre blending popular entertainment (as in vaudeville) with an integrated plot (as in operettas) emerged just after the turn of the century.

The earliest **musical comedies,** as the new musical shows were called, were gaudy, boisterous productions barely held together by a thin excuse for a story. Scenery was simply painted on backdrops, and there was little in the way of a stage set. As World War I lessened Americans' enthusiasm for European products, however, we developed a new confidence in our own artistic talents, and the zany entertainment provided by large and talented casts proved irresistible, if unsophisticated, fun.

The eventual great success of the fledgling form was largely ensured by the efforts of one brash Irish American who never gave up—George M. Cohan (Figure 18.3).

George M. Cohan (1878–1942)

George M. Cohan was the child of vaudeville performers and was virtually brought up on the vaudeville stage. In fact, by the time he was in his teens, Cohan was providing most of the material for the family's acts. Completely self-taught, he made up the skits, composed the songs, wrote the lyrics, and promoted the shows, in which he acted, sang, and danced. (Remember Listening Example 30, "Rose," by Cohan.)

FIGURE 18.3

George M. Cohan.

A zealous patriot, Cohan truly Americanized the Broadway theater. His shows, which always had an American theme, were filled with jaunty, flag-waving songs. His first full-length show, *Little Johnny Jones* (1904), usually considered the first real musical comedy, concerned a popular American jockey, of a jaunty character bearing unmistakable resemblance to Cohan, who goes to England to win the derby, is accused of throwing the race when he loses, but successfully restores his honor and wins his girl. (Johnny Jones is modeled on a real, but less fortunate, person named Tod Sloan.) Although the thin plot hardly holds together, the score is filled with tuneful, high-spirited songs, including "Give My Regards to Broadway" (Listening Example 62) and "Yankee Doodle Boy." (Cohan could not resist claiming, as in the latter song, that he was born on the Fourth of July, although his birth date was actually July 3.)

Listening Example 62

"Give My Regards to Broadway"
(from *Little Johnny Jones*)

Composer
George M. Cohan

Performer
Al Jolson

CD 3
Track 1
2:39

Meter
Two beats to the bar (duple)

Tempo
Brisk

Form
Verse-chorus

Orchestral introduction.

Chorus: Eight lines, sung by Jolson. Notice the manner in which his characteristic vocal "slides" add emotional effect to such words as "yearning."

Verse: Four lines, sung by the chorus ("Did you ever see two Yankees part . . .").

Chorus: Eight lines, sung by Jolson.

Chorus: Eight lines, played by the orchestra, which then changes key.

Chorus: Eight lines, sung by Jolson accompanied by the chorus humming and interspersing comments.

The orchestra finishes the piece with two chords, a kind of exclamation point (da-dah!).

Despite competition from highly popular, more sophisticated operettas, Cohan stormed Broadway with show after show that, although not always good, always had catchy tunes and featured American heroes—a reformed gambler, a baseball player, a senator—and rousing patriotic songs. Though to his great regret he was finally replaced in popularity by several more sophisticated composers, Cohan received the highest award our nation can bestow on civilians, the Congressional Medal of Honor, which President Franklin D. Roosevelt delivered to him in person in recognition of Cohan's contribution to national pride and morale during World War I.

James Cagney re-created Cohan's dramatic life in the movie *Yankee Doodle Dandy* (1942), and in 1968 a successful musical—*George M!*—brought the Cohan magic back to Broadway.

Black Musical Theater

Even as minstrel shows waned in popularity, African American musicians continued to be an important influence on Broadway, writing songs for white shows and also writing, directing, and performing in several all-black musicals in the first decade of the twentieth century. The earliest all-black musicals closely resembled minstrel shows, which had themselves become more black than white while still perpetuating the stereotypical African American characters.

The reference to minstrelsy is apparent in the title of a distinctive black show from 1898: *Clorindy, or the Origin of the Cake-Walk.* The composer, **Will Marion Cook** (1869–1944), was a concert violinist who had studied music at Oberlin College in Ohio, in Germany, and later with Dvořák at the National Conservatory of Music. Cook also wrote the music for several other black shows popular during 1900–1910, including *In Dahomey* (1903), the first all-black musical show to play in a major Broadway theater.

Although, as we have seen, the black influence on popular music was particularly strong in the early twentieth century, interest in black musical theater waned for about ten years (from just before until soon after the First World War), despite the generally flourishing state of the musical stage. Then in 1921 *Shuffle Along,* with music by Eubie Blake and words by **Noble Sissle,** became a Broadway hit. This was one of many shows lying somewhere between a revue and a musical comedy, its loosely integrated plot regularly interrupted by scenes of sheer entertainment. Whites laughed uproariously at the satire, much of which was directed at them, and enthusiastically applauded the stunning chorus line, tap dancing, and singing of the black performance troupe. The cast included **Josephine Baker,** who later became a star in Paris theaters; and the composer William Grant Still (see pp. 394–395) played oboe in the orchestra. One of the songs from the show, "I'm Just Wild about Harry," reappeared as a campaign song for Harry Truman years later.

The 1920s witnessed several other popular shows with all-black casts, although some, including two "Broadway operas" to be discussed in Chapter 20, were written by white composers and lyricists. And the landmark show of the decade, *Show Boat,* written by Jerome Kern (see p. 157), addressed interracial relations with sympathy and sensitivity.

Jerome Kern's *Show Boat*

Jerome Kern, whose songs for Tin Pan Alley were discussed in Chapter 9, wrote a number of successful shows for Broadway, most notably in collaboration with the writers Guy Bolton and P. G. Wodehouse. All three artists were committed to creating shows with strong plots and fine songs, and their works are considered a cornerstone of musical theater.

In 1927 Kern wrote *Show Boat,* thereby making musical history in a number of ways. First, unlike earlier musical comedies, which were basically collections of songs and variety acts loosely held together by a thin plot, *Show Boat* had an integrated plot based on a novel by an established literary figure, Edna Ferber. Despite the success of *Show Boat,* however, it was a number of years before the revolutionary concept of a literature-based musical became the norm for many if not most musicals (American and other): *South Pacific* was based on a collection of short stories by James Michener; *Kiss Me Kate* and *West Side Story* on Shakespearean plays; *The King and I* on an autobiography; *Cats* on poems by T. S. Eliot; and *Phantom of the Opera* and *Les Misérables* on French novels, to name just a few.

Further, the story of *Show Boat,* and the song lyrics by Oscar Hammerstein II (see pp. 321–322) addressed highly sensitive social topics, expressing sympathy for the situation of black people in America and even including an interracial love story—astonishing at a time when audiences confidently expected only sheer entertainment from a musical show. This too was prophetic in the sense that serious social, political, and even religious messages have been included in many later musicals. After *Show Boat,* the term musical *comedy* would no longer be appropriate for all musical Broadway shows.

Most important of all, Kern wrote sophisticated music of the finest quality for his show. Melodies associated with particular characters recur throughout *Show Boat,* providing musical and dramatic unity, and his lovely melodies and interesting harmonies are as appealing today as they were nearly eighty years ago. Among them, the classic love song "Why Do I Love You?" the bluesy "Can't Help Lovin' Dat Man of Mine," and the moving "Ol' Man River" (Listening Example 63) seem likely to remain classics in the American song repertoire.

In yet one more way, *Show Boat* proved prophetic of the direction the Broadway musical would pursue. The quality of the music and the serious nature of the plot have caused some to refer to *Show Boat* as an operetta, and indeed the differences between musicals, operettas, and operas, have become less distinct, and largely meaningless, in recent times.

Golden Age of Broadway Musicals (1930–1955)

Before the 1920s, many great songwriters made their living from songs that they created to be published by Tin Pan Alley and possibly included in a Broadway musical. Even Irving Berlin, who became involved with the Broadway musical stage while in his teens, was at his best writing individual

Listening Example 63

"Ol' Man River" (from *Show Boat*)

Composer
Jerome Kern

Lyricist
Oscar Hammerstein II

CD 3
Track 2
3:31

Meter
(Verse) three beats to the bar; (chorus) four beats to the bar

Tempo
Slow

Form
Verse-chorus

Verse: The bass sings the verse, quietly accompanied by the orchestra. The minimal accompaniment and relaxed rhythmic structure emphasize and help to express the words.

Chorus: Perhaps you will notice the change in meter to quadruple, and certainly the more melodic nature of the music. The four lines of the chorus occur in the order **a a' b a"**: that is, the second and fourth lines are related, but not identical, to the first, and the third phrase differs from them in melody and mood.

Eight bars **(a)** (beginning, "Ol' Man River . . ."). The orchestral accompaniment imitates the melodic phrase "Ol' man river. . . ."

Eight bars **(a')** ("He don't plant taters . . .").

Eight bars **(b)** ("You an' me, we sweat and strain . . ."). The chorus sings in the background.

Eight bars **(a")** ("I gets weary . . .") The chorus accompanies the soloist. Notice the dramatic crescendo in voices and orchestra.

Throughout the performance, the orchestra supports and enhances the voice part, filling in the ends of lines and greatly adding to the emotional impact of the song. The rich timbre of the bass voice and the dramatically deep tones at emotionally significant points also add to the drama of this famous song.

songs, and his shows often seemed more like revues than like musical comedies. For example, Berlin's *Watch Your Step* (1914) became a hit despite its thin plot because of Berlin's great songs—and also because it featured the famous dance couple Irene and Vernon Castle performing the tango (Figure 18.4) and other popular dances of the day.

develop such cracks

In the period just before World War I, the Castles helped spark a social
dance craze, which in some sense changed American culture. More and more
people participated in the new social exercise, often dancing to the music of
urban black Americans. And Irene Castle, who remained prominent in public
life after her husband's death in 1918, symbolized the newly independent
American woman, unencumbered by Victorian restraints.

Like Irving Berlin, George Gershwin had a gift for creating delightful syncopated dance rhythms, and some of his shows included outstanding dance sequences. *Lady Be Good!* (1924) had the wonderful song "Fascinating Rhythm"
and featured the famous dance team of Adele and Fred Astaire. These and
many other early musicals provided vehicles for presenting great songs and
dances with little pretence at dramatic unity or integrity.

But during the 1920s and especially the 1930s, after the economic crash of
1929, songwriters' income from sheet music sales drastically declined. Most
people had radios in their homes by then and found it easier and cheaper to
listen to the radio than to buy sheet music and pay for lessons to learn to read
it. Yet somehow tickets to Broadway musicals continued to sell; so Kern,
Berlin, Porter, Gershwin, and the other great songwriters turned their talents
to the Broadway stage, producing an unprecedented quantity of sparkling
popular music.

After 1929, sound movies (see Chapter 19) gave further stimulus to songwriters' talents and another significant boost to their income. Several Broadway musicals were made into sound films that could be shown in any town
with a movie house, and the great songs soon became familiar nationwide.
Throughout the 1930s and 1940s, Broadway's amazingly gifted composers
and lyricists continued to evolve artistically, producing many shows of lasting
quality and beauty.

Rodgers and Hart In a sense, **Richard Rodgers** (1902–1979) had two careers, both of them as a songwriter. Having worked with one lyricist for many years to produce a number of extremely successful musicals, he collaborated on several new shows with a different partner, whose style and character differed markedly from that of the first. Rodgers, who once remarked, "When the lyrics are right, it's easier for me to write a tune than to bend over and tie my shoelaces," effectively adapted the style of his music to suit the words his lyricists provided, thereby greatly furthering the transition from the loosely integrated shows of early musical comedy into unified musical theater.

The lyrics for Richard Rodgers's first outstanding shows were written by **Lorenz Hart** (1895–1943), one of the most talented lyricists Broadway has known. His rhymes—witty, sophisticated, clever, sometimes devilish, and often risqué—typically were unacceptable for the radio stations of his day (which would not play, for example, his famous "Bewitched, Bothered, and Bewildered" until one line was changed from, "Couldn't sleep, and wouldn't sleep, 'til I could sleep where I shouldn't sleep" to " . . . 'til love came and told me I shouldn't sleep").

As the Broadway audience developed a strong fondness for classical ballet, this form of dance assumed an ever larger role in musical theater. The Rodgers and Hart musical *On Your Toes* (1936) was remarkable because the famous **choreographer** George Balanchine designed the dance steps to be integrated with the drama. One magnificent dance scene in particular, "Slaughter on Tenth Avenue," constituted an integral part of the story, advancing rather than interrupting the plot.

Rodgers and Hart's *Pal Joey* (1940), which also included a ballet scene, was remarkable in another way: the main character was an antihero—a two-timing gigolo who took advantage of the innocent to further his own selfish goals. For this reason, in spite of the wonderful music ("Bewitched, Bothered, and Bewildered" is probably the best-known song of the show), the critics hardly knew how to receive it, and the show was much more successful when it was revived twelve years later.

Talented as he was, the erratic Lorenz Hart finally became impossible to work with, for Rodgers never knew when his lyricist would disappear on an alcoholic binge. Finally, Rodgers turned to **Oscar Hammerstein II** to write the lyrics for his next show, *Oklahoma!*

Rodgers and Hammerstein The collaboration between Hammerstein and Richard Rodgers began as Broadway faced daunting challenges. The Great Depression had finally ended, and people wished to enjoy the theater and could afford to do so; but World War II caused a shortage of materials for sets and costumes, making new productions difficult to achieve. Therefore, it behooved the industry to fashion shows of sufficient quality to last for unprecedented numbers of performances; and so they did.

Still, it was widely assumed that *Oklahoma!* would fail, because it had no opening extravaganza, no chorus line, and no interpolation of songs for the sheer sake of entertainment—all considered requisite in a musical show in the 1940s. But Rodgers and his new lyricist, Hammerstein—already well known for his lyrics in several important shows, including *Show Boat*—believed that all music and dance should enhance rather than interrupt the plot and accomplished their ideal with magnificent success in *Oklahoma!* (1943).

Like *Show Boat, Oklahoma!* not only was a great success but also is considered a landmark in the history of the Broadway musical. The story was built upon believable characters and situations, and the choreography, by Agnes de Mille (a niece of the movie director Cecil B. de Mille), revealed her gift for the expressive story-dance. Every aspect of composition and production enhanced the narrative. As Rodgers himself said, "The orchestrations sound the way the costumes look." And unlike *Show Boat, Oklahoma!* changed the course of Broadway musicals, which never again could survive as loosely integrated songs held together by a shoestring of a plot. Most of all, the songs were simply irresistible. The carefree "Oh, What a Beautiful Mornin'," the romantic "Surrey with a Fringe on Top" and "People Will Say We're in Love," the comic "Everything's Up to Date in Kansas City" and "I Cain't Say No," and of course the rousing "Oklahoma!" were instant and lasting hits. Critics, audiences, and composers alike realized that *Oklahoma!* had ushered in a new kind of musical theater.

Rodgers responded to Hammerstein's words, more thoughtful and serious than Hart's, by writing a different kind of music, also more serious and profound than the simple lilting melodies of many Rodgers and Hart collaborations. *Carousel* (1945), like *Oklahoma!* based on a play, had elements of tragedy and included a beautiful "message" song, "You'll Never Walk Alone." "Hello, Young Lovers" from *The King and I* (1951) is another example of a song more serious than any Rodgers and Hart would have produced. Like Jerome Kern's *Show Boat, South Pacific* (1949) addressed the sensitive subject of interracial marriage. Even *The Sound of Music* (1959), perhaps the frothiest of the Rodgers and Hammerstein shows, concerns real characters involved in difficult situations.

Expansion of the Broadway Musical

In a sense, the revolution Rodgers and Hammerstein implemented in the 1940s may be said to have finally overtaken them. As their success faded, other composers and lyricists came to the fore, reflecting in their own manner influences absorbed from the masters of the golden age. Classical and popular art again grew close together, as they were before the nineteenth century drew self-conscious distinctions between them, and this too affects current musical theater.

For example, **Frank Loesser** (1910–1969), a composer who previously had written such delightfully entertaining but traditional musicals as *Where's Charley?* and *Guys and Dolls,* produced in 1956 *Most Happy Fella,* which he referred to as "a musical with a lotta music" but which is often called a popular or Broadway opera. It was performed, in fact, by the New York City Opera in 1991, and many felt the show was more at home in the opera house than on the Broadway stage; for here Loesser demonstrated his heightened sense of *singing* in the Broadway musical. *Fella* requires highly trained voices and a full orchestra, and like Rodgers and Hammerstein's *Carousel* and Gershwin's *Porgy and Bess* (see pp. 352–353), it probes deeply the emotional lives of its characters. While providing plenty of entertainment and generous comic relief, *Fella* requires more of its performers and audience than did the conventional, earlier style of musical.

Lerner and Loewe
The famous Broadway team of **Alan Jay Lerner** (1918–1986) and **Frederick Loewe** (1901–1988) wrote the wonderful shows *Brigadoon, Paint Your Wagon, Gigi, Camelot,* and *My Fair Lady*—the last closely based on George Bernard Shaw's *Pygmalion,* which Rodgers and Hammerstein had considered completely unsuitable for adaptation as a musical. Their particular contribution to the expansion of the musical, in fact, was a heightened sense of the *play,* whose spoken text they preserved as faithfully as its setting to music would allow.

The lyricist Lerner (whose family owned the Lerner women's wear shops) was an American, but the composer Loewe came to the United States from Vienna in 1924. His Viennese background is especially apparent in *Camelot* and *My Fair Lady,* which because of their period costumes, graceful and melodic scores, and magnificent sets are sometimes called modern-day operettas. "I Could Have Danced All Night," "On the Street Where You Live," "I've Grown Accustomed to Her Face," and "If Ever I Would Leave You" are among the great romantic songs from Lerner and Loewe's musicals.

Leonard Bernstein (1918–1990)
Leonard Bernstein (Figure 18.5) was a pianist, conductor, and composer primarily associated with concert music, although he made significant contributions as well to vernacular music and particularly to the Broadway musical stage. Bernstein adapted his early musical *On the Town* (1944) from a ballet he had written still earlier; and the ballet's famous choreographer, Jerome Robbins, participated in directing the new musical, in which the dances were an integral part of the show. Bernstein's *Wonderful Town* in 1953 and *Candide* in 1956 were also successful shows, and his Broadway masterpiece, *West Side Story* (1957), further demonstrated Bernstein's heightened sense of *dance* on the musical stage.

Robbins choreographed the wonderful dance scenes of *West Side Story,* effectively working them into the drama, which is a retelling of Shakespeare's *Romeo and Juliet.* The show is set in the streets of mid-twentieth-century uptown New York City, and although this Juliet (Maria in the show) does not die at the end, the aura of tragedy is palpable from the opening moments. The rough language, realistic characters, lyrical music, and stunning dance scenes had an overpowering effect on Broadway and have become familiar to untold numbers of people through the movie version of the show.

In one of the most effective kinds of music theater scenes, the **ensemble,** several characters present their own points of view, singly and then collectively,

FIGURE 18.5

Leonard Bernstein conducting the New York Philharmonic, November 12, 1988.

singing different words and music at the same time. The ensemble finale, or final scene, to Act I of *West Side Story* (Listening Example 64) vividly illustrates the musical and dramatic impact this affords.

Stephen Sondheim (b. 1930) One greatly gifted and prolific American composer, **Stephen Sondheim,** has continued to impress viewers and critics with imaginative, creative, often startling shows of endless variety. Having studied with avant-garde composer Milton Babbitt (see pp. 400–401), among others, Sondheim intended to become a composer of concert music; but like Jerome Kern, he was early and lastingly drawn to Broadway. His first experiences with musical theater involved writing song lyrics, a technique he studied diligently with Oscar Hammerstein II, his troubled family's neighbor, who became the boy's surrogate father. From Hammerstein, Sondheim learned the importance of emotional and verbal clarity and the necessity to seamlessly intertwine dialogue, melody, and lyrics to further a plot and give it dramatic force. Sondheim vividly demonstrated his own gifts in this area by writing the lyrics to Leonard Bernstein's songs in *West Side Story,* and to *Gypsy* (1959), with music by Jules Styne. He then went on to become America's premier composer for the musical stage.

After his early collaboration with Leonard Bernstein, Sondheim wrote both the lyrics and the music for many important shows. *A Funny Thing Happened on the Way to the Forum* (1962) and *Follies* (1971) were traditional musicals that proved Sondheim could write within the conventions as well as anyone.

"Tonight" (finale from Act I of *West Side Story*)

CD 3
Track 3
3:38

Composer
Leonard Bernstein

Genre (Type of Piece)
Music theater ensemble

Timbres
Vocal soloists, solo and choral ensembles, and orchestra

A gang of assorted Americans, the Jets, have challenged a rival Puerto Rican gang, the Sharks, to a rumble (fight) "tonight." As the finale begins, the Jets and Sharks, each gang singing in unison, make excited threats to destroy each other. Their fast, highly rhythmic song is punctuated by sharp accents in the orchestra.

Anita, girlfriend of the Sharks' leader, enters, singing of her plans for "tonight" to the same music.

Then Tony, the young "Romeo" of the show, who is also a leader of the Sharks, sings the love song "Tonight," expressing his fervent wish that the night and his time with his beloved Maria could last forever. Although the underlying pulse of Tony's song is the same as the "rumble" music sung by the gangs and Anita, his soaring melodic lines and emotional delivery provide a romantic contrast to the other music.

The gangs begin their threatening lines again, and as they continue, we hear Maria in the distance singing Tony's love song. Tony joins her, and finally Anita completes the ensemble, in which all the elements (the two gangs, Anita, and the lovers Tony and Maria) express independent and indeed conflicting plans for "tonight." The beautifully written, tightly integrated ensemble achieves an almost unbearable level of dramatic tension.

Follies, however, masterfully reveals Sondheim's scorn for the old-time Broadway musical's inability—or unconcern—to deal with reality. Several songs in the show, which parodies the Ziegfeld Follies, brutally express the "folly" of trying to live in a rose-colored past, fantasize about a rose-colored future, or deny death—hardly the traditional happily-ever-after musical fare.

Critics admired the elegant *A Little Night Music* (1973), but audiences faulted the show for not having enough "good tunes," although it included the lovely "Send in the Clowns." The show, a musical version of Ingmar Bergman's film *Smiles of a Summer Night* and variously called a musical or an operetta, interweaves a series of bittersweet love stories that find more or less happy resolution in the end. "Every Day a Little Death" (Listening Example 65) is sung by two unhappy wives, Charlotte and Anne, whose husbands are both in

"Every Day a Little Death"
(from *A Little Night Music*)

Composer and Lyricist
Stephen Sondheim

CD 3
Track 4
2:26

Meter
Quadruple

Form
A B A

An unhappy little two-note phrase, delicately enhanced by the harp, introduces the poignant song.

A. Charlotte begins singing, her manner deceptively lighthearted but her words heartbreaking. The gently rocking orchestra lightly accompanies her crisply delivered words.

B. The middle section (beginning "He smiles sweetly, strokes my hair") is smoother, warmer, more intense than A. Here the strings become slightly more prominent, often doubling Charlotte's melody. Anne, listening, suddenly interjects, "So do I!"

C. Anne at first echoes Charlotte's thoughts, then adds her own, again in the light, crisp manner of the beginning. The women sing in unison at the end, symbolizing their like situation and sentiment. After their rather resigned close, the poignant little harp figure ends the piece.

love with a glamorous, though not young, actress, Desirée. Charlotte is perhaps middle-aged; Anne is the teenage wife of Fredrik, an older man. While she cannot love Fredrick as her husband, Anne is terribly jealous when her refusal to consummate their marriage drives him back to the arms of Desirée, with whom he had a passionate affair years before. In the end, Fredrik's young son—who's actually a year older than his stepmother—and Anne have fallen blissfully in love, and Fredrick has decided he might be most content with Desirée after all. But this song is the poignant expression of two unhappy women married—at least for a time—to men who are attracted to someone else.

The unlikely subject matter of *Sweeney Todd: The Demon Barber of Fleet Street* (1979), a grisly story of murder and cannibalism; and *Assassins* (1990), exploring the history of presidential assassination in the United States, shocked the public but won an audience and high critical praise. *Company* (1970) introduced the **concept musical,** a new kind of show treating controversial subjects and intentionally leaving audiences wondering about the show's meaning and its resolution. *Company,* which raises questions and confronts issues it leaves unresolved, indicated important new directions that American musical theater would follow in the 1970s and 1980s. Another of Sondheim's concept musical, *Pacific Overtures* (1976), succeeded several musicals by other American composers also reflecting a strong Asian influence, including *South Pacific* (1949), *The King and I* (1951), *Kismet* (1953), *Teahouse of the August Moon* (1953), *Flower Drum Song* (1958), and *The World of Suzie Wong* (1958). But *Pacific Overtures,* concerning Admiral Perry's opening of Japan to the West as seen from a Japanese perspective, was more serious than the other shows and followed Eastern techniques more literally than Broadway was prepared to receive. It also made the unwelcome suggestion, so soon after World War II, that Americans had erred by imposing Western ways upon the reluctant Japanese. The Asian cast, the Asian musical instruments, and the elements of stylized Japanese (*kabuki*) theater provided fascinating and provocative theater, but the show was not popular with audiences.

More Black Musicals Little in the way of black musical theater appeared on Broadway after the opening in 1943 (and the revival in 1956) of Oscar Hammerstein II's jazzy adaptation of the French opera *Carmen,* which he called *Carmen Jones,* until several black musicals opened in the 1970s and 1980s. They included a black interpretation of *The Wizard of Oz* called *The Wiz,* an all-black version of *Guys and Dolls,* and the all-black revue *Bubbling Brown Sugar,* featuring fondly remembered melodies by "Fats" Waller, Duke Ellington, and Eubie Blake, among others, produced in 1976. *Me and Bessie* (1975), a two-woman show, narrated the tragic history of Bessie Smith and presented the songs she made famous. *Dream Girls,* based on the experiences of the Supremes, had a successful run in 1981.

The all-black show *Bring in 'da Noise, Bring in 'da Funk* (1996) tells the history—a version of the history—of African Americans more in dance than in song, with little if any connection between the scenes.

The Music of Musicals

Broadway has largely ignored jazz (*Jelly's Last Jam,* fashioned from Jelly Roll Morton's vintage jazz tunes being an exception), and it has not encouraged today's writers of hip-hop, rap, and Latin music to create new musicals. *The Capeman,* with music by Paul Simon, opened in 2000 and was billed as the first all-Latino musical, but it was poorly received.

Neither has country music generally been compatible with the musical stage, though a country-rock musical, *Pump Boys and Dinettes,* was nominated for best musical in 1982; and the delightful *Big River* (1985), with Roger Miller's appealing country music, had a modest success. Both shows continue to be revived in regional theaters, and *Big River* returned to Broadway in 2003. But the cultures of Nashville and Broadway spring from different, even conflicting roots: commercial country music evolved from mountain music, with origins mostly traced to Scotland and Ireland, and its songs address hard-working, mostly churchgoing people. Broadway's roots go back to the make-believe world of Viennese operettas; lighthearted, giddy, Gilbert and Sullivan shows; and Yiddish theater based on magical themes and broad comedy. Even the realism that *Show Boat* and *Oklahoma!* introduced to the Broadway stage was highly colored with romance.

Nor does the stark simplicity of the blues lend itself easily to musical theater's expansive way with a story. Two small shows, *Blues in the Night* (1982) and *It Ain't Nothin' but the Blues* (1999), offered no new music but told their stories through the singing of classic blues songs. In 2002, *Thunder Knocking on the Door,* a book musical with an original score of guitar-driven blues and R&B-style ballads by Keb' Mo', drew mixed reviews. Keb' Mo' aptly described the incompatibility of blues and Broadway: "The blues is about being real. And a musical onstage is about being fake."

Even rock has had only limited effect on musical shows. Although several shows in the 1960s and 1970s were based on rock music, they do not seem to have established a discernible trend; in fact, with the advent of rock and roll, pop and show music diverged. *Hair* (1967), billed as a rock musical but more of a revue because it has no integrated plot, addressed concerns of the youth culture and counterculture of the 1960s—drugs, free love, racial prejudice, the Vietnam War, the burning of draft cards, and more. In one notorious seminude scene, "police" ran through the audience as if raiding the show, prophetic of the audience involvement that has become characteristic of many contemporary musicals. The spectacular staging of *Hair* indicated another important trend in modern musical theater. Although the show included the hit song "Aquarius" and unabashedly accompanied its many other compelling melodies with the chromatics, rhythms, and word patterns of rock, ultimately *Hair* attracted audiences more with its notorious "nude scene" than with its rock music.

At least two important shows of the 1960s and 1970s were based on religious themes, and one of them, *Jesus Christ Superstar,* became a wildly popular rock LP album before the show even went into rehearsal. This show's composer, Andrew Lloyd Webber, is British; but the other, nearly contemporary show based on religious themes was *Godspell,* with music by a New Yorker, Stephen Schwartz (b. 1948). In *Godspell,* more successful than *Jesus Christ Superstar* as a theater piece, a small cast interpreted the Gospel according to St. Matthew in a striking new way, singing Schwartz's simple, appealing contemporary revival songs, the best-known of which is "Day by Day."

Grease (1972), a rollicking hit about the rock and roll era, responded to a "nostalgia craze" of the time, as it does when the show is periodically revived. *Grease* attained renewed popularity in its film version as well, but seems to have been a show of a kind, not a precursor of things to come. In 1996, Jonathan Larson offered the highly successful *Rent,* a retelling of the Italian opera *La Bohème* that intriguingly mixes and matches vernacular musics (reggae, gospel, rhythm and blues, hard rock, pop ballads) with classical forms. Of course rock has invigorated other shows as well, but in general rock has not been the music of Broadway.

A recent trend has been to recycle old rock hits in new shows, with great success on and off Broadway. *Mamma Mia!* (2001), which grafts twenty-two hit songs by the Swedish rock group Abba onto a superficial story, was a hit throughout the Western world. *Hairspray* (2002), another Broadway hit (based on the 1988 movie) features an original score by Marc Shaiman, but the songs sound like rock and roll of the 1950s. One much-admired new show, *Movin' Out* (2002), matches songs by Billy Joel, and some of his classical compositions as well, to the choreography of Twyla Tharp. One reviewer compared that show to a choreographed rock concert, which critics and audiences alike have found a joy.

In some ways, hip-hop seems better suited than rock music for the stage. One show based on hip-hop, *Def Poetry Jam,* earned critical acclaim on Broadway in 2003; but it was an evening of poetry, a spoken-word event, not a play in the conventional sense. New York City's Hip Hop Theater Festival is exploring feasible means of merging hip-hop and musical theater, perhaps by using elements of hip-hop, like rapping and DJs; perhaps by presenting conventionally written plays that deal with the concerns of urban youth—the hip-hop generation.

Current Trends

The last thirty years have been difficult for Broadway and disappointing for lovers of musical theater. New York's theater district, which had declined for some years into a sleazy and even dangerous area, has now revived and is again a vibrant, thrilling place to be. But economic pressures affect those on both sides of the footlights, causing ticket prices to soar and producers to cut the size of choruses and the lavishness of sets in an effort to control costs. (*The King and I* cost $360,000 to mount in 1951 and $5.5 million to revive in 1996—a fifteenfold increase.) In commercial theater, four out of five productions fail to pay back their initial investment. It is not surprising, therefore, that the 2004 fall season saw only one new musical open, the pop-rock show *Brooklyn*.

As the expense of producing a new musical on Broadway increased beyond reason, audiences found more and more revivals of old shows opening there. Revivals—including *Cabaret* (1998), *Annie Get Your Gun* (1999), *Oklahoma!* (2002)—and imports, in fact, have kept Broadway alive in recent years. However, more recent Broadway revivals of *Gypsy, Man of La Mancha,* and *Wonderful Town* proved financial failures. The show *Contact* (1999), billed as a musical, won a Tony award without a note of original, or even live, music. It simply costs too much to take a chance on new material.

A further disappointment to musicians is the fact that revivals tend to use fewer musicians than the original productions did. For example, the original published score for *Pacific Overtures* lists twenty-four parts plus a conductor, but the revival in 2004 used only eight musicians, including the conductor.

From Film to Broadway

In this challenging time for new talent, the Broadway musical has tapped one endlessly renewable source: movies. Thus, in a reverse of the tradition of transferring musicals to film, several films recently have become Broadway shows. Perhaps the first such happy turnabout, *La Cage aux Folles,* with music by Jerry Herman, opened in 1983.

Two of the biggest hits on Broadway, *The Producers* and *The Lion King,* were both based on movies, as were *The Full Monty, Forty-Second Street, Beauty and the Beast, Sweet Smell of Success, Thoroughly Modern Millie, The Rocky Horror Picture Show, The Graduate, Hairspray, Chitty Chitty Bang Bang,* and *A Man of No Importance.* Dozens of other films are being converted into musicals for the stage, on the assumption that a known quantity is likely to sell well.

Effects Other Than Music

Staging is a more important element of musical theater than ever before, as stage mechanics and scenic effects integrated into the story propel the action instead of providing background for it, and as visual impact has assumed more significance than the music in many musicals. Thus although questions of economy encourage the production of small or **chamber musicals,** the more widely popular shows feature large casts and sets extravagant in design and breathtaking in effect. Very few new shows offer memorable, singable songs destined to become standards comparable to the innumerable songs by Kern, Porter, Berlin, Gershwin, and Rodgers that we continue to sing in the shower and singers continue to record. (Webber's "Memory," from *Cats;* and Sondheim's "Send in the Clowns," from *A Little Night Music,* are notable exceptions to this rule.)

There is also today increasing interest in **multimedia shows** combining music, dance, drama, and sophisticated special effects. Audience involvement, complex lighting techniques, tape recordings, films, slides, and videos often are part of the modern music theater experience. Some relatively recent lavishly staged musicals on Broadway were foreign imports: Andrew Lloyd Webber's *Cats, Starlight Express,* and *Phantom of the Opera* feature elaborate staging and costumes, as do *Miss Saigon* and *Les Misérables* by the French composer Claude-Michel Schonberg. Roller skates race on ramps behind and over the heads of the audience in *Starlight Express,* a chandelier makes a spectacular fall over spectators at *Phantom of the Opera,* and a helicopter lands on the stage in *Miss Saigon.*

Dance is more important than ever in the Broadway musical. The loose plot of *A Chorus Line* (1975) concerns the way a choreographer selects dancers, and much of that delightful show's entertainment—in both its live and movie versions—is derived from its wonderful dance sequences. The movie *Saturday Night Fever* (1977) reflected in film the same sheer love of dance. The musical *Forty-Second Street* (1980) is an extravaganza of song and dance that continues to have successful runs around the country and abroad, and a revival of Rodgers and Hart's *On Your Toes* was very well received. In *Bring in 'da Noise, Bring in 'da Funk,* a dance show conceived by the dancer-choreographer Savion Glover, the music seems nearly incidental to the rhythmic patterning of feet to rap, tap, and funk.

Another phenomenon of the current Broadway musical scene is a concern to address children, an audience musicals rarely catered to in the past. *Cats,* introduced as a grown-ups' musical, turned out to have broad appeal for children; and since then *Beauty and the Beast* and *The Lion King* have drawn family audiences, happy to be lavishly entertained rather than challenged in Sondheim's way. However, *Seussical,* based on the books by Dr. Seuss (Theodor Geisel), did not prove a success.

The composer of *Seussical,* Stephen Flaherty (b. 1961), although a Broadway veteran, is much younger than the famous elder statesmen of Broadway musicals. In 1998, he and his lyricist Lynn Ahrens celebrated twenty years of collaboration in musical theater, having won awards for *Ragtime,* on Broadway in 1998–2000, and for their show of 2002, *A Man of No Importance* (based on a film of the same name produced in 1994). Several other young composers and lyricists are making their mark in musical theater, though the significance of their contributions is yet to be determined. A show with the unlikely name *Urinetown* (2001), with music and lyrics by Mark Hollman and book and lyrics by Greg Kotis, was a smash success on Broadway and in regional theaters around the country. In 2003 Adam Guettel—a grandson of Richard Rodgers and son of Mary Rodgers, composer of the immensely successful Broadway musical *Once upon a Mattress* (1959)—wrote the words and music to *The Light in the Piazza,* which received enthusiastic reviews. The music of some new musicals has achieved more success on CD than in the theater. Thus the young composer Michael John LaChiusa's *Wild Party* (2000) received poor reviews, but on CD the songs, which re-create—or better, reinvent—authentic period songs of the 1920s with a contemporary bite, make a strong effect. Another young composer, Andrew Lippa, wrote a different version of *Wild Party,* mixing everything from rhythm and blues to Latin to swing to produce a highly eclectic contemporary pop score that also works better, perhaps, as a recording than on the stage.

The "Broadway musical" has become an international phenomenon, with unprecedented creative and technological sophistication and an apparently limitless variety of styles. Certainly the talents of new choreographers, stage designers, and actors offer enormous hope for this indigenous American musical form. Today's Broadway audiences expect the ultimate mating of the arts that used to be considered the sole prerogative of opera, and many contemporary shows are entirely sung, using no spoken dialogue at all. Thus, Broadway has learned what opera lovers have always known—once caught up in the magic of musical theater, we readily allow reality to be superseded by art and enjoy the emotional and aesthetic rewards, which are grand.

Terms to Review

vaudeville   A show with varied acts, including blackface scenes, dogs, circus stunts, songs, and dance.

burlesque   A variety show featuring satirical humor; later associated with striptease acts.

revue   Originally, a show with lavish staging and costumes but with no integrated plot. Later, a series of scenes united by a theme but without a plot.

book shows   Musicals with an integrated plot.

operetta (light opera)   A form of musical theater in which the music and dancing are closely integrated with the plot.

patter song   A feature of Gilbert and Sullivan's operettas, as well as other forms of musical theater, in which humorous words, outrageous puns, and unlikely rhymes are sung very rapidly, with comic effect.

Gilbert and Sullivan operettas   Comic English musicals (words by William S. Gilbert, music by Arthur Sullivan).

musical comedy   A play with music, in which the elements of entertainment are connected by a plot.

Show Boat   Landmark musical, by Jerome Kern, based on a literary work and addressing sensitive social issues.

choreographer   Artist who designs the steps and movements of dancers.

Oklahoma!   Landmark musical, by Rodgers and Hammerstein, integrating all elements of entertainment into the drama.

ensemble   In musical theater, a group of solo singers simultaneously performing independent words and music.

concept musical   A musical show presenting ideas subject to the audience's interpretation and leaving provocative situations unresolved at the end.

chamber musical   A musical for a small cast, requiring economical resources.

multimedia show   Performances including some combination of music, dance, film, slides, tape recordings, and other sound and visual effects.

Key Figures

Florenz Ziegfeld	Jerome Kern	Alan Jay Lerner
George M. Cohan	Richard Rodgers	Frederick Loewe
Will Marion Cook	Lorenz Hart	Leonard Bernstein
Noble Sissle	Oscar Hammerstein II	Stephen Sondheim
Josephine Baker	Frank Loesser	

Suggestions for Further Listening

Excerpts from any of the shows, or by any of the composers, introduced in this chapter.
   (Some can be heard on the Internet.)

Suggestions for Viewing

Yankee Doodle Dandy (film biography of George M. Cohan)
Videos or DVDs of *Show Boat, Oklahoma!, West Side Story,* and other Broadway musicals.

Critical Thinking

What changes do you think would be required to successfully transpose a film musical to Broadway? A Broadway musical to film?

The composer and singer Adam Guettel has said, "Melody is memorable." Compare the opening phrases of "Oh, What a Beautiful Mornin'" from *Oklahoma!* and "The Star Spangled Banner." Both songs are celebratory, both are in triple meter, and both feature wide leaps in the melodic line. Which melody do you find more memorable? Why?

When Jerome Kern's *Show Boat* was revived some years ago, many people refused to see the show, considering it "racist." Do you think they showed moral rectitude in boycotting the show? Or do you think they should have seen the show before reaching conclusions about it? On the basis of what you've learned about the show, do you believe Kern's intentions were racist? Should terms originally used in Edna Ferber's 1926 novel and in Kern's 1927 musical, considered racist today, be altered in contemporary revivals of the show in the interest of political correctness?

Go to www.mhhe.com/ferrisaml5 for a list of additional Web-based resources that relate to the content in this chapter.

Music for Films

usic was closely associated with and highly important to theatrical performances since well before the ancient Greeks staged their magnificent choral dramas. In modern times, it has been inextricably intertwined with film since the motion picture industry began, about 1895. In fact, as the famous American composer Aaron Copland (pp. 386–391) pointed out, a film score is simply a new form of dramatic music.

Whereas movie musicals, such as *West Side Story* or *A Chorus Line,* and film stories of great composers, such as *Rhapsody in Blue* (Gershwin) or *Amadeus* (Mozart), are best known and best remembered for their music, audiences seldom pay much attention to the music of documentaries, cartoons, and feature films having no inherent musical content. Yet for these, too, music serves as far more than accessory to the finished product, continually pushing our emotional buttons in subliminal fashion whether we "hear" it or not, while accomplishing a number of mundane technical chores as well. Imagine *Gone with the Wind* without "Tara's Theme," *Lawrence of Arabia* without Maurice Jarre's sweeping score, *The Third Man* without its prickly little zither theme—or the shower scene in *Psycho* without Bernard Herrmann's shrill, stabbing strings.

Functions of Music in Film

Film music evokes moods, defines cultures, authenticates historical periods, and reveals personality traits more subtle but often more telling than spoken dialogue. Like any other work of art, the music for a movie, called the **film score,** is based on principles of variety and repetition. It builds a sense of continuity throughout the movie while filling "holes" or awkward pauses in action or dialogue. Music alters the pace of action by changes in tempo, and the sense of space by altering the level of volume, while decorating dull scenes and holding shaky ones together. Musically mimicking, or **Mickey Mousing,** a character's actions adds sub- or semiconscious humor to a scene, while suggestive melodic lines or harmonies effectively foretell or reinforce dramatic events.

Sometimes music actually negates a visual image, in ironic denial of what appears or is said on the screen.

Having drawn the viewer from reality into the atmosphere of a film, music subtly identifies the movie's structural units, indicating the beginning and conclusion of significant scenes and bringing the film to an effective close. But while the show goes on, by lessening our defenses and increasing our susceptibility to suggestion, a good film score allows us to suspend disbelief and become gloriously immersed in the unreal—the superreal—world of cinema.

Source versus Functional Music

Some film music emanates from a source, such as a radio, phonograph, or musical instrument, apparent to the characters and the audience alike. Such **source** or **diegetic music,** as it is called, often provides a thematic anchor for the images onscreen. In films featuring dance, for example, such as *Saturday Night Fever* (1977), *Fame* (1980), *Flashdance* (1983), *Footloose* (1984), *Dirty Dancing* (1987), and *The Mambo Kings* (1992), recorded music forms the natural accompaniment for the action. The rock and roll classics heard as source music in *American Graffiti* (1973) establish period authenticity, and the radio or jukebox songs in *The Last Picture Show* (1971) further suggest specific social values and moral attitudes—country-western music implying purity of character, timeworn tradition, and innocence, whereas Tin Pan Alley pop tunes suggest corrupting influences (money, greed, power) associated with urban life.

Movie convention also readily accepts **functional,** or **nondiegetic, music,** heard by the spectators but not by the characters in the film. When director Alfred Hitchcock expressed skepticism that viewers would accept music in his 1944 film *Lifeboat* (which takes place in the middle of the ocean), film composer David Raksin famously retorted, "Show me the source of the camera and I'll show you where the music comes from!"

Relationships between source and nonsource movie music are frequently complex, and the differences between them are easily blurred; but together they constitute an aural telling of the story parallel to the scenes viewed on the screen.

History of Music in Films

Even before movie theaters were wired for sound, music constituted an essential enhancement of the audience's pleasure, and thousands of musicians made their living in movie theater orchestras. Live musical shows performed before the film began, on a scale less lavish than but related to the concept of today's Radio City Music Hall extravaganzas, had much to do with attracting audiences; and a pianist, a theater organist, or even a chamber orchestra accompanying silent films not only heightened the dramatic tension but also disguised the noise of the projector.

Silent Films Knowing that familiar songs evoke associations with their text, time, and mood, accompanists made frequent references to songs familiar to the audience, thus subliminally adding the songs' unheard texts to the silent films' emotional and informative content. For smaller theaters relying on keyboard as opposed to orchestral accompaniment, musicians used stock musical phrases and harmonies to bring to viewers' minds the sounds and emotions associated with railroads, horse chases, love scenes, comic predicaments, and other formulaic situations. A book published in the 1920s titled *Motion Picture Moods* provided keyboard players with numerous pieces evoking images from gruesome to chaotic, humorous, sentimental, or impassioned. Of course this early movie music raised some questionable associations. Music often depicted women and African Americans unfavorably, and music associated in the public mind with the American Indian was then—as it remained in the lavish golden-era movie westerns and unfortunately often is today—highly stereotypical.

Early Sound Films

Although *The Jazz Singer* (1927), starring Al Jolson, was neither the first major motion picture to use sound nor the first to make notable use of music, its enormous popularity encouraged a succession of imitative efforts, many of which were greeted with resounding enthusiasm only to be almost immediately forgotten by the public. But by 1930, music accompanied film in radically varied ways, some films remaining "silents," some containing a sound track with music but no dialogue, some having intermittent dialogue and sparse music, and some constituting full "talkies" with or without musical accompaniment. (The **sound track** includes all of the dialogue, sound effects, and music of a film, whereas the term *film score* refers to the music only.) More and soon most theaters were wired for sound, forcing movie-house musicians out of their jobs.

By 1934, major developments in recording technology made it possible to accompany dialogue with background music, immeasurably enhancing the emotional potency of a film without dominating or drowning out the spoken words. Hollywood hired classical composers to write the music, thus bringing the stirring sound of orchestral music to a new, highly appreciative, audience. Most of the classical composers working in Hollywood were Europeans, but two outstanding American composers, better known for their music written for the concert hall or opera house, also devoted serious attention to writing film scores. The first major American composer of concert music to write for films was Virgil Thomson (see pp. 351–352), who composed the scores for several government-sponsored documentary films, most notably *The Plow That Broke the Plains* (1936). Aaron Copland's film scores include *Quiet City* (1939), *Of Mice and Men* (1939), *Our Town* (1940), *The Red Pony* (1948), and *The Heiress* (1949), which brought him an Academy Award.

Movie musicals, too, became enormously popular, as Hollywood pounded out hundreds of adaptations of Broadway shows and musicals developed specifically for the movie screen. Sound films continued the tradition of sending programmatic messages through familiar tunes: In *Gone with the Wind* (1939), for example, "Dixie" is heard when war is declared and later as the anxious citizens of Atlanta review casualty lists; the defeated Confederates return home accompanied by "When Johnny Comes Marching Home"; "Marching through Georgia" signifies Northern advances; strains of "Dixie," "Swanee River," and the somber bugle call "Taps" underscore the final shot of the tattered Confederate flag waving in the breeze; and competing phrases of "Dixie" and "The Battle Hymn of the Republic" suggest the military conflict pervading the period of the film.

Although familiar songs provide an audience with a comfortable frame of reference, the introduction of a pleasing new song often enhances sales not only of the movie sound track but also of tickets to the film itself. Several films made during the 1930s and 1940s brought Irving Berlin's music to great numbers of people far from Broadway but able to view feature films in their local movie houses. *Holiday Inn* (1942) introduced Berlin's "White Christmas," one of the most popular songs of the twentieth century; and in 1948 *Easter Parade* gave the title song, written by Berlin for a show in 1933, a new lease on life. These and innumerable other movie songs live a healthy and seemingly endless life quite independent of the films that launched or popularized them.

The Hollywood Sound

The Hollywood studio system, contracting thousands of actors and artisans, gave opportunities to vast numbers of composers, conductors, arrangers, and performers who from the 1930s through the 1950s produced film music of increasing complexity and increasing reliance upon nondiegetic scores. Using the lavishly varied sounds of orchestral instruments, composers drew upon a body of musical conventions to produce what became known as the **classical Hollywood film score.**

Unlike such well known Broadway composer-songwriters as George Gershwin, Irving Berlin, Jerome Kern, and Richard Rodgers, whose scores supported numerous movie musicals—and unlike such concert music composers as Virgil Thomson, Aaron Copland, and Leonard Bernstein, who also wrote for films—the Hollywood triumvirate of **Alfred Newman, Max Steiner,** and **Erich Korngold** are best remembered for the music they created for Hollywood films of the 1930s and 1940s. They applied the highly romantic European concert music techniques of lush orchestral scoring, rich harmonies, and sweeping melodies to achieve the grandeur characteristic of films of Hollywood's golden era. Largely ignored or taken for granted for years, their film scores now are recognized as dramatic music of a high level of composition and performance. There even seems to be some relenting of an entrenched prejudice among the serious concert public against the concert music of film composers who produced symphonic music unrelated to their film careers. The Viennese composer Erich Korngold (1897–1957), for instance, received lavish international praise for his choral, piano, opera, and orchestral music before he settled in Hollywood; but he died unforgiven by the establishment for the lush romantic music with which he had captivated the movie audience. Now, however, his symphonic music is receiving belated but respectful attention in recordings and live performances. Korngold's Symphony in F-sharp Major and his rhapsodic Violin Concerto are among numerous compositions he wrote independent of any association with film music.

FIGURE 19.1

John Williams's two-note "shark" motif (da-da, da-da), probably the most famous motto in film music history, clearly warns of impending terror in *Jaws*.

When in the 1950s science fiction spectaculars adopted the large-sounding effects of the full-blown orchestral score enhanced by increasingly sophisticated synthesized sound, the classical Hollywood score soared to new heights of popularity. Especially, **John Williams** returned the romantic sound of the classical film score to popular favor, adapting the symphony orchestra for the modern recording studio in his stunning scores for the disaster films *The Poseidon Adventure* (1972), *The Towering Inferno* (1974), *Earthquake* (1977), and most notably *Jaws* (1975) (see Figure 19.1), as well as *Star Wars* and *Close Encounters of the Third Kind* (both 1977), *Superman* (1978), and *Raiders of the Lost Ark* (1981). More than any others, the scores for the *Star Wars* films brought about a tidal wave of emotional film scoring that fully returned such overwhelming symphonic film scores to mainstream filmmaking.

The original *Star Wars* score, with its stirring, majestic opening and moments of mysterious quiet for young Luke (Listening Example 66), told the audience what to feel, while the visuals showed what was going on (see Figure 19.2). The film, which lasts 121 minutes, includes eighty-eight minutes of symphonic music, starting with the opening credits. As in certain operas, melodic and rhythmic motives represent characters, ideas, and events, allowing the music to carry dramatic and even narrative responsibility. Thus motives

FIGURE 19.2
Luke Skywalker, Princess Leia,
and Han Solo in a scene from
Star Wars.

Listening Example 66

Star Wars Main Title

Composer
John Williams

CD 3
Track 5
5:48

Luke's famous theme accompanies the opening shots, showing
an imperial star destroyer chasing a Rebel blockade runner.
Brass instruments boldly state the martial theme—which strings
continue, however, in sweeping melodic lines, adding a dashing, romantic dimension to Luke's motive.

After a very brief reference to Princess Leia's quiet, more delicate theme
(1:29), the brass defiantly play the Rebel spaceship **fanfare**—a
brassy flourish—as the Rebel blockade runner appears on the screen
(1:43).

Luke's theme returns at 2:32.

Finally, Williams segues to music from the end of the "End Title" music,
making this "Main Title" music the equivalent of an opera orchestral introduction, or *overture* (see p. 353).

for Luke, Princess Leia, Darth Vader, Yoda, and other characters recur in varied form, as their personalities and experiences evolve. Motives representing objects (such as the Death Star) and ideas or concepts (such as the love shared by Han Solo and Leia, or the Force) also are transformed throughout the film.

The maniacally mechanical *Empire March* of the second *Star Wars* movie, *The Empire Strikes Back,* was so compelling in its evil that it made viewers want to join the dark side. In *Return of the Jedi,* the third movie of the series, the musical themes of good and evil collided and resolved. The music in the fourth movie—Part I of the series—perfectly enhances the spoken and visual melodrama of the film. And John Williams's score for Part II, *Attack of the Clones,* was widely praised, though the movie was not. In all the *Star Wars* movies, pyramiding brasses signal danger, trumpet fanfares on repeated notes signal battle, percussion points to something strange or illusory, and hymn-like writing indicates moments of public civil order or moments of private introspection.

Pop Scores

Around 1950, many composers began to accompany their films with pop music rather than the symphonic Hollywood film score. Soon movie songs were achieving unprecedented popularity. Although Anton Karas's zither theme for *The Third Man* (1949) became a pop instrumental hit, and adaptations of Scott Joplin's rags in *The Sting* (1973) stirred enthusiasm for ragtime among a new generation of listeners, songs are more likely than instrumental pieces to become hits. (By the summer of 1996, the album of songs from *Forrest Gump* had sold more than 6 million copies worldwide, whereas Alan Silvestri's score album had sold only about 100,000.) Sometimes words are even added to an instrumental movie theme for the purpose of popularizing both theme and film. Thus, noticing that audiences were enraptured by the lovely melody David Raksin composed as his theme for *Laura* (1944), studio executives commissioned Johnny Mercer to set lyrics to Raksin's music—whereupon "Laura" soared to the top of the Hit Parade, attracting new viewers for the film.

By the 1950s, many movie scores included or largely consisted of popular songs, such as "Do Not Forsake Me, Oh My Darlin'" (sung by Tex Ritter in *High Noon*) and the title songs from *Three Coins in the Fountain* (1954), *Love Is a Many-Splendored Thing* (1955), and *Around the World in Eighty Days* (1956). Also during the 1950s, jazz accompanied several important films, including *A Streetcar Named Desire* (Alex North, 1951), *The Man with the Golden Arm* (Elmer Bernstein, 1955), *Ascenseur pour l'échafaud* (*Elevator to the Gallows,* Miles Davis, 1957), and *Anatomy of a Murder* (Duke Ellington, 1959).

Pop scores achieved even more emphasis in the 1960s, attracting younger-than-ever audiences to films whose songs frequently outshone other features of the score and earned more money than the films that introduced them. (Few people today associate Henry Mancini's "Moon River," for example, with *Breakfast at Tiffany's,* the film that introduced it in 1962.) Burt Bacharach's scores epitomized film music of that decade and the next, beginning with *What's New Pussycat?* (1965), continuing with *Alfie* (1966), and attracting unprecedented attention with "Raindrops Keep Fallin' on My Head" in *Butch Cassidy and the Sundance Kid* (1969). Unlike movie songs that seem almost independent of the films that feature them, the pop songs providing the title sequence for James Bond films recur in instrumental as well as sung versions to underpin the drama throughout those movies. John Barry's title song for *Goldfinger* (1964), for example, is heard with lyrics also and is integrated into the instrumental score. Songs included in Paul Simon's score for *The Graduate*—"Sounds of Silence," "Mrs. Robinson," and the English folk song "Scarborough Fair"—subtly suggest and support mood changes and dramatic shifts in the narrative.

Randy Newman, whose uncles Lionel, Alfred, and Emil Newman composed some of the most famous movie scores of the 1930s, 1940s, and 1950s, produced several pop albums before establishing his own career as a film composer, which finally took off in the 1970s with *Cold Turkey,* and continued with numerous other well-received films, including *Toy Story 2* (1999), *Scabiscuit* (2003), and *Meet the Fockers* (2004). His beautifully orchestrated film scores typically incorporate echoes of Americana. Stephen Sondheim, apparently not interested in composing a full film score, wrote five songs for Warren Beatty's *Dick Tracy* (1990), effectively capturing in his music the period flavor of the film.

Sometimes the marriage of movie and music is less than ideal, of course, but the sound tracks of two hit films of the 1990s found commercial success while effectively expanding the vision of the filmmakers. The sound tracks for Quentin Tarantino's *Pulp Fiction* and Oliver Stone's *Natural Born Killers* used pop music to heighten the claustrophobic atmosphere of murder and chaos. Further, the sound track for *Pulp Fiction* sprawls from the crooning of the 1950s to the soul of the 1960s to the funk of the 1970s, enhancing the viewers' shifting sense of reality as we lurch from one decade to another.

But loose collections of pop songs, packaged by Hollywood for an audience shaped by MTV and Madison Avenue, increasingly displace integrated orchestral scores in motion pictures today. Electronic editing and other computer-driven techniques allow many young film composers never to develop the basic musical skills once essential in fashioning a score, to the detriment of the field according to some—to its enhancement, in the view of others.

Electronic Music Today, of course, we take electronic effects for granted in movie music (and every other kind of music) but the eerie sounds of the **theremin,** the earliest electronic musical instrument (invented in 1920 by the Russian physicist Léon Thérémin), aroused unprecedented sensations of suspense. The theremin, a wooden cabinet on legs with antennas that respond to the slightest movement of the hands or body in the surrounding space, had prominent effect in *The Bride of Frankenstein* (1935), in Miklos Rozsa's score for Hitchcock's film *Spellbound* (1945), and in *The Thing from Another World* (1951)—an effect colored by the very unfamiliarity of the music's timbre.

In the late 1960s, composers began to use analog techniques, although they were difficult to work with, hard to keep in tune, unreliable, and woefully inconsistent. Nevertheless, Giorgio Moroder's score for *Midnight Express* (1978) proved so effective it became the first electronic film score to win an Academy Award.

With the advent of digital systems in the early 1980s and sampling techniques developed later in that decade, exciting and almost limitless new possibilities appeared, and since then synthesized sounds have enlivened the sound tracks of numberless films. More flexible and less cumbersome than the early machines, the new technologies offered far more than new timbres suggesting otherworldly and futuristic effects. Whereas early keyboards allowed production of only one tone on one keyboard at a time, the new multiple-voice keyboards could be played like pianos or other keyboard instruments. And the new machines afforded extensive editing capabilities, enabling people with less experience as composers to create highly effective film scores. Further, a synthesized music track score, such as the nonacoustic score written by Maurice Jarre for *Fatal Attraction* (1987), needs no performing artist but may be accomplished by an "electronic ensemble" under the control of one individual.

Movie Musicals Revived

Movie musicals, popular during the 1930s and 1940s, lost favor in subsequent decades. However, during 2000 and 2001, at least three new Hollywood films—*Dancer in the Dark; O Brother, Where Art Thou?;* and *Moulin Rouge*—were billed as musicals, though none of them qualified as an original movie musical in the traditional sense: the first merely quotes numbers from *The Sound of Music,* the second uses music popular in the South during the Great Depression, and the third draws on the music of the Beatles, Madonna, and such contemporary musicians as Moby, Beck, U2, Massive Attack, and Fatboy Slim. *Moulin Rouge* had a big impact on movie audiences, and the Oscar-winning film *Chicago,* in 2002, strengthened the perception that the movie musical had returned to favor. The musical biography of the songwriter Cole Porter, *De-Lovely* (2004), seemed to confirm this new, or renewed, enthusiasm.

Current Trends

Today all kinds of music, from classical to pop and from full-blown orchestral scores to synthesized sound tracks, accompany feature films. Some film scores raid the classics. The scores of two poignant films (*Elephant Man,* 1980; and *Platoon,* 1986), for example, quoted Samuel Barber's lovely *Adagio for Strings* (Listening Example 76) to accentuate the extreme pathos of those films. Audiences sometimes accept in films "ultramodern" music that they might reject in the concert hall, finding that dissonant harmonies, wide melodic leaps, instrumental timbres stretched beyond normal limits, and other extreme effects (discussed in Chapters 21 and 23) effectively raise their level of tension and emotional involvement. Henry Mancini used **quarter tones**—those lying halfway between the half steps of the major or minor scale—in *Wait Until Dark* (1967). John Williams's modernistic percussion effects in *Images* (1972) greatly strengthened the emotional effect of that score. And the *minimalist* techniques (pp. 413–414) used by Philip Glass in his Hopi-titled films *Koyaanisqatsi*

(*Life out of Balance,* 1983) and *Powaqqatsi* (*Life in Transformation,* 1988) co-ordinated well with the visual effect of nonnarrative, time-lapse photography. In 1999 and 2000, the academy award for best film score went to classical composers: first John Corigliano for *The Red Violin,* then Tan Dun for *Crouching Tiger, Hidden Dragon.* And John Williams's score for *Minority Report* (2002) is interlaced with striking excerpts from masterworks by Bach, Haydn, Schubert, and Tchaikovsky.

Jazz continues to be a vital component of many movies today. Films featuring country-western, either as source or nondiegetic music, include *Nashville* (1975), *Honeysuckle Rose* (1980), *Coal Miner's Daughter* (1980), *Sweet Dreams* (1985), and *The Last Picture Show.* In 1987, *The Big Easy* brought the exuberant sounds of Cajun music to a wide new audience. For the Civil War saga *Cold Mountain* (2003), the producer J. Bone Burnett effectively wove to-gether original music, traditional folk songs, and standard music score fare.

Ethnic music often flavors film scores—to more or less legitimate effect. Although the adaptations of North American Indian music in *A Man Called Horse* (1970) and *Dances with Wolves* (1990), for example, pander to familiar, often inaccurate stereotypes, Barry Goldberg's score for *Powwow Highway* (1988) gives a more realistic portrayal of American Indian music. John Williams's score for the powerful Holocaust movie *Schindler's List* (1995) combines classical and folk-ethnic references: a winding, eastern European–flavored tune with a folk dance pulse evokes feelings of sad remembrance, and later thematic fragments accompanying harrowing scenes of genocide acutely express human anguish. Hispanic American and African American music enriches many films, recently including *Girlfight* (2000), accompanied with a distinctive blend of hip-hop, flamenco, and hand clapping. And Hans Zimmer's score for *The Lion King* (1994), which includes several songs by Elton John, combines Hollywood symphonics and African chant in an unlikely but highly effective representation of harmony among all peoples and species. Spike Lee's *Bamboozled* (2000) satirized racial stereotypes (white and black) in a modern take on minstrel shows.

By the 1980s composers had become highly skillful at integrating premarketed popular songs into a film score. The score of *When Harry Met Sally* (1989) consists entirely of songs, with no orchestral underscore whatsoever. Giorgio Moroder's songs in *Flashdance* (1983) genuinely support the film; and in *Philadelphia* (1995), songs by Bruce Springsteen and Neil Young replace the conventional orchestral scoring to profound effect. During the latter film's opening scene, as the camera roams over the slums of Philadelphia, Springsteen (as a homeless man staring at his reflection in a store window) sings to himself his melancholy and compelling ballad "Streets of Philadelphia": "Oh brother are you gonna leave me/Wastin' away/On the streets of Philadelphia?" And later in the film, toward the end of a poignant passage in which we view home movies of Tom Hanks (whose character now has AIDS) as a child, Neil Young sings in a small, cracked voice his moving ballad "Philadelphia," whose lyrics ("I won't be ashamed of love") refer obliquely to the gay lawyer who has been dismissed from his firm.

Rock has been used to accompany films since Bill Haley and the Comets performed "Rock around the Clock" in *Blackboard Jungle* (1955). They were succeeded by Simon and Garfunkel's songs in *The Graduate* (1968), the Bee Gees's hits for *Saturday Night Fever* (1978), Pink Floyd's music in *The Wall* (1982), and songs by Prince for *Batman* (1989), to name just a few examples. The rock hits in *Forrest Gump* (1995), which surveys four decades of American life from the view of a rock fan of the 1960s, unify the film by identifying periods and styles: Creedence Clearwater Revival and Jimi Hendrix and the Doors bring to mind the Vietnam years, the Mamas and the Papas praise the hippies in "California Dreamin'," and "Running on Empty" and "On the Road Again" accompany Forrest on his run across America. The songs in *Pulp Fiction* (1994) also help identify periods (the 1950s and 1970s) and give insight into characters. Here the wail of surf music, normally associated with idyllic California beaches, ironically accompanies scenes of gangsters' carnage, the incongruity of this juxtaposition strongly heightening the horror.

Recent rock groups have produced scores varying in style from fusion to classical, and rock stars have taken more serious roles now than in earlier films—Sting in *Dune* (1984) and the Byrds and Danny Elfman for Tim Burton's *Pee-wee's Big Adventure* (1985) and *Beetlejuice* (1988) come to mind. The soft rock phenomenon of the 1980s known as **new age** music, providing soothing, repetitive blocks of gentle, unassuming sounds produced by synthesizers or acoustic folk instruments, most notably affected Michael Convertino's score for *Children of a Lesser God* (1986).

Even opera has been welcomed into the broad realm of mainstream feature filmmaking. A number of movies produced during the 1980s and 1990s include entire scenes from famous operas that pack a potent emotional punch for unsuspecting listeners having little or no experience with this grandest form of music theater. *Fatal Attraction, Moonstruck, A Room with a View, The Witches of Eastwick, Someone to Watch Over Me, The Untouchables, Hannah and Her Sisters,* and *Prizzi's Honor* are only a few of the many films giving more than token attention to famous opera scenes. The powerful recording of Maria Callas singing "La Mamma Morta" (from *Andrea Chenier* by Umberto Giordano) heard as source music toward the end of *Philadelphia* nearly overwhelms the viewer as well as the film's afflicted star; the power and beauty of this serious music offer forceful contrast to Bruce Springsteen's and Neil Young's contemporary, relevant, and highly appealing ballads.

The Composer's Perspective

Arnold Schoenberg (see p. 378) once was asked under what conditions he would work with a movie studio. "I will write music," Schoenberg replied, "and then you will make a motion picture to correspond with it."

Desirable as such an unlikely scenario might appear, composers of film music generally find themselves in the awkward position of writing music hardly intended to be heard. To this end, they read the script, listen to the **temp,** or temporary score (consisting of existing music prepared to demonstrate to the composer the type of music desired for the film) if one is provided, and perhaps scrutinize the film, laboriously determining when and how much music should occur and what sorts of music would serve the specific needs of each scene. Composers vary in their desire to view "dailies"—the detailed footage shot each day, which can be dull and tedious and so can inhibit the composer's emotional response to the action—and their preference to wait for the "rough cut," which tells the story from beginning to end with most of its elements in place. (The latter method allows composers to capitalize better on their first emotional reaction to the film, which is likely to mirror that of the eventual audience.) Some composers favor working from a script; some prefer talking with the director; some work from storyboards; some visit the set and talk with actors; some begin their composition and orchestration only when the film's final edit is complete.

Aaron Copland
"Film music is like a small lamp that you place below the screen to warm it."

Techniques Film composers have developed a vast repertoire of methods, musical and technical, by which to accomplish their practical and aesthetic goals. They know, for example, that the harmonic system of *tonality* offers nearly unlimited means to create anxiety, expectation, or reassurance. Unresolved harmonies build suspense; unorthodox chord progressions effect surprise; and the change from major (often understood to suggest order or stability) to minor (more chromatic and therefore less stable) commonly darkens the mood. Similarly, tonal ambiguity or the use of foreign, artificial, or unfamiliar scales subconsciously affects listeners who are quite unaware of the intellectual reasons for their emotional response. As we know, listeners differ in their perception of *dissonance,* which some scholars believe in any case is a learned rather than innate phenomenon; but skillful composers use relationships between consonant and dissonant sounds to profound dramatic advantage. Extreme dissonance, suggesting disorder or instability, for example, may be relieved by consonant resolutions.

Timbre also has potent influence on our sensibilities: Orchestral strings tug our own emotional strings, and a trumpet's proud blare evokes within us ecstasies of patriotic pride. We can hardly imagine these instruments' roles reversed, whatever the melodic or rhythmic content of their music.

Thus, working at least from detailed charts of the length and description of scenes, with reference perhaps to a temp score as well, a film composer writes new music or adapts excerpts from existing classical or popular music to be heard as source music or skillfully woven into the fabric of the underscore. John Williams, who composes at a piano, has a projection room nearby where he views scenes from a film and compares them with cue sheets and with developing drafts of his musical conceptions.

Finally, the finished score is subjected to the indignities of being cut, mixed with dialogue and other sounds, and further altered by the director and assorted editors and sound engineers. Composers have been heard to lament that they scarcely recognize their own work in the finished product. Today's film composers also often complain of being asked to meet impossible deadlines, of having their music drowned out by deafening sound effects, or—worst of all—of having their scores rejected for entirely capricious reasons.

Film Score Performances and Recordings

Film music sometimes comes to attention independent of the film to which it belongs, through live or recorded performance. Discovering during the 1950s and 1960s the degree to which films sold music and vice versa, Hollywood's composers avidly entered the recording business, producing sound track or film score recordings including some, most, or all of the music of a film. Also, composers sometimes write a suite comprising significant sections of music from the complete score, such as Leonard Bernstein's suite of dances from *West Side Story* and his symphonic suite from *On the Waterfront*. From his sound track for Spike Lee's *Malcolm X,* which brilliantly documents the popular black music of the era, jazz composer and trumpeter Terence Blanchard excerpted *The Malcolm X Jazz Suite,* integrating the disparate moods of the movie score in eleven segments performed by a quintet of saxophone, piano, drums, bass, and trumpet in a highly effective independent composition.

Recently, movie music—suites, excerpts, or themes from popular films—has become a favorite focus of orchestral pops concerts, and such well-known pieces as John Barry's "Romance for Guitar and Orchestra" from the film *Deadfall* (1968) and Korngold's Cello Concerto from his score to *Deception* (1946) are among several movie compositions sometimes heard on the concert stage. The director of *The Red Violin,* released in 1999, commissioned John Corigliano to write an original score and then made the movie around it; and Corigliano fashioned a concert piece, *The Red Violin Chaconne,* from the movie music (for which he won an Oscar).

In 1999, Philip Glass achieved a sort of combination film-concert experience by composing an original score to accompany the classic horror film *Dracula* (1931). No musical score had ever been written for that early movie, which appeared just as silent films were giving way to talkies, when sound technology was in rudimentary stages of development. Glass's score is performed onstage by the well-known Kronos (string) Quartet while the film is projected on the screen.

Would we listen to the film score of a film we had never seen? Judging from sales of sound track and film score recordings, people do, in considerable numbers; sound track albums are selling at unprecedented rates and dominating sales charts more than ever before. Availability on popular recordings of the beautiful themes for *Chariots of Fire, Dances with Wolves,* and *Out of Africa* greatly enhanced ticket sales for those movies; and Elmer Bernstein's score for *The Magnificent Seven* (1960), which may be the most famous score ever written for a Hollywood western, became a classical crossover best-seller more than thirty years later when it was voted best sound track recording of 1994.

Since about 1990, sound track and film score collecting has accelerated among people who, although largely unaware of the music as they viewed a film, discover that the music allows them unlimited opportunity to "re-view" it.

Although instrumental scores appear on best-seller lists infrequently, albums from *Apollo 13* and *Braveheart* have done very well; and the sound tracks for *Pulp Fiction* and *Natural Born Killers* (1994), which use pop music to heighten the claustrophobic atmosphere of murder and chaos, reached the Top 40 on *Billboard*'s album chart. The number one album of 1998 was the sound track to the movie *City of Angels,* a film which made little impact in theaters, but whose sound track spawned two hit singles ("Uninvited" by Alanis Morissette and "Iris" by the Goo Goo Dolls) and stayed firmly lodged in the Top 40 for months. And the number of sound tracks released in a single year climbed steadily throughout the 1990s: in 1990, sixteen sound tracks appeared on *Billboard*'s album chart, and in 1998 there were more than fifty. We may note, however, that some "sound track" albums, exemplified by *Godzilla,* actually have music "inspired by" the film, including songs not heard in the movie at all.

Studies of screen music came to the fore in the 1980s and 1990s with the improving quality and growing popularity of sound track recordings, and today movie music is recognized as a subject worthy of serious musicological consideration. Increasingly, movies are recognized as a source of concert music—a love scene, or a march, for example—equivalent to ballets and operas of the nineteenth century. Universities, libraries, and other institutions of higher learning are carefully preserving Hollywood film scores, and anthologies of articles, essays, score analyses, and memoirs about Hollywood film music attract favorable attention from scholars and film buffs alike.

Terms to Review

film score All of the music accompanying a film.

Mickey Mousing Musically mimicking or accenting an action.

source or **diagetic music** Music heard by characters in the film as well as by the film audience.

functional or **nondiagetic music** Music heard by the audience only.

sound track All of the dialogue, sound effects, and music of a film.

classical Hollywood film score Lush orchestral scores particularly associated with films of the 1930s, 1940s, and 1950s.

fanfare A brief, dramatic phrase or piece for brass instruments (and perhaps percussion), with the character of an announcement or a celebration.

theremin The earliest electronic musical instrument.

quarter tones Tones lying halfway between half steps.

new age A soft rock style providing soothing, repetitious blocks of gentle, unassuming sounds produced by synthesizers or acoustic folk instruments.

temp Temporary film score, composed of existing music independent of the film, offered to demonstrate to a film's composer the type of music desired.

Key Figures

Alfred Newman
Max Steiner

Erich Korngold

John Williams

Suggestions for Further Listening

Source or **Diagetic Music:**
Saturday Night Fever
Dirty Dancing
American Graffiti
Functional or **Nondiagetic Music:**
Lifeboat
Documentary:
The Plow That Broke the Plains
Scores by Aaron Copland:
Quiet City
The Heiress
Scores by John Williams:
Jaws
The *Star Wars* films
Pop Music Scores:
High Noon
Butch Cassidy and the Sundance Kid
Pulp Fiction
When Harry Met Sally
Philadelphia
Jazz Scores:
A Streetcar Named Desire
Anatomy of a Murder

Electronic Music Scores:
Spellbound
Midnight Express
Rock Scores:
Blackboard Jungle
The Wall
Beetlejuice
Opera in Film Scores:
Fatal Attraction
Moonstruck
A Room with a View
Philadelphia
Film Score Suites:
Leonard Bernstein: Suite of dances from *West Side Story*
     Symphonic Suite from *On the Waterfront*
Terence Blanchard: *The Malcolm X Jazz Suite*
John Corigliano: *The Red Violin Chaconne*

For further information, including interviews and sound clips, go to npr.org (the National Public Radio site) and search for "film music."

Critical Thinking

To what might you attribute the American public's apparent revived taste for movie musicals?

If you know the songs "Things Have Changed" (Bob Dylan, from *Wonder Boys*, 2000), "If I Didn't Have You" (Randy Newman, from *Monsters, Inc.,* 2001), and "Lose Yourself" (Eminem, Jeff Bass, and Luis Resto, from *8 Mile,* 2002), do you associate them with the films for which each won an Academy Award for best song?

The next time you view a film, notice as much as you can about the music. Who wrote it? Who performs it? What is the style of the music? How does it affect the movie? Is there both source and functional music in the film? Could the music stand alone as an album of the film score? Could it be arranged into a suite for orchestral performance?

Go to www.mhhe.com/ferrisaml5 for a list of additional Web-based resources that relate to the content in this chapter.

American Opera

Almost since the first opera appeared in Italy, early in the seventeenth century, Italians have hummed their favorite opera tunes while strolling down the street. Other Europeans also have long delighted in the emotional intensity and high drama or comedy of wonderful operas in various styles.

But many Americans until recently considered opera an elite and unlikely form of entertainment, and a characteristically American opera was almost inconceivable. The nineteenth-century American composer William Henry Fry (see pp. 125–126) fully intended operas to sound Italian. Other well-meaning opera enthusiasts sought to attract an American audience by translating Italian, French, or German operas into English. But neither ploy made the medium accessible or meaningful to most American listeners.

Yet opera, the grandest of all the arts, combines singing, acting, orchestral music, drama, staging, costuming, dance, and lighting effects in a form infinitely greater than the sum of its parts. And although opera took a very long time to assume the vital role in American musical theater that it finally has today, since World War II a significant number of American opera companies have been formed, and performances in the major opera houses around the country are regularly sold out. Saturday afternoon broadcasts of Metropolitan Opera performances have been widely listened to since 1931. During the 1980s, films of two Italian operas by Giuseppe Verdi (1813–1901)—*La Traviata* and *Otello*—were commercially successful at popular American movie theaters; and Chapter 19 names some of the many recent commercial films featuring generous opera scenes. Recently network television has been offering full-length live performances of great operas from many countries and periods. The number of professional productions of North American (including Canadian) operas doubled in the decade 1990–2000.

Finally, then, Americans have discovered that there are as many kinds of opera as there are movies or books. Although the complexity of opera requires more preparation from the audience than any other form of art or entertainment, its combined visual and musical effects offer unparalleled rewards.

Opera

An **opera** is a drama that is sung instead of spoken. Like a play, it may be long or short, comic or serious, grand or modest—good or bad. Because ordinary conversation is of course not naturally sung, the opera viewer must abandon or suspend rational thought to become immersed in the art—the magic—that is opera; but this is not as difficult as it sounds, for even skeptical viewers quickly become caught in a great opera's spell and forget to notice that the dialogue is being sung instead of spoken. As noted in Chapter 18, many modern musicals use this same technique, which Broadway audiences have come to expect. After all, it is the role of art to express human feelings at a level beyond the limits of ordinary communication. As our emotions become involved and the real world slips away (or gets out of the way), the most artificial aspects of art somehow seem more real than reality itself.

Solo and Ensemble Singing

In an opera, the exchange of dialogue occurs through **recitative** (from the same root as "recite"), a style of singing in which the words are expressed clearly and economically so as to move the drama along. The melody of a recitative often resembles the inflection of the words as they would be spoken; and the rhythm, free and flexible, also accommodates the text. As you might expect, recitative involves little repetition of phrases, because its purpose is to further, not delay, the action. *Dry recitative* is accompanied by a keyboard instrument only or, in early operas, by a keyboard and another instrument doubling the bass line. The more expressive *accompanied recitative* has orchestral accompaniment.

An **aria,** usually more melodic and often more expressive than a recitative, constitutes a dramatic soliloquy in song, with the emphasis upon the music rather than the text. Time is simply suspended as a character reflects upon and expresses the deepest emotions aroused by situations in the story. Arias fully display the beauty and range of a singer's voice, often allowing the performer to indulge in virtuosic singing, because here the words are less important than the expression of emotion. There also may be considerable repetition of text ("I love you, I *love* you . . .") to enhance the emotional impact.

Unlike recitative, an aria has metered rhythm and is organized according to musical principles of design. The most familiar aria form is called **da capo,** which means "from the beginning" and may be illustrated as **ABA:** The composer writes the first section, **A,** and a contrasting second section, **B,** and then instead of writing out the third part indicates that the first section is to be repeated "from the beginning." Here custom offers further opportunity for vocal display, a singer often improvising elaborate embellishments to the repetition of section **A.**

In an aria, the orchestra may provide far more than simple support for the vocal line, perhaps playing an introduction and concluding passage as well as interludes between sections or verses. Further, instruments may introduce or imitate the singer's melodic phrases throughout the piece or provide sound effects, such as birdcalls or thunder, independent of the singer's melodic line. Sometimes the orchestra even assumes a dramatic or psychological role, contradicting the singer's words by making musical reference to conflicting ideas, for example.

Ensemble scenes add excitement to opera as to all forms of musical theater. The members of an opera **chorus** (a large ensemble with several voices singing each line of music) generally represent characters in the drama, such as guests at a wedding or soldiers returning from battle. And again as in musicals, *solo ensembles*—duets, trios, quartets, quintets, or even larger group of soloists—add thrilling drama as well as magnificent contrapuntal musical effect to the opera stage.

Opera in America

Before the twentieth century, the few American opera houses confined their repertoire almost entirely to foreign operas, because, as we know, little was available or would have been accepted of native work. French opera had strong appeal in New Orleans, where many people spoke French; and New York City had a small but enthusiastic audience for German and Italian operas. But besides Italian-style works such as those of William Henry Fry, no further American operas were presented for a long time.

Then during the first half of the twentieth century, several American composers sought to establish a national opera style by writing operas with American Indian settings. **Mary Carr Moore** (1873–1957) was among the more successful composers of operas on Indian themes; but the idea, although popular for a time, was short-lived.

The ragtime composer Scott Joplin wrote at least two operas, one of which, **Treemonisha,** was published in 1911 in what is called a "piano score"—that is, without orchestration. Joplin wrote the words as well as the music of *Treemon isha,* whose story illustrates his belief that blacks must acquire education in order to improve their social and economic situation. Joplin's opera includes some ragtime and other dance pieces, as well as more conventional operatic arias. In the very effective finale, the large, brightly costumed cast celebrates the happy ending by dancing a stately "slow drag" (Optional Listening Example).

The lack of interest during Joplin's lifetime in an opera by a black composer prevented him from ever achieving a proper performance of *Treemonisha.* However, in the early 1970s the opera was scored for orchestral instruments by Gunther Schuller, and it has been performed, with Schuller's or other orchestral accompaniments, numerous times since then, live and on public television.

Curiously, two operas by white composers, each with an all-black cast and both performed in Broadway theaters rather than in an opera house, first brought American opera to a broad and appreciative audience.

Virgil Thomson (1896–1989) Convinced by the time he graduated from Harvard University that concert music had become overly complex, **Virgil Thomson** imposed a refreshing simplicity upon his own compositions, which were often based on the folk songs, hymns, and Civil War songs he had heard as a child in Missouri. While continuing his music education in Paris with the extremely talented and influential teacher Nadia Boulanger (see p. 386), Thomson discovered that the French shared his appreciation for musical simplicity; they thought, as he did, the purpose of music is to amuse and entertain rather than to improve the listener. Thomson stayed in this congenial atmosphere for fifteen years but was eventually driven home by the impending catastrophe of World War II.

Among Thomson's most stimulating experiences abroad was his collaboration with **Gertrude Stein** (1874–1946), an American writer who spent most of her life in Paris. Stein used words for their sounds rather than their meanings, producing attractive, often funny combinations of syllables regardless of their sense or lack of it. Gertrude Stein wrote the words, or **libretto,** and Virgil Thomson wrote the music of *Four Saints in Three Acts,* the first American opera to appeal to the American public.

This stunning show, which actually concerns fifteen saints and has four acts, makes little if any sense but ravishes the eyes and ears with the most delightful entertainment. When the show opened in 1934 in New York City, its enchanting sets elegantly constructed of brightly colored cellophane—to the dismay of the city's fire department—provided a magnificent stage. Thomson's choice of an all-black cast seems curious, because the characters are (apparently) Spanish and have nothing to do with black culture, but simply reflect the daily blend of meditative creativity and ordinary socializing that Stein and Thomson experienced in Parisian life. (Thomson claimed that Stein patterned the opera's leading characters, St. Theresa and St. Ignatius, after herself and James Joyce.) In any case, although Thomson's declaration that he simply admired the appearance and voices of the black singers may seem racist in today's more sensitive environment, his intentions were artistic and aesthetic, and he would have been astonished to think his genuine esteem might be considered discriminatory.

Thomson set Stein's nonsensical but appealing libretto beautifully to music, although it had been thought that American speech did not lend itself to musical settings; this was, in fact, the first time an American libretto was effectively and idiomatically set to an opera score. This, together with Thomson's folklike melodies, attractive hymn tunes, lovely choruses, colorful sets, and imaginative orchestration, won the appreciation of Broadway audiences accustomed to more frivolous entertainment.

Revived on Broadway in 1986, the show—on a Catholic theme, written by a Jew and a Protestant—seemed as fresh and bold as ever. Further, some reviewers recognized it as a direct antecedent of the nonnarrative, minimal music theater practiced now by Robert Wilson and Philip Glass (see pp. 356–358), David Byrne, Laurie Anderson, and John Adams.

George Gershwin's *Porgy and Bess*
The same year that *Four Saints* opened on Broadway, songwriter and symphonic jazz composer George Gershwin read a novel by DuBose Heyward based on the lives of real people who lived in a black tenement area in Charleston, South Carolina. Profoundly moved by the novel and by the play based on it, Gershwin decided to write an opera on the subject.

In preparation, this New Yorker spent a summer in the Charleston area, where he listened to people talk and sing. Then, having steeped himself in the sounds of the vegetable sellers' calls, the work songs of the men, the lullabies women sang to their babies, and the shouts and hymns performed at church on

Sundays, he returned to New York to write *Porgy and Bess*. The new opera opened on Broadway a year after Thomson's opera—also with an all-black cast.

Porgy begins with an instrumental piece, usually called an **overture** but simply called an introduction by Gershwin, who intended his show for a Broadway audience. Like a conventional opera overture, Gershwin's introduction sets the appropriate mood for the show and includes some of its important themes.

Porgy, a poor man so crippled that he gets around only by goat cart, falls deeply in love with Bess, a "loose-living woman" from New York who gives up her "big city ways" to live and love with him. Their story, tender and moving, has flashes of wit and humor and plenty of tense drama. A number of the songs (Gershwin also avoided the term *aria*) became so popular that, finally, Americans were humming opera tunes in the streets!

The love duet in which Porgy and Bess eloquently express their devotion to one another is one of the most beautiful in the opera literature of the world (see Figure 20.1 and Listening Example 67).

Gian-Carlo Menotti (b. 1911)

Gian-Carlo Menotti, another composer who has written operas well received by a Broadway audience, reversed the prevalent trend by coming from his native Italy to America to study music. A child prodigy who had written two operas by the time he was thirteen, Menotti arrived in 1928 at the Curtis Institute of Music in Philadelphia, Pennsylvania, where he became a close friend of another famous American composer, Samuel Barber (see pp. 391–393).

In 1947, Menotti wrote a two-act thriller, *The Medium*, which because of its modest resources—five singers, one dance-mime role, and an orchestra of only

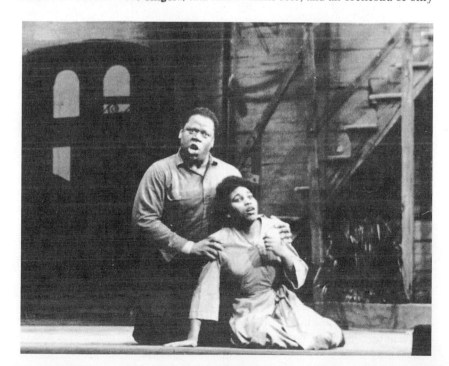

FIGURE 20.1

A scene from Gershwin's *Porgy and Bess.*

"Bess, You Is My Woman Now"
(from *Porgy and Bess*)

Composer
George Gershwin

Genre (Type of Piece)
Opera duet

CD 3
Track 6
5:13

Poignant falling figures in the strings introduce this beautiful duet, in which Porgy (*bass voice*) declares his love for Bess and insists that she must "laugh an' dance for two instead of one," because he is physically unable to get around. The strings double Porgy's passionate melody, enhancing the emotional impact of the music. The verse has five lines of text, yet seems superbly balanced.

Bess (*soprano*) responds with her fervent declaration of love for Porgy, declaring she will go nowhere without him. At first her melody is the same as Porgy's, but soon she soars to rapturous high notes, as if overwhelmed with love and joy.

Notice as they sing together that Bess generally carries the melody whereas Porgy's comments add contrapuntal interest and harmony. Also notice the orchestra's contributions, including melodic support, harmony, and independent "commentary." You will hear expressively inflected blue notes throughout, derived as we have seen from black performance practice and associated with blues, jazz, and many styles of black music.

fourteen players—may be called a **chamber opera.** (It is also quite brief, Menotti intending it to be performed with another miniature opera of his, *The Telephone*.) Broadway audiences found *The Medium*'s eerie mood, memorable melodies, and dramatic libretto, which Menotti wrote himself, moving and exciting indeed.

Menotti's next major work, *The Consul,* opened on Broadway in 1950, had a long, successful run, and won the Pulitzer prize and Drama Critics' Award. The story concerns the frustration and ultimate tragedy of a family desperately trying to escape from their country but confronted with bureaucratic nonsense in response to their urgent pleas for assistance. *The Consul,* written at the time of the cold war, specifies neither country nor time, allowing us to relate the drama's events to our own knowledge, experience, or imagination. The moving aria "To This We've Come," eloquently expressing the rage and despair of a woman prevented by bizarre circumstances from saving her doomed family, is an Optional Listening Example.

The next year (1951), the National Broadcasting Company (NBC) commissioned Menotti to write the first opera conceived especially for television. Menotti based the resulting work, *Amahl and the Night Visitors* (Figure 20.2), on a painting formerly, but no longer, attributed to Hieronymus Bosch and on

FIGURE 20.2
A scene from Menotti's *Amahl and the Night Visitors.*

his own childhood memories. Amahl, whose simple, naive story and lovely music consistently appeal to children and, as Menotti says, to "those who like children" as well, has been performed at Christmastime every year since, often on television, and also by amateurs in church and community settings.

Menotti has written symphonic and choral works as well as several other operas, but he is primarily a man of the theater, whose gift for melody and drama seems to have been best expressed in his early operas written for Broadway or television audiences.

The Trend toward Realism

Although traditionally operas have dealt with fiction, fantasy, myth, or ancient history, increasingly opera composers choose topics from recent history and even from everyday life. As early as 1937, Marc Blitzstein addressed the traumas of the Great Depression in a Broadway opera (sometimes called a musical play) about the struggle for labor rights: *The Cradle Will Rock,* in which much of the music was popular in style and the words reflected the ethnic speech of city streets. A movie, *Cradle Will Rock* (2000), dramatized the formation of the pro-union musical, the attempts to shut it down, and the fascinating manner in which the show finally was performed. Douglas S. Moore wrote about American pioneer life in *The Devil and Daniel Webster* (1939); and in 1958, he set another opera, *The Ballad of Baby Doe,* in the nineteenth century and included some of the musical styles popular then. Aaron Copland's *The Tender Land,* about a midwestern American farm family, also appeared during the 1950s.

FIGURE 20.3

A scene from John Adams's *Nixon in China*.

An opera by Ulysses Kay, *Between Liberty and Oppression* (1991), concerns the life of Frederick Douglass, a hero in African American history.

Beginning in the 1980s, operas based on recent or even current social and political events began to appear, sometimes raising controversy among still-living participants in the events. Philip Glass's *Satyagraha* (1980) tells of the early struggles of Mahatma Gandhi; *X: The Life and Times of Malcolm X* by Anthony Davis (1986), concerns that black nationalist leader; John Adams's first opera, *Nixon in China* (1987), describes President Nixon's visits to and negotiations with that country (Figure 20.3); in 1990, an opera called *Manson Family,* about the Californian mass murderer Charles Manson, was written by John Moran; and in 1991, John Adams presented a new opera, *The Death of Klinghoffer,* which describes the highjacking of the ship *Achille Lauro* in 1985 and the murder of a wheelchair-bound Jewish American passenger. Still another genre, science-fiction opera, has recently been approached by some composers.

Novels sometimes stimulate the creation of operas as well. To mention a few examples, composer John Harbison's *The Great Gatsby,* based on the novel by F. Scott Fitzgerald, achieved some success at the Metropolitan Opera in 1999 and continues to be performed occasionally around the country. *Dead Man Walking* (2000), with music by Jake Heggie and a libretto by the playwright Terrence McNally, is based on Sister Helen Prejean's book of the same name, which also inspired a movie in 1995. **Carlisle Floyd** (b. 1926) one of the foremost opera composers and librettists in the United States today, interpreted John Steinbeck's great American tragedy *Of Mice and Men* (1970) and adapted the comic opera *Cold Sassy Tree* (2000) from Olive Anne Burns's novel of the same name.

Philip Glass, in collaboration with the playwright-director Robert Wilson, wrote a five-hour plotless opera, *Einstein on the Beach* (1976), based on a historical individual but highly unusual in its organization as well as its music: Three visual themes (Train, Trial, and Field), each with its corresponding music, are associated with Albert Einstein's thoughts and experiences. The visual themes, having three scenes each, are presented in four acts, sandwiched between five short connecting pieces called "Knee Plays" that allow time for changing sets and scenery. (Listening Example 68 is the last scene before the last Knee Play of the opera.) Though there is no intermission, audience

Einstein on the Beach: Act IV, Scene 3, "Spaceship"

Composer
Philip Glass (in collaboration with Robert Wilson)

CD 3
Track 7
3:56

Timbres
In this scene, the Philip Glass Ensemble plays flute, electronic organ, bass clarinet, alto saxophone, keyboards, and a violin (representing Albert Einstein). There is also a female solo voice, as well as a small chorus.

Tempo
Varies; often incredibly rapid.

Text
There is no libretto as such: rather, the singers pronounce solfège syllables (do, re, mi, etc.), representing the melody; and numbers, representing the rhythmic structure of the music. Thus the text describes the music itself. You will hear the female chorus sing "mi, fa, mi, re," for example, and the men's chorus count (very rapidly), "One-two-three-four, one-two-three, one-two-three-four," etc.

The opera is a true collaboration between Glass and the great American dramatist Robert Wilson, who shares Glass's concern for apparent motionlessness and seemingly endless durations during which significant things happen or are understood. The title, which refers to Nevil Shute's novel of nuclear holocaust, On the Beach, suggests that Einstein perhaps pondered the possible consequences of his own scientific discoveries. Beginning with a nineteenth-century train (a reference to toy trains Einstein played with as a child), the opera ends inside a twentieth-century spaceship—perhaps the symbol of potential liberation from worldly disaster.

Throughout the work, harmonic and rhythmic structures are linked, integrating rhythm, harmony, and melody in a complex fashion that yet sounds simple and repetitive. Audiences having no idea of the complexities of Glass's conception have found the opera enchanting, almost hypnotic in its deceptively naive appeal. Rigorously intellectual in concept, the music achieves a calm, dreamlike, mystical effect. The electronic organ and the choral voices might even suggest a religious atmosphere, though this is never implied by Philip Glass.

members can come and go at will, as the music gradually unfolds lengthy repetitions and evolutions of small motives.

Opera or Musical: Which Is It?

Today many Broadway and London musicals are sung throughout, and operas by Philip Glass and John Adams, for example, often seem closer to Broadway productions than to opera in the traditional sense. How, then, to distinguish between these forms of musical theater? With difficulty, if at all! There are opera singers who sing musicals and musical theater performers who sing opera. The old definitions of a *musical* as a play with occasional music, an *opera* as a musical drama with no spoken drama, and an *operetta* as something between the two extremes are largely meaningless. Audiences both on Broadway and in the opera house have come to enjoy grand entertainment on a lavish scale and of unprecedented variety and scope.

Still, some suggest that a significant difference between operas and musicals lies not so much in the music, which has increasingly overlapped, but in the words. Whether one understands the language in which an opera is written or not, it is often difficult to understand the words as they are sung. Although many opera composers are famous for their music, the names of few opera librettists come readily to mind, and those who do are remembered more for their story than for the particular turns of phrase with which they delivered it. Broadway lyrics, on the other hand, full of puns and intricate rhymes, must be clearly understood to be appreciated and in fact assume a full share of importance together with the music. Great lyricists such as Lorenz Hart, Ira Gershwin, and Oscar Hammerstein II retain their reputations, and we admire the songs of Cole Porter and Stephen Sondheim as much for their words (written by the composers) as for their music.

Others propose the role of the orchestra as defining the critical difference between the two genres; that is, in opera the orchestra often plays a central role in the telling of the story, while in musicals the orchestra generally plays a supportive role. Advocates of this theory suggest that musicals in which the orchestra takes a more central and dramatic role, as in *West Side Story,* move toward opera, whereas the supportive role of Stephen Sondheim's orchestra relegates his works—for all their emotional power and dramatic subtleties—to the world of musicals. The fact that most opera composers orchestrate their works and most composers of musicals do not lends credence to this possible distinction. On the other hand, the orchestrator Jonathan Tunick refers to Stephen Sondheim's *Sweeney Todd* as neither opera nor musical but a successful American musical drama.

Stephen Sondheim himself suggests that the difference between Broadway and opera is in the expectations of the audience, going so far as to say that in his opinion, when Menotti's *The Medium* and *The Telephone* were performed on Broadway they were "sung-through" shows, and when they were performed in opera houses—for opera audiences—they were operas. In other words, for him the object changes in terms of how it is viewed.

Beverly Sills, who retired from singing opera to become chair of Lincoln Center for the Performing Arts, distinguishes between the vocal requirements for singing opera and singing musicals. Broadway theaters are usually about a third the size of an opera house, and even in the smaller theaters Broadway singers often rely on amplification, whereas opera singers are taught to project their voices, at soft or loud levels, for impressive distances over sustained periods of time.

Still another difference between the genres was recently voiced by an editor of musical scores, who described a musical as something made up by many people—designers, producers, directors, actors, orchestrators, choreographers, dancers, and maybe more, besides the composer and lyricist, all having creative input—whereas an opera normally is the product of one controlling consciousness.

American Opera Today

Although tightened budgets have put serious constraints upon the world of opera, whose complex presentations are exceedingly expensive to produce, Americans today are interested in all varieties of opera, old and new, domestic and foreign, funny and sad, short and long, simple and complex. Many American cities have an opera house and their own resident opera company, and virtually all Americans have access to live or taped performances on radio or television. Foreign operas often are performed in English translation, or, alternatively, English surtitles are projected above the stage to avoid interfering with the visual presentation. The American audience seems finally to have recognized opera as the marvelous form of entertainment it was always intended to be.

In 2004, however, a latent but smoldering issue came to the fore, when a famous and beloved American soprano, Deborah Voigt, was forced out of a production in London because the director deemed her too heavy to be suitable for the role she was to play. While vocal beauty has always mattered in opera, physical beauty is commanding ever more significance, as audiences require opera stars to look as well as sound their part. Opera singers, whose voices are never amplified, and who require extraordinary physical stamina to project their voices (even when singing pianissimo) to the back and the top of a theater, sometimes look as oversized as the melodramatic roles they portray; yet audiences increasingly require them to appear, as well as sound, beautiful. We will probably hear more of this debate concerning the significance of vocal versus physical beauty in the immediate future.

Terms to Review

opera   A drama that is sung, usually with orchestral accompaniment.

recitative   A declamatory setting of a text, used in opera and other dramatic vocal works, with rhythms and inflections related to those of speech.

aria   A songlike setting of a text, musically expressive, accompanied by the orchestra.

da capo   "From the beginning." An aria with a three-part design: the composer writes the first section and a contrasting middle section; the performer repeats the first section, adding embellishments.

chorus   A large vocal ensemble, with several voices on each part.

Treemonisha   An opera by Scott Joplin.

libretto   The words of an opera or another dramatic vocal work.

overture   In musical theater, an introductory instrumental piece that sets the mood and that may include melodic themes from the opera or show to follow.

chamber opera   An opera for a small number of performers and limited resources.

Key Figures

Mary Carr Moore
Virgil Thomson

Gertrude Stein
Gian-Carlo Menotti

Carlisle Floyd
Philip Glass

Optional Listening Examples

Gian-Carlo Menotti: "To This We've Come" from *The Consul*

Scott Joplin: "A Real Slow Drag" from *Treemonisha*

Suggestions for Further Listening

George Gershwin: Overture, "Summertime," "I Got Plenty o' Nothin'," and "It Ain't Necessarily So" from *Porgy and Bess*

Gian-Carlo Menotti: *Amahl and the Night Visitors*

Critical Thinking

Why do you think Americans have been slow to develop enthusiasm for opera? And why do you think operas (American and other) are increasingly popular here now?

Why do you think movies and television commercials often use famous opera themes to heighten emotion or to sell products? Do you think repeated hearing of an excerpt from opera in a radio or television commercial increases the popularity of the music or detracts from its appreciation?

Do you believe it is possible to "suspend disbelief" and forget that opera singers are singing rather than speaking their lines? Is this suspension of disbelief more likely to occur while you are viewing an opera or a musical (movie or live)? Why?

Where do you think opera directors should place their primary emphasis, when hiring singers: on acting? stage presence? singing? physical appearance? other?

Go to www.mhhe.com/ferrisaml5 for a list of additional Web-based resources that relate to the content in this chapter.

PART 5
Summary

After the Civil War, musical theater became increasingly popular in America, as the minstrel show waned in popularity but vaudeville and burlesque flourished. Revues, more elegant and sophisticated than the other variety shows, continue as a popular form of entertainment today.

European operettas, which have an integrated plot, soon stimulated composers to write operettas for an American audience. Gilbert and Sullivan's operettas provided hilarious entertainment; but most influential upon the American music stage was the Viennese operetta, with its romantic stories and make-believe settings.

Early musical comedies combined elements of operetta and variety shows. By writing several shows that had a story but included the song, dance, and comedy routines of vaudeville, George M. Cohan was most influential in accustoming the Broadway audience to the new style. Jerome Kern's *Show Boat* proved that a Broadway musical could be based on a literary work and could address serious subjects effectively. *Oklahoma!* by Rodgers and Hammerstein successfully integrated all the entertainment scenes with the drama. Each of these shows had a profound effect upon the development of the Broadway musical.

The 1920s and 1930s are considered the Golden Age of the Broadway musical because so many outstanding shows were produced. Since then, musical theater has become more complex and more sophisticated. Composers have revealed their heightened sense of singing (Frank Loesser's *Most Happy Fella*), the integrity of the play (Lerner and Loewe), and the importance of dance (Leonard Bernstein), and Bernstein and Stephen Sondheim are among several composers who have applied their classical and popular interests in various ways to the musical stage. Many of today's musicals are multimedia affairs combining technologically complex aural and visual effects.

From the earliest days of commercial films, live music introduced and accompanied a movie; and with the advent of sound films, the film score emerged as a new form of dramatic music. Film music, whether heard by the characters in the film (source or diegetic music) or by the viewing audience alone (functional or nondiegetic music), underpins the movie's emotional effects while serving innumerable practical functions as well.

Classical music, pop, jazz, rock, electronic music, and even opera effectively support feature films, setting a mood, establishing a time period, enhancing characterization, and bridging awkward gaps between scenes. Composers vary widely in their techniques of writing film scores, and all face the inevitability of having their music drastically altered by the director, various editors, and sound engineers. Some, however, compose orchestral suites from portions of their scores, allowing their music to be heard as they conceived it by a concert audience or on a recording.

Opera, too, is newly, but immensely, popular in America today. An opera is a grand combination of literary, visual, and musical arts. Although some composers include spoken words in their operas, traditionally opera dialogue was sung in recitative and emotional reactions were expressed in solo arias, duets, and large or small ensembles.

In the 1920s, several American operas were enthusiastically received. Both Virgil Thomson's *Four Saints in Three Acts* and George Gershwin's *Porgy and Bess* succeeded on Broadway, as did Gian-Carlo Menotti's operas nearly three decades later. Thomson sought an elegant simplicity in music, Gershwin spoke in the spirit of jazz, and Menotti represents the Italian tradition of lyrical melodies and good theater. Today's mainstream and progressive composers are producing a wealth of new American operas, and this form of entertainment is increasingly visible on Broadway, in the opera house, and on television and movie screens.

PART 6

Tradition and Innovation in Concert Music

Music for the Concert Hall: Historical and Cultural Perspective

The twentieth century witnessed an unprecedented diversity of concert music styles, as new historical and cultural awareness broadened concepts of timbre, pitch, melody, harmony, and rhythm. The political and social turmoil of much of that century, and the many important new technological resources, all had strong cultural repercussions, as artists in every medium found their way along traditional paths or forged entirely new avenues of expression.

During the 1920s, several talented young Americans set out to make their living as composers of concert music, never before considered a viable profession in this country. Whereas earlier American composers had largely depended on income-producing careers as teachers or performing musicians, these young people intended to survive as successful professional composers. They meant to write music not radically different from the masterpieces of the European musical heritage, yet sounding distinctively American and of the twentieth century. We may consider that they took an *evolutionary* approach to furthering the history of music.

Other twentieth-century Americans took a *revolutionary* approach to the composition of music. With the energy, curiosity, and independence characteristic of the pioneering spirit, a number of Americans explored musical sound as never before, so extending the boundaries of the definition of the art as to constitute a veritable revolution in the concept of music.

Interaction between the Arts

Throughout the twentieth century, visual and literary artists continued close interaction, sharing an expanded perception of their own disciplines and an interest in the interrelationships among them all. This close association among the arts—often enhanced by new technology—persists today, resulting sometimes in a kind of collision of artists exulting in their own independence and in the collage-like results of the interdependence they share. Some compare this congenial friction, if we can call it that, to the modern urban experience, in which widely disparate elements form a complex, somewhat fragmented whole.

The theater, requiring the services of painters, set designers, writers, musicians, dancers, choreographers, and actors, has always represented a collaborative form of art, and, as we have seen, nineteenth-century artists formed other, less traditional, liaisons as well. But today the visual, literary, and various performance arts influence and interact with music even more than in the past.

Dance, liberated from the expectation that it will tell a story, may or may not be accompanied by or set to music today; but although some dances are entirely independent of music or sound, most choreographers still consider music an inherent and vital dimension of dance. Jazz rhythms and electronically produced sounds as well as other popular and classical music dramatically widen the range of the dance experience.

Literature, too, is affected by the new intimacy among the arts. Several twentieth-century writers chose words for their sounds, rather than their meanings. For example, neither Gertrude Stein's libretto for Virgil Thomson's *Four Saints in Three Acts* (p. 352) nor the stream-of-consciousness prose of William Faulkner, attempts to follow the rules of grammar or syntax. Further, poetry may have visual as well as intellectual values, as when *shaped poems* are placed on a page in a manner conceived to visually enhance the meaning of the words. Each of these literary concepts (or conceits) can be related to a painter's subjective choice of colors, regardless of their relation to real visual experience, and to a composer's choice of pitches for their timbre rather than for functional value.

Multimedia Performances.

The unprecedented degree of collaboration recently occurring among painters, dancers, poets, playwrights, and musicians has produced a wealth of interdisciplinary performances, awakening a healthy appreciation for the arts among audiences whose previous interest in and exposure to art were minimal. Some performances constitute "happenings" combining live or taped music with film, slides, speech, and lighting as well as dance, gestures, or movement of some kind, sometimes with audience participation. Painters and sculptors have combined shapes, colors, and sounds in large "environmental" works.

Because music for tape often requires visual or dramatic interest to sustain an audience's attention in the absence of live performers, some recent compositions involve a combination of live and taped music. Complex multimedia compositions simultaneously address two or more of the senses, and invite spectators to actively participate in their performance.

Relationships between the Visual Arts and Music.

Shared interests and philosophies of art are not only revealed in such collaborative efforts but also individually expressed in each medium of art. Much in the way that *pointillist* painters treat spots of pure color as entities in themselves, for example, composers sometimes treat particular tones or timbres as isolated phenomena with independent, as opposed to interdependent, values. In the machines, advertisements, and commercial objects painted by

Andy Warhol and other pop artists, we see the simplicity and repetition characteristic of musical *minimalism* (pp. 412–414), generally considered a part of the art or concert music experience, but of strong appeal to listeners more accustomed to popular than to so-called "serious" music. Visual artists often depict musical instruments or, more subjectively, the *experience* of listening to music.

Since the early twentieth century, texture has been a source of interest and experimentation throughout the arts. Painters such as Romare Bearden (pp. 143–144) often add a third dimension to their work by affixing pieces of fabric or other foreign objects to their surfaces. Other painters build up their surfaces by applying multiple thick layers of paint. Similarly, composers may vary musical texture by superimposing unrelated timbres or chords, or by combining complex layers of sound. Considering timbre, composers today find sounds of nature, of machinery, and of computer-generated effects to offer a virtually unlimited palette of musical sound, much as sculptors may replace traditional materials like marble and bronze with plastic or with various found materials.

The Value of Chance

Artists have long recognized the value of the unintended and the unexpected in the creative process. An ancient Roman treatise tells of an artist throwing a sponge at his canvas in a fit of rage and being delighted with the "effect of nature" resulting in his picture, and a ninth-century Chinese work describes an artist "who excelled in splattering ink to paint landscapes." Even Leonardo da Vinci advised aspiring landscape painters to visualize landscapes when looking at a wall spotted with stains.

During the 1950s and 1960s, the concept of leaving significant details of their work to chance attracted many visual artists and musicians. *Op art,* like the chance music we shall consider in this part of the text, involves active rather than passive participation, as op artists combine lines and colors to create optical illusions that "activate" the eye instead of "acting upon it" in the traditional way. Jackson Pollock (1912–1956) led the Abstract Expressionist

The Virtuoso, by David Adickes, 1983, 36 feet tall. This whimsical sculpture, which stands in front of an office building in downtown Houston, is one of the countless works of art inspired by musical instruments.

painters, who developed various means to achieve random effects: Pollock, for example, dripped or sprayed paint onto a large surface, carefully choosing the colors, direction, and density of his paints but allowing chance, or serendipity, to determine the result of his work. Like many artists intrigued with chance, Pollock considered the act of creating art a spiritual experience, more significant than the result. He did not create his work to be hung on museum walls but considered it to be as ephemeral—perhaps even as spiritual—as Navajo sand paintings.

Sculptors attracted to the idea of (literally) moving art experimented with motors, bands, and pulleys,

Jackson Pollock, *Number 1*, 1948, oil on canvas. Pollock's abstract expressionist paintings, expressive of the energy and rapid tempo of American life in the 1940s, involve imaginative interaction between chance and the artist's creative intent.

Untitled, a mobile by the American sculptor Alexander Calder, 1976. Aluminum and steel.

whereas Alexander Calder (1898–1976), finding such mobiles too predictable, created small, delicate sculptures to hang in space, subject to the whim of the lightest breeze. Just as one performance of chance music is never like another, Calder's small mobiles never appear exactly the same from one moment to the next.

Chance occurs in literature, too, when novels written in *hypertext* allow readers to choose on their computers which subplots they wish to follow, as through a maze, rendering a book's form and even its conclusion indeterminate.

American Concert Music

We cannot identify, either in Europe or in America, a unifying Western musical language such as prevailed in the several preceding centuries. Rather, the century we were born into gave us a rich multiplicity of musical tongues, which became ever more diverse as composers mixed the great Western tradition with the sounds of other cultures and other times. Experimental, often deliberately provocative music interested some twentieth-century American composers; others chose to follow more traditional paths.

In the first decade of a new century, we can scarcely imagine what musical riches lie in store. Considering how significantly the music of each preceding era differed from the predominant styles it succeeded, we may expect the music of the twenty-first century to chart numerous new and adventurous courses. ♪

Experimental Music: Revolution

21

Three musical pioneers initated the **experimental** movement in America, one a Connecticut Yankee who explored the manifold characteristics of sound, the second a Californian who discovered new ways to use the piano, and the third a European, Edgard Varèse, who dreamed of new instruments that would create *new* sounds and lived to see his dream come true.

Charles Ives (1874–1954)

Charles Ives (Figure 21.1) derived his musical inventiveness from his father, George, an amateur musician who taught his son to play several instruments and (more significantly) to be ever curious about music and musical sound. George Ives continually conducted sound experiments in the family barn, to the annoyance of his neighbors and the fascination of his son.

FIGURE 21.1

Charles Ives.

His father also taught Charles Ives to value each piece of music for its own sake, and all his life the younger Ives valued Stephen Foster's music as highly as Bach's and a good rag as much as a good symphony, viewing each piece according to its own particular merits and considering differentiation among genres of music in terms of quality a form of musical snobbery.

Ives studied music at Yale under Horatio Parker (see p. 133), whom he respected for his accomplishments but considered dogmatic and incapable of pursuing or appreciating new ideas. Convinced by his college experience that his broad musical concepts exceeded those of his contemporaries, and declaring that he did not intend to let his family starve on his dissonances, Ives devoted his professional life to his own highly successful insurance business. (He is remembered in that industry as the father of estate planning and the author of a training manual, *The Amount to Carry,* still in use in the 1980s.) This left him free to write music only at night, on weekends, and during vacations.

Philosophy of Music

An inveterate romantic, Ives had strong literary interests and expressed himself effectively in words as well as in music. He valued the substance, or character, of a piece over its manner, as he referred to music's superficial beauty, which to Ives was "like a drug that allows the ears to lie back in an easy chair." Ives believed that music should be strong and challenging, never "nice"—he equated "niceness" with being weak or superficially polite, while he found dissonant sounds "clean and virile" and labeled people who feared them musical cowards.

Instrumental Compositions

Most of Ives's instrumental compositions are program pieces, many reflecting the New England environment he knew and loved. He dedicated his famous *Concord Sonata* to the transcendentalists, whom he admired and whose ideas he shared; each of the four movements of this substantial piano composition describes the ideas and character of one or more members of the famous group (Ralph Waldo Emerson, Nathaniel Hawthorne, Amos Bronson Alcott, Louisa May Alcott, and Henry David Thoreau). Ives prefaced this work with *Four Essays Before a Sonata,* explaining there in words the ideas expressed in the musical composition.

One of Ives's best-known programmatic pieces, "General Putnam's Camp" from *Three Places in New England* (Listening Example 69), depicts a small boy's fantasies as he enjoys a Fourth of July picnic held at a former Revolutionary War campsite. This brash and exuberant piece includes snatches of patriotic tunes that Ives altered in the most imaginative and sometimes amusing ways, a technique characteristic of much of his music. Whereas composers often quote familiar melodies in their own original compositions, Ives had a peculiar manner of distorting tunes and also combining them in layers of sound intriguing and sometimes puzzling to the listener's ear.

Songs

Ives also wrote about 150 songs, covering many subjects, with settings that range from simple to complex. He frequently based his songs, like his instrumental pieces, on familiar tunes, quoting fragments, phrases, or complete melodies from American hymns, rags, marches, patriotic songs, Stephen

"General Putnam's Camp"
(from *Three Places in New England*)

Composer
Charles Ives

CD 3
Track 8
5:38

Genre
Program music

Form
A loose **A B A'**

Texture

Basically polyphonic. The texture is so dense that repeated hearings generally reveal tunes and fragments previously unnoticed or unrecognized. This is *linear polyphony*, in which each melodic line should be heard independently and the resulting combination of tones, which may be quite dissonant, is not considered to produce chordal harmony.

This programmatic work depicts a small boy's fantasies and dreams as he enjoys a Fourth of July picnic at a former Revolutionary War campground.

The movement opens with a raucous blast (a sound dear to Ives's ears) and continues with a wonderfully virile and highly unorthodox march theme (**A**). Snatches of John Philip Sousa's marches and patriotic American tunes emerge from the subsequent confusion, as does a parodic quotation of "Yankee Doodle."

The boy wanders off and falls asleep, to dream of the hardship and suffering of the soldiers from long ago (**B**). He imagines that he hears the American General Putnam coming over the hill to save the troops. There is an amazing juxtaposition of two bands (one for strings and woodwinds, the other for piano, drums, and trumpet) that approach and pass each other—as they might in a parade—playing different tunes, in different keys and in different meters. (Here the conductor must mark four beats to the measure at one tempo with one hand and three beats to the measure at a different tempo with the other.)

The boy awakens, hears sounds of celebration, and rejoins his friends at the picnic (**A'**). With a jaunty reference to "The Star Spangled Banner," the piece ends on as raucous a note as it began.

Foster's melodies, and the music of Bach and other composers, altering and juxtaposing them into complex layers of sound.

More simply, "At the River" (Listening Example 70) turns a well-known tune into a new composition with its own Ivesian sound.

"At the River"

Composer
Charles Ives

CD 3
Track 9
1:19

Form
Verse-chorus

Tune and Text
Robert Lowry

Accompaniment
The piano introduction sets a tentative, questioning mood. The piano then accompanies the familiar hymn tune with richly dissonant chords, adding competing melodic interest toward the end of the verse. A brief piano interlude occurs between verse and chorus.

Rhythm
Although the listener clearly feels the *quadruple meter* (four beats to the bar), the rhythm is quite free and flexible, contributing to the "questioning" quality of the piece.

Basically retaining the original tune, Ives alters the end of the verse and the chorus with odd turns of phrase that, together with the imaginative harmonies, enhance the tentative mood of this simple and moving song.

Other Characteristics of Ives's Music

Consistently delighted by the irregular and unconventional, Ives experimented with unusual tunings of musical instruments, sometimes deliberately achieving the intriguing effect of instruments being played slightly out of tune. Although generally respecting the concept of tonality, he considered allegiance to one key at a time confining and occasionally indulged in **bitonality** (two keys at once) and **polytonality** (multiple simultaneous keys). His use of all twelve tones of the chromatic scale in some pieces foreshadowed by some years the *atonal* music of other composers.

Ives also conceived extremely complex rhythmic relationships, frequently combining two or more rhythmic patterns into simultaneous **polyrhythms.** Recognizing the continuum of pitches lying between the half steps of a keyboard instrument, he availed himself of quarter tones and **microtones** in some of his music.

The qualities of sound were a further source of endless fascination for Ives, who made space and the manner in which sound traveled through it a significant element in some of his compositions. He also valued a degree of spontaneity in performance, anticipating what later became known as "chance music." Both timbre and chance play more than the usual role in *The Unanswered Question* (Optional Listening Example), a rather mystic, programmatic piece in which a solo trumpet poses "The Perennial Question of

Existence." A group of woodwinds, positioned at a distance from the trumpet, attempts to find "The Invisible Answer," while a string ensemble, located offstage, plays slow, quiet, mysterious music, oblivious of the squabble taking place onstage. Six times the trumpet poses "The Question" and rejects the woodwinds' increasingly agitated replies. Finally, "The Question" is heard once more, to remain unanswered.

In his prefatory instructions for performing this piece, Ives indicated that "The Question" may be posed by any instrument that can play the trumpet's pitches, and the woodwinds may either be all flutes or a combination of instruments from the woodwind family. He also suggested that "The Answers" need not begin at the points where he notated them in the score but could as well come a bit early or late. Thus, space (instruments widely separated from each other) and chance play a small but significant role in this fascinating piece, which has earned a distinguished place in the American repertoire. The Moody Blues ended their album *Knights in White Satin* ("... we decide which is right,/And which is an illusion???") with a brief quotation of "The Question." The moving sounds of *The Unanswered Question* have been heard in many media and contexts; for example, the piece was played with haunting significance at President John Kennedy's memorial service, and it is heard to poignant effect on the music track of *The Thin Red Line* (1999), a war film that hovers between layers of consciousness and leaves many disturbing questions unsolved.

May 5, 1947.

Charles Ives
"Music—that no one knows what it is—and the less he knows he knows what it is the nearer it is to music—probably."

Ives's Place in History   Ill health prevented Ives from continuing his musical explorations after the 1920s, but it was twenty years after that before his music came to public attention and to high if belated recognition. His Third Symphony, written about 1904 but first performed in 1947, won a Pulitzer Prize; and other pieces by Ives have since received similarly prestigious awards. Although many of his innovations have become part of today's normal music experience, the spark of his invention, the verve, the very nerve of his style remain fresh and invigorating today.

Henry Cowell (1897–1965)

By the time of the birth of **Henry Cowell** (Figure 21.2), the American frontier had been pushed all the way to the West Coast, where Cowell was born, in San Francisco, into an eclectic environment whose varied influences are reflected in his highly original compositions. Cowell based some programmatic pieces upon Irish folklore absorbed from his own Irish American family; and childhood friends introduced him to Chinese music, beginning a lifelong interest in the music of East Asia. Further musical experience was afforded by an organist friend who allowed the budding young composer to attend his practice sessions, where Cowell absorbed the modal sounds of Roman Catholic church music. Cowell also was attracted to early American hymn and fuging tunes, using some of them as inspiration for an attractive set of instrumental pieces.

Early Compositions   Having decided by the time he was eight years old to become a composer, Cowell taught himself to play the piano his own way,

FIGURE 21.2
Henry Cowell.

creating sounds he found interesting and eventually using those sounds for imaginative programmatic purposes in his highly original compositions. For example, while still in his teens Cowell wrote a piano piece, "The Tides of Mananaun" (Optional Listening Example), in which the performer uses the flat of the hand or forearm to play large *clusters* of keys in the lower range of the piano, evoking the sounds of the rolling, roaring ocean tides. The extremely dissonant result effectively suggests the deep, unstable, ever-changing sounds he wished to achieve.

Cowell, who believed simply that dissonant combinations evoke strong emotions whereas consonance suggests simplicity, was astonished to learn later that some people tend to hear dissonance and consonance as "bad" or "good" sounds. He and others came to recognize dissonant **tone clusters** as a new kind of chord, built upon seconds rather than the thirds of conventional tonal harmony. Although they later became friends, Cowell and Ives did not know each other's music at the time they both began using clusters, and it was only later that both men discovered they had "invented" the same idea at about the same time.

Piano Experiments Although Cowell wrote many kinds of music, the piano particularly interested him, probably because it was the most readily accessible musical instrument. Desiring to extend the range of sounds the piano could produce, for programmatic reasons or to achieve non-Western effects, he discovered he could do this by playing directly on the strings of the piano as on any other string instrument.

Cowell wrote several pieces in which the piano strings are to be stroked, strummed, plucked, or struck, each technique producing an entirely different effect. He achieved even further variety of sounds by having the pianist either depress some of the keys while manipulating the strings, or mute (stop) the strings with one hand while playing on the keyboard with the other. The techniques he applied to manipulating the piano strings in "The Banshee" (Listening Example 71) and other pieces are very similar to those indicated in the tablature notation used by Chinese and Japanese players of various string

"The Banshee" (excerpt)

Composer
Henry Cowell

CD 3
Track 10
1:41

Program
According to Irish (and Scottish) folklore, a banshee is a fairy-woman who foretells death by materializing nearby one doomed to die and wailing her long, howling cry.

Techniques
To achieve just this effect, "The Banshee" requires two performers: one is seated at the piano depressing the damper pedal, and the other stands in the crook of the piano and manipulates the strings. Cowell specified the following techniques, indicating in prefatory notes how they could be read in the score:

1. Sweeping the strings from the lowest note to a specified note with the flesh of the finger.

2. Sweeping the strings up and back.

3. Sweeping the length of one string with the flesh of a finger.

4. Plucking the strings.

5. Sweeping the strings with the back of a fingernail.

6. Sweeping the strings with the flat of the hand.

instruments and flutes, indicating what their fingers should do in order to produce the required notes, rather than the notes themselves (Figure 21.3). These and other piano experiments proved particularly fruitful for other composers, suggesting the possibility of also producing effective new sounds by playing other traditional instruments in nontraditional ways.

Sources of Inspiration

Cowell was among the first Americans to be fascinated with the music of central and eastern Asia and to be gifted in reflecting the sounds of Persia, Japan, and even Iceland in music that bore the distinction of his own style. The music of the East encouraged Cowell to explore elements he felt had been neglected by Western composers; that is, whereas they had concentrated primarily on melody and harmony, Cowell and soon many other American and European composers found that timbre and rhythm offered them many new and stimulating ideas.

Cowell divided rhythms by five, seven, or other numbers as well as by the conventional two, three, or four; and like Ives, he invented complex polyrhythms, difficult to notate and to perform. Cowell even devised a new rhythmic notation in order to write down his sophisticated concepts. In collaboration with Léon Thérémin (inventor of an early electronic instrument that

3. The Banshee

FIGURE 21.3

For "The Banshee," Cowell modified traditional music notation by the addition of circled letters, each identifying a specific technique for manipulating the piano strings.

The Banshee
Explanation of Symbols

FIGURE 21.3
(Concluded)

"The Banshee" is played on the open strings of the piano, the player standing at the crook. Another person must sit at the keyboard and hold down the damper pedal throughout the composition. The whole work should be played an octave lower than written.

R. H. stands for "right hand." L. H. stands for "left hand." Different ways of playing the strings are indicated by a letter over each tone, as follows:

(A)   indicates a sweep with the flesh of the finger from the lowest string up to the note given.

(B)   sweep lengthwise along the string of the note given with flesh of finger.

(C)   sweep up and back from lowest A to highest B-flat given in this composition.

(D)   pluck string with flesh of finger, where written, instead of octave lower.

(E)   sweep along three notes together, in the same manner as (B).

(F)   sweep in the manner of (B) but with the back of fingernail instead of flesh.

(G)   when the finger is halfway along the string in the manner of (F), start a sweep along the same string with the flesh of the other finger, thus partly damping the sound.

(H)   sweep back and forth in the manner of (C), but start at the same time from both above and below, crossing the sweep in the middle.

(I)   sweep along five notes, in the manner of (B).

(J)   same as (I) but with back of fingernails instead of flesh of finger.

(K)   sweep along in manner of (J) with nails of both hands together, taking in all notes between the two outer limits given.

(L)   sweep in manner of (C) with flat of hand instead of single finger.

bears his name, see p. 341), Cowell developed a machine called the *rhythmicon,* which made it possible to reproduce rhythms of a complexity beyond the capacity of human performance. Of course the rhythmicon has since been replaced by computers and electronic instruments, but in its time it allowed composers greatly to extend their rhythmic creativity.

Writings Like Ives, Cowell wrote about his ideas and ideals, beginning with a book called *New Musical Resources* while still a college student. Deploring the way conventional publishers ignored American experimentalists, he founded a quarterly journal, *New Music,* in which he published provocative works (and to which Ives apparently gave anonymous financial support). The term **New Music,** in fact, came to mean music of an advanced or experimental nature. Cowell also edited a collection of essays by important contemporary composers, and he and his wife Sidney Cowell collaborated on a book about Charles Ives, with whom they became friends. Cowell was among the first to bring Ives's music to public attention.

Writer, teacher, lecturer, editor, inventor, theorist, and composer, Henry Cowell contributed immeasurably to the cause of experimentalism and opened many doors to the future of American music. He traveled extensively, seeking instruction from others and also sharing his own ideas. He played his compositions to appreciative audiences in Europe and was the first American to give concerts in what was then the Soviet Union (1928), thus arousing interest abroad in the new experimental American music.

Concrete Music

During the 1940s, a number of composers of different nationalities working in Paris experimented with recorded musical and nonmusical sounds, which they manipulated to form a new kind of music called **musique concrète,** or, in English, **concrete music.** Having altered the sounds electronically—a process made all the more versatile with the invention of magnetic tape after World War II—they used the products of their manipulations to create musical compositions, rendering the music *concrete* in the sense that it could not be performed or interpreted but existed only on tape.

Five processes are involved in the composition of concrete music:

1. *Selecting* the sounds to be taped. The sounds may include those of traditional instruments, such as piano or voice; sounds of nature, such as raindrops or birdcalls; or sounds of machinery, including a vacuum cleaner or jet plane. Any sound, in fact, may provide the raw material with which the composer works.
2. *Recording* the sounds. In order to alter the sounds and produce a work of art, the composer must have them on tape.
3. *Manipulating* the sounds. Sounds played backward, or faster or slower than normal, may become unrecognizable. Composers use these and other techniques to manipulate sounds as they please.
4. *Mixing* the sounds. This is the step in which the composer combines the sounds he or she has created, much as the traditional composer orchestrates a piece.
5. "Cutting and pasting" the tape—a process called *montage*—to achieve the form of the completed composition.

John Cage (1912–1992)

A true soul mate of Charles Ives's, **John Cage** (Figure 21.4) explored endlessly creative means of varying timbres and, in fact, the very concept of musical sound. For a time, Cage studied with an influential Viennese composer, Arnold Schoenberg, who lived and taught in the United States after World War II. Schoenberg devised a means of arranging all twelve tones of the scale into a series, or *row,* giving each tone equal significance and thus negating the concept of tonal relationships. Cage sampled both magnetic tape methods and Schoenberg's **twelve-tone** technique but soon rebelled against the technical, mathematical, and intellectual control these imposed on a musical composition.

FIGURE 21.4
John Cage.

The son of an inventor, Cage consistently addressed his musical problems with an inventor's ingenuity and creativity. Like Cowell, Cage was born on the West Coast and felt less tied to European traditions than did many German-trained composers in New England and New York. Profoundly interested in Asian philosophies, religions, and musical styles, he soon turned from traditional Western instruments to those producing an intriguing variety of sounds similar to the music of the East. Because he wished to use pitches not in the Western chromatic scale, such unusual "instruments" as cowbells, automobile brake drums, and anvils, combined with Japanese temple bells, Chinese gongs, and other exotic non-Western percussion instruments, attracted him and met his early purposes.

Gamelan Music Cage discovered that an elegant Indonesian percussion ensemble called a **gamelan** *(GAH-meh-lahn)* produced many of the sounds and pitches he desired. The gamelan is an orchestra, in the sense that it is a combination of instruments from various families; but unlike the Western string orchestra, the gamelan consists primarily of percussion instruments (Figure 21.5). These include *metallophones,* which are sets of metal keys suspended over a bronze or wooden frame and struck with a mallet; tuned gongs of various sizes, usually arranged in a semicircle; and drums. The gamelan ensemble also includes a few wind and string instruments that play sustained pitches and add color to the sound. Listening Example 72 gives a brief indication of the delicate and varied sounds of gamelan music.

Although Cage included a gamelan in some of his early compositions, the ensemble—visually as well as aurally stunning—is too expensive to be widely available (although gamelans are in fact becoming increasingly familiar in the West). Therefore, Cage invented a method of altering the grand piano in order to approximate many of a gamelan's sounds.

Prepared Piano In 1938, challenged by the dance company he was accompanying to extend the range of timbres in their performance music without exceeding the limits of their budget, Cage discovered that the grand piano

FIGURE 21.5

A Javanese gamelan.

Listening Example 72

Kebjar Hudjan Mas   (excerpt)

Genre

Balinese gamelan music

CD 3

Track 11

1:03

Form

A series of variations evolves over relentlessly repeated ostinatos, which provide stability and seem to anchor the composition.

Timbres

The metallic sounds of gongs and metallophones, dominating the beginning of the piece, suggest the meaning of "kebjar"—to flash or flame, as in a burst of light. Soon the full gamelan accompanies the joyous peals of sound.

could be altered or "prepared" so as to change the timbres and pitches it produced. By applying pieces of wood, metal, and rubber to the strings of the piano, he slowed the rate at which the strings vibrated, slightly changing the pitch as well as the quality of the sound. His new, or modified, instrument is called the **prepared piano.**

As most keys on a piano keyboard control three strings each, nuts, bolts, screws, bamboo strips, or other materials may be placed on one of the strings, between any two, or touching all three. A composer indicates precisely which strings of which keys are to be prepared, what foreign materials are to be used, and at what distance from the soundboard they are to be placed (Figure 21.6). When the hammers strike the prepared strings, timbres and tones similar to those of a gamelan or a Western percussion ensemble are sounded. A wide variety of sounds and pitches may be achieved in this way, all on a readily available instrument and at the control of an individual performer. Further, the

These measurements apply to a Steinway, L, M, O, A or B

TONE	MATERIAL	STRINGS (left to right)	DISTANCE from Damper (inches)	MATERIAL	STRINGS (left to right)	DISTANCE from Damper (inches)	TONE
	Rubber	1-2-3	15/16*				E
	Rubber	1-2-3	1 7/16*				B
	Rubber	1-2-3	1 7/16*				E
	Weather Stripping	1-2	1	Screw and Nuts	2-3	2¼	D
	Rubber (damper to bridge = 4 9/16; adjust measurements accordingly)	2-3(B♭)-1	3⅜	Screw	2-3	1 7/16	B
	Weather Stripping	1-2	3¾	Bolt and Nuts	2-3	2¼	A♭
	Weather Stripping	1-2	2	Bolt	2-3	1¾	E
				Bolt (small)	2-3	4	D♭
	Weather Stripping	1-2	6	Screw and Nuts	2-3	1½	B♭
	Weather Stripping	1-2-3	4				A♭
	Weather Stripping	1-2-3	3	Weather Stripping	1-2-3	3½	G
	Rubber	1-2-3	5				F♯
	Weather Stripping	1-2-3	8½				E
	Bamboo Slit	1-2	4⅛	Bolt	2-3	4	E♭
	Weather Stripping	1-2-3	11				D
	Double Weather Stripping	1-2	13	Screw and Nuts	2-3	12	D♭
	Double Weather Stripping	1-2	7	Screw and Rubber Washer	2-3	6¾	B♭
	Weather Stripping	1-2-3	4½				G
	Bamboo Slit	1-2	2¼	Bolt	2-3	2	F
	Weather Stripping	1-2	¼	Bolt	2-3	1	D
	Screw and Weather Stripping	1-2	3⅞				F
	Screw and Weather Stripping	1-2	5				D
	Screw and Weather Stripping	1-2	7				B♭
	Screw and Weather Stripping	1-2	14				A♭
	Wood and Cloth	1-1	2¾				E-F

*Measure from Bridge

FIGURE 21.6

The notated tone (left column) indicates the pitch (identified by its letter name in the column on the right) that should be "prepared" by applying the material specified to one or more of its strings at a certain distance from the *dampers* (small pieces of felt-lined wood attached to piano strings).

pianist may also strike the wooden parts and metal braces of the instrument with the hand or an implement, producing even more varied sound effects. Many musicians were impressed with Cage's several independent compositions for prepared piano, and soon other composers also were writing pieces in which a few, or many, strings were to be prepared.

Cage is thought to have written his suite for prepared piano *The Perilous Night* (Listening Example 73) at a time when he was lonely and sad. To express the terror unhappy love can bring, he based his piece on a collection of Irish folktales concerning a "perilous bed," whose wheels rest on a slick floor of polished jasper, and whose occupant suffers attack by mysterious creatures. (Cage's artist friend Jasper Johns—perhaps attracted by the reference to his first name?—interpreted the tale, or Cage's piece, in his painting *Perilous Night*, Figure 21.7.)

Listening Example 73

The Perilous Night (excerpt)

Composer
John Cage

CD 3
Track 12
12:53

Genre
Composition for prepared piano

Preparation
The score directs the pianist to apply nuts, bolts, washers, strips of bamboo, and pieces of weather stripping at measured points between specific strings, creating a variety of wooden, metallic, and indeterminate sounds reminiscent of the Balinese gamelan. The preparation, which affects all characteristics of the piano's sounds, takes an experienced prepared piano performer about half an hour. (See Figure 21.6.)

Form
Suite, consisting of six untitled pieces of varied character, mood, and tempo, expressed within the enormous range of timbres afforded by the prepared piano.

Piece 1. The meter is 4/4, but the rapid tempo and rhythmic ambiguity (accents occurring on weak beats or between beats, some measures of silence) make it difficult to feel a sense of beat. Ostinatos beginning on different beats of the measure further obscure the meter. Rhythmic intensity varies from complex to very simple.

Timbres include the wooden sounds of the brief melodic phrases, punctuated by a shimmering metallic sound (similar to a tambourine?) and accompanied by insistent drumlike low pitches.

The narrow melodic pitch range primarily lies within two half steps (F#-G-Ab). Notice the several melodic ostinatos, which lend unity and stability to the piece. The bass note pitches are particularly indistinct.

—Continued

Listening Example 73—Concluded

The Perilous Night (excerpt)

Dynamic markings vary from *ff* to *pp*, but the muted strings limit the range of volume the instrument can produce. The score indicates a final crescendo to *fff* (one level louder than *ff, or* fortissimo).

The form evolves from a series of sections: the first introduces the three timbres and the narrow melodic intervals; the second (1:01) repeats the tone F#, accompanied by insistent metallic-sounding eighth notes; the third (2:30) suggests drums accompanied by metallic-sounding instruments; the fourth (3:17) stresses the narrow "wooden" intervals; the fifth (4:30) suggests quiet drums; etc. Notice the tumbling drumlike figures that lead to the dramatic, percussive ending.

Piece 2. The rapid tempo of this busy piece suggests perpetual motion. The driving rhythm includes frequent syncopation.

The timbres are primarily metallic.

The dynamic level is quieter than in the first piece.

The wider melodic range includes some very high-pitched ostinatos.

Perhaps you will notice three rather distinct levels of pitch: low, medium, and high.

This brief piece is unified by its ostinatos, each occupying a line or so of the score. The first short sections play with a rising melodic figure; the second seems to emphasize falling patterns. The texture becomes more dense, then lightens again as the piece approaches its simple conclusion.

FIGURE 21.7

Jasper Johns: *Perilous Night.* A detailed interpretation of this painting can be found at the National Gallery of Art Web site, www.nga.gov.

By the 1950s, John Cage had become the dominant figure of American experimental music, as we shall see in Chapter 23.

Terms to Review

experimental music   Music challenging accepted concepts of musical sound.

bitonality   Two keys at the same time.

polytonality   More than two keys at the same time.

polyrhythms   Two or more simultaneous rhythmic patterns.

microtone   Any interval smaller than a half step.

tone cluster   A chord, usually of several tones, built upon seconds. Clusters are often played with the flat of the hand, the arm, or a board cut to a specified length.

New Music   A term used for music of an experimental nature.

musique concrète (concrete music)   Music created by manipulating taped sounds.

twelve-tone   A technique of organizing music, developed by Arnold Schoenberg, in which all twelve tones of the octave are of equal significance.

gamelan   An Indonesian percussion ensemble.

prepared piano   A grand piano on which some or all of the strings have been "prepared" by placing foreign materials on them, thereby altering pitch, timbre, and dynamic level.

Key Figures

Charles Ives   Henry Cowell   John Cage

Optional Listening Examples

Charles Ives: *The Unanswered Question*   Henry Cowell: "The Tides of Mananaun"

Suggestions for Further Listening

Charles Ives: "*Hallowe'en*" (orchestral)   Henry Cowell: *Hymns and Fuging Tunes*
Ives: "Serenity" (song)   John Cage: *Sonatas and Interludes* (prepared piano)

Critical Thinking

Today there is much talk about "high (classical) art" and "low (popular) art." How do you think Charles Ives would have addressed this subject? John Cage? Do you believe music and other art should be classified as high or low? What criteria might such a distinction be based on?

Do you consider Charles Ives's "At the River" an original piece? How does it differ from an arrangement?

How are Henry Cowell's and John Cage's piano experiments related? In what ways do they differ?

Can you conceive of ways in which musicians might continue to experiment with sound, other than by electronic manipulation?

Go to www.mhhe.com/ferrisaml5 for a list of additional Web-based resources that relate to the content in this chapter.

Early Twentieth-Century Mainstream Concert Music: Evolution

Unlike their experimentalist colleagues, many twentieth-century composers took an *evolutionary* approach to furthering the development of music. Some, notably William Schuman (1910–1992), found a source for their compositions in American subjects or tunes. Several American composers found useful material in jazz and other vernacular sources. Since folk and popular dances have long enlivened European concert music, it seems natural for contemporary classical musicians to draw ideas from popular musics, now more varied and sophisticated than ever; but in the 1920s and 1930s, many Americans found this a novel and intriguing concept. Although some musicologists now dispute the view, until recently it was generally acknowledged that Europeans preceded Americans in recognizing jazz as a source of inspiration and material for concert music. Almost from the start of jazz, such European composers as Darius Milhaud, Béla Bartók, and Maurice Ravel integrated the distinctive rhythms, timbres, and performance techniques of the new American vernacular music in their classical compositions.

George Gershwin's *Rhapsody in Blue* (1924, an Optional Listening Example), originally conceived for jazz band and piano, though today it is more often performed by piano and orchestra, confused American critics, who were not sure on what grounds to attack it. They found the piece too jazzy for concert music, but unacceptable as jazz because it involved no improvisation. The public, by contrast, greeted *Rhapsody* with enthusiasm, and it remains among the best-known and best-loved symphonic compositions in the world. But Charles Ives's appreciation for good jazz, equal to his appreciation for good symphonic music, struck many as a veritable aberration.

In any case, evolutionary, often nationalistic, works constituted the mainstream of twentieth-century American concert music.

The Parisian Scene

Most of the eager young composers of the 1920s and 1930s traveled to Europe to study, as America did not yet offer comparably advanced music training. They turned not to Germany, however, as had the Second New England School

385

composers, but to France, which became the world center of artistic creativity after World War I. Not only musicians but also poets, writers, painters, dancers, and choreographers from all over the world met in Paris, where they shared ideas—disparate but fresh and invigorating—and stimulated each other to reach new heights of creativity.

The young American composers found their study in France a liberating experience indeed, for unlike the German masters who insisted on teaching the "correct" way to compose, the French encouraged them to develop their individuality and explore new ideas. Especially, a young French organist, composer, and highly gifted teacher, **Nadia Boulanger** (1887–1979; Figure 22.1), offered superb instruction to this generation and several successive generations of composers, brilliantly teaching skills and technique without inflicting style upon her students. Recognizing each young composer's distinctive talents, she defined the ways each might reach his or her best potential.

The first American to study with Boulanger was a young man destined to become known as the dean of American composers: Aaron Copland.

Aaron Copland (1900–1990)

Aaron Copland (Figure 22.2) was born in Brooklyn, New York, to a family not particularly interested in music. He decided while still in his teens to become a composer of serious music. To this end, Copland spent three years during his early twenties studying in Paris with Nadia Boulanger.

To his astonishment, Boulanger suggested that Copland borrow jazz techniques as one means of giving his music a distinctively American sound. In any case, several of Copland's early pieces, including a suite for small orchestra titled *Music for the Theater* (1925—the year after Gershwin's *Rhapsody in Blue*) and a concerto for piano and orchestra completed the next year, certainly reflect the rhythms, melodies, harmonies, and timbres of jazz.

Although appreciative of these fresh and nationalistic effects, Copland soon found jazz emotionally limited, and he sought inspiration in other American

FIGURE 22.1

Nadia Boulanger.

FIGURE 22.2
Aaron Copland.

sounds, including cowboy songs and early American hymns. An avid proponent of American music from both north and south of the Mexican border, Copland also captured the flavors and spirit of Mexican folk and popular music. First performed in 1937 in Mexico City, his delightful *El Salón México,* a musical potpourri of his own versions and orchestrations of Mexican folk tunes, remains among the favorite Copland works today.

Depression and War Years
Determined to develop an American audience interested in hearing music by American composers, Copland and another prominent American composer, Roger Sessions (1896–1985), organized and supported a series of programs from 1928 to 1931 at which American concert music was performed, heard, and reviewed; thus important new American compositions received public and critical attention at a time before musicians could rely upon recorded music to reach a wide audience. The Copland-Sessions concerts had inestimable value in encouraging the development of American music.

The music Copland wrote just before and after the stock market crashed in 1929 is rather difficult, austere, and uncompromising, although beautifully written and stunning in effect when performed well. Many believe, in fact, that *Piano Variations* (1929) is his finest composition. But the Great Depression profoundly affected the development of an American repertoire, as it affected every phase of American life: people simply were not able to address new subjects and cultivate new tastes at a time when their energies were absorbed by private and public tragedies. Copland, deeply sympathetic to the conservative attitude of the shocked and saddened American people, urgently wished to communicate with them through his music, on which he deliberately imposed a new simplicity. Thus most of his works from the Depression period through the years of World War II are readily accessible and reflect Copland's great interest in all of America.

Intending his music to have a practical as well as an aesthetic purpose, Copland diligently provided scores for radio, films, schools, amateur musicians, and ballet companies. In 1942, he stirred the wartime audience's patriotic spirit with *Lincoln Portrait,* a musical composition that quotes fragments of Stephen Foster's songs and American folk tunes accompanied by the narration of some of Abraham Lincoln's well-known speeches. (After Copland was charged with having communist affiliations, a performance of his *Lincoln Portrait* was canceled just two weeks before its scheduled inclusion in a concert for the inauguration of President Dwight D. Eisenhower. Ultimately, Copland was vindicated of the charges against him.)

A festive fanfare, also written in 1942, has become one of Copland's most famous works. Although a fanfare usually celebrates a royal or state personage or occasion, Copland affirmed his respect and appreciation for the ordinary citizens of America by calling this wartime piece *Fanfare for the Common Man.* Its dramatic theme, based on a rising motive introduced by a solo trumpet, is variously treated by combinations of brass instruments, forcefully punctuated by percussion.

One of several fanfares written in response to a challenge issued by the conductors of the Cincinnati Symphony Orchestra, Copland's *Fanfare* (Listening Example 74) is often performed at occasions of patriotic significance and pride, such as the Olympic Games. It has stirred pop and classical musicians

---

Listening Example 74

Fanfare for the Common Man

Composer
Aaron Copland

CD 3
Track 13
3:14

Timbres
Brass and percussion—characteristic of a fanfare, which is intended to make a dramatic and emphatic musical statement.

Melody
Bold ascending and descending leaps in the melody line lend strength and drama to the piece.

Key
Fanfare begins in B♭ major and moves through abrupt and startling key changes, keeping the piece harmonically interesting, to end in D major.

The piece opens with a mighty pounding of the drum, succeeded by the breathtaking trumpet theme, which is then expanded by the rest of the brass. The dramatic, emotionally uplifting thrust up to the final chord brings the brief composition to a thrilling conclusion.

alike: Keith Emerson arranged a rock version, and the Rolling Stones played their version as a concert opener on their American tour in 1975.

Music for Dance

The interest Americans developed in stage ballets within the Broadway musical and modern dance during the 1930s and 1940s remained very strong; and Copland's best-known works include his dance compositions, usually called *ballets,* although in fact they represent *modern dance.*

Classical ballet is a formal, stylized dance form in which steps, gestures, and positions, together with mime, describe characters and dramatize a story. Particularly characteristic of classical ballet are the female dancers' positions *en pointe,* or on the points of their toes. (The language of ballet, which evolved in seventeenth-century France at the court of Louis XIV, remains French today.) The movements of the dancers (classical or other) are determined by a choreographer, who may set steps to existing music or to music composed especially for a particular dance. Choreography used to be handed down by tradition only, but methods of notation have been developed—some of them quite recently—that make it possible to preserve a choreographer's ideas accurately. Videotape provides another effective tool for this purpose.

Copland's "ballets," however, are examples of **modern dance** (Figure 22.3), a twentieth-century American contribution with steps and gestures more varied and less stylized than those of classical ballet. The costumes of modern dance also are simpler, and the dancers perform barefoot rather than in the rigid, tightly laced shoes that allow ballerinas to dance *en pointe.*

Copland's busy year, 1942, also produced (besides *Lincoln Portrait* and *Fanfare*) his famous ballet *Rodeo,* commissioned by the choreographer Agnes de Mille (who also choreographed *Oklahoma!*). The ballet relates the story of a cowgirl who dresses and acts like a man but wins the love of the head wrangler by appearing at a Saturday night dance wearing a dress, with a bow in her hair. Feminist critics have complained that the capitulation of this tomboy is politically incorrect; some others suggest the cowgirl represents a closeted

FIGURE 22.3

American modern dance.

"Hoedown" from *Rodeo*

CD 3
Track 14
3:29

Composer
Aaron Copland

Genre
Music from modern dance

Meter
Duple

Tempo
Fast

Melody
Based on two old-time fiddle-tunes—"Bonyparte" and "McLeod's Reel"

Form
Three-part (**A B A**)

Under the fanfare-like introductory music, we hear the fiddle "tuning up."

A simple rocking figure (0:18), repeated several times, introduces section **A** (0:40), a jiglike treatment of "Bonyparte." (The music reflects the excitement of the Cowgirl, who has put aside her cowpoke duds and reappeared as the prettiest girl in the room.) Frequent repetition of the jolly phrase makes the music immediately familiar, and the buoyant rhythm almost compels a physical response. (Notice the wood blocks' contribution from the percussion section.)

Initially lighter, less boisterous, section **B** (1:39) treats the other old fiddle tune. Preserving the festive mood, this section becomes increasingly energetic, as strings and brass call and respond to each other.

A brief interlude (2:25) suggests that the music (and the dancers?) may be running down; but (at 2:50), section **A** returns, fully revived. The happy piece ends with three triumphant unison exclamations.

homosexual male, giving the story quite a different flavor. (Copland, though openly homosexual, never advertised the fact.)

The rollicking "Hoedown" from *Rodeo* (Listening Example 75), reminiscent of old-fashioned barn dance or square dance music, is familiar today through television commercials as well as frequent orchestral performances.

Later Works In the 1950s, Copland wrote two sets of *Old American Songs* and an opera with an American setting called *The Tender Land* (mentioned in Chapter 20). He also surprised many people by writing several works based on progressive principles, including twelve-tone technique. In fact, throughout his career, Copland demonstrated an unusual variety of tastes and talents, never remaining committed to a consistent trend or direction. Among his large body of works are choral pieces, film scores (including *Our Town,* 1940; *The Red Pony,* 1948; and *The Heiress,* 1949, for which he won an Academy Award), chamber music, large orchestral works, an opera, and other ballets or dance pieces. He also wrote several very readable books about music.

Samuel Barber (1910–1981)

Beginning in the 1920s, many American composers followed Copland to Paris to study with Nadia Boulanger. Most, like Copland, were basically **traditionalists,** who sought progress of an evolutionary kind. Many were at the same time **neoromantics** ("new romantics"), who organized their compositions according to programmatic rather than strictly intellectual concepts, emphasizing lyrical melodies and richly dissonant harmonies and imbuing their music with warm emotional expression.

Prominent among the latter was **Samuel Barber** (Figure 22.4), whose best-known works include several beautiful art songs. One, "Knoxville: Summer of 1915" for soprano and orchestra (Optional Listening Example), is a setting of a beautiful text written by James Agee in 1938 (later placed by Agee's literary executors, after the author's death, as the Prologue to his Pulitzer-Prize-winning novel *A Death in the Family*). So strongly was Barber attracted to song and the singing voice that even his instrumental pieces have lyrical, songlike melodies rendering them among the most accessible and appreciated compositions of this century.

In 1936, noticing that audiences particularly responded to the slow movement (Adagio) of one of his string quartets, Barber arranged that movement to be played by a larger group of string instruments; and as an independent piece in this more sensuous guise, his *Adagio for Strings* (Listening Example 76) has become fondly familiar to the American public. This quietly solemn piece, acknowledging the reality of sadness but offering solace and rest, was played

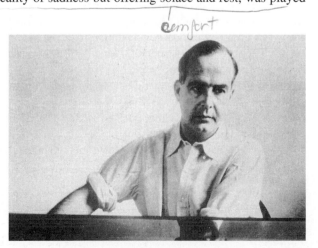

FIGURE 22.4
Samuel Barber.

Listening Example 76

Adagio for Strings

Composer
Samuel Barber

CD 3
Track 15
9:02

Genre
Neoromantic chamber music

Form
Arch form. Gently rounded to end much as it begins, the *Adagio* forms an asymmetrical arch, building through most of the piece to its emotional climax and coming soon thereafter to a quiet close.

Melody
The lovely main theme winding gently throughout the piece is long and irregular, unbounded by conventional concepts of balance or symmetry. Introduced by the violins, it is repeated *sequentially* (at changing—in this case higher and higher—levels of pitch), to intense emotional effect.

Harmony
Tense dissonances alternate with soft, sensuous harmonic resolutions to raise and release the level of intensity. Notice that the relentless rise in pitch level leading toward the climax of the piece coincides with particularly tense harmonies and a dramatic crescendo; and notice, too, the overwhelming effect of the moment of silence succeeding the climax.

---

during the radio announcement of Franklin Delano Roosevelt's death in 1945 and has frequently been performed at solemn state occasions since. It was heard in its entirety at the end of the poignant film *The Elephant Man* (1980) and was the musical theme of *Platoon* (Best Picture of the Year, 1986).

Some critics suggest that the long, asymmetrical, rhythmically relaxed melody of this emotionally expressive yet unpretentious piece, clearly unfettered by preconceived rules and measurements, characterizes the American spirit. Yet Barber was inspired to write the *Adagio* by a passionate poem of Virgil from the *Georgics;* and indeed, the wavelike motion of Barber's melody and the sensuous tension and release of the harmony seem closely linked to the subject of sexual abandon and fulfillment. The poem (as translated by the former poet laureate Robert Pinsky) begins:

> As when far off in the middle of the ocean
> A breast-shaped curve of wave begins to whiten
> And rise above the surface, then rolling on
> Gathers and gathers until it reaches land

Huge as a mountain and crashes among the rocks
With a prodigious roar, and what was deep
Comes churning up from the bottom in mighty swirls
Of sunken sand and living things and water . . .

Harlem Renaissance

The **Harlem Renaissance** was a movement of the 1920s in which African American painters, sculptors, poets, playwrights, musicians, novelists, and essayists broke from convention to "promote racial advancement through artistic creativity." Stimulated by poet Langston Hughes, writer Zora Neale Hurston, and many others, black artists in every field traveled to Harlem (in uptown New York City), seeking within the heady environment of this unprecedented concentration of African American talent to effect a true renaissance—a rebirth—of black "high art."

Although treated primarily as a literary movement, the Harlem Renaissance inspired visual artists as well to express modern urban life from the African American point of view. And the movement used and was supported and accompanied by music. Among the musicians it attracted to New York, Eubie Blake created *Shuffle Along* on Broadway, W. C. Handy ("father of the blues") established his music publishing house, Fletcher Henderson and especially Duke Ellington drew huge numbers of white people to Harlem to hear jazz, James P. Johnson and Thomas "Fats" Waller virtually created jazz piano, and Bessie Smith sang the blues. These were prominent among many others who introduced, developed, and promoted the black popular music and jazz of the Harlem Renaissance.

Primarily it was in the realm of concert music, however, that musicians of the Harlem Renaissance sought to develop folk materials from the black cultural heritage into artistic creations commanding the respect of white as well as black artists and intellectuals. Blacks who had begun to gain access to American and European conservatories and universities were eager to synthesize their own musical heritage with their new skills and perspectives, having as their primary goal the "elevation" of spirituals, blues, and jazz to symphonic form. Harry T. Burleigh and Robert Nathaniel Dett, for example, were among the most successful black composers basing classical compositions on familiar spirituals; and the singers Marian Anderson and Paul Robeson brought these eloquent songs to a large and appreciative concert audience. Although the Harlem Renaissance ended (with the onslaught of the Great Depression) before many composers could fully develop their skills, the accomplishments of these and countless others reveal the rich cultural milieu in which black intellectuals made high art in the Harlem Renaissance. Yet the subject remains controversial, many black musicians resenting the idea that mastery of classical techniques somehow advanced black music. Here we explore the sensitive issue from the point of view of those who were involved in a movement that at the time seemed meaningful and important to them.

FIGURE 22.5

William Grant Still.

Preeminent among the composers, William Grant Still became the first black composer to have a symphony played by a major symphony orchestra, the first to conduct a major symphony orchestra, and the first to have an opera produced by a major American company.

William Grant Still (1895–1978)

As a child, **William Grant Still** (Figure 22.5) showed both an interest in and a talent for music, studying violin and listening avidly to his stepfather's opera recordings. But as a young black living in the American South, he found it difficult to be taken seriously as a classical musician.

Nevertheless, Still won a scholarship to the prestigious Oberlin Conservatory of Music in Ohio, and after earning his degree continued his studies with

Listening Example 77

Afro-American Symphony, third movement

Composer
William Grant Still

CD 3
Track 16
3:23

Tempo
Animato (animated, rapid)

Form
Variations on a theme

Following a cymbal crash, a brief introduction sets the carefree mood, whereupon the syncopated theme enters, accompanied by a banjo brightly marking the backbeat. This unorthodox orchestral instrument has much to do with the programmatic character of the movement, intended to reflect happier moments in the African American experience. The theme soars to raptures of unalloyed pleasure.

A solo oboe begins the theme again, lightly, delicately, passing it to other instruments, which respond in call-and-response fashion. A four-note motive ("dum-te-dum-dum") extracted from the lighthearted theme is tossed sequentially higher and higher, then passed through the ranges of the instruments.

A second theme, bluesy in mood, smooth (*legato*) rather than bouncy, almost—but not quite—of a plaintive tone, momentarily sobers the effect, blue notes heightening the poignancy of this brief passage. But soon the irrepressible main theme returns with its confident banjo backbeat. The orchestra sounds increasingly jazzy as it accompanies the saucy tune to its happy conclusion.

the evolutionary composer George Chadwick (of the Second New England School) and a revolutionary (European) composer, Edgard Varèse, who considered all sounds, including those called noise, valid for use in a musical composition. For several years, Still played in dance bands and variety shows while working for a popular music publishing company, and before becoming definitively involved with concert music. Then, during a long and successful career, he wrote several operas and ballets, some film scores, and many songs and choral pieces.

Still, whose racial heritage was mixed, had a personal interest in American Indian and Spanish American music but identified primarily with black Americans, and it was their experience he wished to express. Declaring his purpose to "elevate Negro musical idioms to a position of dignity and effectiveness in the field of symphonic and operatic music," Still allied himself with the Harlem Renaissance during the pre-Depression years, producing his fine *Afro-American Symphony* in 1930 (Listening Example 77).

Many American composers of the late twentieth century, including those discussed in Chapter 24, shared the ideals so eloquently expressed in the music of Copland, Barber, Still, and other early mainstream composers. Indeed, their accomplishments inspire much of today's American music.

Terms to Review

classical ballet   A formal, stylized dance form that evolved in seventeenth-century France.

modern dance   A contemporary American dance form, less stylized than classical ballet, although today many dancers and choreographers combine the two techniques.

traditionalist   A composer who makes no radical departures from the conceptions of earlier music.

neoromantic   A contemporary composer whose music reveals nineteenth-century melodic, harmonic, and expressive characteristics.

Harlem Renaissance   A cultural movement centering in Harlem in the 1920s in which African American artists in every field achieved high art.

Key Figures

Nadia Boulanger   Aaron Copland   Samuel Barber   William Grant Still

Optional Listening Examples

George Gershwin: *Rhapsody in Blue*
Aaron Copland: Variations on "Simple Gifts" from *Appalachian Spring*

Samuel Barber: "Knoxville: Summer of 1915"
William Grant Still: *Afro-American Symphony,* first movement

Suggestions for Further Listening

Aaron Copland: *Music for the Theatre*
Copland: *Piano Variations*
Copland: *El Salón México*
Copland: Concerto for Piano and Orchestra
Copland: *Billy the Kid* Suite

Copland: Third Symphony
Samuel Barber: Piano Concerto
Rhapsody in Black: Music and Words from the Harlem Renaissance (four-CD boxed set, Rhino Records)

Critical Thinking

What images does Aaron's Copland's "Hoedown" bring to your mind? What musical elements evoke those images?

Having read the beginning of Virgil's poem that inspired Samuel Barber to write his famous *Adagio,* do you hear the music as primarily sensual, or elegiac? Tragic, or comforting?

What are your views on the Harlem Renaissance? Did its gifted black poets, writers, painters, and musicians choose the best route to secure economic, social, and cultural equality with white artists? What other recourse might they have had? Did efforts to raise spirituals and blues to "high art" enhance or detract from these forms? (To form and support your views, try to listen to recordings by Marian Anderson, Paul Robeson, and others.)

Go to www.mhhe.com/ferrisaml5 for a list of additional Web-based resources that relate to the content in this chapter.

The Avant-Garde, Continued

Experimentalism, which romantically denies traditional boundaries, abandons established rules of composition, and explores new concepts of the very meaning of music, appeals strongly to Americans, a romantic people, creative, inventive, independent, and accustomed to freedom and space. It is not surprising, then, that Americans have often been in the forefront of the experimental movement in music.

Experimentalists both here and abroad have followed diverse paths, some choosing an intellectual, controlled approach to their music, and other avant-garde composers remaining detached from the compositions they produce, leaving important aspects to be decided by the performers, listeners, or simply chance. Some composers of new music include elements of both romantic and classical styles in their work.

Rhythm and Timbre

By the mid-twentieth century, rhythm and timbre had replaced melody and harmony as the elements of primary interest for many American composers. Experimentalists carried forward the work begun earlier in the century by Ives and Cowell, altering traditional instruments or playing them in new ways in order to produce unusual sounds. Today many composers use traditional instruments, including the human voice, to produce sounds—such as whispers, shouts, groans, or teeth clicks—that do not conform to the traditional concept of beauty. Instrumentalists may be directed to produce breathy, squeaky, or raucous sounds, sometimes but not always for programmatic effect. Several composers have found that the resonant timbres of mallet instruments, such as the marimba, xylophone, or glockenspiel, offer an attractive alternative to traditional orchestral or other Western sounds; and the precise rhythmic effects expert players can achieve on mallet instruments further enhance their appeal for many composers today.

Harry Partch (1901–1974) Some composers, of whom **Harry Partch** is best-known, invented entirely new musical instruments. Known as the hobo composer because during the Great Depression he actually did spend

FIGURE 23.1

Harry Partch's Quadrangularus Reversum, 1972. Some of his instruments can be heard, and even "played," on the Web.

time on the rails, Partch designed and built an amazing array of exotically named instruments, including the kithara, crychord, marimba eroica, and spoils of war, among many others (Figure 23.1). He constructed his mazda marimba of lightbulbs, and he made an instrument of tuned beer and wine bottles reminiscent of Benjamin Franklin's glass harmonica.

Considering the division of the octave into twelve equal intervals both limiting and false, Partch divised a forty-three-tone scale, whose microtones more naturally reproduce the sounds of spoken, as well as sung, texts. Many of his inventions produce lovely, delicate tones, seemingly more suited to the world of nature than are traditional western band and orchestral instruments.

Tape Music and the Electronic Synthesizer

In the early 1950s some German musicians experimented with **tape music,** storing electronically generated sound materials on tape and then manipulating them, much as the French, a few years earlier, had manipulated prerecorded sounds to develop concrete music. Composers achieved the pitch they desired on the new **electronic synthesizer,** an instrument of seemingly unlimited capabilities, by plugging into electronic **oscillators.** ("Oscillation" is another word for vibration.) A **fingerboard** allowed players to slide through a range of pitches, unlimited by frets or keys. By plugging into other outlets on the synthesizer, the player altered the shape of the sound waves, determining the timbre of the sounds to be produced. Electronic **filters** selected out high and low ranges of a broadly spread sound, such as industrial or machinery noise,

High pitches

Low pitches

Mer - ri - ly   we   roll   a - long . . .

= Machinery noise

= A melody tone

= Narrow band of sound achieved by filtering out
  high and low pitches

FIGURE 23.2

On an electronic synthesizer, high and low pitches can be filtered out of machinery noise to produce a narrow band of sound or a melodic line.

producing a narrow band of melody of an interesting but nontraditional timbre (Figure 23.2).

The first synthesizer in the United States, the RCA Mark II (sponsored in 1959 by Princeton and Columbia universities and located at Columbia, in New York City), filled most of a room and was driven by a strip of paper with holes punched in it; but huge and cumbersome as it sounds today, it offered a new world of sound and unprecedented accuracy of rhythm and pitch. Not only did synthesizers and other electronic means enable composers to achieve sounds never heard before, but composers could hear their compositions immediately, instead of waiting for a live performance, which was sometimes difficult to achieve. Further, composers could save the sounds they liked on tape. It was not necessary to rehearse a piece and rely on the abilities of (or pay a salary to) performers, because the composer might produce all the sounds of a piece, independent of human assistance. The new electronic techniques offered a thrilling range of experience to composers interested in creating new sounds and exercising total control over their performance.

Today computers aid composers in the process of notating music, rendering the procedure faster, more accurate, and more efficient than in the past. Computers also allow the use of tempos too fast and rhythmic combinations too complex for human accomplishment, as well as nontonal intervals very difficult for musicians to hear and reproduce with accuracy. In fact, computers often control every facet of electronic music-making today. For example, in the electronic music lab shown in Figure 23.3, an electronic keyboard and two computers generate the sounds indicated by a musical score; the sounds are fed into a computer which functions as the mixer; and another computer records the resulting composition. Synthesizers and further recording equipment are no longer necessary in the modern studio.

FIGURE 23.3

Electronic music workstation including sophisticated equipment with which to compose, perform, and record music.

FIGURE 23.4

Milton Babbitt, 1965, with RCA Mark II Electronic Music Synthesizer.

Milton Babbitt (b. 1916)

While a student at New York University, **Milton Babbitt** (Figure 23.4) used the twelve-tone technique to achieve the mathematical precision he desired in his musical compositions; soon, he extended the orderly concept to other aspects of composition besides pitch. He arranged patterns of rhythms and durations, for example, into series that are systematically repeated throughout a composition. In some pieces composed according to this extension of the twelve-tone technique, called **total serialism, serialization,** or **serial technique,** the various series are mathematically related to each other; in other pieces, they are independent.

Babbitt also was one of the earliest enthusiasts and primary exponents of electronic music, codirecting the establishment of the RCA Mark II Synthesizer. It was several years later before synthesizers became available to composers in other parts of this country.

Babbitt, who finds rhythm and timbre more interesting to work with than melody and harmony, uses electronic techniques to achieve his exotic sounds and complex rhythms. A brilliant man who composes challenging music and deplores mistakes or misinterpretations by performers, Babbitt writes pieces which exist only on tape and for which there is no score, knowing that these will always be heard as he intended. Together with the resources of the electronic synthesizer, computers, and magnetic tape technique, total serialism allows Babbitt to achieve the highly ordered and logical music he prefers.

"Ensembles for Synthesizer" (Listening Example 78) is an early classic of this kind of electronic music.

Listening Example 78

"Ensembles for Synthesizer"
(excerpt)

Composer
Milton Babbitt

Genre
Concrete music

CD 3
Track 17
1:01

Form
This piece is a mosaic of tiny fragments (ensembles), each distinguished by a characteristic timbre, range of pitch, rhythmic pattern, dynamic level, and texture.

Timbres
Babbitt programmed the synthesizer to produce various metallic, wooden, and mysterious airy sounds, with occasional references to the sound of an electronic organ.

Rhythms
The rhythmic patterns are varied and complex, and are sometimes played at extremely rapid tempos, requiring electronic performance techniques.

Pitches
All twelve tones are used, although not according to Schoenberg's row technique. The ranges of pitch level are extreme.

Because this music is conceived and constructed differently from traditional compositions, it must also be approached differently by the listener. Concentration on and appreciation of the highly sensuous sounds and the fascinating rhythmic techniques yield intense listening pleasure.

John Cage and Chance Music

Some musicians turned away from the taut control provided by twelve-tone and tape techniques, preferring to leave certain aspects of the performance of their music to *chance.* Their counterparts in the visual arts were by the Abstract Expressionist painters, led by Jackson Pollock; and the moving sculptures of Alexander Calder, among many others. Free jazz musicians brought chance to the world of vernacular music, and John Cage the leading experimentalist of the 1950s and 1960s, led the movement toward chance, or indeterminacy, in the concert world.

Cage found the lack of spontaneity afforded by twelve-tone and concrete music profoundly dissatisfying, and his primary interest for many years was **chance** or **aleatory music,** in which the composer leaves significant aspects of each performance to chance. His commitment to Zen Buddhism, which he found less judgmental and dogmatic than Western philosophies and religions, inclined him to resist hierarchical determinations as to what in music is proper and desirable. Like Partch, Cage resisted the ancient Greeks' determination that division of the octave into seven tones constituted the most satisfactory system of scales. Cage proposed that the octave might as well be divided by ten, twenty, or any other number of intervals.

Improvisation is one form of such **indeterminate music** (as chance or aleatory music is also called), requiring performers to make certain decisions concerning melody, rhythm, and harmony; but aleatory music encompasses much more than this. *Aleatory* comes from the Latin word for dice, and throwing dice is among the ways of determining various aspects of an aleatory piece—for example, melodic or metric patterns, or the number of repetitions of a phrase or section. Other imaginative techniques used by composers of chance music include graphic notation that may be interpreted in many different ways; performance decisions based on the Chinese *Book of Chance,* called *I Ching* (pronounced "E Jing"); scores that may be read backward, forward, or upside down; and circular scores that may be read clockwise or counterclockwise.

The degree of possible indeterminacy ranges from minimal, as in Ives's *Unanswered Question,* to **random** music, in which almost all of the composition changes from one performance to another. Thus Cage scored *Imaginary Landscape no. 4* (1951) for twelve radios, indicating specific positions on the radio dials, dynamic levels, durations, and even the degree of abruptness with which each sound begins and ends; but of course different material will be broadcast at each "performance."

As we reexamine the meaning of music in our time, respected opinions on the subject of what constitutes music and musical sound vary. Some people argue that Cage's *Imaginary Landscape no. 4* is random sound as opposed to music, whereas others believe that the piece is clearly "organized sound" and therefore meets that broad definition of music. Still others insist that the quality of the sounds determines whether a composition is music or simply a listening experience. Certainly Cage was a disciplined artist, who clearly defined the freedoms he introduced into his compositions. "Freedom is one thing," he said, "but liberty is, so to speak, going too far."

JOHN CAGE

SEPTEMBER 5, 1912 – AUGUST 12, 1992

SILENCE

AMERICAN SOCIETY OF
COMPOSERS, AUTHORS & PUBLISHERS

MORTON GOULD
P R E S I D E N T

FIGURE 23.5

This full page appearing in the Sunday issue of the *New York Times* the week of Cage's death gave poignant tribute to this influential composer.

Silence We have seen that composers notate rests, or periods of silence, as carefully as they notate pitches (see Table 1, p. 2). But Cage discovered that although specific sounds may cease, there are always other sounds that continue; thus true silence is never part of the human experience. Traditionalists call the continuing sounds "noise" as opposed to "music," but Cage considered all sounds worthy of attention and encouraged us to be aware and appreciative of them. In fact, he flatly stated that "silence" is an absurd concept and simply does not exist.

To demonstrate the nonexistence of silence, Cage placed himself in a soundproof chamber, as silent as technicians could make it—in which his own bloodstream and nervous system produced clearly audible sounds. Next he wrote a book titled *Silence* (1961) and composed the notorious "4′33″" ("Four Minutes Thirty-Three Seconds") for "any instrument or combination of instruments," the score indicating three movements, each marked *tacet*—the term musicians use to mean "be silent." According to Cage, although the instruments make no sound at all, the audience has "a profound listening experience" throughout the duration of this noncomposition.

John Cage became the most controversial and influential American composer of the twentieth century. When he died, the American Society of Composers, Authors, and Publishers (ASCAP) expressed profound respect and regret with the full-page black-bordered announcement shown in Figure 23.5.

Other Composers of Chance Music

During the 1950s, three composers based in New York City became closely associated with John Cage while developing related ideas of their own. Like him, they intended to achieve objectivity in their music by refusing to specify details in the traditional way: in other words, they allowed their music to "come into its own."

Morton Feldman (1926–1987) sometimes used graphic notation to indicate his general intentions, leaving specific pitches and their durations to be determined by the performers. In one piece, he indicated the notes but left rhythms unspecified, allowing them to evolve within a general tempo established by the conductor at the beginning of each performance. Feldman is among those experimentalists whose imaginative scores sometimes also constitute works of visual art. Feldman's *Projection 2,* for example, is a series of rectangles indicating periods of time, small triangles placed within the rectangles suggesting when to play and how long tones should endure, and the vertical placement of the triangles giving a general idea of approximate levels of pitch.

Earle Brown (b. 1926), another associate of Cage, reflected in his music the mobility of Alexander Calder's sculptures and the spontaneity of Jackson Pollock's paintings, claiming to have composed some pieces so rapidly and spontaneously that they represented "performances" rather than "compositions." Brown, too, developed intriguing and attractive graphic notations for his scores, such as *December 1952* (Figure 23.6), written on one page as a series of vertical and horizontal lines that indicate only in a general way the

FIGURE 23.6

Excerpt from the score for *December 1952* from *FOLIO* by Earle Brown.

direction, dynamic level, duration, and pitch of the sounds. A decade later Brown further demonstrated the affinity between music and visual art by composing *Calder Piece 1963–1966,* for which Alexander Calder made a large mobile sculpture expressly for use as an instrument in the work.

The third New Yorker who was an associate of John Cage, Christian Wolff (b. 1934), like Feldman wished to "set sounds free," and like Cage was interested in silence as well as sound. His tones sometimes seem suspended in air, surrounded by space that lets them "breathe." Wolff has written some chamber pieces for which neither the instrumentation nor the duration of the tones (which *are* notated) is specified. The score for *1, 2, or 3 People* is a good example of the artistic nature of Wolff's original notation.

The ever-adventurous Henry Cowell wrote at least one piece of genuine chance music, *26 Simultaneous Mosaics* (1963), for clarinet, violin, violoncello, piano, and percussion. These brief pieces, written for each of the instruments individually, may be played in any order chosen by the players, who also, according to Cowell's instructions, may start and stop playing as they please.

Indeterminacy continues to be significant in today's concert music among so-called mainstream as well as New Music composers. Many who desire a degree of indeterminacy in their largely structured music have devised ingenious techniques for indicating the limits within which performers are to interpret their compositions.

Notation

Chance musicians such as Morton Feldman, Earle Brown, and John Cage are not the only composers who have created original means of notating their music. **Theater scores,** for example, require performing musicians to act as well as sing and play musical instruments, and such scores often require original methods of notation as well. **Laurie Anderson** (b. 1947), one of today's best-known performance artists, uses a variety of media, including film, electronic and acoustic music, slides, costumes, and other effects in her live performances, which defy traditional means of notation. Anderson's albums, too, demonstrate her technical wizardry and avant-garde vision.

Other characteristics of new music necessitating new kinds of notation include unusual techniques of playing on traditional instruments, passages to be sounded so rapidly that composers notate only their start and finish, clusters showing the number and range of tones but not the actual pitches, extremely complex divisions of beats, and extremely long durations better expressed in seconds of time than in quarter, half, and whole notes.

Graphs serve some composers as a means of notating the bounds within which pitches, rhythms, durations, and metric patterns are to be determined. Several composers have devised different means of notation to accommodate the specific demands of each new piece. And visual interest and appeal continue to attract many of them (see Figure 23.7).

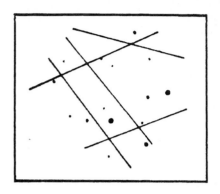

FIGURE 23.7

Nontraditional notation by John Cage.

Since about 1950, in fact, music notated as art has become quite usual. And as music looks more like visual art, art is looking more like performance—many museum pieces, for example, requiring movement or interaction between the artist or viewers and the visual work.

Pauline Oliveros (b. 1932)

Pauline Oliveros began composing music in a traditional manner but soon became fascinated with the qualities of all sounds, including those produced by nature (raindrops, wind) and by machinery. She avoids the meter and pulse characteristic of Western music in favor of rhythms that shift, expand, and contract more or less systematically, and her heightened sensitivity to timbre has led her to explore and experiment extensively with vocal and instrumental colors, often to stunning effect.

Oliveros is among the composers who have chosen to give up the idea of individual control over their music. She prefers to guide a group—often of music amateurs—through a shared creative experience. For example, she once asked the members of a large audience each to sing a pitch of their choice, sustaining it for the length of one breath. Coming to the end of that breath, they were to listen to someone as far away as possible and respond to his or her pitch. For the next fifteen minutes, extraordinary waves of harmony washed over the room, thrilling "composer" and performers alike.

Listening Example 79

Sound Patterns

Composer
Pauline Oliveros

CD 3
Track 18
4:03

Timbre
Mixed chorus, a cappella.

The score indicates very precise and quite difficult rhythms to be realized by singers improvising pitches within specified ranges. The singers also must produce various sounds, including tongue clicks, whispers, shouts, lip-pops, and finger-snaps. The effect, although entirely the result of human performance, suggests electronic enhancement and is somehow—unaccountably—whimsically humorous.

In Oliveros's *Sound Patterns* (Listening Example 79), a choral work with no text, the voices produce abstract sounds as unrelated to traditional concepts of melody and harmony as are abstract paintings to the shapes and colors of representational art. Yet like John Cage, Pauline Oliveros clearly structures even her pieces that rely heavily on free improvisation. Her conceptual score for *Portrait of the Quintet of the Americas,* for example, consists of circles and spokes all mapped out with the look of computer graphics, and each of the five performers has a set of assigned pitches based on his or her astrological chart. No two performances will be the same, but the performers' options are limited by restrictions imposed by the composer. Using tape and other electronic techniques, Oliveros creates distinctive pieces of sound imagery, haunting in their seductive sonic beauty.

Technology, of course, offers experimentalists possibilities dreamed of but unrealized by Ives, Cowell, and their cohort. On the simplest level, microphones placed inside a musical instrument amplify and alter or distort its sounds and may produce echo effects. Quarter-note flutes can play twice as many notes as a conventional model, and a device exists to give pianos "fluid tuning," releasing them from confinement to the eighty-eight tones created by their keys. A Hypercello and a Hyperviolin use electronic enhancement to expand what musicians can do with those instruments.

Our final chapter concerns other, more conservative, composers who also, in more traditional ways, have profoundly enriched America's musical landscape.

Terms to Review

tape music   Electronically generated sounds that have been recorded on tape and manipulated to create a music composition.

electronic synthesizer   An electronic sound generator capable of producing, imitating, and altering sounds.

oscillators   The means by which pitch is determined on an electronic synthesizer.

fingerboard   A board on the synthesizer, uninterrupted by keys or frets, allowing a player to slide through a continuum of pitches.

filters   On a synthesizer, electronic instruments that filter high and low pitches from a wide band of sound to produce a narrow band of melody.

total serialism   Also called **serialization** or **serial technique.** Application of twelve-tone concepts to other aspects of a composition (timbres or durations, for example), which, like tones, may be arranged into series and repeated.

aleatory music   Sometimes referred to as **chance** or **indeterminate** music, aleatory music leaves significant decisions to the performer of a composition, or to chance. An extreme example of aleatory music may be called **random** music.

theater score   A concert piece that includes visual and dramatic elements as well as music.

Key Figures

Harry Partch   Milton Babbitt   Laurie Anderson   Pauline Oliveros

Optional Listening Example

John Cage: *Aria* and *Fontana Mix* (aleatory)

Suggestions for Further Listening

Harry Partch: "The Letter—A Depression Message from a Hobo Friend" (1943)

Partch: "Plectra and Percussion Dances" (1949–1952)

Harry Partch Collection (four CDs, New World Records)

Milton Babbitt: *Three Compositions for Piano* (serialism)

Critical Thinking

John Cage said that fear in life is the fear of change. Do you agree? Can change be avoided? Should art (of any kind) be a fixed idea?

What do you think John Cage meant when he said that freedom is one thing, but liberty is going too far? The Latin root of *liberty* suggests release from bondage (separation), and *freedom* shares Northern European origins with *friend* (connection). Do you think these concepts are relevant to Cage's remark?

In classical music, there has been a change in emphasis from melody and harmony to rhythm and timbre. Can you relate this to changing tastes in pop music? Do you consider the modern urban experience relevant, or irrelevant, to changes in artistic preferences?

Given a choice between attending a concert of traditional orchestral music and a concert involving new (experimental) instruments, which would you choose? Why?

Go to www.mhhe.com/ferrisaml5 for a list of additional Web-based resources that relate to the content in this chapter.

The Recent Mainstream

By the 1950s, Americans enjoyed unprecedented access to a broad range of concert music. They could purchase long-playing records (LPs), listen to many hours of concert music a week on radio stations, and watch live performances on television. Centers for performing arts were being built at many places around the country, and important conservatories in several American cities offered music training of the highest quality. All this activity stimulated large numbers of American composers to write music intended for concert performance.

Many of these composers, choosing to write music rooted in the past, entered the modern American mainstream rather than joining the avant-garde. They may be seen as traditionalists, desiring to continue the evolution of music in a logical and orderly, rather than a revolutionary, manner. Yet their music, like that of their revolutionary colleagues, also reveals modern trends.

The Elements of Music

While the elements of music remain the fundamental materials with which composers work, today even mainstream composers often approach the elements in new ways. Harmony in recent music, for example, is often entirely dissonant, never resolving to or even alternating with traditionally consonant sounds. And while some composers retain a firm preference for lyricism, others have been accused of writing music with no melody at all. A contemporary piece rarely has "no melody"; but modern melodies often have a more angular contour than the songlike melodies of the nineteenth century, making them difficult to recognize. A few composers continue to base their melodies on twelve-tone and serial techniques, no longer considered avant-garde; and some choose melody tones far distant from each other, perhaps including microtones unfamiliar to Western ears. The fact that such techniques make it challenging to follow a melodic line, however, is not to say that no such line is present.

Still, modern traditionalists, like experimentalists, often focus on rhythm and timbre, rather than on melody and harmony, as the elements of primary interest and potential development.

New Concepts of Form

Some contemporary composers adapt the symphony, concerto, and other traditional forms to meet their personal creative needs. Others, however, consider such forms too tied to earlier concepts of symmetry and tonal relationships to stimulate their own creativity. Modern concepts of form are more likely to be based on principles of repetition with variation, as exemplified by *minimalist* music (see pp. 412–414), than on the complex development of motivic ideas characteristic of music in the Classic style. Some composers actually invent a new form for each piece they write, allowing characteristics of the particular piece to determine its organizing principles.

The many significant twentieth-century American mainstream composers include the New Yorker William Schuman and the westerner Lou Harrison.

William Schuman (1910–1992)

William Schuman, a rather conservative composer with a strong interest in musical nationalism, reigned as one of the giants of twentieth-century American music. He began composing while in high school, when he also formed a jazz ensemble (in which he played violin and banjo) and played in the school orchestra. After years of writing popular songs (many with the famous lyricist Frank Loesser, none of them a hit), he finally realized that his real gift lay in the composition of orchestral and other concert literature—often flavored, however, with jazz and with the sounds of American folk traditions. Schuman also had strong executive talents, serving as an officer of several organizations: he was, for example, president of Juilliard, first president of Lincoln Center for the Performing Arts, and chairman of the MacDowell Colony.

Schuman's orchestral music is mostly for a large orchestra, featuring distinct blocks—as opposed to delicate lines—of color. His long melodies soar over strong rhythmic foundations, giving much of his music an aura of majesty. Among his compositions based on American tunes, the three-movement *New England Triptych* includes sections on two tunes we have studied: William Billings's "When Jesus Wept" and "Chester" (Listening Example 80).

Lou Harrison (1917–2003)

Though born in Oregon, **Lou Harrison** revealed the spirit of California in his interests and in his style of composition. Like the Californian Henry Cowell, Harrison early grew familiar with Chinese opera and Gregorian chant, absorbing the sounds of Spanish and Mexican culture as well. The music of the Pacific Rim also fascinated Harrison throughout his life, as it had Cowell. While serving as music critic at the New York *Herald Tribune,* Harrison generously brought long overdue attention to Charles Ives, surely his opposite in character and temperament: it was Harrison who prepared and conducted the first performance of an Ives symphony—the Third, in 1947. However, unashamedly gay (whereas Cowell feared exposure as a homosexual), Harrison never felt

New England Triptych, third movement, "Chester"

Composer
William Schuman

CD 3
Track 19
2:50

Form
Rather free, a fantasy based on Billings's famous tune

Timbre
Orchestra

Meter
Quadruple

The movement begins slowly and quietly (the score is marked "Religioso") as the woodwinds play a relatively straightforward version of "Chester." The last phrase of the tune, begun by a solo bassoon, is picked up by a bass clarinet and tapers off. After a suspenseful pause, brass and strings abruptly introduce a fiery new section (0:49), allegro in tempo and percussive in effect. At 0:55 the meter changes to duple as the woodwinds play the theme in unison, punctuated by short (staccato) chords in brass and strings. Beginning at 1:07, rapid figures swirl throughout the woodwinds, until at 1:23 the strings begin a rapid new pattern, accompanied by a drone in the bass instruments (tuba, cello, and double bass). At 1:35, the horns sound a fragment of the theme, answered by the trombones and tuba. Soon other brasses and woodwinds sound a celebratory fanfare. Trumpets take the melody at 1:54, snare drums lending a military flavor. A long crescendo leads to the exciting final section, introduced by dissonant trombones and horns at 2:14 to bring the movement to a rousing, resounding conclusion.

comfortable in New York City, preferring the gentle climate and receptive atmosphere where he lived on the coast of Monterey Bay.

Like another Californian, John Cage, with whom he worked closely for a time, Harrison accompanied dancers early in his career, wrote music for percussion instruments, and became entranced with the Indonesian percussion orchestra, the gamelan. Always seeking new timbres, he studied the aesthetics, instruments, tuning systems, and compositional techniques of Asian music, learning to use them in his own original manner rather than imitatively. Ethnic music of the Americas fascinated him as well. His Symphony No. 4 ("Last Symphony"), for example, concludes with three Native American coyote tales narrated in singsong style.

Harrison disparaged the trend toward complexity in the music of some of his contemporaries, and he directly challenged Ives's contempt by declaring himself happy to write music that sounds pretty. Another famous composer, Ned Rorem, describes Harrison's melodies as infectiously beautiful; Harrison said they were "the audience's take-home pay."

Minimalism

Minimalist art, which strips objects to their elemental geometric shape and makes no attempt to symbolize or represent any real object or experience, often takes the form of sculpture or installations, such as Robert Smithson's *Spiral Jetty* (Figure 24.1). During the 1960s, some composers carried **minimalism** to music, writing simple, restful sonorities that changed very slowly over a drone. Just as visual minimalists restricted colors, values, shapes, lines, and textures, composers used minimal changes in melody, harmony, and rhythm, allowing the structure of a composition simply to evolve as the music quietly continued. Terry Riley is considered to have introduced this musical style, and Philip Glass has been closely associated with it.

Terry Riley (b. 1935)   The composer and pianist **Terry Riley** pioneered minimalist music in the mid-1960s, writing music reflective of the rhythmic subtleties of the classical music of India, where Riley studied for a time, and also revealing the improvisatory characteristics of jazz. He experimented with tape loops (varying the synchronization of repeated patterns by altering the length of tape, for example). Then, influenced by his experiences with non-Western music, and by the work of another American composer,

FIGURE 24.1

Robert Smithson's monumental earthwork, *Spiral Jetty* (1970), located on the Great Salt Lake, Utah.
(Art © Estate of Robert Smithson / Licensed by VAGA, New York, NY)

La Monte Young, he composed a number of pieces in what has come to be called minimalist style.

Riley's composition *In C* (1964) in a sense reinvented the whole process of listening to music. *In C* consists of fifty-three brief motives, each consisting of tones chosen mostly from the octave beginning on middle C. The number or kind of instruments required to perform the piece is not specified, although usually a piano is included in the ensemble. While someone—usually the pianist—marks a pulse by repeatedly playing two very high C's at the same time, the other musicians each play each of the motives, starting together with the first motive and proceeding to the next motives, in order, as they individually choose. Each musician may repeat a motive any number of times (or not), moving to the next motive when ready, regardless of where the other players are in the piece. Each musician chooses how to phrase each motive, where to put the downbeats, and how long to rest between motives, with the piece ending when all musicians finally reach Motive 53. The sound of the music, which has an almost hypnotic effect, has been described as a highly appealing, continually evolving tonal tapestry; and certainly it constitutes a kind of chance music.

Terry Riley remains an active, creative musician involved in a vast array of projects around the world, including music for theater and for films. For NASA, he composed *Sun Rings for String Quartet* (2002), incorporating sounds of the planets recorded by the Voyager mission on its journey to deep space. His projected scores for 2004 included *The Cusp of Magic* for string quartet and pipa (a Chinese string instrument) and *Melodious Junkyard* for prepared piano.

Philip Glass (b. 1937)

Philip Glass (Figure 24.2) has been among the leading exponents of minimalism. Having studied traditional composition techniques with Nadia Boulanger and others, he developed a strong interest in

FIGURE 24.2
Philip Glass.

sonority, leading him to linger on interesting sounds for such long periods that all sense of pulse became obscured. Impressed by the sophisticated rhythms of the music of Africa and India and thinking he might somehow adapt them to his needs, Glass studied with Ravi Shankar, a famous Indian sitar player, who interpreted various complex and subtle Indian rhythmic techniques in a manner Glass might apply to his own compositions.

From Indian practice, Glass derived a rhythmic system unlike the Western metric system, which divides measured units (see Table 1, p. 2). Glass's is an additive procedure, starting with a simple rhythmic pattern, repeating it for some time, and then altering it very gradually by systematically adding or removing units.

Glass, like so many contemporary musicians, finds affinities with colleagues in the visual arts. For example, he says that the work of certain sculptors, who stripped their art of all superfluous lines to produce figures of extreme simplicity, inspired him to vary the slowly evolving sounds in his minimalist music by occasional abrupt shifts of timbre or harmony.

More interested in the sound than in the form of a piece, Philip Glass often requires performers of his music to have creative as well as interpretive skills beyond those of the usual ensemble player. Therefore, he formed his own Philip Glass Ensemble, consisting of players—for whom some of his music is specifically conceived—who are able and willing to perform in this new and challenging way. The ensemble, which Glass himself directs, consists of two electric organs, four woodwind players who double on several amplified wind instruments, and a female singer who uses her voice as another, wordless "instrument." Glass often leaves the choice of instrumentation of a piece to the ensemble members, so that the sound of a particular composition is actually determined at the time of each performance and may differ considerably from one concert to the next.

Although some listeners consider Glass's music monotonous, it has attracted many enthusiasts who find it soothing, easy to follow, and stimulating in a new, even a spiritual, way. Its cosmic sense of ongoing time addresses an increased interest in various non-Western concepts and techniques, including meditation and an unhurried, relaxed, less organized approach to life. The music is controlled but not intellectual, and its simple, naive effect has been compared to that of popular music. A visit to Glass's Web site indicates his continuing prolific contribution to American music: for example, in 2002 he wrote the stunning score for the feature film *The Hours;* his ninety-minute work *Orion* premiered as part of Cultural Olympiad 2004 in Greece.; and the National Symphony Orchestra commissioned his Symphony No. 7 to celebrate the sixtieth birthday, in 2005, of the conductor Leonard Slatkin.

Women in Music

No longer routinely denied educational and professional opportunities in music, women are earning prestigious reputations on a par with their male colleagues as composers, conductors, and performers. An arbitrary, by no means

FIGURE 24.3
Gwyneth Walker.

definitive list of well-known and highly successful composers of recent years would include, besides Pauline Oliveros and Laurie Anderson, Louise Talma (1906–1996), Vivian Fine (1913–2000), Joan Tower (b. 1938), Barbara Kolb (b. 1939), Ellen Taaffe Zwilich (b. 1939), Meredith Monk (b. 1943), and one of America's most frequently performed living composers: Libby Larsen (b. 1950). Indeed, a composer's gender becomes of increasingly, and refreshingly, less significance with every year.

Gwyneth Walker (Figure 24.3), a resident of Vermont, retired from her position on the faculty of Oberlin College Conservatory in 1982 to become a full-time composer and since then has created a large catalog of works for orchestra, chamber ensembles, choral ensembles, and solo voice. "Maggie and Millie and Molly and May" (Listening Example 81) is the fourth in a set, or *cycle,* of five art songs with words by the American poet e. e. cummings and by Gwyneth Walker. (An art song is a concert setting of a poem, usually by a well-known poet, to music.) The song cycle takes its title from a line in the first song: "do not fear, though love be a day, we will go a-maying."

"Maggie and Milly and Molly and May"
(from the song cycle *Though Love Be a Day*)

CD 3
Track 20
1:08

Composer
Gwyneth Walker

Poet
e. e. cummings

Genre
Art song

Meter
Duple

Timbre
Soprano and piano (Walker wrote the song for a "high voice"—soprano or tenor)

Form
Through-composed

The lighthearted, lively, and whimsical music for this song is beautifully responsive to the text. The brief, perky introduction sets the mood for the girls' romp on the beach; and the piano anticipates, accompanies, or echoes their feelings throughout the piece. Notice the wide leaps in the melodic line, challenging to sing but expressive of the motions of the skipping girls.

maggie and millie and molly and may
went down to the beach (to play one day)

and maggie discovered a shell that sang
so sweetly she couldn't remember her troubles, and

millie befriended a stranded star
whose rays five languid fingers were;

and molly was chased by a horrible thing
which raced sideways while blowing bubbles: and

may come home with a smooth round stone
as small as a world and as large as alone.

For whatever we lose (like a you or a me)
it's always ourselves we find in the sea.

The poems include many references to fingers and to the number five; and Walker says she made subconscious decisions to set five songs, use five words in the title, and use quintuplet figures in the music of some songs (not this one).

A Promise of New Sounds

Compared with music in the first half of the twentieth century, music in recent decades has remained relatively stable. Largely because of prevailing economic conditions, for example, the symphony orchestra has changed relatively little in recent years. Traditional pieces, which make up the bulk of orchestral programming, call for traditional instrumentation; and orchestras struggling to fill seats are reluctant to challenge audiences with the unfamiliar.

In fact, orchestras around the country are trying to make new listeners comfortable by developing programs to help them understand the language of classical music. One concert hall offers devices something like a Palm Pilot that allow audience members to read commentary on pieces in "real time," like program notes cued to particular parts of a piece. Another has tried oversize television screens to bring members of the orchestra to the audience in close-up. The New York Philharmonic tried an experimental personal digital assistant (PDA) providing live visuals of the orchestra and descriptive listening guides.

Thus for economic reasons as well as their own personal reasons, contemporary mainstream composers have reached out to audiences with modest, accessible works. Yet it seems inevitable that, to transform themselves into twenty-first century media, orchestras must come to terms with electronics and amplification, and many mainstream as well as avant-garde composers today are seeking ways to combine electronic and acoustic sounds effectively. To their considerable advantage is the fact that performance standards have improved significantly in the last quarter century, as performers have become familiar with new instruments and with new techniques applied to conventional instruments. And much to the advantage of audiences is the new musical polylingualism, as composers mix the great Western tradition with music of other cultures and times. New timbres and new levels of amplification may well require new performance spaces, suggesting that concertgoing may soon acquire a new character and new dimensions.

Scientific discoveries and the capabilities of recent technology have dramatically altered our perceptions, not just of music, but of the meaning and goals of human life and the role art plays in it. Laws of relativity, for example, replacing comfortably established laws of science and nature, have weakened our sense of stability while expanding the range of our imagination. We have come, in fact, to *expect* the unpredictable, for we know that in life (and certainly in art) things are not always as they seem. But we know that the human experience will continue to be explored and reflected in our visual, literary, and performing arts.

We also know that all the arts will continue to explore and reflect the human experience and the wonders of our changing sensibility, to our lasting benefit and joy.

Term to Review

minimalism   A style of music based on many repetitions of very simple melodic and rhythmic patterns.

Key Figures

William Schuman   Terry Riley   Gwyneth Walker
Lou Harrison   Philip Glass

Optional Listening Example

Steve Reich: *Drumming* (minimalism)

Suggestions for Further Listening

William Schuman: *American Festival* Overture
Schuman: "Chester" Overture for Symphonic Band
Philip Glass: *Music in Fifths*

Glass: *Music with Changing Parts*
Ellen Taafe Zwilich: Symphony No. 1
Libby Larsen: *Deep Summer Music*

Critical Thinking

Do you share Charles Ives's scorn for "music that sounds pretty," or do you agree with Lou Harrison's concept that accessible melodies are the audience's "take-home pay"?

The performance artist Laurie Anderson has said, "Writing about music is like dancing about architecture." How do you interpret her thought?

The art critic for *The New York Times,* Hilton Kramer, said, "The more minimal the art, the more maximum the explanation." What do you think he meant, and do you agree?

Do you imagine that women entering such traditionally male professions as orchestral conductor face obstacles their male colleagues do not experience? If so, what might these obstacles be? How might they be addressed (by women, and by men)? Research the experience of Marin Alsop, appointed Music Director of the Baltimore Symphony Orchestra in 2005.

Go to www.mhhe.com/ferrisaml5 for a list of additional Web-based resources that relate to the content in this chapter.

PART 6
Summary

Like pioneers defying geographic boundaries, some early twentieth-century Americans extended the horizons of music, breaking ground for succeeding generations of experimentalists by exploring and widening the concept of musical sound. Charles Ives, curious about the properties of sound, equated dissonance with strength and composed in a bold, complex, independent style. Scoffing at the musically timid and encouraging adventurous listening, Ives greatly expanded the sounds and the meaning of music.

By directly manipulating piano strings, Henry Cowell proved that conventional musical instruments could produce new timbres. Cowell, who was among the first Western composers to draw inspiration from cultures to the East rather than from Europe, also extended the range of rhythmic complexity and actively supported New Music. Harry Partch, also interested in Asian music, invented many new instruments of his own.

Both revolutionary and evolutionary modern composers have often shown more interest in rhythm and timbre than in melody and harmony. Those preferring music that is highly organized, such as Milton Babbitt, may use the twelve-tone or total serial technique or render their music "concrete" by electric manipulations recorded on tape. John Cage and other composers of aleatory music moved in the opposite direction, requiring performers not only to interpret their music but also to share in its creation.

Although the mainstream of modern American music remains varied and changing, its new modes of expression are derived from the past. Most of America's first professional composers studied in Paris with Nadia Boulanger. The first of them, Aaron Copland, based some of his early music on jazz and later used other means (folk, religious, and cowboy music, for example) to give his music a nationalistic stamp. Seeking to please his audience during the trying years of the Great Depression, Copland wrote orchestral, vocal, and dance compositions with tuneful melodies and catchy rhythms. Some of his more challenging later works have yet to become part of the familiar American repertoire. Other mainstream composers include Samuel Barber, whose music is melodically lyrical and warmly expressive; William Grant Still, who addresses the experience of black Americans; and William Schuman, whose interest in American folk traditions and in jazz flavors much of his music. Minimalism, of particular interest to Terry Riley and Philip Glass, among others, has disappointed some critics while at the same time attracting new listeners to the concert hall.

Whereas the symphony orchestra has remained relatively stable in recent years, the meaning and concepts of music and art have changed more significantly in the last half century than during the previous 300 years. As the visual arts, dance, literature, and music offer an unprecedented variety of individual and multimedia experiences, we enjoy increasingly ready access to them, thanks to advances in technology and increased opportunity for travel by creators, performers, and audience members alike. More than ever, the arts play a vital role in everyday American life.

The Charge

You are now well prepared to enjoy all kinds of American music. You know about the music of the Yankee pioneers, conceived for utility but considered art today. You have learned about our vernacular musics—from Stephen Foster's songs and Sousa's marches through ragtime, jazz, rock, and musicals. You have followed the development of American concert music and have seen how Americans became leaders in experimentalism. You understand that American music, rooted like the American experience itself in the cultures of Europe, Africa, Asia, and Latin America, stands now, brave and free, a monument to *our* culture and a source of infinite pleasure and stimulation.

The new and unfamiliar will not intimidate the initiated listener: of course it is safe to listen to a work long acknowledged as a masterpiece, but it is exhilarating to hear the first performance of a potential masterpiece of our own culture and day. To condemn a piece for having "no melody" may be as absurd as to condemn a doughnut for having no center, a piece by Mozart for having no electronic synthesizer, or an African dance for not being accompanied by a symphony orchestra.

And so, armed with the experience you have gathered through this course, with a sense of adventure, and in a spirit of curiosity and happy expectation, may you venture forth to join the ranks of adventurous, prepared, receptive, creative listeners absorbing the many musics of today. Enjoy!

Glossary

A

a cappella   Unaccompanied choral music.

acid rock   Sometimes called "psychedelic rock." Music that attempts to evoke the sensations experienced by a person under the influence of LSD.

acoustic instrument   The natural, as opposed to electric, instrument.

alabado   A religious song of praise, belonging to Spanish and Mexican folk traditions.

Alberti bass   An accompaniment pattern consisting of rhythmically regular broken chords.

aleatory music   Sometimes referred to as **chance** or **indeterminate** music, aleatory is music in which the composer has left significant decisions to the performer or to chance. An extreme example is called **random** music.

alternative country   Variously defined style, blending punk and rock-and-roll effects with country sounds.

alto or **contralto**   The low female voice.

American operettas   Musical shows adapted from the Viennese style, written for the Broadway stage.

American Society of Composers, Authors, and Publishers (ASCAP)
Performance right licensing agency formed in 1914 to protect the rights of music creators.

answer   The second presentation of the fugue subject, on the dominant.

anthem   A through-composed religious song, usually with a biblical text, for performance by a choir rather than a congregation.

aria   A songlike setting, musically expressive, accompanied by the orchestra.

armonica or **glass harmonica**   A musical instrument invented by Benjamin Franklin, consisting of tuned, wet glasses that were rubbed to produce sound.

arrangement   In jazz, a written musical score that includes most or all of the notes to be played.

art rock   A blend of rock and symphonic or concert styles.

art song   Concert setting of a poem, usually by a well-known poet, to music.

atonal   With no tonic note or tonal relationships.

augmentation   A rhythmic variation in which note values are doubled, making a theme twice as slow as it was originally.

B

backbeat   Heavy accent on normally weak second and fourth beats of a measure in quadruple meter.

baile   Traditional Spanish social dance, popular in areas of the southwestern United States.

ballad   A folk song, strophic in form, that tells a story.

ballad opera   An English form of musical theater setting comedy and satire to popular tunes.

banjo   A string instrument derived from the African *banjar*.

barbershop style   Unaccompanied (traditionally male) voices singing popular songs in close harmony.

bass   The low male voice.

bass clef (𝄢)   Symbol often used to notate lower pitches.

Bay Psalm Book   The first book printed in America, a psalter that first appeared in 1640.

bebop   A complex, highly improvised jazz style, largely developed by Charlie Parker and Dizzy Gillespie.

big bands   Popular dance ensembles of the 1930s and 1940s, consisting of twelve to eighteen players. The bands had brass, reed, and rhythm sections.

bitonality Two keys at the same time.

blue notes Flexible tones derived from African scales.

bluegrass A commercial instrumental style derived from mountain music.

blues A black vocal folk music.

bomba Puerto Rican couple dance derived from Africa.

bones A folk percussion instrument consisting of a pair of castanets tied together and held in one hand.

boogie-woogie or piano blues A popular piano style with the form and harmony of the blues, but a faster tempo and a dance beat.

book shows Musicals with an integrated plot.

bossa nova Brazilian rhythm, slower, more subtle than Cuban dances, reflecting the influence of cool and progressive jazz.

break A dramatic, unstable, strongly rhythmic section, as in a march.

Broadcast Music, Inc. (BMI) Performance right licensing agency formed in 1940 to protect the rights of music creators.

broadside A written ballad, printed on a large sheet or in a set of sheets called a *songster.*

burlesque A variety show featuring satirical humor; later associated with striptease acts.

C

cadenza Solo passage.

Cajun music A country music of the Cajuns (Acadians), vibrant, light hearted, often with a strong dance beat.

cakewalk A plantation dance with syncopated melodies, including the *short-LONG-short* figure that became characteristic of ragtime.

call-and-response A solo voice alternating with a chorus of singers. The effect may be applied to instrumental music as well.

calypso Caribbean song style with humorously satirical topical texts.

canon A polyphonic composition in which all of the voices perform the same melody, beginning at different times.

cantata A relatively short choral work on a religious or secular subject, accompanied by organ or orchestra.

chachacha A slower version of the mambo, with a double beat added between the last and first beats of each measure.

chamber musical Musical for a small cast and economical resources.

chamber opera An opera for a small number of performers.

chamber orchestra A small orchestra with a few instruments per line of music.

chance music See **aleatory music.**

changing meters A different number of beats to the measure within a piece or section.

chantey Folk song about sailors and the sea.

character piece A relatively short piano piece, often in ternary form, in a characteristic style or mood.

chord A meaningful combination of three or more tones.

chordal texture The texture in which a melodic line is accompanied by chordal harmony. Also called **homophonic texture.**

choreographer Person who designs the steps and movements of dancers.

chorus A large ensemble, with several voices on each part.

chromaticism Use of tones not belonging in a particular major or minor scale.

classical A restrained, objective style of art. Spelled with a capital letter, refers to music of the eighteenth-century Classical period.

classical ballet A formal, stylized dance form that evolved in seventeenth-century France.

classical Hollywood film scores Lush orchestral scores particularly associated with films of the 1930s, 1940s, and 1950s.

classic blues Professional, stylized blues, conceived for performance in theater and clubs and on commercial recordings.

clef A sign placed on the staff that fixes the pitch of each line and space.

coda Closing section.

collective improvisation Simultaneous improvisation by some or all members of a combo.

combo A small jazz ensemble.

compound meter Each beat in a measure is divided by three.

concept musical A musical show presenting ideas subject to the audience's interpretation and leaving situations unresolved at the end.

concert band An instrumental ensemble including brass, woodwind, and percussion instruments.

concertina A kind of accordion or portable reed instrument. Melody and chords are achieved by depressing buttons or keys, and the wind is supplied by a folding bellows.

concerto A multimovement (usually three-movement) work for orchestra plus solo instrument or instruments.

concerto grosso A Baroque composition for orchestra and a small group of solo instruments. The form has been revived by some twentieth-century composers.

conga Cuban carnival dance-march, performed in a chain, with a heavy kick marking every fourth beat.

conjunto Ensemble accompanying dance and song in norteño music, north and south of the Mexico-Texas border.

conservatory A professional music school.

consonance Musical sounds that seem to be passive or at rest. Adjective: **consonant.**

contrapuntal Another term for **polyphonic.**

cool jazz A style introduced about 1950 for large bands that included some symphonic instruments.

Copland-Sessions concerts A series of concerts sponsored by Aaron Copland and Roger Sessions from 1928 to 1931 for the purpose of promoting music by American composers.

corrido Storytelling song, with roots in Mexico and the southwestern and western United States.

countermelody A melody performed together with another melody.

country-western Western music with a country flavor, including western swing, honky-tonk, and cowboy songs.

cover, cover recording A re-recording by a different performer of a popular record, sometimes intended to appeal to a broader audience than the original recording addressed.

Creole In nineteenth-century New Orleans, a person born in America of a family native to another country. Later the term was used for people of mixed racial heritage.

crossover Music that appeals to more than one kind of audience.

cu-bop Dizzy Gillespie's fusion of Latin rhythms with bebop.

D

da capo "From the beginning." A three-part design. The composer writes the first section and a contrasting middle section of a da capo aria, and the performer repeats the first section with embellishments.

diminution A rhythmic variation in which note values are halved, making a theme twice as fast as it was originally.

disco Commercial dance music popular in the 1970s.

dissonance Musical sounds that imply tension, drive, or activity. Adjective: **dissonant.**

Dixieland A white imitation of New Orleans jazz, introduced in Chicago; faster, more intense than New Orleans jazz.

Dobro A wood-body guitar with a metal resonator and an aluminum cone for amplification.

dominant The fifth tone of the major or minor scale, the tone most closely related to tonic. Often represented by the Roman numeral V.

doo-wop The name given to background vocal ensembles that accompanied Motown singers, often by singing neutral or nonsense syllables.

drone A single tone, sounded continuously or repeated.

dynamic level The level of volume (loudness or softness) of a musical sound.

E

eight-to-the-bar Ostinato that accompanies a boogie. Each of the four counts in a measure is divided into a long and short beat.

electro (nu-wave) Machine-like sounds, revived from the 1980s.

electronic synthesizer An electronic sound generator capable of producing, imitating, and altering sounds.

elements of music The basic materials of which music is composed.

ensemble In music theater, a group of solo singers, performing their own words and music at the same time.

experimental music Music challenging traditional concepts of musical sound.

exposition The first section of a fugue.

F

falsetto The singing voice above the normal (full or chest voice) range.

fanfare A brief, dramatic phrase or piece for brass and perhaps percussion instruments, with the character of an announcement or celebration.

field holler An emotional vocal phase, sung as a long, loud call, developed by blacks as a kind of communication with fellow workers.

fife and drum corps An early band, consisting of fifes and drums, which performed for military and later for entertainment purposes.

film score   All the music accompanying a film.

filters   Devices to select out high and low pitches electronically from a wide band of sound to produce a narrow band of melody.

finale   In music theater, the final scene of an act or of the show.

fingerboard   A board on the synthesizer that is uninterrupted by keys or frets, allowing a player to slide through a continuum of pitches.

First New England School America's first composers. Also known as Yankee pioneers and singing school masters, they lived in New England in the late eighteenth century and wrote music for practical purposes.

folk hymn   Another name for a white spiritual.

folk music   Usually music of unknown origin, transmitted orally and enjoyed by the general population.

folk rock   The addition of light rock effects to urban folk music.

form   The organization or formal design of a musical composition.

forte   Loud.

free jazz   A style of free improvisation introduced by Ornette Coleman in 1960.

fret   A strip of material attached to the fingerboard of a string instrument, allowing players to stop the strings at specific pitches.

fuging tune   A song in two sections, the first homophonic and the second polyphonic in texture.

fugue   A polyphonic composition, originally for keyboard instruments, in which the imitative entrances of

the voices alternate between tonic and dominant.

functional or nondiegetic music Film music heard by the audience only.

funk   Rock music rooted in soul but with lyrics that express interracial concerns.

G

gamelan   An Indonesian percussion ensemble.

genre   Kind or type of musical composition.

Gilbert and Sullivan operettas Comic English musicals (words by Gilbert, music by Sullivan).

glee   A part-song with three or more lines of music, in chordal or homophonic texture, with the melody usually in the top voice.

glissando   An expressive slide between pitches.

gospel   Folklike religious songs. White gospel includes camp-meeting spirituals; black gospel has had far more influence on popular music.

Grand Ole Opray   The world's longest-running radio show, which continues to present country music's top performers.

Gregorian chant   Term for Roman Catholic plainchant since the sixth century.

grunge   The Seattle sound, a hybrid of pop, heavy metal, and punk.

H

habanera   Cuban dance, whose rhythm is the basis of the tango.

half step   The smallest interval on a keyboard, and the closest interval in traditional Western music.

hard bop   Simple tunes accompanied by repetitive rhythms.

Harlem   A black neighborhood in uptown New York City that became an important center for jazz.

Harlem Renaissance   A cultural movement centering in Harlem in the 1920s in which African American artists in every field achieved high art.

harmony   The meaningful combination of two or more different tones.

heavy metal   Loud, heavily electronic music, often with distorted sound.

heterophony   The simultaneous sounding of two or more different versions of the same melody.

hillbilly music   A term applied to early country music.

hip-hop   Music (sounds) accompanying rapped lyrics.

homophonic texture   The texture in which a melodic line is accompanied by chordal harmony. Also called **chordal texture.**

honky-tonk   A Texan vocal style with harsh, honest lyrics.

hymn   A religious verse set to music suitable for congregational singing.

I

improvisation   The simultaneous invention and performance of music.

indeterminate music   See **aleatory music.**

interval   The distance between two tones.

irregular meters   Meters other than duple, triple, or quadruple (usually five or seven to the bar).

J

jam   To improvise together informally.

jazz   A means of performing music. There are many moods and styles, but improvisation is an inherent characteristic of jazz.

jazz-rock or fusion   Rock instrumentation blended with the improvisation and flexible rhythms of jazz.

K

Kansas City jazz   A light, spacious, relaxed style based on melodic riffs.

key   The name of the tonic upon which a tonal piece is based; also called **tonality.**

L

legato   Smooth, uninterrupted.

libretto   The words of an opera or another dramatic vocal work.

lining out   Practice whereby each line of text is sung by a leader and echoed by the congregation.

M

MacDowell Colony   An artists' colony established on the estate of Edward MacDowell in Peterboro, New Hampshire.

major, minor scales   The tonal scales.

mambo   Afro-Cuban form of big band dance music

mariachis   Mexican strolling groups of musicians, including strings and often led by one or more trumpets.

mazurka   A Polish folk dance of varying character, in triple meter.

melody   A meaningful succession of pitches.

meter   The organization of rhythm into patterns of strong and weak beats.

Mickey Mousing   Musically mimicking or accenting an action.

microtone   Any interval smaller than a half step.

minimalism   A style of music based upon many repetitions of simple melodic and rhythmic patterns.

minstrel show   An entertainment in which (originally) white men performed music and comedy in imitation of stereotypical African Americans.

modern dance   A contemporary American dance form, less stylized than classical ballet.

modes   Seven-note scales within the range of an octave, including but not limited to the scale patterns we call major and minor.

modulate   To change key systematically, usually by using one or more tones common to each key as pivotal.

monophonic texture   The musical texture consisting of one melodic line.

Moravians   Europeans who settled in Pennsylvania and whose music compositions and performances were of a highly professional quality.

motive   A short melodic phrase, subject to development.

Motown   A highly successful black company that recorded, published, and sponsored black popular music.

movement   A section of a complete work that has its own formal design and a degree of independence but is conceived as a part of the whole; usually separated from other movements by a pause.

multimedia shows   Performances including some combination of music, dance, film, slides, tape recordings, and other sound and visual techniques.

musical comedy   A play with music, in which the elements of entertainment are connected by a plot.

musique concrète or concrete music   Music that has been created by manipulating taped sounds. Any sounds may be selected for this purpose.

N

Nashville sound   Country music's commercial response to rock and roll, with country themes, pop instrumentation, and a heavy beat.

nationalism   A nineteenth-century movement in which artists of many nationalities sought to express the particular characteristics of their own cultures.

neoclassicism   The preference of some twentieth-century composers for the small performing ensembles, emotional restraint, and formal designs of the Baroque and Classical periods.

neoromantic   A twentieth-century composer whose music has nineteenth-century melodic, harmonic, and expressive characteristics.

new age   A soft rock style providing soothing, repetitious blocks of gentle, unassuming sounds produced by synthesizers or acoustic folk instruments.

New Music   The term used for music of an experimental nature.

New Orleans jazz   Virtuosic improvisation by members of a jazz combo on a given melody.

new wave   A term encompassing several styles, all conceived within the context of modern studio and electronic techniques.

norteño   Texas Mexican-American style of music.

notes   The symbols with which music is written down.

nu-wave (electro)   Machine-like sounds, revived from the 1980s.

O

octave   The interval of an eighth.

octave displacement   The choice of a note of the same name from a distant octave.

Oklahoma!   Landmark musical, by Rodgers and Hammerstein, integrating all elements of entertainment into the drama.

opera   A drama that is sung, usually with orchestral accompaniment.

operetta or **light opera**   A form of music theater in which the music and dancing are closely integrated with the plot.

opéra bouffe   A French style of operetta, featuring satirical humor and visual spectacle.

oratorio   A dramatic work based on a religious subject and performed by vocal soloists and chorus with orchestral accompaniment.

oscillators   The means by which pitch is determined on the electronic synthesizer.

ostinato   A repeated melodic or rhythmic pattern.

overture   In musical theater, an introductory instrumental piece.

P

patter songs   A feature of Gilbert and Sullivan operettas (and other forms of music theater) in which humorous words are sung very rapidly, with comic effect.

payola   The acceptance by disc jockeys of money and gifts in return for plugging recordings.

pentatonic scale   A five-note scale within the range of an octave.

piano   Soft. Also, the pianoforte, a keyboard instrument.

piano roll   Perforated paper roll on which pianists recorded their performances.

pitch   The highness or lowness of a sound.

player piano   Instrument for playing piano rolls by pumping pedals, forcing air through the holes in a piano roll as it wound over a tracker bar.

polymeters   Two or more meters performed simultaneously.

polyphonic texture   The musical texture in which two or more melodic lines are simultaneously combined.

polyrhythms   Two or more simultaneous rhythmic patterns.

polytonality   Multiple simultaneous keys.

powwow   A contemporary pan-Indian gathering for singing, dancing, rodeo, carnival, and other celebrations.

prepared piano   A grand piano on which some or all of the strings have been "prepared" by placing foreign materials on them to alter pitch, timbre, and dynamic level.

process music   Steve Reich's term for music whose form can be heard to evolve from the repetition of patterns slightly out of synchronization with each other.

program, programmatic music   Instrumental music that describes a story, scene, idea, or event.

progressive jazz   A symphonic approach to jazz, introduced by Stan Kenton.

psalm tunes   Tuneful settings of the psalms in versions suitable for congregational singing.

psalms   One hundred fifty inspirational verses found in the Old Testament of the Bible.

psalter   A collection of the psalms in metered and rhymed verse, suitable for setting to simple tunes.

punk   A British reaction to flagrantly commercial rock and roll.

Q

quarter tone   The interval halfway between half steps.

R

race records   The term used before 1949 by the popular music industry for recordings intended for an African American audience. (Later called rhythm and blues.)

ragtime   A written piano music, duple in meter and moderate in tempo. The left hand generally marks the beat and the right hand plays a syncopated melody.

random music   See **aleatory music.**

rap   Rapid spoken patter accompanied by funk-style rhythms; derived from reggae performance practices.

recitative   A declamatory setting of a text, with rhythms and inflections related to those of speech.

Used in opera and other dramatic vocal works.

reed organ (parlor organ, cabinet organ, cottage organ, melodeon) A keyboard instrument, popular in the nineteenth-century for its relatively small size and price, the variety of sound produced by adjusting stops, and the small amount of maintenance it required.

reeds Wind instruments in which the player causes small, flexible pieces of material called reeds to vibrate. Clarinets and saxophones are single-reed instruments: oboes and bassoons have double reeds.

refrain A section of melody and text that recurs at the end of each verse of a strophic song.

reggae A blend of rock and African Jamaican styles.

rests Symbols indicating the cessation of musical sound.

revue Originally, a show with lavish staging and costumes but no integrated plot. Later, a series of scenes united by a theme but without a plot.

rhythm The arrangement of time in music.

rhythm and blues (R&B) Broadly, black popular music of the 1950s. More specifically, a black popular style in quadruple meter, with strong backbeats and a danceable tempo.

riff A repeated melodic or rhythmic pattern that provides unity in a jazz composition.

rock A collective term encompassing many styles of popular music that evolved from and succeeded rock and roll.

rock and roll A popular music of the mid-1950s to mid-1960s that combined characteristics of rhythm and blues and country-western music.

rockabilly A close amalgamation of country music and rock and roll.

romanticism Emotional, subjective approach to art. So romantic was the period from about 1825 to 1900 it is referred to as the Romantic period of music.

rondo A musical form in which various episodes alternate with the opening material: **A B A C A.**

round A circular canon, which may be repeated indefinitely.

row The term for the arrangement of pitches on which a twelve-tone composition is based.

rubato Flexible rhythm and tempo. The word means "robbing" and refers to stealing from the tempo at some points and roughly repaying the lost time at others.

rumba Group of Afro-Cuban musical and dance forms, with many variants.

rural (country) blues Folklike vocal blues.

S

The Sacred Harp A popular nineteenth-century collection of hymns and spiritual songs.

salsa Popular Cuban dance band music with rhythms derived from African American dances.

samba Most famous Brazilian song-dance; duple meter.

scale A stepwise rising or ascending pattern of pitches within the range of an octave.

scatting or **scat singing** Improvising on nonsense or neutral syllables.

Second New England School The first American composers to write significant works in all of the large concert forms. Sometimes referred to as the Boston classicists.

sequence The repetition of a melodic figure at different levels of pitch.

shape-note notation A method that assigns a shape to the notated pitches of *fa, sol, la,* and *mi,* placing them on the staff in normal position.

shout, ring shout A lively dance, performed at religious services with shuffling but vigorous steps by dancers in a ring, accompanied by the singing of a religious song.

Show Boat Landmark musical by Jerome Kern, based on a literary work and addressing sensitive social issues.

simple meter Each beat in a measure is divided in half.

singing school masters America's first composers. See **First New England School.**

singing school movement An effort by music amateurs to teach New Englanders to read music and to sing. The movement began in the early eighteenth century.

slack key guitar Hawaiian guitar with loosened strings, having a characteristic resonant sound.

sonata A multimovement form for one or more solo instruments.

song plugger A music store employee who played popular songs on the piano to demonstrate them for customers.

soprano The high female voice.

soul A fervent, emotional black style rooted in gospel and the blues.

sound track All the dialogue, sound effects, and music of a film.

sound wave Longitudinal pressure waves. As the shape of the sound wave is altered, the timbre of the sound changes.

source or **diegetic music**   Music heard by characters in a film as well as by the audience.

spiritual   A folklike religious song with a simple tune.

staccato   Short, detached tones.

staff   Five lines and four spaces upon which music is notated.

steel drum, pan   Percussion instrument made by pounding the bottom of an oil drum into a concave shape and hammering grooves for the notes.

steel guitar   Guitar with metal strings, held on the lap, played by sliding a metal bar along the strings with the left hand while plucking the strings with the right hand.

stops   Levers or buttons that allow the player to adjust the timbres produced by certain keyboard instruments.

strain   A melodic section in a rag, march, or other vernacular form of music.

stride piano   A jazz piano style in which the left hand alternates low bass notes (on *one* and *three*) with midrange chords (on *two* and *four*).

strophic form   Most common song form. Two or more stanzas are set to the same melody.

style   A characteristic manner of composition or performance.

subdominant   The fourth tone of the major or minor scale, represented as IV.

subject   The principal melodic theme of a fugue.

suite   An instrumental work composed of several dances or other semi-independent pieces. A suite from a film includes several sections of music from the film score.

surfing songs   Songs by the Beach Boys and other groups reflecting the easy California lifestyle.

sweet jazz   Music with the sound and flavor of jazz, but arranged so that playing it requires little improvisation.

swing   A term with many meanings, including (1) a mood of lilting spontaneity, and (2) a danceable music played by the big bands in the 1930s and 1940s.

symphonic jazz   Concert music that has some of the sounds of jazz.

syncopation   The occurrence of accents in unexpected places.

T

tambourine   A small drum with metal disks that jingle when the instrument is struck or shaken.

tango   Graceful, sensuous Argentinean dance, the first of the Latin rhythms to become popular in the United States.

tape music   Electronically generated sounds that have been recorded on tape and manipulated to create a music composition.

techno   Futuristic electronic music featuring hard, driving sounds and rhythms.

tejano   Music of Mexican Americans born and living in South Texas.

temp   Temporary film score, composed of existing music, offered to demonstrate to a film's composer the type of music desired for the film.

tempo   The rate of speed at which music is performed.

tenor   The high male voice.

texture   The manner in which melodic lines are used.

theater scores   Concert pieces that include visual and dramatic elements as well as music.

theme and variations   An instrumental form in which a theme or melody recurs to provide unity, but in altered guises for variety.

theremin   The earliest electronic musical instrument.

third stream   Term coined by Gunther Schuller, referring to the combination, but not the blending, of jazz and classical music. The term is loosely used today to refer to avant-garde jazz styles.

through-composed   A song form containing new music throughout, as opposed to setting new text to the repetition of music as in strophic form.

timbre   The characteristic quality of the sound of a voice or instrument.

Tin Pan Alley   The popular music publishing industry from the late nineteenth through the first half of the twentieth centuries. Also, the neighborhood in New York where the publishing houses were then located.

toasting, dubbing   A technique developed by Jamaican disc jockeys of rapid patter-talking over the sound of spinning records.

tonality, tonal system   The system of harmony that has governed Western music for nearly four centuries.

tone   A sound with a specific pitch.

tone cluster   A chord, usually of several tones, built upon seconds. Clusters are often played with the flat of the hand, the arm, or a board cut to a particular length.

tonic   The first and most important note of a tonal scale, often indicated by the Roman numeral I.

total serialism   Also called **serialization** or **serial technique.** Application of the twelve-tone technique to other aspects of a composition, which may also be arranged into series and repeated systematically.

traditionalist   A composer who makes no radical departures from the styles and conceptions of earlier music.

transcription   An arrangement of a piece originally composed for a particular instrument or ensemble so that it can be played by a different instrument or combination of instruments.

treble clef (𝄞)   Symbol often used to notate higher pitches.

Treemonisha   An opera by Scott Joplin.

triad   The most basic chord in the tonal system, consisting of three alternate pitches or two superimposed thirds.

trio   A strain that is lighter in texture, softer in dynamic level, and more melodic than the others in a march or rag.

tune   A melody that is easily recognized, memorized, and sung.

twelve-bar blues   The classic form of the blues, consisting of three-line stanzas with four bars or measures in each line.

twelve-tone   A technique of organizing music in which all twelve tones of the octave are of equal significance.

two-step or **fox-trot**   An American dance derived from ragtime. The meter is duple, the rhythm syncopated, the tempo moderate.

U

ukulele   Small Hawaiian guitar-like instrument with four strings.

unison   The same pitch at the same octave or different octaves.

urban blues   Blues pieces written for publication and professional performance.

urban folk revival   Socially conscious movement popular in the 1960s, relating country music and mainstream pop.

V

vaudeville   A show with various acts including blackface scenes, dogs, circus stunts, songs, and dance.

vernacular   The common language. In music, refers to popular music.

verse-chorus form   Common song form in which the *verses* relate the story and a tuneful *chorus,* or refrain, is repeated after each verse.

vibrato   A slight variation in pitch that adds warmth and intensity to vocal or instrumental sounds.

Viennese operettas   The style of operetta written by Johann Strauss, Jr., and other Viennese composers, featuring exotic settings and romantic plots.

virtuoso   A performer who possesses dazzling technical brilliance.

vocables   Neutral syllables, sometimes called consonant-vowel clusters.

W

Wa-Wan Press   A publishing company established by Arthur Farwell and dedicated to the publication of American music.

walkaround   A lively plantation song-and-dance routine often forming the finale of a minstrel show.

walking bass   A steadily moving pattern in the plucked string bass that has melodic as well as rhythmic implications.

waltz   A ballroom dance in triple meter.

western swing   The Texas swing band style, influenced by Mexican and Hawaiian sounds and by jazz.

whole step   An interval equal to two half steps.

work song   Song sung to relieve tension and to regulate the movements of people working alone or in unison with others.

Y

yodel   A singing technique that involves changing rapidly back and forth between the normal and falsetto voices.

Z

Ziegfeld Follies   Elegant revues produced by Florenz Ziegfeld nearly every year from 1907 to 1932.

zydeco   A rock-flavored black Cajun style of country music.

Credits

Part 1

pages 16: Archive Photos;
17: © National Museum of the American Indian; **19:** Historical Pictures / Stock Montage; **20 (left):** Corbis Images;
20 (right): Yale University Art Gallery, Gift of Mrs. E. A. Giddings;
21: National Park Service / Department of the Interior; **23:** Courtesy of the Harvard University Portrait Collection, Harvard University, Cambridge, Massachusetts. Bequest of Ward Nicholas Boylston in 1828;
24 (left): Gift of Mrs. George von Lengerke Meyer. Courtesy, Museum of Fine Arts, Boston;
24 (right): Philadelphia Museum of Art, The George W. Elkens Collection

Chapter 1

Figure 1.1: © National Museum of The American Indian;
Figure 1.2: © Smithsonian American Art Museum, Washington, D.C. / Art Resource; **Figure 1.3:** © 1980 by J. Richard Haefer. Used by permission;
Figure 1.4: © 1980 by J. Richard Haefer. Used by permission;
Figure 1.5: Getty Images

Chapter 2

Figure 2.1: Brown Brothers;
Figure 2.3: (LC-USZ62-115201) Library of Congress;
Figure 2.4: (LC-USZ62-76295) Library of Congress

Chapter 3

Figure 3.1: Courtesy of the Trustees of Boston Public Library;
Figure 3.2: © Historical Pictures / Stock Montage; **Figure 3.3:** © Philadelphia Museum of Art / CORBIS;

page 58: AP / Wide World Photos;
Figure 3.4: The Granger Collection;
Figure 3.7: © 1992 National Gallery of Art, Washington

Chapter 4

Figure 4.1: Louisiana State Museum;
Figure 4.2: The Metropolitan Museum of Art; The Cosby Brown Collection of Musical Instruments, 1889;
Figure 4.3: Corbis Images;
Figure 4.4: Art & History Archives, Berlin; **Figure 4.5:** © Fridmar Damm / Leo de Wys, Inc.

Part 2

pages 78: The Granger Collection;
80 (both): Corbis Images;
81 (top): Smith College Museum of Art, Northampton, MA. Purchased with funds given anonymously by a member of the class of 1952;
81 (bottom): © 1992 National Gallery of Art, Washington, D.C., 1844 / 1845, Paul Mellon Collection; **82:** Courtesy of the New York Historical Society, New York City; **83:** Collection of the New York Public Library. Astor, Lenox and Tilden Foundations; **84 (top):** Courtesy City of San Jose Public Library, CA., **84 (bottom):** Philadelphia Museum of Art

Chapter 5

Figure 5.1: © Smithsonian American Art Museum, Washington, D.C. / Art Resource; **Figure 5.2:** From B. F. White and E. J. King, *The Sacred Harp,* 1844. Copyright © Sacred Heart Publishing Company, Atlanta, GA. Reprinted by permission.

Chapter 6

Figure 6.1: Hampton University Museum, Hampton, Virginia;

Figures 6.2 and 6.3: Corbis Images;
Figure 6.4: Culver Pictures, Inc.;
Figure 6.5: EKM-Nepenthe

Chapter 7

Figures 7.1, 7.2, and 7.3: Corbis Images; **Figure 7.4:** Reproduced from Theodore Thomas: *A Musical Autobiography,* ed. George P. Upton, 1905, rpf. New York: Da Capo Press, 1964. Used by permission.

Chapter 8

Figures 8.2 and 8.3: Corbis Images

Part 3

pages 142 and 143: Hulton Getty Picture Archive; **144:** © Smithsonian American Art Museum, Washington, D.C. / Art Resource

Chapter 9

Figure 9.1: Copyright 1983, U.S. Postal Service; **Figure 9.2:** Jane Kramer / EKM Nepenthe; **page 151:** AP / Wide World Photos; **Figure 9.3:** Corbis Images; **Figure 9.4:** The Cole Porter Musical and Literary Property Trusts; **Figure 9.5:** Corbis Images

Chapter 10

Figure 10.1: Jerry Howard / Stock Boston; **Figure 10.3:** © Cheryl Higgins 1989 / Decisive Moment, Inc.
Figure 10.4: Frank Driggs Collection / Archive Photos

Chapter 11

Figure 11.1: Getty Images / X188;
Figure 11.2: Photo © by Chris Strach Witz, courtesy of Arhoolie Records, 10341 San Pablo Ave, El Cerrito, CA 94530. From the booklet of Arhoolie CD

307: "Zydeco—The Early Years.";
Figure 11.3: Frank Driggs Collection /
Archive Photos; **Figure 11.4:** AP / Wide
World Photo

Chapter 12

Figure 12.1: Collection of Archie
Motley and Valerie Gerrard Browne /
Chicago Historical Society;
Figure 12.2: North Wind Picture
Archives; **Figures 12.3 and 12.4:** Frank
Driggs Collection / Archive Photos;
Figure 12.5: © Washington Post.
Reprinted by permission of the D.C.
Public Library; **Figure 12.6:** Corbis
Images; **Figure 12.7:** © Frank Driggs
Collection; **page 211:** Everett Collection

Chapter 13

Figure 13.1: Culver Pictures, Inc.;
Figure 13.2: Metronome / Archive
Photos; **Figure 13.3:** Courtesy of Ray
Avery; **Figure 13.4:** Corbis Images;
Figure 13.5: © Ray Avery;
Figure 13.6: © Shooting Star

Chapter 14

Figure 14.1: Bob Parent / Archive
Photos; **Figure 14.2:** © 2001 The
Pollock-Krasner Foundation / Artists
Rights Society (ARS), NY;
Figure 14.3: Historical Pictures / Stock
Montage; **Figure 14.4:** Courtesy of
Atlantic Records; **Figure 14.5:** Reuters /
STR / Archive Photos; **Figure 14.6:** AP /
Wide World Photo

Part 4

page 252: © 2001 Andy Warhol
Foundation for the Visual Arts / Artists
Rights Society (ARS), New York

Chapter 15

Figure 15.1: The Kobal Collection;
Figure 15.3: Bob Parent / Archive
Photos; **Figure 15.4:** Photo © by Susan
Titelman, courtesy Brazos Films, 10341

San Pablo Ave, El Cerrito, CA 94530.
From the film: *Chulas Fronteras;*
Figure 15.5: Corbis Images

Chapter 16

Figure 16.1: AP / Wide World Photos;
Figures 16.2 and 16.3: Corbis Images;
Figures 16.4 and 16.5: Hulton Getty
Picture Archive; **Figure 16.6:** Corbis
Images; **Figure 16.7:** AP / Wide World
Photos; **Figure 16.8:** Joseph Sia /
Archive Photos

Chapter 17

Figure 17.1: Tom Gateo / Archive
Photos; **Figure 17.2:** Hulton Getty
Picture Archive; **Figure 17.3:** Corbis
Images

Part 5

pages 306 and 307: Photofest

Chapter 18

Figure 18.1: Corbis Images;
Figure 18.2: Courtesy *Opera News;*
Figure 18.3: Culver Pictures, Inc.;
Figure 18.4: © Frank Driggs Collection;
Figure 18.5: AP / Wide World Photos

Chapter 19

Figure 19.1: The Kobal Collection;
Figure 19.2: The Everett Collection;
page 345: Photofest

Chapter 20

Figure 20.1: Courtesy of *Opera News;*
Figure 20.2: Corbis Images;
Figure 20.3: © Andrew Popper / Picture
Group

Part 6

pages 364: AP / Wide World Photos;
366: Courtesy of David Adickes;
367 (top): © 2001 The Pollock-
Krasner Foundation / Artists Rights
Society (ARS), New York;
367 (bottom): Gift of the Collectors

Committee, © 1992 National Gallery of
Art, Washington, D.C., 1976

Chapter 21

Figure 21.1: Corbis Images;
page 373: AP / Wide World Photos;
Figure 21.2: Corbis Images;
Figure 21.3: Copyright © 1930 by W. A.
Quincke & Company, Los Angeles, CA.
Copyright Renewed 1958 by Henry
Cowell. Copyright Assigned 1959 to
Associated Music Publishers, Inc. (BMI)
International Copyright Secured.
All Rights Reserved. Reprinted by
Permission. **Figure 21.4:** © Steve
Kagan / Photo Researchers, Inc.;
Figure 21.5: © George Holton / Photo
Researchers, Inc.; **Figure 21.7:** © Board
of Trustees, National Gallery of Art,
Washington

Chapter 22

Figure 22.1: Courtesy of Milton
Babbitt; **Figure 22.2:** American
Symphony Orchestra League;
Figures 22.3 and 22.4: Corbis
Images; **Figure 22.5:** © Frank Driggs
Collection

Chapter 23

Figure 23.1: Danlee Mitchell / Harry
Partch Foundation; **Figure 23.3:** Photo
by Dud Ferris / Courtesy Arizona State
University; **Figure 23.4:** © Oscar
White / CORBIS; **Figure 23.5:** Courtesy
of American Society of Composers,
Authors & Publishers;
Figure 23.6: Copyright © 1953
(renewed) Associated Music Publishers,
Inc. International copyright secured. All
rights reserved. Used by permission.

Chapter 24

Figure 24.1: Art © Estate of Robert
Smithson / Licensed by VAGA, New
York, NY; **Figure 24.2:** AP / Wide
World Photos; **Figure 24.3:** Christian
Wideawake

Index